MEDIEVAL
&
RENAISSANCE
DRAMA
IN ENGLAND

Editorial Board

MEDIEVAL & RENAISSANCE DRAMA IN ENGLAND

An Annual Gathering of
Research, Criticism,
and Reviews

II

EDITOR
J. Leeds Barroll, III

ASSOCIATE EDITOR
Paul Werstine

AMS PRESS
New York

Medieval and Renaissance Drama in England welcomes essays on the English drama before 1640. There is no limitation on length other than appropriateness to the task at hand. Footnote references should conform to the style found in this journal; articles should be accompanied by return postage. Articles may be sent either to the Editor, Department of English, University of Maryland, Baltimore County, Catonsville, Maryland 21228 USA or to the Associate Editor, Department of Modern Languages, King's College, 266 Epworth Avenue, London, Ontario N6A 2M3, Canada.

ISSN 0731-3403
Set ISBN 0-404-62300-X
Volume II ISBN 0-404-62302-6
Library of Congress Catalogue Card Number: 83-45280

Manufactured in the United States of America

Contents

LIST OF ILLUSTRATIONS

Foreword

THIS second volume of *MaRDiE* is issued with our thanks to those who have been so encouraging in their reception of its predecessor. We also continue to welcome contributions from scholars in all areas of the world, and we note that papers are not restricted to any specific length. We particularly invite the work of of scholars concerned with medieval drama, just as we continue to welcome proposals for reviews or review-articles. For although reviews are ordinarily invitational, proposals will be given most serious consideration.

Please communicate with the Editor or the Associate Editor, E. Paul Werstine, on these matters.

— J. LEEDS BARROLL, III
Editor

Notes on Contributors

JOHN H. ASTINGTON is Associate Professor in the Department of English, Erindale College, and the Graduate Center for the Study of Drama, University of Toronto. His research interests lie in the history of playhouses and of staging in the sixteenth and seventeenth centuries.

PAUL BERTRAM is Professor of English at Rutgers University. He is author of *White Spaces in Shakespeare: The Development of the Modern Text*.

LEE BLISS is Associate Professor of English at the University of California, Santa Barbara, and author of *The World's Perspective: John Webster and the Jacobean Drama* as well as articles on Beaumont, Chapman, Fletcher, and Shakespeare.

STEPHEN BOOTH is Professor of English at the University of California, Berkeley. His most recent book is called *"King Lear," "Macbeth," Indefinition, & Tragedy*.

JACKSON CAMPBELL BOSWELL is Professor of English Studies at the University of the District of Columbia. Author of *Milton's Library*, he has forthcoming articles on the English literary reputations of Bacon, Erasmus, More, and Sidney. Among his other interests is the history of exploration and discovery.

ROBERT E. BURKHART is Professor and Chair of English at Eastern Kentucky University. He has authored *Shakespeare's Bad Quartos* and articles on Chaucer, Spenser, and Shakespeare.

S. P. CERASANO is Assistant Professor of English at Colgate University and currently at work on a book-length manuscript about Edward Alleyn and the Fortune Playhouses.

LAWRENCE M. CLOPPER is Professor of English at Indiana University. He has edited the dramatic records of Chester for the *Records of Early English Drama* and published essays on medieval drama in *Modern Language Quarterly*, *Chaucer Review*, *Modern Philology*, *Leeds Studies in English*, and other journals.

SCOTT COLLEY is Associate Professor of English and Associate Dean at Vanderbilt University. Author of many articles on English Renaissance drama, he is co-editor of the forthcoming New Variorum *Richard III*.

WILLIAM EDINGER is Associate Professor of English at the University of Maryland, Baltimore County. He is author of *Samuel Johnson and Poetic Style* and of articles on eighteenth-century British literary criticism. Currently he is working on a book on tradition and innovation in British criticism, 1700–1765.

CHARLES R. FORKER is Professor of English at Indiana University and has published numerous articles on Shakespeare, Webster, and other Renaissance dramatists. His annotated bibliography of *Henry V* has recently been published by Garland Publishing.

WILLIAM INGRAM is Professor of English at the University of Michigan and author of a number of studies of the Elizabethan stage.

HARRY KEYISHIAN is Professor of English at the Madison, New Jersey campus of Fairleigh Dickinson University. He is Chairperson of the Editorial Committee of Fairleigh Dickinson University Press and co-editor of *The Literary Review: An International Journal of Contemporary Writing*.

NORMA KROLL is an Assistant Professor of English at the University of Massachusetts, Boston, currently working on studies of the cosmology in the Corpus Christi Cycles and of the structure of time and space in the twelfth-century romances of Chretien de Troyes.

DOUGLAS M. LANIER is the John L. Lievsay Instructor of English at Duke University. He has written on John Marston and is completing a book-length study of self-fashioning in the works of Ben Jonson.

WILLIAM B. LONG has taught English Renaissance drama at Washington University in St. Louis and at The City College of New York and currently is an editor at AMS Press, New York. His introductory survey of problems in Elizabethan-Jacobean-Caroline manuscript playbooks, "Stage-Directions: A Misinterpreted Factor in Determining Textual Provenance," has been published in *TEXT*, II (1985).

DAVID MCPHERSON is Professor and Associate Chairman of English at the University of New Mexico. He has published a monograph on Ben Jonson's library in *Studies in Philology*, plus a dozen articles on topics related to Elizabethan literature and drama.

LENA COWEN ORLIN is Acting Director of Academic Programs at the Folger Shakespeare Library. Her article is part of a longer study of Elizabethan and Jacobean domestic tragedy.

ELAINE UPTON PUGH, Assistant Professor of English at the University of Massachusetts, Boston, is active in feminist criticism of Shakespeare, having presented papers at the Ohio Shakespeare Conference and written reviews of feminist criticism of Shakespeare for *Women's Review of Books*. Currently she is working on a book exploring the concept of the heroine in five Shakespearean plays.

PHILIP B. ROLLINSON is Associate Professor of English at the University of South Carolina. He has written *Classical Theories of Allegory and Christian Culture* (1981) as well as many articles on Old English Literature, Spenser, and Milton.

ROBERT M. SCHULER teaches English at the University of Victoria. His works in progress include a study of Renaissance scientific poetry and a history of the English georgic before 1700; among his recent publications is "The Renaissance Chaucer as Alchemist," *Viator*, 15 (1984).

ALICE-LYLE SCOUFOS is an English Professor at California State University, Fullerton. She is the author of *Shakespeare's Typological Satire* (1979) and numerous articles and reviews in scholarly journals.

CATHERINE M. SHAW teaches at McGill and Concordia Universities in Montreal. She has written a two-volume work *The Masque in English Renaissance Drama* and *Richard Broome*. In addition she has edited *The Old Law* by Middleton and Rowley and has published articles in *Shakespeare Survey*, *University of Toronto Quarterly*, and other scholarly journals.

ALAN SINFIELD is Reader in English at the University of Sussex. His recent publications include *Literature in Protestant England 1550–1660* and *Society and Literature 1945–1970*. Just published is *Political Shakespeare: New Essays in Cultural Materialism*, edited with Jonathan Dollimore.

ROLF SOELLNER is Professor of English at the Ohio State University. His works on Shakespeare and Renaissance drama include *Shakespeare's Patterns of Self-Knowledge* (1972) and *Timon of Athens: Shakespeare's Pessimistic Tragedy* (1979).

J. A. B. SOMERSET is Associate Professor of English at the University of Western Ontario. He has edited *Four Tudor Interludes* and is currently at work on the records of Shropshire and Staffordshire for the Records of Early English Drama and on a Catalogue Index of the Stratford, Ontario, Shakespearean Festival Archives.

GEORGE WALTON WILLIAMS, Professor of English and Chairman, Duke University, is the author of articles published in *Studies in Bibliography*, *The Library*, *Shakespeare Quarterly*, and other journals. He has been Textual Reviewer for *Shakespeare Survey*, 1978–83, and is currently chairman of the Modern Language Association Group on Bibliography and Textual Criticism (1985) and of the Shakespeare Association of America Seminar on Text (1986).

WILLIAM PROCTOR WILLIAMS is Professor of English at Northern Illinois University, Editor of *Analytical and Enumerative Bibliography*, General Editor of the English Political Dialogues, compiler of *Jeremy Taylor: An Annotated Checklist*, and co-author of *An Introduction to Bibliography and Textual Studies* for the Modern Language Association of America.

Local Drama and Playing Places at Shrewsbury:
New Findings from the Borough Records

J. A. B. SOMERSET

IN THE first issue of this annual volume, Professor John Wasson demonstrated some of the ways in which our views about the activities of provincial travelling players are being modified as a result of the research being conducted for Records of Early English Drama (REED).[1] His focus was upon travellers, and his evidence was drawn from across Britain. To complement his findings I propose here to turn to the local dramatic activities of a particular borough, Shrewsbury, whose records I have been investigating for several years. We are fortunate that the early records of Shrewsbury are remarkably complete and well-preserved—perhaps the most complete collection for any borough in the country.[2] They provide a comprehensive picture of early drama in Shrewsbury that reverses many previous assumptions about early civic plays.

I

I will consider only Shrewsbury's local plays here, although there existed other well-organized civic ceremonial activities. The annual Corpus Christi procession and guild feasts occurred from at least the mid-fifteenth century, survived the Reformation in altered form, and were only finally suppressed in the nineteenth century. An annual celebration known as the "Shearmen's Tree" can be reconstructed in detail because of an acrimonious court case in the 1590s that arose over an attempt to suppress the festivity. The opposition to this attempt reveals how loyal was the following for such public festivals in the town. Occasions for public ceremonial were also afforded by the repeated efforts of the burghers to lure the Council in the Marches of Wales to the town; on many occasions the Council (and sometimes other dignitaries) were lavishly welcomed and entertained with parades, feasts, speeches, and plays.

Civic playing in Shrewsbury covers a long span and is typical of the range of activities observable in boroughs that did not possess a cycle of civic religious plays (we now realize that far fewer localities in England had such cycles than had saint plays, miracle plays [as at Croxton], folk plays, and the like). Shrewsbury staged a variety of plays at Pentecost, May, Whitsun, or thereabouts; the earliest record occurs in 1445–46 with payments for a Pentecost play performed "extra muros,"[3] and plays are last mentioned in 1575 with the dismantling of the town's stage.[4] Between these dates over twenty-five civic plays are mentioned in the records.

1

While it is beyond our limits here to consider all these references in detail, we must examine the titles which survive. Of the thirteen records that clearly indicate the type of play involved, six point to religious drama:

Feliciane et Sabine (1516–17)
The Three Kings of Cologne (1517–18)
The Play of Saint Katherine (1525–26)
The Passion of Christ (1561)
Julian the Apostate (1564–65)

Mr. Thomas Ashton, then Headmaster at Shrewsbury School, was author of the last two, and so we may safely assign his "third great play" (as the record calls it) to the group of religious plays. The other seven records indicate folk plays; these were a Robin Hood play (produced in 1552–53) and a play produced six times (1521, 1523, 1532, 1542, 1547, and 1551). It is variously named after, presumably, its main character, the Abbot of Mayvoll, Marall, or Marham (Mardol is the name of a street that runs through the market area in Shrewsbury, and this may have some connection with the nonsense-name). The Shrewsbury records clearly suggest that this was a play. At nearby Willenhall, in Staffordshire, the name crops up in a Star Chamber deposition, and this evidence indicates that a gathering of money took place when the event was staged there.[5] Such a gathering was normal during folk-play perform-ances, King ales, King games, Robin Hood ceremonies, and the like.

Irrespective of the type of play, May, Corpus Christi, or Whitsun was the usual time for productions, and so among the other records we cannot guess with any confidence that a play at Pentecost would have been religious in nature. The evidence contradicts the view of V. A. Kolve (as expressed in the title of his study) that there was a definable "play called Corpus Christi" and that towns' choices of dramatic fare at that feast were limited to cycle plays or miracles of the host.[6] In view of the vehemence with which the reformers attacked shrines, relics, and cults of saints, I think it is significant that there is a gap in the performances of religious plays—between 1525–26 and 1561 the evidence of named plays points to folk-drama. The winds of religious controversy no doubt alarmed the town officials, and the best way to avoid trouble probably was to look elsewhere for entertainments. This prudent action might explain why there is no clear evidence of governmental inter-ference with saint plays—probably there were few or none with which to take issue. Later in the REED project, when it becomes possible to list activities from across Britain in chronological order, I would be surprised if such decisions are not indi-cated in many places.

II

In England, far more civic religious plays were produced upon fixed stages (using "place and scaffold" staging arrangements) than upon processional pageant wagons. In fact, we must no longer think of the large processional cycle plays as typical of medieval dramatic activities, although their texts loom disproportionately large in our library of surviving texts (probably because of their size and their nature as civically sponsored annual events).

When we turn to consider fixed playing places we are frustrated by lack of evidence. Traces survive from all parts of Britain of fixed outdoor playing places, but traces are all that remain. E. K. Chambers surveyed the subject before 1903 for his indispensable appendix to *The Medieval Stage,* "Representations of Medieval Plays," and came up with the following list, which indicates the variety of places used:

Bassingbourn, Cambridgeshire	(a field)
Bungay, Suffolk	(a churchyard)
Chelmsford, Essex	(the "pightell", a small enclosed ground)
Harling, Norfolk	(at the church gate)
Louth, Lincolnshire	(the markit-stede)
Perran, Cornwall	(a *plan-an-gware*)
Reading, Berkshire	(the forbury)
Shrewsbury, Shropshire	(St. Chad's churchyard, the abbey, a quarry)
Yarmouth, Norfolk	(the game house)
London	(Clerkenwell fields)

As well, there are three from outside England:

Aberdeen	(le Wyndmylhill)
Dublin	(Hoggin green)
Kilkenny	(the market-cross)

The geographical scatter convinces one that fixed outdoor stages could have been found anywhere. What were the "inhonestos ludos" (plays? games?) that were condemned by bishop after bishop in the thirteenth century as unfit to be allowed in churchyards? One's curiosity is aroused by this ban, just as it is teased by the "honestos ludos" that the bans seem to imply. Only two of the playing places in the list, we note, are churchyards. On the other hand, it is relevant to note that there are records of almost as many performances inside churches as within town halls or guildhalls, as Professor Wasson has observed (compare Note 1). We cannot assume that episcopal disfavor was always vigorously applied or that it governed local practice.

In the eighty years since Chambers, some further examples of outdoor fixed playing places have come to light:

Bodmin, Cornwall	(the "church hay" or church enclosure)
Carlium Castle, near Truro	(a *plan-an-gwary*)

Carlisle, Cumberland	(in foro civitatis)
Coventry, Warks	(the little park)
Glastonbury, Somerset	(in "la Belhay")
Kendal, Westmoreland	(the street)
Walsham-le-Willows, Norfolk	(the game place)
Lydd, Dorset	(the hyghe strete)[7]

Again the geographical distribution is widespread. Seeing a bald list like this, referring to places most of which have disappeared or have been altered beyond recognition, one gains an impression of improvisation, making do, and artlessness. This
misconception has colored many accounts of medieval drama, leading commentators
to speak of the artless simplicity of our forefathers and of the "greater need for
Shakespere to arise, [and] replace the old Religionism with the new humanity...."[8]

Where we have some detailed evidence, or where there are some surviving
remains (in only a few localities), these lead us to think that the impression of
unsophistication is perhaps mistaken. We have the impressive *plan-an-gware* at
Perran, Cornwall, and the production of the Cornish cycle there in the 1960s is
remembered by many. At Clerkenwell fields, in London, we know that scaffolds for
spectators were erected in 1409 and that King Henry attended the performance.[9]
The records of Great Yarmouth, Norfolk, have recently been completely transcribed
by Professor David Galloway, and many new details have come to light. The game
place there had a house attached to it, and the property was under town control as
early as 1491–92. A lease drawn in 1538–39 provides a description and dimensions:

> a certeyn Garden lyeing on the sowthe syde of the parsonage garden extendyng in lenght
> by the same parsonage wall xxxvj foote & in brede xxj foote & it abbutith vpon the town
> wall ageynst thest to gether with acerteyn hous Calde the game place house....[10]

The plot was small but was used together with the house for performances, since
the lessee had to agree to "permitt & suffre all suche players as their audiens to haue
the plesure & ese of the seid hous & Gameplace at all such tyme & tymes as eny
interlud*es* or playes ther shalbe ministred or played at eny time."

Another game-place has been discovered by Professor K. M. Dodd at Walsham-
le-Willows (a village much smaller than Great Yarmouth). Working from early
maps and descriptions Professor Dodd has located a circular game-place of astonishing size—approximately 165–180 feet in diameter.[11] How could such a small village
have used such a large game-place? Why are its dimensions so different from those
at Great Yarmouth? Nothing whatever is known about productions or staging, but
such questions prevent us from generalizing too easily, even about playing customs
within a county. Finally, at Chelmsford, Essex, Professor John Coldewey has uncovered an early map that locates the "pightell" near the church. There survives
abundant evidence for a one-time production in the pightell in 1562; the churchwardens sought to raise money for church repairs by sponsoring a lavish production
(which was, alas, a financial failure). Professor Coldewey suggests that they may

have produced the Digby plays; the evidence from lists of costumes, props, and stage-effects is compelling, and particularly relevant is the fact that a former owner of the manuscript, Miles Blomfield, lived in Chelmsford at the time.[12]

Mention of the Digby plays reminds us that the surviving plays written for stationary outdoor performance make extravagant demands upon the producer—they are big theater, not improvised or patched together. The Digby *Mary Magdalene,* for example, took three days to perform and required such scenic devices as a temple to be destroyed by earthquake and fire, and a ship capable of moving about the place while holding half a dozen actors. Similarly ambitious production demands are made by *The Castle of Perseverance,* the drawing of whose stage-plan has had a great influence upon our notions about fixed stages. As interpreted by Mr. Richard Southern, it calls for a massive circular theater, approximately a hundred and twenty feet across, with a castle in the middle to hold eight actors as required by the text; as well, five scaffolds are called for around the perimeter of the circle. Whether or not one agrees with Southern that a vast moat and embankment were constructed for the performance of this play, it was a very large undertaking.[13] The production of the play in Toronto (1979) demonstrated that a sizable castle is needed to accommodate eight actors; to keep this in proportion necessitated a "round" of considerable size, as did the pageantry, color, and action that the text of the play requires.

Since the publication of Southern's book in 1957, scholars have tended to conceive of only two types of medieval staging, the processional theater of pageant wagons or fixed "in the round" staging. Rounds have become orthodoxy and virtually all stationary productions have been assumed to be in the round, because (as we saw in listing the playing spaces involved) virtually no details about production are forthcoming, other than from *The Castle of Perseverance* plan and the plans for the Cornish plays *Origio Mundi* and *Buenans Meriasek.* We extrapolate, of course, from the known to the unknown, but we must be careful to avoid circular argument.

One might suggest that the drawing of the *Castle* stage-plan may survive because its singularity caused a scribe to copy it as evidence of an unusual staging method for a play whose banns indicate touring. As well, we should observe that the only surviving "round" place associated with plays is in Cornwall, and there such circular earthworks had existed for centuries before being used for a production. As Schmidt notes, the evidence for specially erected *plan-an-gwarys* in Cornwall is late and problematical.[14] The round at Walsham-le-willows, insofar as it can be reconstructed, seems to have had only a circular stage or "table" as a fixed central feature. On the evidence, it would not be unreasonable to suggest that medieval producers adapted existing topographical features for use as theaters and that we therefore must approach the definition of "the place" more tentatively.[15]

Production "in the round" has seemed so attractive that it has been at various times proposed (in spite of the unmistakable recorded evidence for processions) as the method used to stage the Chester cycle, the York cycle, and the Towneley cycle; partly because of difficulties that processional staging arrangements appear to some scholars to involve, "round" production seemed set to engulf all medieval theater.[16] It is not necessary to review the history and disposition of this controversy in order to observe that we are in danger of becoming subject to the tyranny of circles—of seeing "round" theaters as the only type of fixed medieval theater space. The title of a recent article, "Medieval Rounds and Wooden O's," may be selected as one among many that make an implicit assumption about early fixed stages.[17]

Discovery of surprising new evidence makes us more cautious about such generalizations. There are records of three playing-places at Shrewsbury, but we find that two of them have disappeared without physical trace (the normal fate of such early outdoor places). St. Chad's Church collapsed in 1780 and was rebuilt on a site some distance away; so one cannot uncover details of its churchyard in which a play was once recorded as being produced. The abbey was also the site for a production. It survived the Reformation but was substantially dismantled in the nineteenth century. The third locale was the quarry. That the quarry at Shrewsbury was a theater "in the round" was suggested, soon after Southern's book appeared, by Professor Arthur Freeman.[18] His article is based upon earlier scattered references in print to the quarry and maybe a visit to the site where he perhaps saw a roughly circular area that might have been a playing-place. His comments have become the basis of later assumptions about Shrewsbury, including my own when I began work on the records for REED. Schmidt (p. 315) questions Freeman's conclusions, and suggests that "the plays were given in a real quarry." She had not apparently been able to view the grounds in question and hence did not realize that the nearly circular place alluded to by Freeman is a surviving feature. The area where the stage formerly stood used to be called "behind the walls" and was a town pasture; it survives as a public park, now called "The Quarry", on the southwest side of the town. The shaded water garden in the center of the photograph (Figure 1) (where plays could conceivably have been given in the round) is now called the "Dingle" and was, in Professor Freeman's view, the quarry of the old records. It is roughly elliptical and about 120 to 160 feet in diameter with sloping banked sides. Nothing in the previously known financial records of the borough or the Assembly Minute Books would contradict the hypothesis that the Dingle was the early playing-place (because they say little beyond barely mentioning the early quarry). Neither of the early maps of Shrewsbury shows a trace of any playing-place here or elsewhere, or any other feature of these lands for that matter (see Figure 2).

The assumption that the Dingle was the quarry theater of the old records, I have come to see, is incorrect; the Dingle was not the site for the plays, nor was Shrewsbury's medieval theater in the round. I begin with new evidence that I have uncovered. Although this evidence is latest in date of all the records that mention the quarry, it does a great deal, by tying together other evidence, to locate the quarry and establish its shape for us.

A good part of the land "behind the walls" was once owned by an Augustinian friary, which lay just to the north of the lands before it was suppressed in the 1530s. The abbots at various times had entered into long-term leases with several persons for parcels of land behind the walls, and these leases had in turn been bequeathed from generation to generation. Over the years, the bailiffs and burgesses increasingly came to assume that all the lands behind the walls were common lands, perhaps because a growing number of civic events took place there. Events came to a head in the 1570s when the bailiffs in their turn granted leases to parts of these lands "behind the walls"; litigation over the validity of leases had begun by 1581 and an earlier generation of Jarndyces awaited the outcome of a series of suits that lasted thirty years.

In 1609-10 the last lawsuit took place. One testamentary leaseholder, Roger Pope, sued the bailiffs of Shrewsbury in Chancery over his disputed claim to a part of the lands called "behind the walls"; although the bailiffs had been paying him rent for years for the use of his plot of ground, they inexplicably defended the suit and claimed that the ground was theirs. (It gives me some pleasure, by the way, to say that they lost and, after refusing to negotiate a settlement, were forced to buy out Pope's lease at a price established by the Court.) The suit was investigated by Commissioners sitting for Chancery at Shrewsbury; apparently such informal attempts to hear cases in advance and drive the parties to agreement were common. For a defence, the bailiffs chose to try to demonstrate that they had been in *de facto* control of the lands for many years. They drew up a list of twenty-one interrogatories or questions and called three witnesses of very advanced age: Richard Higgons (84 years), Humfrey Leaton (63 years), and John Perche (60 years). This method of hearing evidence and testing claims inevitably produces formulaic affirmative answers to the questions posed, since there was no opportunity for cross-examination. But in any case the claims of the bailiffs, sworn to by these three, do give us a good deal of information about the lands behind the walls.

Questions eleven, fourteen, fifteen, and sixteen are of special interest. Question eleven asks if the townspeople have, with the bailiffs' license, "digged and gotten stone and clay in the said close or pasture called behind the walles in severall places thereof. . . ."[19] There were apparently two or more quarries, in which were carried on do-it-yourself operations for the supply of private building-materials for which, I suppose, townspeople paid the bailiffs for each load removed. Question fourteen asks if "behind the walls" was a public ground used for musters and militia training; fifteen asks if it was a meeting place for guilds and a recreation ground for schoolboys and others; and sixteen focuses on the "quarell" or quarry:

> Item whether hath one parcell of the saide close next adioyneinge to the scite of the saide ffriery called the | dry quarell from tyme to tyme dureinge your remembrance bene vsed and imployed by the burgesses and Inhabitants of the saide towne for bearbaytings bullbaitings makeinge butts and shootinge for stage plaies and Common playes siluer games wrestling Runninge Leapinge, and other like actiuities and recreacions, And whether haue they as occasion serued at their will and pleasure made scaffolds erected boothes and tentes [tenements] made stayres and digged and troaden the ground & soyle aswell within the compasse of the saide drie quarell as in other parts of the close aboue the saide quarell for the better beholdinge and takeinge the pleasure of the said Common plaies and other exercises and disports without licence or Restraint of the said complainaunte. . . .[20]

The deponents, as I mentioned, agreed in all respects with the questions posed, but one distinction they drew is of interest. The deposition asks about "stage plaies and Common playes"; this is the terminology of Richard Higgons's reply, but the other two vary slightly from it. Leaton speaks of "stage playes and other playes," while Perche refers to "stage playes and other like activities and recreacions."[21] One wonders if these distinctions are like those in the records for the game house at Great Yarmouth, where we read about "eny interludes or plays," or for John Rastell's stage in Finsbury, where he had stage plays in the summer and interludes in winter.[22] Perhaps, on the other hand, stage plays are to be distinguished from other types of "play" or recreation.

These Chancery interrogatories clearly imply that there was more than one quarry (why else specify the "dry" one?); they tell us a great deal about how the "dry quarry" (and the land in the close adjacent to it) were made ready for plays and about the great variety of activities that took place there. This "dry quarry" is perhaps also located, depending upon how we punctuate one phrase of the interrogatory: either

> one parcell, of the saide close next adioyneinge to the scite of the saide ffriery ...

or

> one parcell of the saide close, next adioyneinge to the scite of the saide ffriery. . . .

If the former punctuation were correct, the surviving dingle, which is in the middle of the lands that adjoin the former site of the friary, might have been the "dry quarry" as Freeman appears to suggest, despite the fact that it now contains an ornamental pond. Could not a formerly dry quarry have later become partly wet by the addition of a pond? If the latter punctuation is correct, the parcel of land in question must have adjoined the site of the old friary. I believe that this is the case.

I mentioned that this lawsuit was the conclusion to a series of litigations extending over thirty long years; depositions from a suit in the Court of Requests in 1582, in which one Joyce Baynes (Roger Pope's predecessor) went to law over her claims to land behind the walls, come into the picture here. While the evidence in this earlier case says nothing whatever about plays, two of the deponents make comments about quarrying activities. One George Higgons deposed that "the Inhabitants of the sayde Towne of Shrewsbury haue been vsed to digge claye in the pasture behinde the Walles, in A hole neere the middest of the same pasture, and sometymes in the syde thereof. . . ." Richard Owen deposed that "the Towne and Inhabitants of Shrewisbury haue bine accustomed heretofore to digge or gett claye at ther pleasures without restrainte and that the same claye hath bene goten At a place ther Callyd the water Quarell beinge in the middle of the said pasture. . . ."[23] Here two quarries are identified, with the water quarry being in the location of the present dingle, in the middle of the pasture lands, and another quarry significantly located as "in the syde" of the pasture. I will return to that phrase later, but now I wish to turn for further elucidation to a later description of the lands.

In his *History of Shrewsbury* (1779), Thomas Phillips (a local antiquary) described the environs of Shrewsbury by a sort of walking tour, and he explained how the parklands behind the old walls had come by his day to be known as The Quarry; he points out that it "probably received its present name from a small quarry of red stone worked there in the Dingle" (p. 200). "Dingle," a word that came into common use only in the seventeenth century, means a secluded hollow or fold; by Phillips's day it was an apt description for the former water quarry, long out of use, and by his day (and until 1879) a swampy and wild refuge for slowworms, snails, and other nasties much sought after by the boys of the town. The Horticultural Society in 1880 levelled it, dried it up, created an ornamental pond, and converted it to its present function as a municipal water-garden. In fact, the water quarry has become (at least partly) dry, as early photographs of its former state can testify.

Thomas Phillips describes the other, "dry" quarry, during the same description of the parklands: "In the reign of Queen Elizabeth one Aston exhibited several dramatic performances here ... the place of exhibition was on the top of the rope walk, a bank cut there in the form of an amphitheatre, with seats thereon still visible" (p. 201). The two sites, then, were still clearly distinguishable in 1779. Although the rope walk is not now identifiable, Phillips gives another clue about the location of the dry quarry when he describes the public walkways then in use in the park, and he mentions a lateral pathway at "the top of the hill near the dry dingle."

We should now recall the earliest description of the quarry (1582) as being "in the side" of the lands behind the walls. A visit to the site today shows what George Higgons no doubt meant by these words. The lands behind the walls slope gently (approximately fourteen meters in 290 meters) from the line of the old town walls in a southwesterly direction toward the river Severn. But at the northeast corner there is a far more abrupt slope northwards toward the former site of the old friary—approximately ten meters in thirty meters. The dry quarry was excavated at this side of the lands behind the walls, into the face of this steeper slope, and in time a saucer-like semicircular depression was dug into this steeper northern slope of the hill. We must remember that, lacking modern machinery, the townspeople would have followed this line of least resistance in obtaining their building materials, which they were able to remove by cart through a nearby gate in the town walls.

If we consider the clues from these lawsuits and Phillips's description, we can locate the dry quarry on maps and views of the town that date from early in the eighteenth century; as well, we can gain from them at least some idea of what the site looked like then, and probably earlier as well. Phillips's assertion that seating was still visible in 1779 implies that not a great deal of quarrying had taken place after 1575; this is not surprising because the lands had been *sub judice* for a generation, between 1575 and 1611.

Eighteenth-century views and maps offer a series of impressions of the appearance of the site. The first surviving view, by John Bowen, an early eighteenth-century antiquarian, shows the quarry from the southwest (Shrewsbury's photogenic side, fortunately) before the parklands had been planted with rows of lime trees along the pathways in 1709. (The state of development of these lime trees allows us to date approximately the various views of the lands.) The value of Bowen's view is its suggestion (in the line of the town wall) of the steep incline at the northeastern edge of the lands where the dry quarry had been located (Figure 3). Next is a prospect dated 1732; here the lime trees are growing, the sudden incline of the wall toward the north is clear, and the dry quarry was just over the brow of the hill (Figure 4). In 1739 there was a great frost, and a view (unfortunately badly preserved) records the activities of the townspeople walking on the frozen Severn beside the parklands. A detail from this view clearly shows the semicircular quarry, in which a building apparently has been erected (Figure 5).

Such pictorial representations can be complemented by another means of recording topographical features, which eventually replaced them: maps. After the Burleigh map (Figure 2) and the Speed map of 1611, we must move forward to 1746 for the Rocque map (not noted for its accuracy), on which the quarry is depicted, or at least suggested (Figure 6). Shortly afterwards, in 1760, a survey was undertaken of the town lands whose income was then devoted to the support of the foundling hospital; these included Kingsland (across the river) and the lands under discussion, which were then leased as pasture. A detail from this clearly shows the quarry, but without a building. This survey is more trustworthy for locating the walkways across the lands, which, you will recall, were described by Phillips nineteen years later (Figure 7). Finally, to conclude the early maps, we have two maps from 1832, one of which clearly shows a building in the quarry, while the other does not (Figures 8 and 9).

The Ordnance Survey has produced three distinct surveys of the town, in 1882, 1902, and 1963; with their efforts the depictions of Shrewsbury attain topographical accuracy from which it is possible to obtain scale measurements. As well, the town's project in the 1890s to erect public swimming baths in the old dry quarry resulted in an exterior site plan that shows the dry quarry very clearly. The 1882 Ordnance survey shows the building depicted on one of the 1832 maps and suggests that some landscaping had resulted from its erection (Figure 10). The town's plan again shows the building, with the proposed baths to be erected next to it (Figure 11). The baths were not built exactly as depicted in this design, but the 1902 Ordnance survey shows us what was erected (Figure 12). Finally, the 1963 Ordnance survey (see Figure 13) shows the results of renovating and extending the baths in 1960; the rear wall of the quarry has disappeared, and the dry quarry has, in a sense, become "wet."

Clearly, the former site of the stage and amphitheater has now been obliterated by Shrewsbury's large swimming pool, and so to visit the site today does not arouse any hopes for reviving theater in the quarry. A visit is useful, however, to gain some impression of the size of the original site and its elevations. The dry quarry occupied about as much space as is now taken by the 1960 addition to the baths, and the construction work has no doubt obliterated the rear slope and any trace of the seating once "digged and troaden" into the old quarry, which was pointed out by Thomas Phillips. A photograph of the baths from the main entrance to the park leaves an

Figure 1. Modern aerial photograph, showing the Quarry Park.

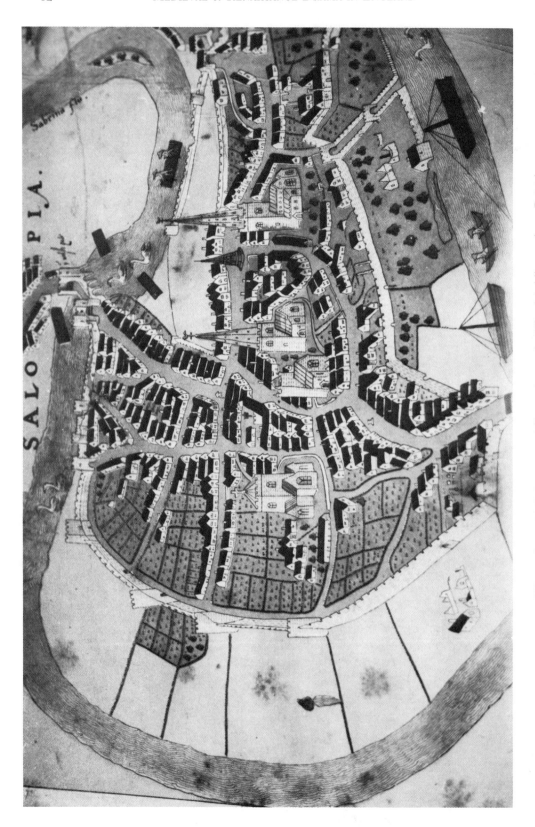

Figure 2. The earliest surviving map of Shrewsbury, the "Burleigh" map from British Library MS Royal 18.D.iii, f. 89.

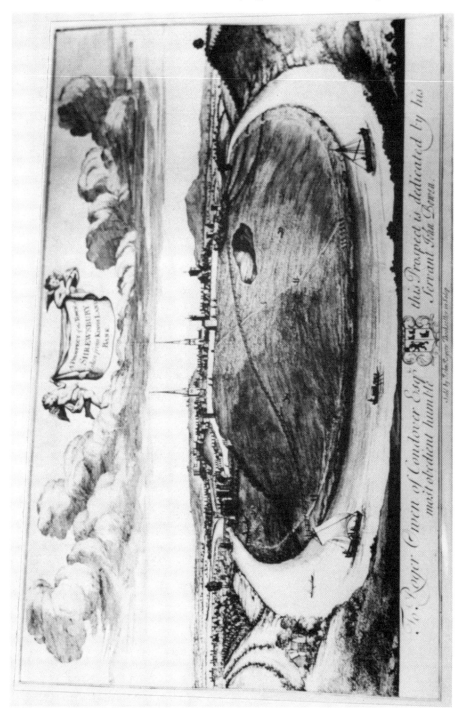

Figure 3. The Bowen view (*ca.* 1700).

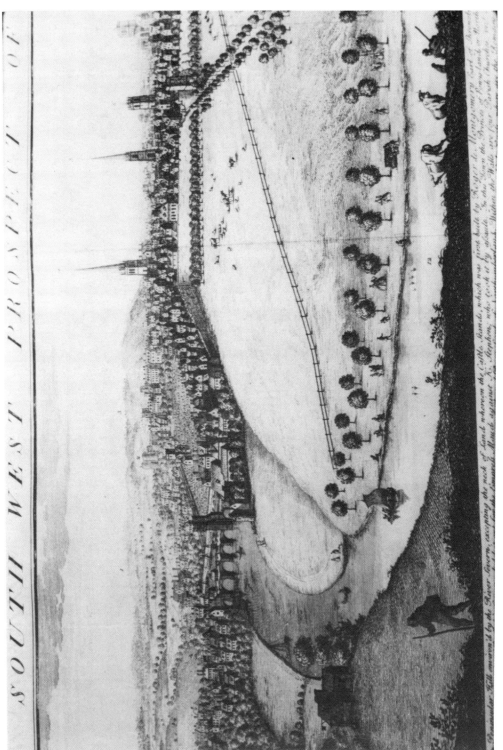

Figure 4. Prospect of Shrewsbury (1732).

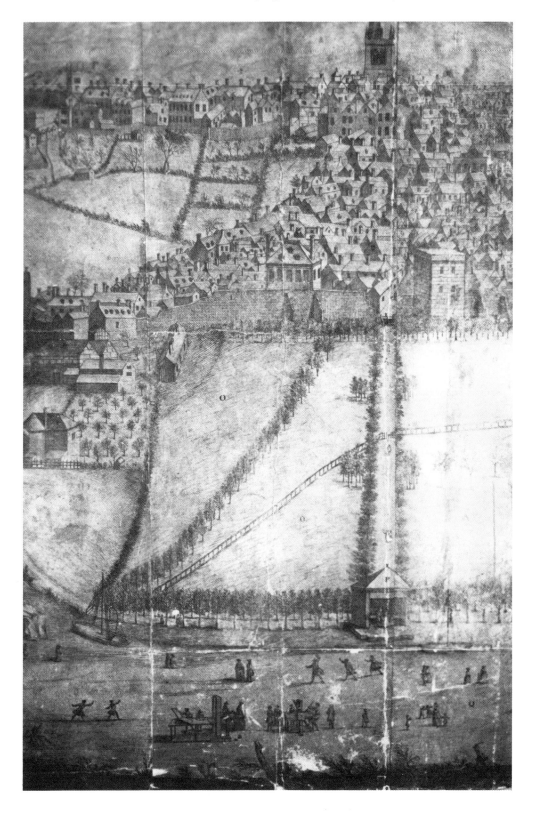

Figure 5. Part of the 1739 view of Shrewsbury during the Great Frost.

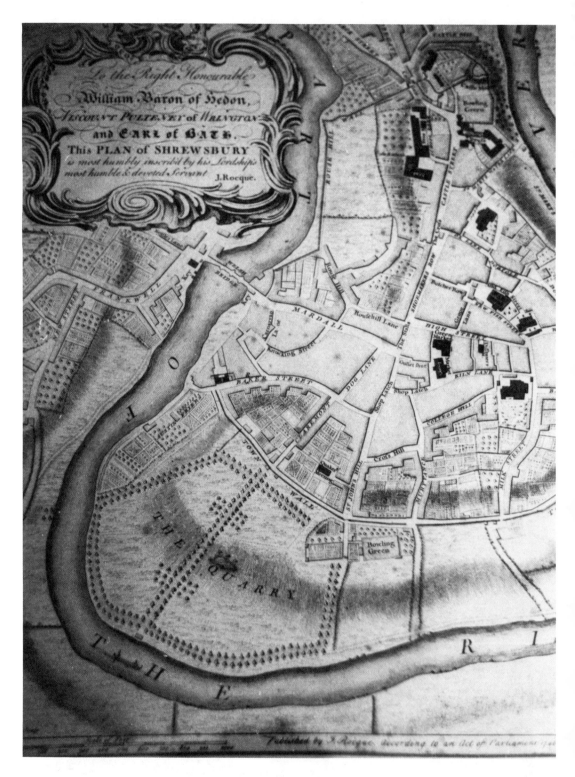

Figure 6. The Rocque Map (1746).

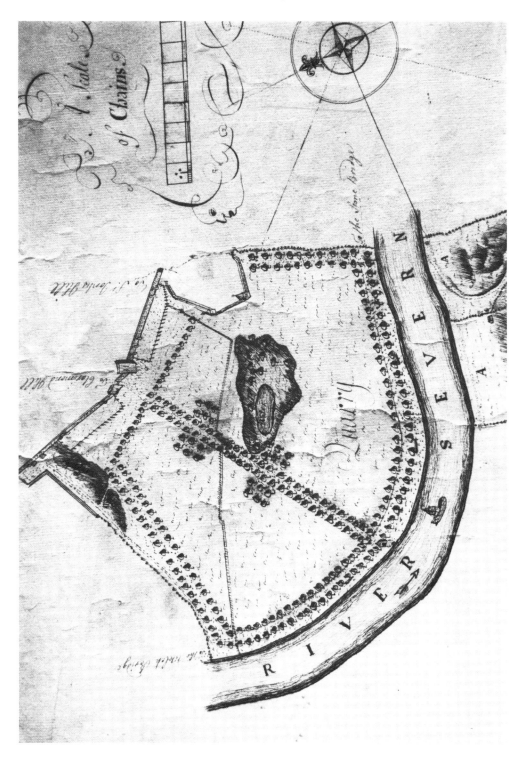

Figure 7. Part of Survey of Town Lands (1760).

Figure 8. Map of Shrewsbury, 1832, showing no building in the quarry.

Figure 9. John Wood's map of Shrewsbury (1838).

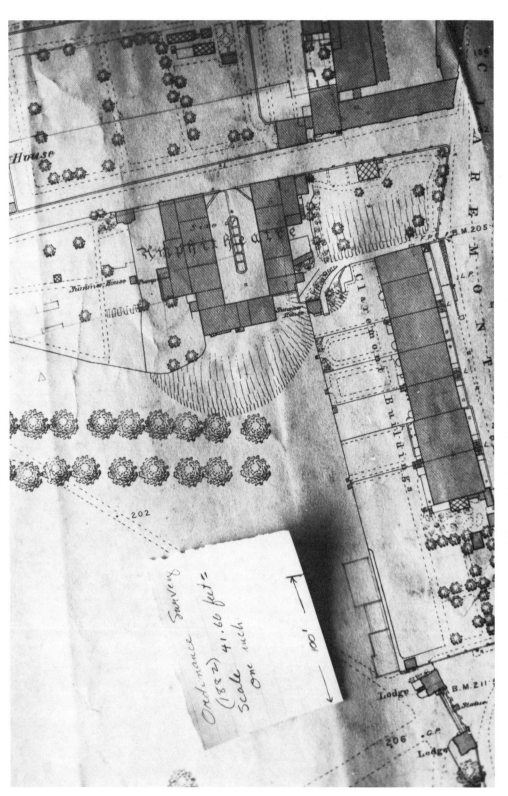

Figure 10. Part of the Ordnance Survey of 1882.

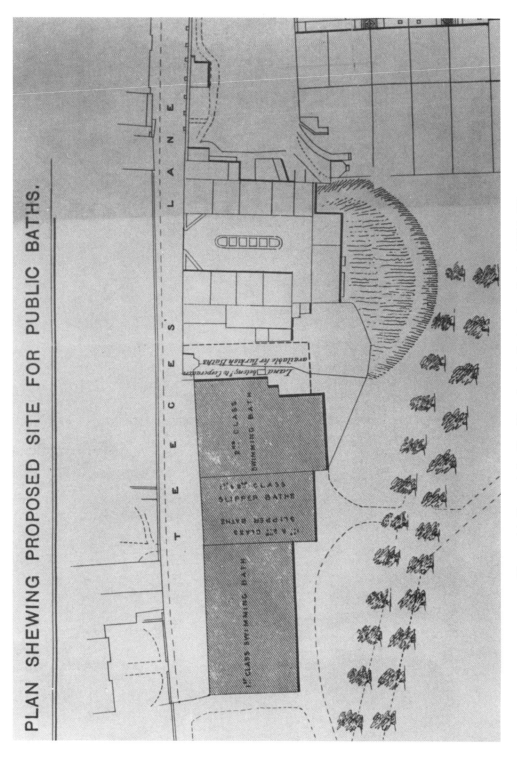

Figure 11. Part of the Site Plan for the Swimming Baths (1890–95).

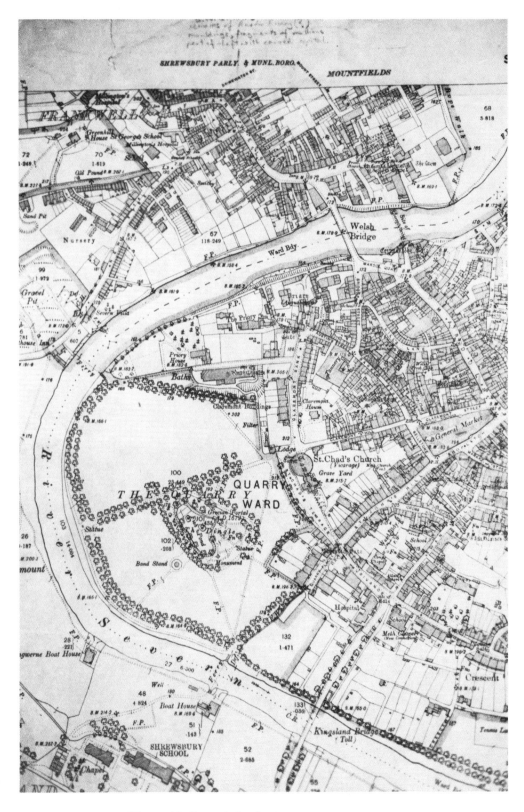

Figure 12. Part of the Ordnance Survey of 1902.

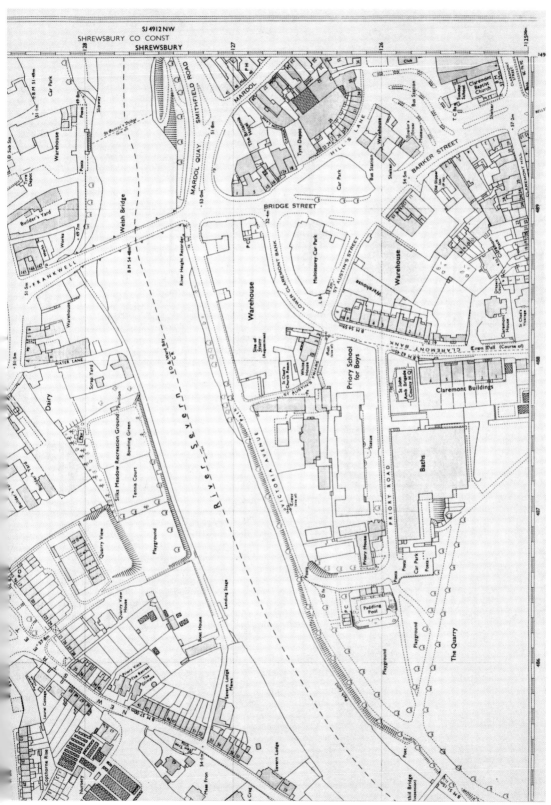

Figure 13. Part of the 1963 Ordnance Survey, SJ 4912 NW, showing the present public baths on the site of the quarry. Copyright H. M. Ordnance Survey.

Figure 14. Photograph of the Dry Quarry (1983). Taken by the author.

impression of the size of the new bath (the large white building) and hence of the former quarry which it stands upon. The lateral pathway along which the camera is pointed is, I suggest, the "rope walk" mentioned by Phillips. One can also see that the new baths have interrupted the course of another pathway to the river, which was clearly depicted on early maps (Figure 14).

Having gained an idea of the size, shape, and location of the dry quarry, let us now return to the early records, to trace its history as a playing-place. It surfaces in the bailiffs' accounts and Assembly Minute Books only when a civic occasion in the quarry entailed a payment from town funds; hence the various activities mentioned by the deponents in the early lawsuits pass almost entirely without mention in these financial records. For example, one visiting bearward was paid for performing there in 1519–20, in addition to the money collected from the audience "in quarera pone muros." Since exactly the same arrangements were recorded many times, it is not unlikely that other visiting performances took place there and that the scribe simply omitted to mention the place of performance when recording the payments.[24] Probably some of the local events supported from town funds also took place in the quarry even though the records of payment for such events do not mention the place of performance—mentioning the place, again, is probably just a chance occurrence. We cannot assume that the quarry remained unchanged through the hundred and twenty-five years when it was used as a theater—quarrying activities continued to take place there, as the deponents indicated. While we are not sure of the exact appearance of the quarry at any given time, its location in the side of the hill, near the bottom of which was no doubt the wall of the friary grounds, allows us confidently to conclude that the theater shape was semicircular.

III

Glynne Wickham is likely right in asserting that weather was the determining factor in choosing May or June as the usual season for local plays. At Shrewsbury, the stage or playing area in the quarry faced southeast, and so that time of year (when the sun was high) would have been most suitable. As already noted, religious drama at Shrewsbury was "big" theater, and the motives of the producers doubtless combined devotion to God and to profits. At the first recorded civic play, in 1445-46, which lasted two days (implying either two performances or a lengthy play), the town spent 7s. 6d. entertaining Lady Talbot, the guest of honor; she saw the play "in Mansione sua [in her structure] ad lusum extra muros."[25] The dry quarry was established by that time, as we know from an early lease granted by the Augustinian friary that includes the phrase "in nostro nove quarell."[26] (The word *new* is, I think, a relative term, distinguishing the dry quarry from the older water quarry that had been in use for centuries.) The dry quarry was the only suitable playing-place "extra muros," as the evidence of the 1609–10 suit suggests; so we are safe in assuming that this structure was erected at the quarry. It may have been similar in function to the *loggias* erected for important spectators at the *Mystère des trois Doms* at Romans in

1509. This "Mansion" is probably alluded to again in 1532–33, when two shillings were spent to refurbish it for the reception of the Lord President of the Council of the Marches of Wales; then it was described as having two storeys.[27] A final allusion to structures in the quarry comes from 1575, when the Assembly Minutes record:

> that whereas the frame of timber that stood in the quarell behind the walles is taken doune that the same tymber shale presentlye be deliuered to the scholemaster to the vse of the scholle accordinglye as mr ashton hathe at this tyme written the which hath bine red.[28]

As we shall see later, Mr. Ashton (the headmaster) produced several lavish and costly plays in the 1560s; it is likely that this frame of timber refers to one of his constructions; it may have been in fact a stage.

To return to the scale of the town's play-making, the records note that several productions after 1445 lasted more than one day. In 1515–16 three performances appear to have been given, and in 1569 a play produced by Thomas Ashton lasted "all the holly daies"; a contemporary chronicler alludes to a motive for the town's support of such a large venture when he notes that "unto the which cam greate number of people of noble men and others the which was praysed greatly."[29] The local records show that Shrewsbury had solicited contributions from, and no doubt advertised in, neighboring towns and villages for the support of this play, whose purpose was at least partly to promote the trade and interests of the town. The motive of attracting nobility, particularly noted by the chronicler, is detectable elsewhere—two examples have been given, and one could add Arthur, Prince of Wales (1492–93, and 1495), the Abbot of Shrewsbury (1515), and the Lord President, entertained with plays and shows on numerous occasions. A local legend (recorded in the aforementioned chronicle) states that Queen Elizabeth was planning to visit a Shrewsbury play in 1564–65; whether this be true or not, the claim is evidence for the motive of self-advertisement that at least partly lay behind Shrewsbury's civic religious drama.

Usually, the fragmentary records give us little insight into the production style or use of the theater space. Four exceptions survive: there are details for the 1492–93 play, for the St. Katherine play in 1525–26, and for the productions mounted in the 1560s by the headmaster of the free school, Thomas Ashton. We may conclude by looking briefly at these, to see what they reveal about the quarry and the plays. For the 1492-93 production (mounted to entertain the Prince of Wales) no place of performance is mentioned, but there is a payment "pro mancione dictorum ludentum" [for the structure for the said players]; this likely refers to some sort of stage-structure, but it might be another reference to the "Mansion" for noble spectators recorded in 1445–46. Payments for props and costumes include painting, gold foil, and repair of beards (not, we note, new ones). The most remarkable payment is to the "custodiis leonis domini Regis"; one wonders if the King's lion might have been doing his bit to frighten Thisbe away (likely not).[30] Or might the play have had something to do with Daniel? We will never know. With the 1492–93 production we may glance at the records for the St. Katherine play in 1525–26, for which the budget was £5, disbursed in nineteen payments, most of which were, maddeningly, "by bill"—the bills are not preserved. A well-known local comic actor received 6s. 8d. for being "lord of misrule" (apparently folk elements were mingled with the religious story), and a miscellaneous list of costs for the play includes payments for heads of hair, beards, a dizard's head, gold and green foil, gold and green paper, six dozen bells, and materials for staging explosions and smoke—four pounds of gunpowder, camfer, and saltpeter.[31] These details, scattered as they are, indicate that Shrewsbury spent considerable sums to stage lively and colorful theater, although they do not give any evidence about the stage.

The devotion to theater of Thomas Ashton, headmaster of the Grammar School from 1561, was remarkable, but we must remember that he was a pupil of Martin Bucer at Cambridge and likely learned from him a conviction of the value of religious theater.[32] We may safely assume, as well, that St. John's College would have given Ashton a thorough grounding in Greek and Latin language, culture, and letters. He is important because the series of civic religious plays that he staged in the 1560s were enthusiastically supported by the town, were alluded to by an important eyewitness writing in 1587, and were likely the activities in the memories of the three aged witnesses whom I discussed earlier. These men would have been between ten and thirty years old in the 1560s. It is also not at all unlikely that Sir Philip Sidney and Fulke Greville, both of whom were admitted to the school in 1564, participated in Ashton's public plays.

Ashton probably made some changes to the quarry in 1564–65, in which year the town decided to

> confer with mr Assheton to knowe the charges to set furth a play at wytsontyde next and to knowe the benyvolense of All occupations and other persons what they will gyue towardes the settyng furthe of the same.[33]

The sum they gave, £25.13.0, was very large when one considers that it was "ultra pecunias datas per confraternities"; probably some of it at least went into the "frame of timber" that was dismantled and given to Ashton for the school in 1575. For the production in 1569 the town gave Ashton £10 over and above the guild contributions but added:

> yf that mr ashton shale declare by his honestie that there shalbe wantinge of any money rather then the said mr ashton shude thereby bee a looser that then the said money wantinge shall likweis be discharged by the town.[34]

This year the Drapers gave £5 and the Mercers 30s; while other guild accounts are lost, it is likely that they also contributed.

One or another of Ashton's three productions was witnessed by the poet and deviser of shows Thomas Churchyard. He was a native of Shrewsbury and was on one occasion (in 1575) commissioned by the Lord President to prepare a royal welcome at Shrewsbury, for a visit that did not take place. In his poem *The Worthiness of Wales* (1587), Churchyard describes his native town and writes:

> I had such haste, in hope to be but briefe,
> That monuments, in churches were forgot:
> And somewhat more, behind the walles as chiefe,
> Where playes haue bin, which is most worthie note
> There is a ground, newe made theator wise,
> Both deep and hye, in goodly auncient guise:
> Where well may sit, ten thousand men at ease,
> And yet the one, the other not displease.
>
> A space below, to bait both bull and beare,
> For players too, great roome and place at will.
> And in the same, a cocke pit wondrous feare
> Besides where men, may wrastle in their fill.
> A Ground most apt, and they that sits above,
> At once in vewe, all this may see for loue:
> At Aston's play, who had beheld this then,
> Might well haue seene there twenty thousand men.

Churchyard's phrase "both deep and hye," and his reference to "they that sits above" can be used to elucidate a phrase in the interrogatories in the 1609–10 lawsuit (see above, p. 7); it asked if the townspeople had "made stayres and digged and troaden the ground and soyle aswell within the compasse of the saide drie quarell as in other parts of the close aboue." Churchyard implies that the seating arrangements for the amphitheater were constructed above the level of the top of the natural slope of the quarry (by heaping up an embankment), as well as within it; such an arrangement would have been necessary to accommodate the numbers of spectators he claims. Even allowing for hyperbole (understandable from a true son of Shrewsbury like Churchyard), the estimates of audience size are impressive and suggest that Shrewsbury succeeded in its aim of attracting large numbers of people from surrounding towns and villages, and even from further afield. (The contradiction between Churchyard's figures of 10,000 and 20,000 may arise because the latter figure is his estimate of the total attendance at Ashton's play—we know that in 1569 it "lasted all the holly daies." Perhaps Churchyard alludes to two performances?)

Churchyard's marginal note to these verses, praising Ashton as a learned and godly preacher, suggests that the two men were acquainted. Like Ashton, Churchyard was a Cambridge graduate with a sound classical training; I suggest that he could recognize a Greek or Roman theater shape, and that this is what he meant by describing the quarry as being "in goodly auncient guise," not referring to an ancient British (round) theater as Freeman suggested. Ashton "new made" the quarry, as Churchyard reports, but he was not able to alter its basic shape; so we may conclude that the shape of the civic theater at Shrewsbury from 1445 to 1575 was not circular, but semicircular.

As a semicircular amphitheater, Shrewsbury's quarry was (so far as we now know) unique in England. But we should look at this another way, because there are only three other medieval theaters of known shape (Cornwall, Walsham-le-Willows, and *The Castle of Perseverance*). Shrewsbury's amphitheater takes its place among the few certain pieces of evidence about early outdoor fixed theaters. I referred earlier to the habit of extrapolating from the few known (round) theater shapes to the unknown ones, which has led to the assumption that "round" staging was the norm. To extrapolate in this manner in future must mean supposing that other civic outdoor theaters, about which we have records but no evidence of structure, may not have been "round." We will have to begin by assuming that existing topographical features in particular localities would have been employed by townspeople when they sought a place to convert or adapt as a theater; they did not *a priori* think of a circular theater, and they likely had some knowledge of other stage traditions than that of performing "in the round." I have not alluded here to indoor playing-places, or to the later Elizabethan theaters, but we may note in passing that their arrangements did not dictate performance in the round, but with the audience arranged in a semicircle. Perhaps in future we may be able to go so far as to suggest that "round" arrangements, where they were employed, were special and dictated by circumstances and/or tradition in particular places. (Such a conclusion, as I noted earlier, has become the current view of processional staging, which appears to have flourished in only a handful of northern and north Midlands localities.) In conclusion, the importance of this discovery at Shrewsbury is that it will enable us to think afresh about the other records of fixed outdoor playing-places, without necessarily going around in circles.

NOTES

1. "Professional Actors in the Middle Ages and Early Renaissance," *Medieval and Renaissance Drama in England,* I, ed. J. Leeds Barroll, III (New York: AMS Press, 1984), pp. 1–11.

2. According to Charles Gross, *Bibliography of British Municipal History, Including Gilds and Parliamentary Representation* (New York: Longmans, 1897), see "Shrewsbury."

3. Shropshire Record Office, Shrewsbury Borough Records (SRO 3365/377, mb. 5). Cited by kind permission of the Archivist, Mrs. M. T. Halford.

4. Shrewsbury Assembly Minute Books (Guildhall Collection), No. 76, f. 196^v. Cited by kind permission of the Chief Executive, Shrewsbury and Atcham Borough Council.

5. Public Record Office, STAC 2/3/289.

6. V. A. Kolve, *The Play Called Corpus Christi* (Stanford, Calif.: Stanford University Press, 1966), p. 47.

7. See Ian Lancashire, *Dramatic Texts and Records of Britain: A Chronological Topography to 1558* (Toronto: University of Toronto Press, 1984), *passim.*

8. F. J. Furnivall, ed., *The Digby Plays,* E.E.T.S., Extra Series, 70 (London: Oxford University Press, 1896; rpt. 1967), p. viii.

9. Glynne Wickham, *Early English Stages,* 3 vols. (London: Routledge, 1966), I, 162–163.

10. *Dramatic Records of Norfolk and Suffolk,* ed. David Galloway and John Wasson, Malone Society Collections, XI (Oxford: The Malone Society, 1980-81), pp. 12–13.

11. K. M. Dodd, "Another Elizabethan Theatre in the Round," *Shakespeare Quarterly,* 21 (1970), 125–156.

12. John Coldewey, "The Digby Plays and the Chelmsford Records," *Research Opportunities in Renaissance Drama,* 12 (1978), 106–125.

13. Richard Southern, *The Medieval Theatre in the Round* (London: Faber, 1957). Compare Natalie Crohn Schmidt, "Was There a Medieval Theatre in the Round? A Re-examination of the Evidence," in Jerome Taylor and Alan Nelson, eds., *Medieval English Drama* (Chicago: University of Chicago Press, 1972), pp. 292–315. She suggests that the ditch is a moat around the Castle and that the drawing in the Macro MS. is a set-design. The Toronto production adopted her interpretation of the moat but found that a circular place of considerable size was needed to present the scope of the action.

14. Schmidt, p. 309.

15. On hillforts, scattered throughout Britain, see Christopher Hawkes, "Hillforts," *Antiquity,* 5 (1931), 60–97.

16. A. C. Cawley, "Pageant Wagon vs. Juggernaut Car," *Research Opportunities in Renaissance Drama,* 13-14 (1970–71), 204–207.

17. John R. Elliott, "Medieval Rounds and Wooden O's: The Medieval Heritage of the Elizabethan Theatre," in Malcolm Bradbury, *et al.,* eds., *Medieval Drama,* Stratford-upon-Avon Studies, 16 (London: Arnold, 1973), pp. 223–246. I emphasize that it is only the title of Professor Elliott's excellent discussion that provides my example here. Compare Martial Rose, ed., *The Wakefield Mystery Plays* (London: Evans, 1961), pp. 33–40, where the use in early stage-directions of the term "the place" or "about the place" is assumed to be evidence that the acting space was circular.

18. Arthur Freeman, "A Round Outside Cornwall," *Theatre Notebook,* 12 (1961), 10–11.

19. SRO 3365/2501, ff. 16, 19. Grateful acknowledgement is made for permission to reproduce illustrations as follows: Figure 1 (Shrewsbury Museums); Figure 2 (The British Library); Figures 3, 5, 6, 11 (The Librarian, Local Studies Library, Borough of Shrewsbury and Atcham); Figures 4, 7, 8, 9, (Shropshire Record Office); Figure 13 (Copyright H. M. Government. Reproduced by permission of H. M. Ordnance Survey).

20. SRO 3365/2501, ff. 16, 19.

21. SRO 3365/2502, ff. 69–72.

22. Ff. 17–18, 39, 55.

23. A. W. Pollard, ed., *Fifteenth Century Prose and Verse* (1897, rpt. New York: Cooper Square Publishers, 1964), pp. 307–321, prints transcripts of REQ 2/8/14. See E. K. Chambers, *The Medieval Stage,* 2 vols. (Oxford: Clarendon Press, 1903), II, 183–184.

24. SRO 3365/2501, ff. 16, 19.

25. SRO 3365/438, f. 63^v.

26. SRO 3365/377, mb. 5.

27. SRO 3365/2536, no. 20 (Deeds concerning the Quarry).

28. SRO 3365/438, f. 185^v.

29. Shrewsbury Assembly Minute Books (Guildhall Collection), No. 76, f. 196^v.

30. Ancient Chronicle of Shrewsbury (Taylor MS); Shrewsbury School Library. Quoted by kind permission of the Librarian, Mr. J. B. Lawson.

31. SRO 3365/951, mb. 1 dorse.

32. SRO 3365/438, ff. 154, 156^v, 157.

33. For the Latin text of Martin Bucer's *De Honestis Ludis,* part of his *De Regno Christi* (presented to King Edward VI in 1551), see E. K. Chambers, *The Elizabethan Stage,* 4 vols. (Oxford: Clarendon Press, 1923), IV, 188–190; a translation is in Glynne Wickham, *Early English Stages,* II, Part i (London: Routledge, 1967), 329–331.

34. Assembly Minute Books (Guildhall Collection), No. 76, ff. 67[v]–68.

35. Assembly Minute Books (Guildhall Collection), No. 76, f. 117[v].

Cosmic Characters and Human Form:

Dramatic Interaction and Conflict

in the Chester Cycle "Fall of Lucifer"

NORMA KROLL

ANY STUDY of the art of the Chester or of the York, Towneley, or N-town plays must address the ways in which the dramatists transform Christian doctrine and history from sets of principles and sequences of acts into networks of interactions.[1] The Chester play of Lucifer's rebellion differs from the other three versions primarily in its author's use of imagery of the human body not simply as a vehicle for linking episodes or reflecting doctorinal principles but as an integral part of the dramatic action. He subtly manipulates bodily images to humanize God and the angels so that they can engage in the kinds of moral and emotional interactions essential to fully developed dramatic conflicts. Thus the Chester God rules and its Lucifer seeks to rule not as absolute sovereigns but as feudal lords who require the personal cooperation and political support of their subordinates in maintaining the integrity of their governments. Because of the dramatist's artful use of language and unusual reworking of conventional material, his creation play, apparently written a century or more after the other three,[2] requires the kind of careful scrutiny of nuances and motifs that we generally give to Elizabethan drama. Such close study highlights the imagistic patterns underlying the play's more striking dramatic touches and effects—patterns that, cumulatively, give color and form to the Chester play as a whole.

I

To do a close reading of the ways that the Chester playwright built a pattern of images into the action of his creation play, we must first consider not only what liberties the playwright took with his material but also what license he had to balance the constraints of Christian doctrine against the constraints of dramatic form. Such a preliminary consideration has proved difficult because religion and art merge inseparably in the cycle plays' form and content. The difficulties are exemplified in V. A. Kolve's and Rosemary Woolf's diametrically opposing assumptions about the design of the plays, assumptions that they bolster by drawing on the same Lollard polemic, *A Treatise of miraclis pleyinge*.[3] This document argued against attempts to justify the plays either as "gamen" offering religious recreation or as "quike bookis" offering religious instruction to the unlettered. In *The Play Called*

Corpus Christi, Kolve assumes that the cycle plays are a "game" whose very non-seriousness allowed for God, Christ, and Lucifer to be impersonated by human actors without fear of blasphemy.[4] In *The English Mystery Plays,* Rosemary Woolf rejects "game theory" because it has "no literary bearing" and yet accepts the other non-literary assumption, the notion of "quike bookis" or speaking pictures, as the esthetic basis for the plays.[5]

Woolf considers the York playwright the most skillful of the four dramatists because she finds that he "deliberately excluded all action and all dramatic dialogue (Satan and the good angels do not address each other)" to give his work the dignity and symbolic quality of a painting (p. 109). As we might expect, Woolf finds the Chester playwright the most inept because he "raises in his diffuse play a moral and psychological problem that it was well beyond his capacity and intention to answer; he therefore has to show an abrupt and unmotivated change of heart in Satan, and his treatment seems mechanical, even crude" (p. 107). Nonetheless, a close look at the language of both plays reveals that Woolf's theory does not really apply to either. The York representation of events in heaven is not static: things do happen, but as its language reveals, the action is mental, not physical, as it is in the Chester. The York God creates the universe by deciding His "thoghts to full-fyll."[6] Similarly, its Lucifer need do nothing more than think aloud about rebelling to find himself in hell, lamenting his loss but somewhat bewildered as well, since, as he later expostulates, he had "sayde but a thoghte" (I, 114). In fact, the York God's closing explanation confirms the truth of Lucifer's unwitting comment: "Those foles for þaire fayre-hede in fantasyes fell" (I, 129).

Kolve's view of the cycle drama as play-acting, taking the word "playe" in the Chester creation as particular support for his assumption (pp. 7–29), is more fertile because play is an active process. The word did mean a mimic action or representation, but if we look at "playe" in its dramatic context, we see that its other meanings are more pertinent. The loyal angels of the Chester play warn Lucifer against persisting in his "parlous playe," which they equate with "daunce."[7] Both terms refer to an active or interactive physical exercise or work that could be gamelike or, were the play secular, even sexual (*MED*). Clearly the pleasurable associations are meant ironically; in fact, "playe" could also refer to warlike actions or, when used figuratively of people, to rapid movement or change (*OED*). Here the images of "playe" and "daunce" suggest not imitation but a hostile interchange that, metaphorically, takes on the dimensions of a bodily conflict. The implied physicality functions crucially in the context of the play as a whole, for the action that the angels describe as a "parlous playe" is described by Lucifer as moving "Above greate God," an act expeditiously accomplished while the God of this one creation ambulates, quite humanly, about the heavens (I, 182). Such a move suggests not an attempt to imitate God but an attempt to achieve superiority over Him. Lucifer's expectations are akin to those of a feudal lord who assumes that any defeated opponent will become his sworn subject.

The Chester play is not only more dynamic than Woolf supposes, but as a careful reading shows, its dynamics are also more physical than Kolve assumes. Key images of place and of bodily nature function as integral parts of the action, rather than as commentaries on events as in the York play. As a result, the Chester characters' choices and deeds are defined by images of their bodily forms in ways that make them surprisingly human, suggesting that the characters, instead of attempting to imitate God, tend to approximate human beings. This development echoes St. Thomas Aquinas's belief that God's and man's creative acts are analogous because "God is the cause of things by His intellect and will, just as the craftsman is the cause of things by his craft."[8] Singularly, the Chester God decides to "builde" a place for the angels, a term suggesting human craftmanship, and constructs "a heaven without endyinge" in time but defined by "a comely compasse / by comely creation" in space (I, 38–41)—a line that strongly suggests not natural boundaries but official or political limits to the area that He chooses to rule. Within this domain, God places the angels, not infinitely far from Him, as Christian doctrine teaches, but physically as well as emotionally close, as human companionship requires: "here I set you nexte my cheare, / my love to you is soe fervente" (I, 88–89). In keeping with this physical and emotional closeness, the Chester God and angels, unlike their counterparts in the other creation plays, not only share the same territory but also interact verbally. When God warns, "Touche not my throne" and let not "pride fall oughte in your intente," Lucifer readily and helpfully promises, "Ney, lorde, that will we not in deed" (I, 91–94). Thus the playwright allows for the possibility of both emotional and political relationships, with all the psychological ambiguities and risks involved in such interactions.

As we shall see, the physicality of the angels' and God's natures makes their interactions virtually a matter of necessity as well as of desire. The Chester God requires the angelic hierarchy to help Him govern, delegating authority over the angels to Lucifer while He inspects other parts of the heavens (I, 110–113). God apparently needs such support because He has taken on bodily form—a "brighte face" and "fygure" (I, 116–121)—which limits Him spatially. Correspondingly, the Lucifer-Demon seeks the same kind of assistance in heaven, calling upon the angels to kneel to him, and in hell, enlisting the aid of his subordinate, the Second Demon, to draw men into "myne order" (I, 257–258). This kind of interdependence presumes trust and makes the play's cosmic characters as emotionally vulnerable to each other as human characters would be.

The Chester playwright's humanization of God and the angels, as well as the less radical York, Towneley, and N-town versions, became possible in the later Middle Ages because of the complex evolution of medieval doctrine. If the cycles' Christ-centered subject matter reflects the Franciscan concern with Christ's human sufferings,[9] the cycles' opening plays of God's creation and the angels' rebellion build on both St. Augustine and St. Thomas Aquinas's teachings about the nature of God's and the angels' acts.[10] The York, Towneley, and N-town authors drew on Augustine and Thomas to represent the angels' rebellion without compromising God's ineffably superior power and position by engaging Him in a struggle with His creatures. These dramatists suggest rather than develop a struggle by alternating between the good and bad angels, who maintain opposing points of view but who do not interact with God; indeed, they state their respective positions without even addressing each other (with the exception of the Towneley good angels' brief but unanswered warning).

This pattern reflects St. Augustine's justification of human evil for esthetic purposes: " 'Antithesis' ['opposition' or 'contraposition'] provides the most attractive figures in literary composition" just as "there is beauty in the composition of the world's history arising from the antithesis of contraries"—a kind of eloquence in events, instead of in words (*City of God,* XI, 18). Because the three playwrights portray just such a quick shift from good to bad angels, they suggest a conflict and generate sufficient sense of tension to offset the tensionless ease of God's victory. But because they create no more than the impression of conflict, their representations can be described more accurately as dramatized exposition than as drama.

In contrast, the Chester playwright engages God in a dramatic interaction and conflict with the angels and Lucifer. This development is extraordinary because it requires involving an omnipotent and unlimited Creator and a more than humanly powerful but still limited Lucifer in a moral struggle as opponents who, if not equal, are at least equally vulnerable and who find the outcome equally vital. The difficulty lies in finding a way to narrow the incommensurable distance between God and Lucifer since interaction and conflict depend on limits, on the ways that the characters struggle against the bounds imposed by their own natures, by others, or by circumstances. The Chester playwright builds the necessary personal and political limits in a very human image that closely echoes St. Thomas's notion that scriptural images of the angels' physical activity represent their moral propensities. For Thomas, "by *walking,* we are to understand the movement of [the angels'] free-will tending towards good" (*Summa,* I, Q.63, A.7, R.1).

The Chester God sanctions the angels' proper moral conduct by commanding that "iech one with others, as it is righte," must "walke aboute the Trenitie" (I, 66–67). The metaphor implies circumscribing but of a particular kind, for the command also includes two phrases which subtly qualify what is "righte." The first, "iech one with others," suggests that the angels must interact as well as act. In this one play, the angels do speak to each other and do influence each other's as well as God's acts: for example, Lucifer delays acting on his rebellious inclinations to argue at length with the loyal angels. The second phrase, "to walke aboute the Trenitie," suggests that the angels' activity somehow encompasses and perhaps even involves God. Indeed, the Chester God, unlike His counterparts in the other cycle plays, is hurt by the loss of the rebellious angels: "my meirth thou hast made amisse. / I maye well suffer; my will is not soe / that they shoulde parte this from my blesse" (I, 275–277). While the Chester God cannot be overthrown by the rebellious angels, He can be emotionally overcome. Thus this play's God and Lucifer can and do face each other in a moral struggle, are mutually vulnerable, and are deeply touched by the outcome. In the world of the play, God is increasingly affected by Lucifer's struggle because He has chosen to create angels for the sake of a quite human desire for personal involvement: "What have I offended unto thee? / I made thee my frende; thou arte my foe" (I, 223–224). In sum, the playwright cleverly subverts doctrine by transforming God's love, the conventional motive ascribed to Him, into the desire for friendship, which calls for personal participation and closeness, rather than the traditional *caritas* or impersonal expression of divine goodness and universal love.

The Chester dramatist's humanization of the creation differs radically from the York, Towneley, and N-town versions in the ways that he uses the freedom to rework doctrine implied in the fourteenth-century Nominalist separation of theology from philosophy. By the time the cycle plays were composed, philosophers focused on problems of epistemology and physical science, while theologians argued such issues as free will, grace, and God's absolute power.[11] These theological arguments simultaneously exalted God's acts and moved His nature and power beyond man's rational comprehension.[12] Thus the Nominalists narrowed the scope of doctrine and, correspondingly, broadened the domain of what could be treated in non-religious contexts. Implicitly, they freed Augustinian, Thomistic, and even their own teachings for use as dramatic metaphors by the cycle playwrights.

The York as well as the Towneley and N-town dramatists draw on the traditional view of God's omnipotence and omniscience: by virtue of His divine Ideas or Forms, God creates as well as knows all that was, is, and will be (*City of God,* XI, 21 and XII, 27; *Summa,* I, Q.9, A.1); in the words of the God of the N-town creation, "all þat evyr xal haue beynge / it is closyd in my mende."[13] Very differently, the Chester playwright's singular emphasis on God's direct intervention appears, at first glance, to incorporate Nominalist views of His absolutely unqualified nature and power,[14] for as Kathleen Ashley recognizes, He creates by building directly, unlike his York, Towneley, and N-town counterparts who work by means of traditional divine Ideas or Forms.[15] Yet the Chester playwright omits any reference to divine Forms not so much to stress the absolute nature of God's power in any Nominalist sense as to downplay traditional notions of His omnipotence in order to make Him similar enough to His creatures to interact with them. Where the three earlier dramatists represent a God who is and remains the absolute creator and ruler of the universe, the Chester author portrays a God who progressively tempers and limits His power for the sake of interacting with the angels as well as with the human characters in the cycle as a whole.

II

By the artful use of metaphors, the Chester playwright humanizes God's interactions with the angels without destroying the spirit of Christian history. He begins with conventional images of light, sanctioned by Augustinian theology, and progressively incorporates images of the human body, justified both by scripture and by Thomistic identification of bodily form with the soul (*Summa,* I, Q.75–76) as well as by the sixteenth-century celebration of the human body as a metaphor for properly organized political and personal health.[16] Thus this late cycle dramatist bridges the gaps between medieval and Renaissance world views and dramatic techniques. He quickens his images by building them into the characters' interactions, a technique that we commonly expect of Renaissance dramatists, and by constructing an elaborate and interconnected pattern of physical acts, unlike anything attempted in the other three cycle creation plays. As a result, the vehicle for the dynamics of the play's dramatic interaction is a concrete but subtle pattern of bodily images and action that functions both figuratively and literally to define and limit the characters' natures and deeds.

In the Chester play, the characters' development is built around three successive sets of metaphors—of their light as a diffuse radiance, of their light as emanating from their bodily forms, and of their human forms as the source of their powers. The change from one stage to the next occurs as God and the angels move through three stages of activity—first establishing their potential to act, then supporting each other mutually, and finally contending with each other. Since each character changes as he acts and interacts, his development is independent, shaped by his individual choices, as well as interdependent, shaped by his need for others. As a result, we have an interwoven pattern of metaphors that provides a remarkable contrast to the few random images for God and the virtual lack of any images except light for Lucifer in the other three creation plays.

In the first stage of the characters' activity, the Chester dramatist uses a traditional image of light to represent a God who establishes His dramatic potential to create and to change: "My beames be all beawtitude; / all blisse is in my buyldinge" (I, 13–14). The idea of God's light diffusing itself in every direction and dimension, bringing eternity and infinity and time and space into existence, became a commonplace in Augustinian and Franciscan thought during the later Middle Ages.[17] In a theological context, the image establishes God's omnipotence. But it is the dramatic context in which God celebrates His beams, rather than the language itself, that makes the image extraordinary. The Chester God, unlike His three counterparts, speaks before, not as, He creates. Accordingly, He highlights His potential to create, instead of His act of creation. By implication, before the creation the Chester God is neither omnipotent nor immutable but omnipotential, which allows both for His divinity and His development.

We can see how suggestive of potential mutability the Chester-play image of God's light is by looking at the other three creation plays, whose characterizations of an immutable God are consistent in every respect with Christian theology of divine Forms. No character in these plays even mentions God's light, although light is an eminently traditional way of linking Him to the angels. Thus in each of these three plays, God remains ineffably distant from and unlike the angels, untouched by His creatures no matter what changes they bring about within the universe or in their own manifold dependence on Him.

Very differently, the Chester playwright prepares for the gradual humanizing of God's nature not only by interposing an image of God's diffused "beames" at a point in the play that suggests a state of potentiality but also by buttressing the image with an unconventional and difficult metaphor: "The might of my makeinge / is marked in mee, / dissolved under a deadem / by my devyne experience" (I, 32–35). These curiously ambiguous lines take on particular importance, given the playwright's precise use of language in the play as a whole, for they suggest that God's power is originally formless. The key terms are "marked," "dissolved," "deadem," and "experience." Although "marked" evokes an outline or a formal design, the word is qualified by "dissolved," which referred then as now to the absence or disintegration of form or structure (*MED*). In effect, God's power to create is distinguished not by inherent Forms or Ideas but by its diffused or inchoate state.[18] The Chester God Himself recognizes and approves this formlessness of His power, proclaiming its exaltation under His diadem, which crowns His divine existence.

The key to our understanding of the inherent processes shaping the Chester God's character is the phrase "by my experience." "Experience" meant a test or operation to ascertain some truth, a proof by trial or practical judgment, as well as the actual observation of events as a source of knowledge (*MED*). These all suggest that the original state of God's knowledge, like that of His power, was somehow still in the process of being formed, emphasizing the possibility of quite human ways of acquiring knowledge. These meanings also anticipate the bodily experience or trial that is Christ's human incarnation. By implication, we can assume that God's deeds, like men's, are in some way experimental, so that He too learns by practical encounters and observations just as His human creatures do.

Correspondingly, the Chester playwright uses imagery of light to portray Lucifer's original potential for action and development, thereby transforming a traditionally static figure into a dynamic character who can either remain loyal or rebel and who can also reverse his opposition to God, at least before he falls into hell. Scholars have tended to read Lucifer's (and Lightborne's) initial speeches as unquestionably insincere; however, the strong emphasis that the playwright gives to these declarations in the responses made by God and the other angels before the mutiny seems more consistent with a view of these speeches as expressions of the angels' complex capacity for moral development. The whole pattern of action, in fact, differs significantly from the paradigm employed in the other three creation plays, where Lucifer is created, immediately glorifies his own light, and promptly falls, forever denied any possibility of redemption. Thus each of these Lucifers begins and remains eternally fixed in opposition to God (*Summa,* I, Q.64, A.2). In contrast, the Chester playwright's extension of the span of action between the creation and the fall allows scope for representing Lucifer's original light not as an impetus to rebellion but as a sign of his potential to choose and change:

> Ney, lorde, that will we not in deed, / for nothinge tresspasse unto thee.
> Thy greate godhead we ever dreade, / and never exsaulte ourselves soe hie.
> Thou hast us marked with great might and mayne, / in thy blesse evermore
>   to byde and bee,
> in lastinge life our life to leade. / And bearer of lighte thou hast made me.
>   *(I, 94–101)*

Lucifer's potential is of course different from God's. While God celebrates His ability to create, the first angel confirms his ability to act morally by choosing and sustaining obedience over disobedience. Although he, like his counterparts, is extremely pleased with his own brilliance, his initial act, unlike theirs, is neither excessive nor obsessive, making his pleasure a sign of his inherent capacity to be with and to support God forever. Just as Lucifer's light reflects God's, his claim to be "marked with greate might" echoes God's proclamation that the "might of my makeinge / is marked in mee." Lucifer's rightful sphere of activity, like his state of potentiality, parallels God's.

To emphasize and expand upon these metaphoric correlations that prepare for the characters' political interactions, the playwright invents the supporting character Lightborne (sustained or carried by light, *OED*), who stands in relation to Lucifer as Lucifer stands to God. As the first angel's lieutenant, Lightborne elaborates on his superior's affirmation of the blessings accruing from service to God: "And I ame marked of that same moulde. / Loveinge be to our creator / that us hase made gayer then goulde, / under his dieadem ever to indure" (I, 102–105). Lightborne repeats the term "marked," echoing both God and Lucifer and thus emphasizing the similarities in the natures of all three. Lightborne also claims to be of the "same moulde" and, in effect, to have the same power and potential as they. Although *mold,* like *marked,* suggests shape or form, the complementary image—"gayer then goulde"—evokes only the purity and probity of the angels' light. Since the light of God's originally "dissolved" creative power is the source of the angels' strength, "moulde" emphasizes that Lucifer and Lightborne share a formlessness akin to God's during this first stage of their existence. God's phrase "dissolved under a deadem" becomes Lightborne's "under his dieadem ever to indure." The addition of "ever" intensifies our sense of the angels' similitude to God—the angels are for all intents and purposes eternal—while "dieadem" indicates the angels' closeness to God. This repetition thus makes God's crown a symbol not of His absolute power but of His and the angels' shared sphere of existence and perhaps of sovereignty.

Before we look at the possibilities for close involvement, however, we must explore the reverse side of Lucifer's moral potential and power. Appropriately, images of light reflect the paradox central to the Chester angel's nature, for his light gives him the potential not only for loyal participation in heavenly activities but also for treasonous behavior. Well before he acts on his rebellious desires, therefore, the Chester Lucifer competitively pits his light against God's:

> Aha, that I ame wounderous brighte, / amongest you all shininge full cleare!
> Of all heaven I beare the lighte / though God hymselfe and he were here.
>   *(I, 126–129)*
>
> ... I commaunde you for to cease / and see the beautie that I beare.
> All heaven shines through my brightnes / for God himselfe shines not so cleare.
>   *(I, 142–145)*

These declamations verge closely on defiance, but integrated as they are into the first stage of Lucifer's dramatic development, they express his sense of his potential to rule, should he decide to make himself master of the heavens. Although he claims to be more brilliant than God, not equally brilliant or like God, Lucifer calls only for the other angels' admiration of his light, not their allegiance. The line between disobeying God's injunction against self-exaltation and rebelling against God is a fine one, but Lucifer as yet clearly does not act to turn competition into contention. This distinction, however fine, is an important one for two reasons. First, in this one play the characters can and do develop morally (or immorally) and emotionally as well as physically. Such development stems from ambiguities inherent in their essential natures. Lucifer's light, for example, makes him extremely proud, but his pride could lead him either to act with unswerving loyalty or to preen himself dangerously, even before he is actually prepared to move against God. Second, the action is compounded of the characters' interactions, so that Lucifer's inertia when unaided offers a striking contrast to his activity once he is fully supported by Lightborne.

This complex imagistic pattern differs significantly from the straightforward York, Towneley, and N-town use of light imagery for Lucifer, as we can see by looking at the key images in the Towneley Lucifer's speech: "Syn that we ar all angels bright," "this mastre longys to me"; "I am a thowsand fold / brighter then is the son."[19] He claims unequivocally that his light makes him like God and therefore qualifies him to displace his Creator. Indeed, he also acts immediately on his belief, taking God's seat in the course of his exhortation. His speech differs from its York and N-town parallels only in the Towneley Lucifer's brief allusions to his bodily light—"I am so bright of ich a lym" (I, 106)—and bodily nature—"I am so semely, blode & bone" (I, 102). But the playwright does not build these corporeal images into the action, for the Towneley good and bad angels respond solely to Lucifer's assessment of his brilliance.

In the Chester play, however, images of bodily light and bodily form function as the vehicle of the angels' interactions and of further changes in the scope of God and Lucifer's political power. The second stage of the characters' development and interactions is marked by a shift from formlessness to bodily form, with the might of both God and Lucifer represented by the light emanating from their bodies. This shift not only begins the process of humanizing God and Lucifer but also signals radical changes in conventional views of God's strength. Even though the power of God's light remains unchanged, so that He remains the God of the play's universe, His assumption of bodily form involves the kind of limits inherent in physical existence:

> For I will wende and take my trace / and see this blesse in every tower.
> Iche one of you kepe well his place; / and, Lucifer, I make thee governour.
> Nowe I charge the grounde of grace / that yt be set with my order.
> Beholde the beames of my brighte face, / which ever was and shall indewer.
> This is your health in every case: / To beholude your creator.

Was never none so like me, soe full of grace, / nor never shall as my fygure.
Here will I bide nowe in this place / to be angells comforture.
To be revisible in shorte space, / it is my will in this same houre.

(I, 110–125)

To emphasize that God's bodily form imposes limits that become integral to the action, the playwright uses the most striking poetic devices—repetition, alliteration, and rhyme. Within the *ababababab* pattern, seven of the eight *a* rhymes (including "face" and the alliterative phrase "grounde of grace") and six of the *b* rhymes imply that God and the angels exist and function as if in space and time. These rhymes, "trace" (path or direction), "tower," "order," "place" (repeated twice), "space" (period of time), "houre," and "grounde of grace," indicate that temporal and spatial restrictions prevail in the heavens. Given that God now has both "face" and "fygure" (geometrical shape or outline and living body, *MED*), His power is limited to whatever place He occupies, as if corporeally, so that He must move from place to place in order to oversee His creation. But this constraint, inherent in any metaphoric humanizing of God and the angels (perhaps the reason the other creation plays have no such images of God), functions literally in order to prepare for God's interaction with the angels. He requires each of the angels to "kepe well his place" and appoints Lucifer to serve as "governour" in His stead, while He inspects the outlying regions of His domain. Thus the Chester playwright uses imagery to portray a more dramatically active God who not only includes the angels in His sphere of existence but who also shares the responsibilities of governing with them.

This representation of God's power differs considerably from the portrayals in the other creation plays. The York, Towneley, and N-town Gods are as unquestionably omnipresent as they are omnipotent: they neither employ Lucifer nor move about in order to govern. The N-town God speaks of Himself as "walking in þis wone [place]," but He does so as "þe ffadyr of powste," reflecting His absolute nature whether He occupies or leaves His throne (I, 15–18). The York God governs, knows Lucifer's intent to rebel even before the angel begins, and instantly throws Lucifer into hell without needing to move from His place at all. The Towneley God does leave His throne, but the move is a technical device, noted only in the rubrics, which allows Lucifer to occupy His seat momentarily. The text has only God's unqualified claims to omniscience—"ffor all is in my sight" (I, 15). Because the move does not enter into the dialogue, no conflict develops—a striking contrast to the Chester play in which Lucifer's assumption of God's throne becomes the subject of an extended struggle between the angels.

The Chester playwright uses metaphors of bodily light in the second stage of Lucifer's development, making these images the dramatic focus of the angels' sense of potency as well as of their subsequent interactions. Just as God's command, "Behoulde the beames of my brighte face," serves as a rallying point for the angels' support of His government, so Lucifer's bodily brightness stirs his follower Light-borne to offer the support that Lucifer needs to persist in his intention to rebel:

"Therfore you shalbe set here [in God's throne], / that all heaven maye ye behoulde. / The brightnes of your bodie cleare / is brighter then God a thousandfoulde" (I, 162–165). The second angel thus provides Lucifer with the necessary political support for a struggle against God, assuring him of his power to rule by maintaining that Lucifer's own body, rather than God's, is the source of his light and his power.[20]

Henceforth, the Chester angels respond to the destructive power generated by Lucifer and Lightborne's use of their bodily light. The angels who oppose Lucifer not only perceive the light emanating from the rebellious angels' bodies but also recognize that the "brightnes of your fayer bodyes / will make yee to goe hense" (I, 176–177). The situation anticipated by the loyal angels is of course an ironic echo of the earlier scene in which God's bodily light was linked to His movement about the heavens. Yet, the implicit parallel also reinforces Lucifer's credibility as an adversary to God because even the angels who resist Lucifer acknowledge the brilliance of his and Lightborne's bodies.

To dramatize the third stage of the characters' development, the playwright employs images of the bodies of God and Lucifer as the source of their power and the crux of their interaction. This third shift in imagery allows the playwright to make the strength manifested by God and Lucifer sufficiently alike to allow for a conflict without contravening doctrine too radically by engaging them in an actual physical clash. Yet their battle centers upon their relative physical positions and upon their bodily dominance over the angels. The Chester Lucifer, unlike his counterparts, exalts his body to justify his move into God's seat:

> Goe hense? Behoulde, sennyors one every syde, / and unto me you caste your eyen.
> I charge you angells in this tyde / behoulde and see now what I meane.
> Above greate God I will me guyde / and set myselfe here; as I wene,
> I ame pearlesse and prince of pride, / for God hymselfe shines not so sheene.
> Here will I sitt nowe in his steade, / to exsaulte myselfe in this same see.
> Behoulde my bodye, handes and head— / the mighte of God is marked in mee.
> All angells, torne to me I read, / and to your soveraigne kneele one your knee.
> I ame your comforte, bouth lorde and head, / the meirth and might of the majestye.
>
> *(I, 178–193)*

By flouting God's light rather than His bodily strength, Lucifer both denigrates God's power and avoids a direct challenge while focusing the other angels' attention on his own "bodye, handes and head" as the source of his power. His body, he believes, reveals that "the mighte of God is marked in mee" (an echo of God's earlier proclamation that the "might of my makeinge / is marked in mee") and qualifies him to move "Above" God. Similarly, Lucifer's pledge to be the angels' "comforte, bouth lorde and head" builds upon God's earlier vow to remain awhile "in this place / to be angells comforture." These adaptations of God's claims suggest that Lucifer now feels empowered as the corporeal ruler of the angels and of God. But Lucifer also requires the other angels to abase themselves physically before him—to cast their "eyen" on him and to "kneele one your knee." Just as God's travels about the heavens made the security of His government dependent upon the first angel's willingness to support His position, so Lucifer's rebellion depends upon the angels' consenting to make their acts conform physically to his.

The Chester playwright uses metaphors of bodily action and interaction in Lightborne's response to Lucifer's assumption of God's throne in order to dramatize the importance of the characters' bodily strength for political developments in heaven. Lightborne offers the equivalent of feudal fealty, promising to participate in the rebellion as "nexte of the same degree, / repleth by all experience," because if he "mighte sit him [Lucifer] bye / all heaven shoulde doe" them "reverence" (I, 194–197).[21] Lightborne's use of *replete* ("physically or materially stuffed," *OED*) and his reiteration of God's term "experience" suggest that he sees the act of seating himself with Lucifer as both a measure and a test of bodily strength. But when Lightborne refers competitively to God—"we shoulde him passe by our fullgens"— he, like Lucifer, ignores God's bodily form, thus deflecting the angels' attention from God's might and avoiding a too-precipitate challenge to God's power.

The angels who oppose Lucifer and support God also respond to the metaphoric shift in the locus of each character's strength. They too now use images of bodily movement to warn the two rebellious angels of the physical punishment awaiting them, if they persist:

> our soveraigne lorde will have you hense / and he fynde you in this araye.
> Goe too your seates and wynde your hense. / You have begone a parlous playe.
> Ye shall well witt the subsequence— / this daunce will torne to teene and traye.
>
> *(I, 204–209)*

The choice that the Dominations offer Lucifer and Lightborne is an extraordinarily human one, made possible by the playwright's reworking of St. Thomas's distinction between evil in human situations and evil in nature. Thomas saw natural evil as Augustine did, as the absence of good and thus as nothing in itself, but he saw moral evil as "constitutive," as having intrinsic qualities that can change (*Summa,* I, Q. 48, A.1, R.2). Since good and evil alike were "something," they could act upon each other so that "from this evil in morality, there may be a return to good, but not from any sort of [natural] evil," such as blindness (*Summa,* I, Q.48, A.1, R.3). Similarly, the Chester Lucifer's rebellious move can be reversed. He can escape punishment even after he takes God's seat if he simply follows the loyal angels' advice and forgoes the interaction set up in his "parlous playe." Because the playwright represents God's power as defined by His body and thus as spatially limited, Lucifer and Lightborne still have time to chose between moving toward disaster or toward joy, providing that they can forgo "this araye" (battle dress and position, *OED*). As "have you hense" and "wynde you hense" also indicate, the journey in either direction is imaged as physical. These images combine with the even more physically suggestive "playe" and "daunce," ironically highlighting the interactive forces at work on the angels' destinies. The Chester playwright's elaboration of the conventionally brief rebellion allows him to develop his dramatic material in two highly effective ways. First, the angels' interactions involve them in a moral struggle that simply does not occur in the other three cycle plays. Second, the Chester playwright makes the angels' interactions crucial to the course of the struggle between Lucifer and God: Lucifer is so emboldened by Lightborne's support and so angered by the loyal angels' opposition that he finally issues a direct challenge to God: "Though God come, I will not hense, / but sitt righte here before his face" (I, 212–213). With dramatic economy, this challenge metaphorically suggests God's physical involvement in the play's conflict without engaging Him physically, a depiction that would stretch Christian doctrine beyond reasonable bounds.

God responds by throwing Lucifer and Lightborne into hell, as is conventional, but the speech accompanying His act singularly links the punishment to the bodily metaphors that shaped the preceding interaction: "Saye, what araye doe ye make here? . . . Therfore I charge this order [Lucifer's] cleare, / faste from this place looke that yee fall. / Full soone I shall chaunge your cheare— / for your fowle pride to hell you shall" (I, 214–221). God's reiteration of "araye" indicates that He, like the angels, sees the struggle for rule of the heavens as akin to a physical venture into battle. His use of "cheare" is an ironic pun, playing upon various medieval meanings of the word—chair, situation, or entertainment, and the earliest of the meanings, facial expression (*MED*). The rebellious angels not only lose all access to God's chair and meet a most dismal sort of recreation but also experience a diametric change in their bodily natures. In effect, God responds to and builds His retribution upon Lucifer's challenge to His face by debasing the angels' physical positions and forms.

III

In the scene in hell, the Chester playwright continues his strategy of using bodily images as the focus of the fallen angels' political interaction and conflict. Not only does the dramatist play upon the conventional transformation of the angels from creatures of light to creatures of darkness, as the York and Towneley authors do, but he also makes the demons' darkened and debased bodies the specific focus of their anger and despair. Just as Lucifer had issued a personal challenge to God's face in heaven, so Lightborne, now the Second Demon, withdraws his earlier support and defies Lucifer, the First Demon, to his face in hell: "And even heither thou hast us broughte / into dungeon to take our trace. / All this sorrowe thou hast us soughte—/ the devill maye speede thy stinckinge face" (I, 234–237). This challenge repeats God's earlier linking of face and trace, implying that the difference between God's "brighte" and Lucifer's "stinckinge face" is a bitter measure of how much the two angels have lost. In essence, the repetition reveals that their bodily natures, however changed, continue to reflect and advance their interactions.

The First Demon simply responds in kind, apparently to throw the blame and the curse back in the teeth of the Second: "My face, false feature, for thy fare! / Thou hast us broughte to teene and treay" (I, 238–239). Yet the epithet "false feature" (perverted form or creature, MED) reminds the Second that his nature, like his acts, still corresponds to the First's. The epithet also implies that the Second's part in advancing the rebellion now makes it necessary that he accept the First's face as his "fare" (both sustenance and way, MED). As in any human relationship, the two angels' interaction, not the unilateral desires or acts of one or the other, led to their present plight. Since the fact of their mutual responsibility is beyond gainsaying, the Second stops accusing the First and turns to lamenting the predicament that they share: "Then shall we never care for woo" (I, 250). The "we" indicates that the Second Demon understands and accepts his and Lucifer's interdependency, something Lucifer had failed to realize in his interaction with God, but the "never care" suggests that the Second believes that their interaction might well be ended, if only because he sees nothing further to be gained by working together.

Much as God had made Lucifer His "governour," the First Demon engages the Second as his next-in-command in a new joint enterprise: "Ruffyn, my frende fayer and free, / loke that thou keepe mankinde from blesse" (I, 260–261). Although conflict now becomes the major form of interaction for man, the Demons, and God, mutual support is as necessary to the success of the Demons' hellish struggle as to God's heavenly works. No matter how ironically the First's acclaim of the Second as his "frende fayer and free" echoes God's disappointed cry "I made thee my frende," the First Demon and God alike manifest their desire, if not their need, for close personal relationship in order to rule their respective domains properly. The Chester cycle scene in hell thus differs radically from those in the York and Towneley cycles because its First and Second Demons' quite human interaction enables them to come to terms politically and emotionally with each other and their situation.

No such personal or political interplay is enacted by the demons in the other cycle plays. The other three dramatists avoid using imagery of bodily form, emphasizing instead the angels' loss of light. The N-town Lucifer simply accepts that he is a "devyl ful derke" in heaven (I, 77), and no scene in hell follows. In the Towneley scene in hell, only the fallen angels speak, expressing regret solely for having lost their light and "waxen blak as any coyll."[22] The York scene in hell, like the Chester, depicts demons who argue coarsely with Lucifer, for the playwright emphasizes that Demons have become incapable of the fine intellectual processes once characterizing their acts in heaven. The York Lucifer also expostulates in return, although the exchange remains a stalled interaction, since it goes no further: "Vnthryuandely threpe ȝhe, I sayde but a thoghte" and "ȝhe ly, owte! allas! / I wyste noghte þis wo sculde be wroghte. / Owte on ȝhow! lurdans, ȝhe smore me in smoke" (I, 114–117). Lucifer's confusion, not his desire to manipulate and use his followers, shapes his response, for he had indeed entertained no more than the thought of rebelling in heaven and now speaks what he believes to be true when he disclaims responsibility for their fate. But because neither the angels nor Lucifer influence each other in any way, the scene ends without any understanding or accommodation between them.

If the Chester Lucifer's interaction with Lightborne seems human because it is manipulative and self-serving, God's interaction with the angels seems human because of the pain that He suffers at losing even two of them:

> A, wicked pryde! A, woo worth thee, woo!
> My meirth thou hast made amisse.
> I maye well suffer: my will is not soe
> that they shoulde parte this from my blesse.
> A, pryde! Why mighte thou not braste in two?
> Why did the that? Why did they thus?
> Beholde, my angells, pride is your foe.
> All sorrowe shall shewe wheresoever yt is.
>
> And though they have broken my comaundement,
> me ruse yt sore full sufferently.
>
> *(I, 274–283)*

Singularly, God feels the loss of the fallen angels as keenly as they feel their loss of heaven. Where the Gods of the other three cycle plays remain wholly detached, either focusing dispassionately on the justice of Lucifer's punishment or ignoring the fact of the fall entirely, the Chester God responds emotionally, as would a human ruler betrayed by one whom he had loved and trusted enough to make his personal deputy. Thus He "maye well suffer" from the experience. Yet His anguish stems not only from the hurt caused Him by the rebellion but also from His perplexity over the motive for rebelling. Even though He thrice reiterates that "pride," the conventional motive, was the cause, God adds "Why did they that? Why did they thus?" Insofar as these questions are rhetorical, they underplay the bewilderment that they suggest, while also emphasizing the subtle humanizing of God that occurs in the course of the play. Like Lucifer and Lightborne, God shows increasingly emotional concern over the changed bodily order, concern that seems acutely personal and human.

Much like a wise and perceptive human being, He understands the pride underlying Lucifer and Lightborne's rebellion; but unlike an omniscient God, He remains puzzled about why they were so susceptible to pride. Also like a human being, the Chester God is vulnerable to the pain of broken trust and friendship, vulnerability built upon his humanly-appearing bodily form and limitations. In fact, God shows himself to be even more deeply and poignantly affected than the Demons by the polarization that divides the universe into opposing camps. The reflexive construction, "me ruse," in the final line of God's lament indicates that He regrets the fall both for His own sake and for the angels'. What began as a beneficial sharing of responsibility among God, Lucifer, and the angels ends as a baneful give-and-take of affliction. In sum, the Chester playwright integrates doctrine and drama to portray a God and a Lucifer who, however stylized, have become well-realized dramatic characters in a fictive world, characters whose struggle illustrates the ultimate interconnectedness of all acts and all beings in ways that intensify the audience's sense of the horror of all evil, for it touches even God.

NOTES

1. Eleanor Prosser, in *Drama and Religion in the English Mystery Plays* (Stanford: Stanford University Press, 1961), for example, follows Hardin Craig's view that the cycle drama's " 'life-blood was religion, and [that] its success depended on its awakening and releasing a pent-up body of religious knowledge and religious feeling' " (p. 10). Her emphasis on religious rather than dramatic concerns as the determinant of the cycle plays' form marks the direction taken by later critics. The most recent study of the Chester cycle, Peter W. Travis's *Dramatic Design in the Chester Cycle* (Chicago: University of Chicago Press, 1982), takes the same tack. He offers a carefully developed argument that the medieval viewers participated by a kind of displaced "late medieval affective piety" (p. 21) in the "illusion of the play" (p. 24). The cycle thus becomes a kind of displaced religion, with the elements of the creation play, from God's circumscribing of space to the final contrast of heavenly light and hellish darkness, reflecting the actual harmony and eternity of the creation. He, like Prosser, believes the "recurring dramatic imperative of the English Corpus Christi plays" to be " 'Behold and believe!' " (p. 201), a call to salvation. I would argue that the cycles represent religious material, but they humanize (which does not mean secularize) their material in ways that satisfy their authors' and audiences' need for drama even more than their need for religion. For a concise overview of the "sources, analogues, and authorities" in the cycle, see R. M. Lumiansky and David Mills's *The Chester Mystery Cycle: Essays and Documents* (Chapel Hill: University of North Carolina Press, 1983), Ch. 2.

2. Scholars at first considered the Chester cycle the earliest of the four. But Lawrence M. Clopper's convincing work on the documents pertaining to the Chester cycle ("The History and Development of the Chester Cycle," *Modern Philology,* 75 [1978], 219–246) has changed scholarly opinion on the date of the plays by demonstrating that all known documents pertaining to the cycle are very late.

3. *Reliquae Antiquae,* ed. Thomas Wright and James Orchard Halliwell, 2 vols. (London: John Russell Smith, 1845; rpt. New York: AMS Press, 1966), II, 42–57. This treatise also confirms that the miracle plays' basic appeal was to the bodily senses—"syth myraclis pleyinge is of the lustis of the fleyssh and myrthe of the body"—but disapproves of the plays because of the author's conviction that "the voyce of Crist and the voyce of the fleysh ben of two contrarious lordis" (p. 44). Indeed, as we shall see, both voices must be valued before non-devotional drama can become possible.

4. (Stanford: Stanford University Press, 1966), p. 19. Kolve's important work is a major beginning to studying the plays as plays. His approach allows him to examine the characters in the plays as dramatic figures, not as Christian icons, even though he believes that the plays were primarily intended to encourage faith and virtue. Where Travis's study thoroughly illuminates the depth of the Christianity subsumed in the plays, Kolve's suggests the vital importance of such dramatic techniques as irony in transforming religion into drama. See also R. W. Hanning's " 'You Have Begun a Parlous Pleye': The Nature and Limits of Dramatic Mimesis as a Theme in Four Middle English 'Fall of Lucifer' Cycle Plays" (*Comparative Drama,* 7 [1973], 22–50). Hanning applies Kolve's theory to the creation plays by reinterpreting game as mimesis. His evaluation of the play contradicts Rosemary Woolf's, for he finds the Chester play the most sophisticated of the four, primarily because he perceptively notes the features unique to this play—for example, the concretization of heaven, the subversion of Lucifer by Lightborne, the human dismay of God, and the extended conflict. But Hanning's assumptions that Lucifer's sin was an attempt to imitate God and that the period between the creation and rebellion of the angel is extended to create suspense obfuscate the significance of these elements in the design of the work. His premises lead away from recognition of the pattern of God's and the angels' interactions—interactions that provide the basis for and give meaning to the conflict.

5. (Berkeley: University of California Press, 1973), pp. 85–101.

6. *York Plays,* ed. Lucy Toulmin Smith (1885; rpt. New York: Russell & Russell, 1963), I, 19.

7. *The Chester Mystery Cycle,* ed. R. M. Lumiansky and David Mills, Early English Text Society, S. S. 3 (London: Early English Text Society, 1974), I, 207–209. Subsequent references to passages from the Chester play are noted in the text.

8. *Summa Theologica,* 3 vols. (New York: Benziger Brothers, Inc., 1947), I,. Q.45, A.6.

9. See Bernard of Clairvaux, *"De Gradibus Humilitatis,"* in *Opera Omnia* (Paris: Apud Faume Fratres, 1939), I, 1277–1293; and "Vitis Mystica: Tractatus De Passione Domini," in *Opera Omnia,* II, 865–988. See, too, St. Bonaventura, *The Mind's Road to God,* trans. George Boas (Indianapolis: Bobbs-Merrill Co., 1953), pp. 27, 32, 42, 43; Etienne Gilson, *The Philosophy of St. Bonaventura,* trans. Dom Illtyd Trethowan and Frank J. Sheed (Patterson, N. J.: St. Anthony Guild Press, 1965), pp. 429–432.

10. Thomas, I, Q.3, A.1–2; I, Q.50, A.1–2. St. Augustine, *The City of God,* ed. David Knowles, trans. Henry Bettenson (Baltimore: Pelican Classics, 1972), XII, 26; *The Confessions,* ed. Harold C. Gardiner, S.J., trans. Edward B. Pusey, D.D. (New York: Washington Square Press, Inc., 1963), XII, pp. 262–265. For the importance of Thomas to Renaissance drama, see George C. Herndl's study, *The High Design: English Renaissance Tragedy and the Natural Law* (Lexington: The University Press of Kentucky, 1970), pp. 88–109. For a fairly detailed account of the continued importance of Thomas's philosophy in the Renaissance, see Armand A. Maurer's *Medieval Philosophy* (New York: Random House, 1962), pp. 327–371.

11. See Gordon Leff, *Medieval Thought* (1958; rpt. Baltimore: Penguin Books, 1965), pp. 294–296.

12. See David Knowles, *The Evolution of Medieval Thought* (New York: Random House, 1962), Ch. XXVI, "The Breakdown of the Synthesis," pp. 311–317 and Ch. XXVIII, "The Harvest of Nominalism," pp. 327–336; see also Leff, pp. 289–302. These two works provide lucid and concise discussions of fourteenth-century views of God, science, and mysticism.

13. *Ludus Coventriae or The Plaie Called Corpus Christi,* ed. K. S. Block, Early English Text Society, E. S. 120 (London: Early English Text Society, 1922), I, 15–18.

14. Knowles, p. 330.

15. "Divine Power in the Chester Cycle and Late Medieval Thought," *Journal of the History of Ideas,* 39 (1978), 387–404. See also Etienne Gilson, *History of Christian Philosophy in the Middle Ages* (New York: Random House, 1955), p. 499. Gilson also offers excellent discussions of the changes wrought by the Nominalists.

16. See Sir Thomas Elyot's exemplary work *The Governor* (New York: Everyman's Library, 1962), p. 332.

17. This image of God's light could well come directly from the Augustinians, who propounded a theology of light. St. Bernard, in *De Consideratione, Liber V, Caput XII* in *Opera Omnia,* I, for example, teaches that God's light reaches everywhere to overcome moral and spiritual darkness (p. 1090). The Chester image of God's light recalls not only the thought of St. Bernard but also that of St. Bonaventura, an Augustinian contemporary of St. Thomas, who taught that God's power radiated out like pure light (see, for example, *Collations on the Six Days,* trans. Jose de Vinck, in *Works,* [Patterson, N. J.: St. Anthony Guild Press, 1970], V, 304–307).

18. Just such an implicit connection between light and a "dissolved" state was made by St. Bonaventura. He expounded a view of God's power both as light and as "a fullness of originating perfection" and "a productive diffusion," for His nature "supremely diffuses itself in a threefold outpouring" which His creatures receive according to the capacity of their finite and imperfect natures (*Collations,* pp. 160–166). Correspondingly, Bonaventura believed that God's absolute good is "self-diffusive" (*The Mind's Road to God,* p. 39).

19. *The Towneley Plays,* ed. George England and Alfred W. Pollard, Early English Text Society, E. S. 51 (London: Early English Text Society, 1897), I, 78, 81, 88–89.

20. This line reflects St. Thomas's view of Lucifer's motive: "that likeness of God which is bestowed by grace, he sought to have it by the power of his own nature" (*Summa,* I, Q.63, A.3).

21. Lightborne's hopes for himself reflect St. Thomas's theory of the lesser rebellious angels' motive: the follower of Lucifer "chooses rather to be subject to an inferior than to a superior, if he can procure an advantage under an inferior which he cannot under a superior" (*Summa,* I, Q.64, A.8, R.2).

22. Towneley, I, 136–138. This play's Lucifer does not speak again until his temptation of Adam and Eve, which is treated not as a separate play but as part of the creation and fall.

Seven Actors in Search of a Biographer

JACKSON CAMPBELL BOSWELL

EDWIN NUNGEZER'S *Dictionary of Actors*[1] has long stood as a handy reference tool on the bookshelves of theater historians. Recent and current research by Glynne Wickham, Daniel Rowan, William Ingram, and others suggests that it is time for a revised, updated edition. Toward such an endeavor, I offer details about seven early English actors, five of whom were omitted by Nungezer, who also misrepresented the other two. The names of six are Thomas Moyle, Simon Fish, John Roo, Richard Spenser, Andrew Hewit, and one Ramsey. The seventh may be a Myles Somelymes, but, since his identity is uncertain, I term him "Dr. Turner's patient" or "an actor in hot water."

In the Christmas season of 1526, some students of Gray's Inn produced a "disguising" for the delectation of their fellows. The play had been, according to Halle's *Chronicle*,[2] "compiled for the most part" twenty years previously by John Roo, a sergeant-at-law. The play has as its plot "that lorde governance was ruled by dissipacion and negligence, by whose misgovernance and evill order, lady Publike wele was put from governance: which caused Rumor Populi, Inward grudge and disdain of wanton sovereignetie, to rise with a greate multitude, to expell negligence and dissipacion, and to restore Publik welth again to her estate, which was so doen." Halle continues, "This plaie was so set furth with riche and costly apparel, with straunge divises of Maskes & morrishes that it was highly praised of all menne, savyng of the Cardinall [Thomas Wolsey], whiche imagined that the plaie had been divised of hym, & in a greate furie sent for the saied master Roo, and toke from hym his Coyfe, and sent hym to the Flete, & after he sent for the yong gentlemen, that plaied in the plaie, and them highly rebuked and thretened, & sent one of them called Thomas Moyle of Kent to the Flete. . . . This plaie sore displeased the Cardinall, and yet it was never meante to hym" (f. 154ᵛ).

Halle does not mention any actors in the drama other than Moyle,[3] but John Foxe names Simon Fish as one of the "gentlemen that plaied." Indeed, Foxe calls him the chief actor who took the part "after all others had refused it."[4] Although Halle strongly discounts any satiric intent against Cardinal Wolsey, Foxe says, "There was a certaine play or interlude made by one Master Roo . . . in whiche playe partly was matter agaynst the Cardinal Wolsey. And where none durst take upon them to play that part, which touched the sayd Cardinall, this foresayd M. Fishe tooke uppon him to do it, whereupon great displeasure ensued agaynst him, upon the Cardinals part: Insomuch as he beyng pursued by the sayd cardinall, the same nyght that this Tragedy was playd, was compelled of force to voyde his owne house, & so fled over the sea unto Tyndale."[5]

51

Robert Persons, writing to undercut and discredit Foxe,[6] gives a somewhat different interpretation to these events, but he concurs that the play was politically inspired. According to Persons, Fish fled England "for having played an opprobrious pagent against *Cardinall Wolsey.*" He fled "to Tyndall in Flanders, & there being well instructed by him, wrote that famous raylinge booke, intituled: *The Supplication of beggars* [*STC* 10883 (1529)], (answered afterward by *Syr Thomas More,* when he was Chancelor of the Dutchy of *Lancaster,* intituling it *The supplication of soules)*" [*STC* 18092 (1529)].[7] Considering the propagandistic motivations of both Foxe and Persons, one tends to give greater credence to Halle than to either of these religious partisans.

Although both Halle and Foxe spell the playwright's name *Roo,* Nungezer spells the name *Roll,* with appropriate cross-references. Nungezer cites John Payne Collier, who, in his usual slapdash fashion, muddies the waters a bit; Collier assigns the play to "Christmas, 1527-8."[8] On the authority of E. K. Chambers, Nungezer also notes that "Roll" was a "Court Interluder" in 1530 and that he died in 1539.

There are, in point of fact, two John Roo's. In addition to the John Roo (or Roll) who was a member of the royal company of Interlude Players in the reign of Henry VIII and who died in 1539, there is John Roo (or Rowe) the distinguished barrister and amateur playwright who was Sergeant-at-law in Gray's Inn; he died 8 October 1544. Nungezer, regrettably, conflates the two.[9]

Three other actors also became embroiled in politico-religious controversy and were burned for heresy in Salisbury in 1541. According to John Foxe, "Richard Spenser in lyke maner priest, leaving his papistrie, toke unto hym a wyfe getting his living with ye sweate of his browes and labours of hys handes. Besides this, forsomuche as he was thought to holde a contrary opinion of the Sacrament against the decrees and lawes in those dayes, he was craftely circumvented and put to death, being burned at Salisbury together with one Andrew Hewyt in the yeare aforesayd."[10] Foxe revised this account shortly afterwards to include several significant facts: "About the same tyme also a certeine Priest was burned at Salisbury, who leavyng his Papistry, had maryed a wife, and become a player in interludes, with one Ramsey and Hewet, which iii. were all condemned and burned: Against whom, and specially agaynst Spenser, was layde matter concernyng the Sacrament of the altar."[11]

Commenting on Foxe's statement about Spenser, Robert Persons names *"Richard Spencer* an Apostata priest" who "became a stage-player for lacke of a better occupation, togeather with his fellow commediants *Ramsey* and *Hewyt."*[12] Persons also assigns Spenser the feast day of 3 November in the Foxeian calendar; Andrew Hewit receives the following day; Ramsey gets left out of the calendar.[13] William Turner's *A Booke of the Natures and Properties, of the Bathes in England* (hereinafter *A Booke of the Bathes)*, contains a reference to Myles Somelymes, an actor in Lord Somerset's company.[14] The reference is somewhat ambiguous and has, I believe, hitherto been misinterpreted. Turner's actor was first noted by John Payne Collier[15] and was later picked up by Nungezer.[16] Depending in part upon Collier's inaccurate transcription of Turner's text, Nungezer lumped together three men whose names are variations on Miles; the resultant confusion is not only misleading but downright inaccurate.

In light of the date and place listed in Turner's Preface to *A Booke of the Bathes* (from Basel on 10 March 1557), it seems that he may have known one of Lord Somerset's players sometime between 1551, after his first appointment as Dean of Wells, and 1553, before his second exile.[17] John Tucker Murray indicates that the Lord Protector's company was in Bristol on 28 April 1551;[18] as Wells, Bristol, and Bath are within a fifteen-mile radius, it is possible that Turner met Lord Somerset's player then.

The Lord Somerset who was Turner's contemporary was Edward Seymour, sometime brother-in-law to Henry VIII. Collier says, "It is not at all unlikely, that on the accession of Edward VI., the Protector, who assumed all the authority of King, took into his pay at least some of the discharged players of Henry VIII: . . . and, although it [the name *Myles*] does not occur among those [listed players] of Henry VIII., at any former period, some of his fellows might have been selected from older theatrical retainers of the crown."[19] Murray also notes that Lord Seymour "seems to have first taken a company of players into his patronage soon after he became Lord Protector, for such a company is not mentioned till 1547-48 when they acted at Canterbury. As they are not heard of after then [22 January 1552], they probably disbanded or passed under other patronage about the time of the Duke of Somerset's execution."[20]

Turner's reference to the actor occurs during a discussion of the efficacy of the waters at Bath; there he says, "The chefe matter whereof these bathes in this citye have theyr chefe vertue and streingth / after my judgement is *brimstone*."[21] Those who would examine the baths as he has done should concur in his opinion, he says, and he cites as evidence of his persuasion the following incident: "When as I was at these bathes wyth a certayn man diseased in the goute / I went in to them my selfe wyth my patiente / and broughte furth of the place nexte unto the spring / and out of the bottom / slyme / mudde / bones and stones / whyche alltogether smelled evidentlye of brimstone" (f. 1). Brimstone, he goes on to say, is the "only mater in these bathes / or ellis the chefe that beareth ruel in them. For they drye up wounder-fullye / and heale the goute excellentlye / and that in a shorte tyme / as wyth diverse other one myles somtyme / one of my Lorde of Summersettes players can beare witnes" (f. 1).

Collier, with his usual disdain for accuracy, transcribes the passage in this fashion: "the writer says: for they [the waters of Bath] drye up wounderfullye, and heale the goute excellentlye (and that in a short tyme), as with diverse other, one Myles, one of my Lord of Summersettes players, can beare witnesse."[22] In spite of the liberties that Collier takes with the text, he may well have caught Turner's intention. Neither *Somtyme* nor *Somelymes,* as it is spelled in the 1586 edition, is a common English surname; neither is listed in the Register of Wills, and neither turned up on the Mormon computer for genealogical research. Considering Turner's difficult hand, his capricious punctuation, spelling, and capitalization—to say nothing of the vagaries of printers—it is entirely possible that the passage was intended to read as Collier transmogrifies it or, alternatively, ". . . as wyth diverse other[s] one Myles / somtyme one of my Lorde of Summersettes players. . . ." It should be noted, however, that the spelling of the player's name remains uniform in all the editions of *A Booke of the Bathes* published in Turner's lifetime. In William Bremer's editions (see Note 14), the spelling changes from *Myles Somtyme* (1562) and *Myles Some-lymes* (1586) to *Miles Somelimes* in 1587; the name continues to be spelled thus in all subsequent editions. Moreover, through all nine editions of the work a pause is consistently marked after *Somtyme/Somelymes/Somelimes* rather than after *Myles/Miles*. Needless to say, although say it I will, just because *Somtyme/Somelymes/Somelimes* no longer seems to exist as a family name, it does not follow that it never existed; indeed, Bremer may have altered the spelling and retained Turner's punctu-ation from some knowledge that we do not possess today. Doubtlessly Bremer's reasons for making the changes were as rational as Nungezer's gratuitous conflation of Turner's patient with Tobias Mils, a member of Queen Elizabeth's company in 1583, and with Tobias Milles, son of Robert Cecil's secretary.[23] It is highly unlikely that a gouty trouper of the reign of Henry VIII is either of these two individuals who flourished in his younger daughter's old age. To list *Myles Somelymes* (or whatever) under the name *Tobias Mils* is, in effect, to deny him his rightful billing in the playbill of the theater history.

Just as the placid pool of Bath yielded up unexpected evidence of healing power along with the slime, mud, bones, and stones, so Turner's *Booke of the Bathes* yields up to us an unexpected find: the name of a gout-plagued player whose aches and pains saved him from anonymity.

NOTES

1. (New Haven, Conn.: Yale University Press, 1929; rpt. New York: AMS Press, 1971).

2. Edward Halle, *The Union of the Two Noble and Illustrate Famelies* (London, 1548); *STC* 12721.

3. For a brief account of Thomas Moyle, see *DNB*.

4. See Fish's entry in *DNB*. For fuller accounts of this episode, see A. C. Pollard, *Wolsey* (London: Longmans, Green 1929), pp. 220–221, and Neville Williams, *The Cardinal & The Secretary* (London: Weidenfield and Nicolson, 1975), pp. 75 ff.

5. John Foxe, *Actes and Monuments* (London, 1570), II.1152-1153; *STC* 11223. In the 1877 edition, IV.657.

6. William Eusebius Andrews, *Critical and Historical Review of Fox's Book of Martyrs, Shewing the Inaccuracies, Falsehoods, and Misrepresentations in that Work of Deception* (London: by author, 1824).

7. Robert Persons [Parsons], *A Treatise of Three Conversions of England* (St. Omer, 1603), II.416; *STC* 19416.

8. Foxe says, "It [the play] happened the first year that this gentleman [Fish] came to London to dwell, which was about AD. 1525" (IV.657). For a more exact date see Pollard and Williams.

9. Actually Nungezer might have sensed something fishy about the coincidence of names, for a sergeant-at-law was a barrister of some standing whose rank was comparable to a doctor of law

in ecclesiastical courts. In the Tudor period all judges of common-law courts had to have served as sergeants-at-law prior to their elevation to the bench. It is exceedingly doubtful that a sergeant-at-law would demean himself by becoming a common player—even in a royal company. See *Black's Law Dictionary.*

10. *Actes and Monuments* (London, 1563), p. 613.

11. *Actes and Monuments* (London, 1570), II.1376.

12. Persons, III.236.

13. Persons, III.sig. ******4.

14. Turner finished his work on healing waters in 1552, and it was first published as *The Second Parte of William Turners Herball* in 1562 (*STC* 24366) and republished as the fourth part of the enlarged *Herbal* of 1568 (*STC* 24367). It was also reprinted in William Bremer's edition of Thomas Vicary's *The Englishman's Treasure* in 1586 and in six subsequent editions (*STC* 24707 *et seq.*) as *The Rare Treasor of the English Bathes. A Booke of the Bathes* is occasionally found bound separately (*STC* 24351 and *STC* 24352).

15. John Payne Collier, *The History of English Dramatic Poetry to the Time of Shakespeare; and Annals of the Stage to the Restoration* (London: John Murray, 1831), I, 140.

16. Pp. 251–252.

17. Although best known to posterity as a naturalist, Turner wrote a number of ardent religious tracts in pursuit of preferment. A devout disciple of Hugh Latimer, he was forced into exile because of his outspoken, impolitic opinions. While abroad he studied natural history and medicine and became friends with Conrad Gesner and other eminent European naturalists. After returning to England, Turner was appointed Dean of Wells Cathedral in 1551, but following the death of Edward VI in 1553, he went into another period of exile to escape the Marian persecutions. He was eventually restored to the Deanery of Wells in 1558. Awarded his doctorate in medicine in Italy during his first exile, Turner proceeded to incorporate for an M.D. at Oxford upon his return, and he combined medical and clerical duties throughout the remainder of his career. See Charles Webster, *Dictionary of Scientific Biography* (New York: Charles Scribner's Sons, 1970–80), XIII, 501–503.

18. John Tucker Murray, *English Dramatic Companies 1558–1642*, 2 vols. (London: Constable, 1910), II, 68.

19. Collier, I, 140.

20. Murray, II, 68.

21. Turner (1562 ed.; *STC* 24365), f. 1. Turner's suggestion that Englishmen bathe for their health was met with some skepticism, but the idea caught on slowly. In his *Almanacke and Prognostication for 1604* (*STC2* 466.6), Thomas Johnson advises readers to enter the baths of Bustons or Bathe only in April, May, or September [sig. A2]. John Neve's advice on bathing in his *Prognostication for 1631* (*STC2* 490.7) is indicative of conservative attitudes and practices prevalent in Turner's time:

> Bathings, are commonly used rather for pleasure then for profit, especially where hot-houses are overmuch haunted, but I mind not to speake of them in this place, otherwise then to advertise those that tender their own health, to be warie and circumspect in resorting unto them without cause, and immediatly after or with such persons as be uncleane. . . . Furthermore if Bathing bee used for health, let the party grieved learne of the wise Physition, whether his sicknesse hath need of moystening, or drying . . . if the sicknesse require drying . . . then let him Bath the moone being in fiery signs, having good aspects of Mars and the Sunne.
>
> Also before you enter into any Bath, your body must be first purged, for if you goe in unprepared & unpurged, peradventure you may be worse then before.

The best time of the yeare to Bath in, is in the Spring and Harvest, and in the moenth of May and September. The best time of the day to goe into the Bath, is one houre after the Sun rising at the least, alwaies provided, that you must walke either an houre or halfe an houre before, and have a stool either by nature or art: you must cover your head well, so long as you be in the Bath, and beware you drinke not cold drinke although you be very thirsty, but forbeare all things that be cold, least when you are hot within, cold strike suddenly into some principall member and so hurt you.

The time of tarying in the Bath, is commonly one houre, but it may be more or lesse, according to the nature of the Bath, or sicknesse of the party, at the discretion of the wise Phisition.

(sigs. B3–B4)

22. Collier, I, 139.
23. Pp. 251–252.

Man's House as His Castle
in *Arden of Feversham*

LENA COWEN ORLIN

STUDENTS OF THE English Renaissance already have some idea of what the private house could mean as an ideal of order from the "great house" literature of Sidney on Kalander's house, Jonson on Penshurst, and Marvell on Nunappleton.[1] But we have come to recognize that we can appreciate the tension and poignancy of Sidney's, Jonson's, and Marvell's encomiums only if we understand their awareness of the larger changes threatening such domestic order. What we should also apprehend is that these changes were experienced by householders of all stations, not just the residents of the great houses, as many "new" men of lower classes acquired land and property for the first time in the expanding economy of the Tudor and Stuart years.

It was Henry VIII's alienation of confiscated monastic lands, deplored by some as an undermining of the integrity of the royal household, that provided the opportunity for the members of a flourishing gentry class to establish themselves for the first time in the sixteenth century as landlords and householders. The position of these new men was reinforced, especially in contemporary conduct-literature, by their depiction as figures of order presiding over domestic microcosms of the state, an analogy that had first established itself in English law. In 1605, Sir Edward Coke was to decide a case before the King's Bench with the observations "That the house of every one is to him his Castle and Fortress, as well for defence against injury and violence, as for his repose. . . . [T]he Law without default in the owner doth abhorre destruction or breaking of any house which is for the habitation and safety of a man." In 1628, in *The Third Institute,* he would repeat that "a mans house is his castle . . . where shall a man be safe, if it be not in his house?" Although Coke is customarily credited with that central metaphor, he undoubtedly borrowed it from William Lambard's *Eirenarcha,* written in 1579: "our law calleth a mans house, his castle, meaning that he may defend himselfe therein." In turn, Lambard credited Sir William Stanford, who, in *Les Plees del Coron,* had written in 1557 that "ma measõ est a moy: come mon castel, hors de quel, le ley ne moy arta a fuer." And Stanford had cited a statute from 1478: "la meason de home est a luy son Castel & son defence."[2]

The cultural ethos suggested by this legal metaphor shaped not only sixteenth- and seventeenth-century great house literature but also a species of drama that made its first appearance in 1592 with the anonymous *Arden of Feversham*. This story of a gentleman householder from Kent who was murdered in his home[3] by his wife and her lover was so often retold that it is evident that it struck a chord of recognition and response. As an elevation of strife and murder in a mere gentleman's household to the genre of tragedy, the play had its counterpart in the nearly contemporaneous social and economic elevation of the gentry. It is even possible that the whole genre of domestic tragedy arises from those contemporary dynamics, and I wish to argue for this point here. Taking *Arden of Feversham* as the best known example of this dramatic genre, this article will sketch the historical context that can allow us then to discuss the tragedy itself as "domestic" tragedy in a particularly Elizabethan sense.

<h1 style="text-align:center">I</h1>

Of particularly far-reaching economic impact was the dissolution of the monasteries, which provoked what Joyce Youings has called "a revolution in landownership, second only to that which followed the Norman Conquest."[4] At least among historians in our secular age, there is nearly unanimous agreement that the monasteries were sufficiently spiritually bankrupt that they played a more important economic role, as landlords, than they did a religious one. The monasteries held perhaps a fourth of the land in early Tudor England, where there were only three types of principal landowners: the Crown, noblemen and gentlemen, and the Church. Beginning with the first Act of Dissolution in 1536, Henry VIII not only disintegrated the monastic institutions but also confiscated their lands and rental incomes—and not for religious or social purposes, but for his own profit. The Tudors had already established the royal authority to confiscate individuals' estates, like those of the rebel Lord Darcy, but this peaceful seizure of land on such a vast scale was unprecedented.

The wholesale transfer of property from Church to state was not accomplished without some complications, challenges, and complaints. Representatives of each monastery had to be induced to renounce their claim, and a local court had in each instance to name the king "founder," that is, legal representative of the actual founding patron of the institution, before its property could escheat to him. The heirs of some original benefactors did make some competing claims, but Henry was rarely unsuccessful even before he nullified such claims in the subsequent acts of dissolution. The shifted estates were so many and so large that Henry also had to create a bureaucracy, the Court of Augmentations, to administer them, to make grants in fee, and to exact feudal dues and rents from tenant farmers. These standing customary and copyhold tenancies, usually held at least for a "life" of twenty-one years, were honored by the Crown, which overthrew only what it called "crafty" leases made during the year before the closing of a monastery in anticipation of dissolution. Undoubtedly this conservative treatment of tenancies quieted much potential dissatisfaction; perhaps the Crown was less able to allay rural distress that local rents would no longer be received by local landlords but would instead be removed to and expended in London.

The repercussions of the transfer of property spread further when the Crown began, almost immediately, to distribute it. Cromwell thought of the new holdings in the old way, as an endowment to the Crown, and he reportedly urged Henry to make grants of land to "the gentlemen of the kingdom . . . that he may thereby gain the hearts and affections of his subjects."[5] Such grants were not outright gifts: they usually ensured a return to the King of political loyalty, knight service, wardship rights, and one-tenth of the annual income of the property; also and more importantly, they often reverted to the Crown with the grantee's death. It was an old and popular sentiment in England that all Crown lands belonged to the monarchic institution, not to an individual monarch. Sir John Fortescue, for example, had warned in the 1470s that alienation of "a king's livelihood is properly called delapidation of his crown, and therefore is of great infamy."[6] The first grant of former monastic property was awarded within two months of the first Act of Dissolution to the Chancellor of the Court of Augmentations, Richard Rich. Of the 234 grants that succeeded it, many were similarly made to officials of the Court of Augumentations or to their families; all likewise followed the established practice of the English monarchy of exploiting the royal estate for political purposes.

But then, in 1539, the first sale of confiscated monastic land was negotiated, and Henry VIII thus initiated a full-scale exploitation of the royal estate for economic gain. All former monastic property was effectively put on the market; only some large estates and some land near older royal holdings were reserved. Henry succeeded in alienating over half of the old monastic estates; his children and the early Stuarts disposed of most of the rest. This new way of thinking about the confiscated property as a source of immediate income for the Crown was to occasion the sixteenth- and seventeenth-century "revolution in landownership."

For the very idea that land was a commodity, subject to sale, was a relatively new one. Land had been sufficiently stable in pre-Tudor England that its ownership had seemed a part of the natural order. The estates of the lords, for example, had been bound by ancient entails to descend by rule of primogeniture to eldest sons. Some lands and annuities had been settled on other noble family members, especially widows, but such grants were usually made only for life and eventually reverted to the patrimony. Some estates had been diminished or divided upon a failure of male heirs, but the redistribution was usually accomplished through wardship or marriage, not sale. Then, during the reigns of the early Tudors, these lords were given the right to break their entails and alienate their property, and many chose to emulate their king by selling land to put money in their purses. The novelty of the idea of the sale of land is apparent in the procedure by which it was accomplished, an awkward adaptation of feudal laws that was as formally complicated as the process by which the King had claimed the monastic estates. The buyer and seller negotiated the transfer by engaging in a legal suit that resulted in the purchaser's being fined in the amount of the purchase price. That price was determined by the appraised income that could be derived from the land—twenty years' value in the early part of the century, thirty years' value later. The more abstract concept of capital value had yet to be employed.

The sale of the old monastic estates did not engender the land market; it was the land market that had already sprung up by the early sixteenth century that made such distribution of monastic property practical and, indeed, conceivable. But the flooding of that market with enormous amounts of property—property available on such a scale for the first time in English history—certainly stimulated the revolution in landownership. By the last two decades of the sixteenth century, a brisk land market had grown into a booming one.

The market in formerly monastic lands has been called speculative because many of those who were awarded commissions by the Court of Augmentations immediately resold parcels of property. Recent scholarship has established that such petitioners were more likely agents than speculators: the procedure of petitioning the Court to appraise a specific piece of property, to fix a price, and to execute warrants and letters patent was a complicated, expensive, and time-consuming one; so it would have been natural for small purchasers to find themselves representatives. It is now clear, moreover, that widespread speculation was unlikely because there was little contemporary conviction that land was a good investment. Had there been, the King would almost certainly have been less eager to alienate such vast tracts. His case was admittedly a special one, because the cost of administering his estates was not insignificant; but the fact remains that he preferred ready money to the prospect of long-term income from rents and produce. Furthermore, the land was not, as had been thought, given away at bargain prices. Its distribution continued over a century because some men spent years accumulating the capital necessary to satisfy their land hunger. Many of those who purchased property were merchants, yeomen, lesser gentry, and younger sons, who were establishing themselves on the land and as householders for the first time. They were trading their hard-earned money for a chance at gentility: to them land signified not profit but status.

Gentle status could be, in this time of social as well as economic mobility, self-defined. Gordon Batho, for example, has noted how often sixteenth-century Englishmen who are called by others "yeomen" chose to call themselves "gentlemen" and how often surviving legal documents identify them in both ways.[7] As "commoners," gentlemen were very clearly distinguished from noblemen. At the same time, however, they were unquestionably privileged, to adopt Ann Jennalie Cook's term.[8] Thomas Wilson, for example, identifies kings and lords as *nobilitas maior* and gentlemen as *nobilitas minor,* and William Harrison defines the gentry hierarchically as, after the King himself, "the prince, dukes, marquises, earls, viscounts, and barons, and these are called gentlemen of the greater sort, or (as our common usage of speech is) lords and noblemen; and next unto them be knights, esquires, and last of all, they that are simply called gentlemen."[9]

In common contemporary understanding, the surest signal of gentility was the ownership of land sufficient for livelihood. William Harrison writes of yeomen who "live wealthily, keep good houses, and travail to get riches"; when they "do come to great wealth, insomuch that many of them are able and do buy the lands of unthrifty gentlemen," and when they leave their sons "sufficient lands whereupon they may live without labor"; then those yeomen "do make them [their sons] by those means to become gentlemen."[10] Most gentlemen did own land, usually of at least ten pounds annual value in early sixteenth-century money;[11] the gentry as a group owned more land than did the nobility. In fact, as the old feudal system dissolved, gentlemen were no longer mere manor lords on the demesnes of the ultimate lords, peers, but were independent landlords in their own right, equal under the law to noble land-lords. An absolute social stratification that evolved during the thirteenth to the seventeenth centuries was that of landlord and tenant.

If land was often a prerequisite to gentility, it was no more than a prerequisite, and style of living was continuing witness to success and status. Thomas Gainsford without apology advises the conspicuous display of material success: "If a Gentleman will be a Farmer," that is, establish himself on a country estate as a member of the landed gentry, then "it is the best to obtain the principall house" in the area—the manor house. Further, "if you can leaue an estate of a thousand markes behinde you, let the passers by, viewing the house imagin it a 1000. pound a yeare."[12] In other words, gentlemen, especially lesser gentlemen, identified themselves by living as gentlemen, notably in houses worthy of gentlemen.

Even seventeenth-century parsons, according to M. W. Barley, "were increas-ingly unwilling to take a living which had no better house than a labourer's. Such livings tended to remain vacant for long periods."[13] An especially revealing glimpse of the social significance attached to a man's house and standard of living is offered in Wallace MacCaffrey's review of the career of an Exeter man named John Wolcott. Wolcott, according to his biographer, John Hooker, was prominent in local civic affairs, but "by reason of his age and his small welthe it was not thought nor ment that ever the office of the mayroltie shold have fallen unto his lott. . . . [H]e was verie poore and lyved yn very meane estate." In 1565, Wolcott was by some chance elected mayor anyway: "The Chamber thereupon ordered his house to be furnished up properly and an allowance made for his housekeeping," as befitted his station.[14]

Standards in housing improved so rapidly during this period that W. G. Hoskins has called the years from 1570 to 1640, and especially 1575 to 1625, the time of the "Great Rebuilding."[15] New domestic ideals of privacy, comfort, and luxury in hous-ing and furnishings encouraged the energy and involvement that William Harrison vividly depicts:

> It is a world to see, moreover, how divers men, being bent to building and having a delectable vein in spending of their goods by that trade, do daily imagine new devices of their own to guide their workmen withal, and those more curious and excellent always than the former. In the proceeding also of their works, how they set up, how they pull down, how they enlarge, how they restrain, how they add to, how they take from, whereby their heads are never idle, their purses never shut, nor their books of account never made perfect.[16]

Perhaps the most profound of the many developments in domestic architecture during the sixteenth century was the adoption of new building materials. For those living at the lower end of the social scale, earth, thatch, and light woods like willow were abandoned: oak was preferred, while noblemen and gentlemen rejected even such hardwood for the stone and brick that were no longer reserved for churches and monastic buildings. Indeed, at a time when the greatest obstacles to building in stone were the difficulty and expense of transporting it from the quarries, ruined abbeys proved a valuable resource to new men establishing their estates. It is William Harrison's reaction, again, that is best known: "And yet see the change, for when our houses were builded of willow, then had we oaken men; but now that our houses are come to be made of oak, our men are not only become willow but a great many . . . altogether of straw, which is a sore alteration."[17]

A more positive and less arguable result of the use of these more durable materials was the new permanence of domestic architecture. For the first time, the poor were able to build houses that outlasted many more than just one or two generations. Those who were not poor justified the money and attention devoted to their houses as birthrights to their descendants and monuments to familial continuity. The Renaissance Englishman's awareness that at least his house could withstand the forces of mutability magnified the value and significance that he attached to it. As early as 1540, Andrew Borde recognized three reasons why a man might build himself a new house or remodel his old one: first, "for his owne proper cõmodyte[,] welth and helth"; second, "for other men, the whiche wyll resorte to hym"; and third, for "his posteryte."[18]

Nearly a century later, Sir John Oglander expressed a similar sense of familial obligation. He compiled "His Rules for Husbandry," in which he warns his readers not to violate the legacy of their ancestors: "Be sure, whatsoever misfortune befalls thee, sell not thy land, which was with much care and pain provided and kept for thee and hath continued so many ages in thy name. Rather feed on bread and water than be the confusion of thy house. . . . [B]e sure not to waste that which was gotten by others' care, pains and industry." In his diary, he reveals a correspondingly active consciousness of his descendants. They are his justification when he is too liberal in improving his property: "I have been so foolish as to bestow more money than a wise man would have done in flowers for the garden. . . . I planted above a hundred elms and ashes, some chestnuts and serviceberries in the grove of my house. . . . I planted them all, most with my own hands. When my successors hereafter reap the fruits of my labours, let them remember the founder." His imagination peoples the concrete, present space of his house and lands with these anticipated followers. But the imagined defeat of time is at least partially circumvented: in 1632 he records, only "with my tears and a foul pen," the death of his eldest son. A later journal entry is wistful: "I have with my own hands planted 2 young orchards at Nunwell. . . . I have now made it a fit place for any gentleman, and had hopes that my son George would have succeeded me and have enjoyed the fruits of my labours."[19]

A Renaissance Englishman's sense of the value of his house would have been intensified, inevitably, by what Peter Clark has demonstrated to be a "sixteenth-century phenomenon," enforced migration.[20] The number of the homeless poor—

including farmers displaced by enclosures and engrossing, masterless men, discharged and deserting soldiers, dismissed servants and runaway apprentices—swelled appreciably during the 1540s, reached its peak during Elizabeth's reign, and did not drop until the 1640s. The Poor Laws of 1575, 1597, and 1601 undertook to house and employ the true poor. But concurrently with the rising number of vagrants came the advent of professional roguery chronicled by, for example, Thomas Harman, Robert Greene, and Thomas Dekker. The most vigorous attention of the State was devoted, as might thus have been expected, to the idle and thriftless poor, who were denounced in statutes, pamphlet literature, and public proclamations; subjected to town watches and searches; and severely punished, imprisoned, and banished. Francis Bacon called them "the seed of peril and tumult in a state."[21] The modern historian, Paul Slack, observes:

> Vagabonds became the scapegoats for all social problems. They were carriers of rumour, sedition, and disease, and they infested others with their "licentious liberty." . . . They were individuals with few household or kinship ties, and they had often fled from masters, husbands, or wives. These traits were determined or confirmed by experience of a rootless insecure existence in forests or towns or armies, and consolidated by the exigencies of an economy marked by seasonal and chronic underemployment. When we see the special class of migrants who were punished as vagrants we can comprehend contemporary reactions to them as representatives of disorder.[22]

To an Elizabethan rogue, his social opposite was, suggests Thomas Dekker, any man with a house. Dekker records, among ten "Articles of their fraternities," the rogues' commandment that "Thou shalt teach no householder to cant, neither confess anything to them, be it never so true, but deny the same with oaths."[23] For a man on the social fringes, to have a house was to achieve respectability. When Thomas Heywood undertakes to defend actors, who had been classed among vagrants under earlier Tudor laws, he protests: "Many among vs, I know, to be of substance, of gouernment, of sober liues, and temperate carriages, house-keepers and contributory to all duties enioyned them."[24] To a workingman at the lower end of the economic scale, what stood between him and vagrancy was his house: it secured for him not only a place of physical refuge but also a place in the social order. Could he have listened to contemporary sermons and government proclamations, heard of agrarian riots and tenant lawsuits, watched rogues whipped and pilloried, or encountered beggars and thieves without valuing his own house, all the more, as his castle? To subscribers to state and church authority, a house was a restraining moral influence upon any individual man, as well as a keystone of a healthy economy and a stable society. Matthew Griffith posits that writing a domestic treatise, as he does, and structuring an ideal family, building a model house, and governing a Christian commonwealth, as he advises others to do, are, equally, ordering activities. In *Bethel: Or a Forme for Families,* Griffith describes the organizing principle of his manual: "this *Building* is *uniforme;* this treatise *Methodicall:* for I here present the *whole body* of the *Oeconomickes,* under a *continued Metaphor* of *building an house.*"[25]

Griffith was one of many writers who promulgated what were pervasive ideological reinforcements for a Renaissance Englishman's concern for his house. The authors of sixteenth- and seventeenth-century domestic economies and conduct books were religiously and politically conservative men, not minority voices. Their sentiments echoed official decisions of the English courts and quasi-official sermons in Anglican churches.

They typically began by comparing the head of the household to a monarch, a priest, a bishop, or even to Christ. William Gouge, for example, in *Of Domesticall Duties,* takes the universe as macrocosm and the house as microcosm in positing such correspondences:

> There may be a resemblance where there is no parity, and a likenesse where there is no equality. The glorious and bright Sunne in the firmament, and a dimme candle in an house, haue a kinde of fellowship, and the same office, which is to giue light. ... So then an husband resembleth not only the head of a naturall body, but also the glorious image of Christ [and, further,] is as a king in his owne house: as a king is to see that land well gouerned where he is king, so he that is the chiefe ruler in an house.[26]

This last analogy had of course been popularized proverbially: "Every Man is King in his House" is the version that John Wodroephe recorded.[27] The correspondence between householder and king was also sanctioned officially by the statute of treasons that had been adopted in 1352 and that was not abolished until 1828: "when a servant slayeth his master, or a wife her husband," the crime committed was not called murder, but petit treason, and those convicted were punished accordingly.[28]

If the head of the household was as a king, then his household could be compared to the state; this was a correspondence that the domestic writers also elaborated. Dudley North explains that *"Oeconomy* is the Art of well governing a mans private house and fortunes, by which appears, that there is no necessary Object of *Oeconomy,* save an Owner with his house and possessions, but it is seldom exercised without Wife and Servants." He continues that a family is "an epitome of hereditary Monarchy"; the master "doth somewhat resemble the Soveraign Prince, his Children the Nobility or second estate, and the Body of Servants beareth some similitude to the Commons."[29] The analogy chosen by the anonymous author of *Counsel to the Husband; To the Wife Instruction* is more often encountered in the domestic economies:

> A familie may bee compared vnto a commonwealth: wherein there are diuers societies and degrees, reciprocally relating, and mutually depending one vpon another. The highest degree or societie is between the husband and the wife; and this is as the first wheele of a clocke, that turneth about all the rest in order. The next societie, is betweene the Parents and the children. The third betweene the seruants one with another, and towards all other superiors in the familie.[30]

Accustomed to conceptualizing society in stratifications of class, North, Gouge, Griffith, and others like Robert Cleaver, William Perkins, William Whately, and George Whetstone thought readily of the "commonwealth" of the household in the same hierarchical terms.

The house itself, the physical structure that Griffith took as an image of order for its inhabitants to emulate, assumed its own importance in these domestic economies. Gouge advises any couple who are *"erecting a new family"* that "their parents house must be left, and the husband and wife must dwell each with other."[31] Recent demographic research, especially that conducted by Peter Laslett, indicates that Elizabethan and Jacobean housing practice accorded with such advice. Only among the greater gentry and nobility were early marriages and multi-generational households fairly common. Upper-class heirs married young so that dowry and property arrangements could be finalized and so that they could undertake their primary obligation to maintain an unbroken line of descendants to inherit the ancestral estate; they stayed with their parents in the houses around which their duties, futures, and very lives revolved. But nuclear families in independent houses were elsewhere the rule. Most men married in their late twenties or early thirties, when they were able to set themselves up in their own homes, and their life expectancies were short enough that their houses would pass to their sons at about the time men of this second generation were, in turn, in their late twenties and early thirties. Marriage, according to Laslett,

> gave the man full membership of the community, and added a cell to village society. It is understandable, therefore, that marriage could not come about unless a slot was vacant, so to speak, and the aspiring couple was fit to fill it up. It might be a cottage which had fallen empty.[32]

For the domestic and political writers, there was ideological, not just economic, warrant for the practice. Jean Bodin, for example, notes that "a Familie should haue but one head, one maister, and one Lord: whereas otherwise if it should have many heads, their commaunds would be contrarie." He further calls it "the law of nature, which willeth, That euery man shuld be maister of his owne house."[33]

In the expanding Tudor and Stuart economy, many men were new to this role in household government. As Erasmus had undertaken "The Education of a Christian Prince," so the authors of domestic economies and conduct books advised the men attaining "kingship" in their houses. Every description of the housekeeper's role, every elaboration of the correspondences, and every assertion of patriarchal authority was given impetus by an immediate reminder of the "duties enioyned," to recall Heywood's phrase. Reiterated were both the economic responsibilities—of providing shelter, food, and clothing for the family, of supervising the budget for the wife, and of ensuring settled and respectable futures for the children—and the moral obligations—of disciplining and correcting children and servants, of encouraging diligence and preventing idleness, of providing Christian instruction and a model for Christian life.

Furthermore, the domestic writers insisted that a householder's responsibilities were not only to his own family but also to church and state. Gouge asks rhetorically: "who knoweth not that the preseruation of families tendeth to the good of Church and common-wealth? so as a conscionable performance of houshold duties, in regard of the end and fruit thereof, may be accounted a publike worke."[34] Bodin refuses to consider "Oeconomicall gouernment" as distinct from "Politicall," or "a Citie from a Familie"; that "can no other wise be done," he asserts, "than if wee should pull the members from the bodie; or go about to build a Citie without houses."[35] In Robert Snawsel's universe, order builds almost mathematically from the starting point of the well-governed house:

> good parents are speciall instruments to make godly children, and good seruants; and godly children and good seruants will make religious men and women; and religious men and womē doth make a flourishing church, and famous common-weale, set forth Gods glory, and establish the Princes kingdome.[36]

In like manner, Josias Nichols describes the "disorder of one priuate familie" as recorded in the Bible and moralizes:

> Behold then what good may come out of a well instructed familie, namely, that it may bee the preseruing of the countrie and Church, in the time of extreame daunger and darknesse, the seedplot against the time of reformation, and a meanes by which God doth multiplie his people and peace in a countrie: and that by the contrarie, an whole countrie may fall into Idolatry and destruction. Whereby euery man may see what honorable seruice I wish him vnto, when I exhort him to the instructing of his family.[37]

To most individual sixteenth- and seventeenth-century men, there must have seemed many dark and dangerous threats to any sense of natural order, threats all the more potent and senses all the more poignant because that order had appeared so recently secure. The monolith that had been the Church had disappeared in a series of religious upheavals and reversals. With the end of the feudal system, another link in the old understanding of strictly parallel degrees and hierarchical relationships had been dissolved. That old order of obligations and trusts had been schematic, nearly mathematical, and thus comprehensible without analysis and accepted without question. Now the lords had lost their old command over men; correspondingly, villeins were no longer assured of what had often been the lords' benevolent protection: they had either to support themselves or to fend for themselves as beggars and vagrants. New men were achieving lordships and landlordships without the old lords' understandings of the obligations of power and wealth. All relationships were distanced—and debased—by a new intermediary, money. As the economic system became more sophisticated, men were removed from the land—men who comprised the first generation of their families not to work the soil, among them, gentry, professionals, and merchants. And even those who still farmed must have sensed, with the rationalization of agricultural methods, that the land was losing some of its mystery and power. There must have seemed no more virgin land: the plow despoiled; the reclamation of waste and the practice of enclosure encroached. With the loss of common ground came inevitably a loss of communal sense. And with the growth of a market in land, the land itself was no longer static, sure, a force of order; it could be traded and, again, debased by equation with monetary value. These radical changes surely threatened man's impulse to possess and control.

Many of these anxieties could not be articulated; some were concerns that would have been impolitic to articulate. And so when Matthew Griffith defines his sense of disorder, it is in terms of individual responsibility, not cultural transformation, with such narrow and specific complaints as these: "Why are our children so disobedient, and our servants so disordered? Why are some wives so unfaithfull, and some husbands so unprofitable members both of *Church,* and *Common-wealth*?"

Griffith's answer to his rhetorical question is that the disobedient, the disordered, the unfaithful, and the unprofitable are not "part of God's building"—that is, not part of a "well-ordered family. . . . That which hath both an orderly head, and orderly members, having mutuall relation to each other." One of his particular concerns is that "some houses are now faine to hop Headlesse"; thus, he advises the head of the household on how to order his house.[38] It may be axiomatic that anxieties for lost order will be expressed in defenses of authoritarianism. Certainly among many Elizabethan and Jacobean authors there seemed a sudden need to articulate and defend patriarchal theory, for the first time called into doubt. The patriarchal theory of family order was used by political writers just as the monarchical theory of government was used by domestic writers, each called upon to validate the other, each having seemed sufficiently a part of the natural order to be understood to have the power to do so.[39]

II

The economic, social, architectural, and ideological changes that impinged upon a Renaissance Englishman's estimation of his house are abstract and generalized phenomena; they become concrete and immediate in life stories like those of John Wolcott of Exeter and Sir John Oglander of Nunwell, in what we know of John and William Shakespeare of Stratford-upon-Avon, and in such case histories as those of Thomas Ardern of Faversham, Master Page of Plymouth, Walter Calverley of Yorkshire, and Jane Shore and George Sanders of London.[40] It is through case history that some of these anxieties came to be expressed on the Elizabethan and Jacobean stage. When Thomas Ardern's story was dramatized, for example, it was as a "lamentable and *true* tragedie" (italics mine).[41] I would suggest that the anonymous dramatist's understanding of Ardern's story can be best approached in light of the contexts that I have sketched.

Thomas Ardern's family background, date of birth, and early years are undiscovered history.[42] He was a gentleman, but evidently not a landed one: Ardern came to Faversham in Kent a "new" man, free to establish himself in a new home and to build his own estate. He arrived there through his service to Sir Edward North, who seems to have been a model for as well as master to the ambitious lesser gentleman. North courted royal favor and was awarded the post of Clerk of Parliament, then the post of Treasurer of the Court of Augmentations (in both positions, Ardern was his assistant) and finally, in 1554, a lordship. North also courted money and twice married wealthy widows. In his turn, North rewarded his assistant with the post of Commissioner of the Port of Faversham, a lucrative office in a thriving center of trade with London. Ardern benefited from his mentor in yet another way when he followed North's example of marrying shrewdly by wedding North's own stepdaughter, Alyce Mirfyn.[43]

That this was a marriage of convenience for Thomas Ardern is further indicated by the fact that Alyce was enamored of one of her stepfather's household servants, a man named Thomas Morsby. Ardern was, however, "yet so greatly gyven to sek his advauntage, and caryd so lytle how he came by it that in hope of atteynynge some benefite of the lord northe by meanes of this mosby who could do muche wt hym, he winkd at that shamefull dysordar and bothe parmyttyd and also invited hym very often to be in his howse," even after the wedding.[44]

Ardern was in fact remarkably successful, by whatever means, in accumulating money and lands. His principal acquisition had belonged to the Benedictine Abbey of Faversham. After its dissolution, the land was first granted to a local knight, Sir Thomas Cheyney, Lord Warden of the Cinque Ports. The property was so extensive that when Cheyney received it and two other small pieces in 1539, he returned to the King more than 283 pounds, paid over two years, as well as knight service and an annual fee thereafter. Included were over forty-two acres of land and "all houses, edifices, barns, stables, dove houses, orchards, gardens" on the land. Five years later, Cheyney, an established gentleman, was willing to trade this property for Ardern's new money. Ardern held these lands and buildings until his death, as is evident from the inquisition post mortem into his estate, which lists them in terms nearly identical to those used in the King's grant to Cheyney. With additional holdings including, notably, a water mill, meadow acreage, seventeen tenanted messuages, and two orchards, the estate was then valued at an annual worth of over forty-five pounds.

Others of Ardern's ventures in real property can be discovered in Edward Hasted's history of Kent. He records grants that Ardern himself received from the King in 1540, 1543, 1544, and 1545 for woods, marshes, meadows, manors, and a priory. Ardern's experience with the Court of Augmentations no doubt facilitated these purchases. One of these manors, which returned him twelve pounds annually in rent, was granted by the King *in tail male* and so reverted to the Crown when Ardern died without a male heir. The woods were let to him only for a "life" of twenty-one years. And Ardern also practiced some land brokerage and immediately resold some of his 1543 grants.[45]

In addition to this wealth of office and rental income, Ardern sought status. Through Alyce Mirfyn, he married into a distinguished family that comprised not only her stepfather, who was to become First Baron North; but also the half brother Roger, who succeeded his father as Second Baron; the half brother Sir Thomas, who was to be remembered as the translator of Plutarch; the half sister Mary, who married Henry, Lord Scrope of Bolton; and another, Christiana, who married William, Earl of Worcester. It was a connection that Ardern evidently chose to evoke, for a window of his house was embellished with the North coat of arms.[46] He and Alyce set up housekeeping on some of his acquired property, in a house attached to the old abbey gate at the edge of town, backing on his abbey lands. There, a two-roomed gatehouse had first been built in the late thirteenth century, then expanded, perhaps into a guesthouse, in the fifteenth. Archaeological evidence suggests that around 1545 Ardern himself built a more commodious residence that incorporated the old stone walls. His house is described in 1671 as "the great house near the Abbey gate eastward" by the antiquarian Thomas Southouse. In a survey of the property that had belonged to the dissolved abbey, Southouse lists twenty-two houses with their annual rental worths: two are valued at something over a pound each, some in shillings, some only in pence, but Ardern's "great house" is said to be worth three pounds.[47] Thus established in Faversham, Ardern also succeeded in getting himself elected as one of twelve town jurats (or aldermen) and finally, in 1548, as mayor.[48]

Despite all these concrete evidences of success, Ardern's quest for status was less fortunate than those for money and land. His mother, who lived in Norwich, enjoyed begging, even though Ardern "assayde all meanes posseble to kepe hir from it." The means included a regular stipend for her support: at one point, she was discovered to have sixty pounds in her possession.[49] Ardern's wife's "euill demeanor," her affair with Morsby, was evidently well known by his fellow townspeople.[50] Some of them complained that Ardern had evicted legally tenured residents of abbey lands when he acquired them or had violated the moral obligation of old tenancies at will. He was described as "wresting" the land from tenants "extorciowsly" and "by vyolence."[51] He also abused his civil authority by arranging for a fair to be held on his own abbey green when it should have been held on town property. For thus cheating the Corporation of Faversham of expected revenue and "reaping all the gaines to himselfe," he was in 1550 deposed from town office and disenfranchised.[52] His wife was convinced that "there was not anie [in the town] that would care for his death," he was "so evell belovyd."[53]

He somehow succeeded, however, in getting reinstated as a jurat before his death. Just how closely this new man identified with the town he had adopted is clear from his will, dated 20 December 1550. Ardern left Faversham some houses and lands worth forty shillings to endow "a sermon to be preached every year in commemoration of the several benefactors, and for the encouragement of others to go and do likewise, the residue to be expended in bread to be distributed to the poor." When his only child and heir married, her husband sued the Corporation for the bequeathed property, with some success. But the town still holds one plot from Ardern's bequest, and the annual sermon was preached in his name well into the nineteenth century.[54]

Thomas Ardern was typical of his time in that so many of the historic patterns described above can be traced through his life. He was like many other men among his contemporaries and in immediately succeeding generations who were social climbers, who sought status and were ashamed of beggary, who bought land and evicted tenants, who built and rebuilt houses, and whose impulses were secular and materialistic. What was atypical about Thomas Ardern—and what accounts for the preservation in such detail of his otherwise unremarkable story—was his death on 15 February 1551 at the hands of his wife Alyce and her lover Morsby.

They were not accomplished murderers. After trying unsuccessfully to poison Ardern's broth, they enlisted the aid of Ardern's serving-man, Mighell Saunderson; his maid, Elsabeth Stafford; and a disgruntled former tenant of Abbey land, John Grene. They then hired two ruffians, "masterless men," Black Wyll and George Losebagg (or Shakebag), who themselves missed killing Ardern in two attempts in London and two on the road. When this group of conspirators finally succeeded in strangling, stabbing, and bludgeoning Ardern to death in his parlor, there was some sentiment in the town that a curse placed upon him by another evicted tenant had impelled his violent death. The murderers had carried the corpse to the disputed land, where, it was reported, a perfect outline of the body was preserved for two years afterward by blighted grass. Both Losebagg and the painter who had provided Alyce with poison escaped after the murder and were "nevar hard of aftar"; Grene and Black Wyll fled as well but were eventually captured and executed. Also executed for Ardern's murder were Alyce, Morsby, Morsby's sister, Mighell Saunderson, Elsabeth Stafford, and an apparently innocent man named George Bradshawe. For the crimes of petit treason against husband and master, Alyce and Elsabeth were burned to death, and Mighell was drawn and hanged in chains.[55]

Ardern's story found its way not only into such local records and histories as the Faversham Wardmote Book, Southouse's survey, Hasted's history of Kent, and Edward Jacob's *History of the Town and Port of Faversham,* but also into the *Breviat Chronicle,* Holinshed's *Chronicles,* Stow's papers and his *Annals,* a London merchant's diary, and Thomas Heywood's *Troia Britannica.* It was an illustration of justice to Thomas Beard in 1597 and to John Taylor in 1630; it was included among a list of such casualties as fire and plague and such wonders as Siamese twins and dolphins by Richard Baker in 1643. The story was worked into a ballad printed in 1633 and into a chapbook probably printed in the early eighteenth century. As late as 1969, it was also the basis of a novel. But the story is best known as it was told in an anonymous play entered in the Stationers' Register in 1592—a play that was reprinted in 1599 and 1633, that toured the provinces in the 1650s, that appeared in a puppet version in 1736, that was undertaken for revision by George Lillo and then completed by John Hoadley in 1759, that was attributed to Shakespeare in 1770, that was transformed into a ballet in 1799, that was abridged for performance by William Poel in 1897 and then revived by him in full in 1925, that was freely adapted as an opera in 1967 and as a La Mama theater-of-cruelty production in 1970, and that has been staged fairly continuously in the town of Faversham. The play known as *Arden of Feversham* is also generally recognized as the earliest surviving English "domestic" tragedy.[56]

Few Elizabethan plays lend themselves to source study as readily as does *Arden of Feversham.* The anonymous playwright probably consulted Holinshed's chronicle account for his plot, characters, "and even, at times, some of his wording"; he may also have known the manuscript account (found among Stow's papers) that differs from Holinshed in only a few particulars, some of which he seems to adopt.[57] To the first modern editor of *Arden,* Faversham antiquarian Edward Jacob, we owe not only the rediscovery of the play and its inclusion among Shakespeare's apocryphal works but also the practice of elaborating it with historical references. In his edition of 1770, Jacob reprinted a third narrative version of the story, his abridgement of the official one in the Wardmote Book of the town of Faversham. Succeeding editors have devoted introductions, notes, and appendices to what is known of the historical Thomas Ardern and to what is generally perceived to be the playwright's remarkable fidelity to his sources.

But the Arden to whom we are introduced, even in the first nineteen lines of the play, seems to me to be strikingly unlike the Ardern of the sources and of the critical consensus:

> *Franklin.* Arden, cheer up thy spirits and droop no more.
> My gracious Lord the Duke of Somerset
> Hath freely given to thee and to thy heirs,
> By letters patents from his majesty,
> All the lands of the Abbey of Faversham.
> Here are the deeds,   6
> Sealed and subscribed with his name and the king's.
> Read them, and leave this melancholy mood.
> *Arden.* Franklin, thy love prolongs my weary life;
> And, but for thee, how odious were this life,
> That shows me nothing but torments my soul,
> And those foul objects that offend mine eyes—   12
> Which makes me wish that for this veil of heaven
> The earth hung over my head and covered me.
> Love letters passed 'twixt Mosby and my wife,
> And they have privy meetings in the town.
> Nay, on his finger did I spy the ring
> Which at our marriage day the priest put on.   18
> Can any grief be half so great as this?[58]

M. L. Wine praises these first two speeches: "On an immediate level of recognition, introduction of character and exposition of theme could not be more rapid and concise." Arden, he says, is established "as an ambitious man whose success is in itself bringing him no happiness and as a more complicated private person, whose grief finds its source in mixed motives of rejected love, shame, and hurt pride."[59] Certainly we see the unhappiness: Arden evidently appears on stage exhibiting the convention-al signs of melancholy that occasion Franklin's first words; later he wishes for death to relieve him of his grief. We also see the success, in Franklin's enthusiastic delight that Arden has been granted the dissolved Abbey property by the Lord Protector to the young Edward VI. But this announcement seems in itself to distance us from the historical Ardern, who purchased the land from Sir Thomas Cheyney in an exchange contaminated by implicit acquisitiveness and by disbursed monies. So do we, as Wine suggests, see ambition? Franklin's delight is not contagious; his assumption that the deeds have power to cheer is not borne out. Although over a third of the modern editors of the play add to line six, "Here are the deeds," the stage direction "*He hands them*," the text suggests that Arden does not, in fact, take them.[60] For Arden is interested not in "letters patents" but in love letters; not in the deeds recording the lands that belong to him but in the ring signaling that his wife belongs to him; not in business but in Alice.

When Arden soon thereafter encounters Mosby, Arden finds his cuckolder outside his house in conversation with his wife. Alice covers hastily, indicating that Mosby has come to see not her but Arden by saying for his overhearing, "Master Mosby, ask him the question yourself" (i.291). Mosby improvises a question designed to put the meeting on a business footing. The Abbey lands have been offered him for sale, he says; does Arden own them outright, or does the Greene who offered them have an interest? Arden dispatches Alice out of earshot and answers tersely, "As for the lands, Mosby, they are mine / By letters patents from his majesty" (i.300–301). Then he turns to an issue that concerns him far more: "But I must have a mandate for my wife; / They say you seek to rob me of her love" (i.302–303). If the protagonist Arden is relentless in anything, finally, it is in his indifference to business dealings.

These immediate indications that the playwright's conception of his protagonist Arden is far different from Holinshed's picture of Thomas Ardern are not isolated ones. Arden also, for example, describes Mosby as a "botcher"—choosing the most disparaging term for a tailor or mender—and then contrasts this occupation with his own station: "I am by birth a gentleman of blood" (i.36). He is, as William Harrison puts it, "defined to descend of three descents [generations] of nobleness, that is to say, of name and of arms both by father and mother" and several removes from the upstart gentleman of newly awarded coat-armor.[61] The dramatic protagonist Arden not only is socially superior to the tailor Mosby, but also is irreproachably above his new and ambitious historical prototype.

The disparities between the Ardern of whom we read in the sources and the Arden to whom we are introduced in the play are important ones. In the sources there is little distinction made between Ardern the man of business and Ardern the husband, for it is his greed that makes him a willing cuckold. Holinshed writes that he "perceiued right well" the "mutuall familiaritie" of his wife and Morsby, "yet bicause he would not offend hir, and so loose the benefit which he hoped to gaine at some of hir freends hands in bearing with hir lewdnesse, which he might haue lost if he should haue fallen out with hir: he was contented to winke at hir filthie disorder." As quoted above, the Harley manuscript also presents an Ardern who "winked at that shamefull dysorder."[62] The story of this wittol's death is less a tragedy than a curiosity; what fascinates is less the character of the man than that of the obsessed wife, single-minded and coldblooded through frustrated attempt after frustrated attempt at mariticide.

The playwright, however, chooses not to make Arden a wittol and thus not to make him contemptible and not to weaken what logic there is in Alice's homicidal obsession. At the same time the playwright chooses not to make Arden a fool, blithely unconscious of his wife's betrayal, and thus perhaps equally contemptible. Instead the play presents Arden as a tragic protagonist who is wise enough to suspect his wife's infidelity and honorable enough to be enraged by it but who is deterred by an external agent from acting on his own right instincts.

The agent who dissuades Arden from action is his "honest friend"—and the author's one addition to the received cast of characters—Franklin. It is Franklin who first hears Arden's doubts about Alice but who dismisses them platitudinously: "Comfort thyself, sweet friend; it is not strange / That women will be false and wavering" (i.20–21). Such flippant remarks are inadequate to calm the enraged husband; he jumps to act on his suspicions, with a towering violence not unfitting in response to the worst of dishonors, cuckoldry. But Franklin counsels inaction: "Be patient, gentle friend" (i.44)—the epithet rings ironically after Arden's bloody vows. Franklin has four further pieces of advice:

> [1] Entreat her fair; sweet words are fittest engines
>   To raze the flint walls of a woman's breast.
> [2] In any case be not too jealous,
> [3] Nor make no question of her love to thee;
>   But, as securely, presently take horse,
> [4] And lie with me at London all this term;
>   For women when they may will not,
>   But being kept back, straight grow outrageous.
>
> *(i.46–53)*

Although Arden objects most strenuously that "this abhors from reason," he finally, in his grief, his confusion, and his misapprehension that the affair is young enough to be yet unconsummated, allows himself to be persuaded: "yet I'll try it" (i.54).

Step by step, Arden follows Franklin's advice. When Alice enters, he greets her with the advised sweet words (that is, with step number one):

> Sweet love, thou know'st that we two, Ovid-like,
> Have often chid the morning when it 'gan to peep,
> And often wished that dark Night's purblind steeds
> Would pull her by the purple mantle back
> And cast her in the ocean to her love.
>
> *(i.60–64)*

Arden is able to dissemble only for the length of this brief nostalgic aubade: he breaks off with, "But this night, sweet Alice, thou hast killed my heart: / I heard thee call on Mosby in thy sleep" (i.65–66). Alice makes excuses for the guilt revealed under the influence of a dream; it is Franklin who interrupts Arden's pursuit of it by reminding him, perhaps in an aside, "Arden, leave to urge her overfar" (i.73). Arden conformably retracts the jealous accusation (step number two) with "Nay, love, there is no credit in a dream" and reassures her (step number three) with "Let it suffice I know thou lovest me well" (i.74–75). Alice, cunning in duplicity, presses the issue: "Now I remember whereupon it came: / Had we no talk of Mosby yesternight?" (i.76–77). It is Franklin who seizes the rational and innocent explanation and smoothes the uncomfortable moment: "Mistress Alice, I heard you name him once or twice" (i.78). Even as Franklin acknowledges that Alice herself brought Mosby's name into their conversation, he excuses her. It is Franklin, far more than Arden, who is credulous.

On cue, Arden concurs with him and then announces that he will soon travel to London, following Franklin's fourth piece of advice. Perhaps Arden allows himself to be persuaded against his own reason and instincts because Franklin's explanations are so rational and his wisdom so conventional: Franklin is both Arden's Horatio and his Polonius. Franklin's aphoristic remarks are by their very nature time-honored. And the first three steps of his counsel are not eccentric: a household manual dating back to 1530 could be a gloss on them:

> Yf yu suspecte the womē of thy house let other persones rather shewethe / than thou shulde be ouer besy to trye out the mater . . . it were better unknowen. For ones knowen it is neuer cured / the wounde is withoute remedy. . . . The [best] & moost easy waye therin: is to dissymule the mater though it were pryuely knowen / and pretende ygnoraunce withoute ony quarell or countenaunce. . . . A noble herte / and hygh gentyll mynde / wyll neuer serche of womens maters. A shrewe wyll sooner be corrected by smylynge or laughynge / thā by a staffe / or strokes. The best way to kepe a waman good: is gentle entreaty / and neuer to let her knowe that she is suspected / and euer to be counseyled & informed with louynge maner.[63]

Franklin's complacent rationalism is finally ineffectual because Alice Arden operates by no rational rules: she is undreamt of in Franklin's philosophy.

The creation of Franklin allows the anonymous author of *Arden of Feversham* to reconcile what would otherwise be two conflicting impulses: Arden's tragic stature and the received plot. To Franklin, Arden reveals himself as neither wittol nor fool. But Franklin deters him from acting on his suspicions and preventing the catalogue of frustrated murder attempts that is the essence of the story line. The playwright is thus able to exploit the episodic nature of that inherited plot to his own artistic ends. In the spontaneous and hastily improvised stratagems, in Alice's rash eagerness "to acquaint each stranger with our drifts" (i.578), in Michael's conflicting emotions, in how much Black Will and Shakebag rely upon chance and coincidence, and in all the repeated failures, the would-be assassins are emphatically delineated by the playwright as figures of disorder.

He adds some further coherence to the received plot by dramatizing the sequence of events as a play-long search for a place to commit a successful murder. After the second attempt on Arden is thwarted in St. Paul's, the assassins reconnoiter. "[L]et us bethink us on some other place," suggests Greene, "Where Arden may be met with handsomely" (iii.85–86). He reiterates, "Let us bethink us on some other place / Whose earth may swallow up this Arden's blood" (iii.117–118). "But, give me place and opportunity," vows Shakebag, and he will show Arden no mercy (iii.109). Their schemes and threats are aimless until Michael crosses the stage on his way to prepare Arden's chamber for the night. He is recruited: "Thy office is but to appoint the place," Black Will says, and Black Will will perform the rest (iii.164). So Michael does provide a place—"This night come to his house at Aldersgate"— and opportunity—"The doors I'll leave unlocked against you come"—for the third murder attempt. He leads his master, he reflects remorsefully, "As unsuspected, to the slaughterhouse" (iii.179, 180, 202).

When this attempt fails because Michael's cry of conscience and cowardice prompts Arden to check and lock Franklin's doors, Michael is quick to protect himself from the assassins by inventing an explanation for the locked doors that he thinks they will accept. And he diverts their attention as soon as possible to a new murder site: "Rainham Down / A place well fitting such a stratagem" (vii.18–19). It is Greene who directs the fifth attempt, to intercept Arden on his way to the Isle of Sheppey: "Black Will and Shakebag I have placed / In the broom close, watching Arden's coming" (x.102–103). And then there is the sword fight in a public way in Feversham that ends with Mosby "going wounded from the place" (xiii.124).

That the successful murder finally came to pass in Arden's house is a matter of historical record, not dramatic invention. But the playwright recognizes tragic potential in this historic fact and devises it so that each time the character Mosby takes an active hand in planning murder, he attempts it in Arden's house: Mosby solicits poison from Clarke, Mosby asks Clarke for a "crucifix impoisonèd" (i.611; the ruse is never tried), and Mosby orchestrates the final "complot" (xiv.92). Finally, it is the playwright's understanding of what Arden and Mosby represent in the little world of Arden's house that makes this tale of domestic violence "The Lamentable and True Tragedie of M. Arden of Feversham in Kent."

Arden's authority as a husband and as a householder is established in the first scene by the challenges to it. He suspects some of them: to Franklin he details how his mistrust of Alice and Mosby has been aroused by their love letters, the exchange of rings, and their "privy meetings in the town" (i.16). Soon after, he describes Mosby as an "injurious ribald that attempts / To violate my dear wife's chastity" and as one who "thinks to defile" (that is, expects to defile) Arden's marriage bed (i.37–38, 40). In this latter understanding of the lovers' relationship, Arden is probably wrong; all subsequent evidence indicates that the affair has in fact been consummated. We are also to learn, however, that in one of his earlier observations Arden is certainly right: Mosby and Alice have met in town but never in Arden's own house. To that extent at least, Mosby has not yet usurped Arden's place. By the end of the first scene, even that will no longer be true, as a direct consequence of Arden's submission to the most dangerous of all Franklin's pieces of advice, to "lie with me at London all this term" (i.51).

In fact, the true nature of Alice's infidelity is rebellion. Only Arden's presence in his house has been any deterrent to her; he has been the "hindrance" that has kept her meetings with Mosby "privy," surreptitious, and in the town. When Arden informs her that "yet ere noon we'll take horse and away," Alice sees him off to the quay and then repeats, but in exultation, "Ere noon he means to take horse and away! / Sweet news is this" (i.92–94).

That she associates Arden's presence with enforced discretion and his absence with heedlessness is confirmed almost immediately when Adam comes from the Flower-de-Luce Inn to bring her word from Mosby. "Be not afraid," says Alice, "my husband is now from home" (i.108). When Mosby appears, he greets her with a rebuff: "Away, I say, and talk not to me now" (i.179). Alice chooses to assume that he merely pretends such strangeness and so reassures him that he "needest not fear." For Mosby too, fear has only one association; he returns, "Where is your husband?" (i.181–182). Only when reassured that Arden is at the quay does Mosby allow himself to stay and be reconciled to Alice by her alternating blandishments and reproaches.

Until Arden is gone from Feversham, however, the lovers must still exercise some caution. In sending for Mosby, Alice asks Adam to suggest that Mosby come "but along my door / And as a stranger but salute me there" (i.128–129). Because the door distinguishes the public from the private, Mosby can preserve the appearance of strangeness by remaining outside Arden's house. "This may he do," Alice asserts, "without suspect or fear" (i.130). But she complains of the restraint that is imposed by Arden's presence:

> I know he [Mosby] loves me well but dares not come
> Because my husband is so jealous
> And these my narrow-prying neighbours blab,
> Hinder our meetings when we would confer.
> But, if I live, that block shall be removed;
> And Mosby, thou that comes to me by stealth,
> Shalt neither fear the biting speech of men
> Nor Arden's looks.
>
> *(i.133–140)*

Finally, she would have him removed more permanently than merely to London; she vows that Arden shall surely die.

> Yet nothing could enforce me to the deed
> But Mosby's love. Might I without control
> Enjoy thee still, then Arden should not die;
> But, seeing I cannot, therefore let him die.
>
> *(i.273–276)*

After the poison attempt miscarries, Alice bluffs her way through Arden's questions about her broth and then through his sentimental leave-taking. She asks him to return quickly "lest that I die for sorrow" (i.406), but her first words when he exits are "I am glad he is gone." Her protestations of love had nearly proved too successful: "he was about to stay, / But did you mark me then how I brake off?" (i.417–418). Arden's absence is Alice's triumph.

When Arden eventually returns from London, Alice is infuriated anew at the curtailment of her liberty that his presence represents. She repeats her challenges to Arden's authority: "Why should he thrust his sickle in our corn"—what right has Arden to interfere with the lovers' happiness? "Or what hath he to do with thee, my love"—what authority does he have over Mosby? "Or govern me that am to rule myself?" (x.83–85). "Forsooth," she exclaims, "for credit sake, I must leave thee! / Nay, he must leave to live that we may love" (x.86–87).

Her lover, however, would establish a different household hierarchy. When Alice had first told Mosby that Arden would be leaving for London, Mosby had answered revealingly, "To London, Alice? If thou'lt be ruled by me, / We'll make him sure enough" (i.224–225). He already enjoys her, but Mosby aspires to rule her—and indeed to rule all that is legitimately Arden's. Franklin's perspective—that it is not strange that women will be false—is not an unusual one, but neither he nor Arden yet realizes that the contest with Mosby is not just for a woman but for all that Arden is master of.

Arden had imaged Alice's possible infidelity as a defilement of their wedding bed; Mosby will picture himself not in Arden's bed, but "in Arden's seat" (viii.31), assuming Arden's authority. This challenge to Arden's authority is underscored when his own man is enlisted to betray him: "I will kill my master," Michael vows (i.162). It is suggested with irony when Alice speaks of usurpation but professes that it is Arden who usurps Mosby's place in her heart (i.98–99). And the challenge is finally theatrically established when Mosby makes his first entrance into Arden's house. In urging "Alice, let's in and see what cheer you keep" (i.636), he anticipates enjoying not only what the hostess has to offer but also what the householder has ceded. The first scene ends with a telling exchange:

> *Mosby.* . . . I hope, now Master Arden is from home,
>   You'll give me leave to play your husband's part.
> *Alice.* Mosby, you know who's master of my heart
>   He well may be the master of the house.
>
>   *(i.637–640)*

Of Mosby, though, more than of Arden, Wine might write of "an ambitious man whose success is in itself bringing him no happiness." For in a later soliloquy, Mosby confesses to himself that "My golden time was when I had no gold; / Though then I wanted, yet I slept secure" (viii.11–12). It is his aspiration that has brought him to a place that now seems inhospitable:

> . . . since I climbed the top bough of the tree
> And sought to build my nest among the clouds,
> Each gentle starry gale doth shake my bed

> And makes me dread my downfall to the earth.
>   *(viii.15–18)*

But Mosby tells himself that he cannot undo what is past: "The way I seek to find where pleasure dwells / Is hedged behind me that I cannot back" (viii.20–21). So he "needs must on" to find security. There is Arden yet to kill; Mosby renews his vows against him and then considers Greene, Michael, and Clarke: as "Chief actors to Arden's overthrow," they may be a threat to Mosby "when they shall see me sit in Arden's seat" (viii.30–31). Thus he must have them dispatched too by way of ensuring his place and authority: only "then am I sole ruler of mine own" (vii.36). His paranoia extends even to Alice: "You have supplanted Arden for my sake / And will extirpen me to plant another" (viii.40–41).

When Alice enters hard upon his vow to "cleanly rid [his] hands of her" (viii.43), she presents him with a newer and nearer threat: she is having doubts and regrets of her own. She thinks to become again "honest Arden's wife" and to abandon Mosby, the "mean artificer, that low-born name" (viii.73, 77). Even after Mosby has persuaded her again, he continues to taunt her: "O, no, I am a base artificer; / My wings are feathered for a lowly flight" (viii.135–136)—she has, that is, suggested that he does not belong with her in the "top bough of the tree." With his further sneering observation that "We beggars must not breathe where gentles are" (viii.139), he provokes from her some reassurances that he befits the place which he has assumed. "Sweet Mosby is as gentle as a king. . . . Himself is valued gentle by his worth" (viii.140–145). It is then dramatically reiterated that the place which Mosby has already assumed is in Arden's house. In direct contrast to her first-scene request that he "come but along the door" to avoid "suspect" and "fear," she urges, "Come, let us in to shun suspicion" (viii.166). Mosby no longer poses as a stranger; he makes himself "as gentle as a king" in Arden's house.

The early Arden suspects that Alice is a rebel and Mosby a usurper. Once Arden leaves his home, for example, his suspicions of his wife grow to conviction. He describes her to Franklin in poetry lush with natural and classical imagery. She is unafraid of the "common speech of men" who "mangle credit," wound with words, "And couch dishonour as dishonour buds"; she will not "turn the leaf / And sorrow for her dissolution"; "she is rooted in her wickedness"; censure only "makes her vice to grow / As Hydra's head that plenished by decay"; she shames him so that "Mosby's name, a scandal unto mine, / Is deeply trenchèd in my blushing brow" (iv.1–17). Arden describes himself with similar extravagance as suffering a "heart's grief" that "rends my other powers / Worse than the conflict at the hour of death" (iv.19–20). Franklin offers only thin consolation. Arden, apparently not even hearing his friend's response, suddenly speaks, in striking contrast to his earlier linguistic exuberance, tersely, simply, and bleakly: "My house is irksome; there I cannot rest" (iv.27).

Franklin suggests, unhelpfully but well-meaningly, "Then stay with me in London; go not home" (iv.28). But Arden knows that "Then that base Mosby doth usurp my room / And makes his triumph of my being thence" (iv.29–30). In this context, "room" carries the sense of "the particular place assigned or appropriated to a person" (*OED*, sb. 11), or of "office, position, or authority" (*OED*, sb. 12b). The image which Arden evokes is that of a man, himself, who has been king in his own house, but who is now in exile, dethroned by a base usurper. As long as Arden remains in London, the pretender will enjoy his superior's place unchallenged.

The first murder attempt had failed when Arden had noticed that "There's something in this broth / That is not wholesome" (i.365–366). During the second attempt, interrupted when an apprentice "lets . . . down his [shop] window, and it breaks Black Will's head," Arden had asked, "What troublesome fray or mutiny is this?" It was Franklin who had dismissed it as "nothing but some brabbling, paltry fray, / Devised to pick men's pockets in the throng" (iii.51s.d., 55, 56–57). And Arden had thwarted the third murder attempt when he thought to lock Franklin's doors, left open to the assassins by Michael. But, while in London, Arden allows himself to be persuaded by Franklin that a premonitory dream is "but a mockery" (vi.40) and thereafter abandons all heedfulness and suspicion. The consequences of an ignored dream were sufficiently established by dramatic convention that little surprise would have attached to the role reversal that Arden and Franklin subsequently undergo.

In depicting the ensuing murder attempts, the playwright focuses on an Arden whose complacency amounts to culpability. On Rainham Down, for example, Arden is blithely interested in what he calls Franklin's "pretty tale" of an unfaithful wife who is majestic in denial even when confronted with evidence of her sin; it is Franklin who is "assailèd" by "so fierce a qualm" that he cannot continue (ix.92,67). This fourth murder attempt is frustrated only by the fortuitous appearance of Lord Cheyne with his men. In a fifth attempt, the murderers are prevented by a fog that obscures their vision; Arden meanwhile jests carelessly with a ferryman about irksome houses, absent husbands, wandering wives, and resultant cuckoldry. Alice and Mosby undertake the sixth attempt by coming before him with their arms entwined, exchanging a "sugared kiss" (xiii.80). When Mosby taunts Arden that "the horns are thine" (xiii.82), Arden is provoked to a sword fight. But Arden is overcome with remorse at Mosby's resultant wounds; it is only Franklin who fully recognizes how Arden has been dishonored. Arden, who cannot do too much to make amends, insists that Mosby "come and sup . . . at our house this night" (xiv.40).

Perhaps because Alice reveals that she has grown so desperate for Arden's death that she has nearly murdered him in his sleep, Mosby at this time determines once again to take a hand in the arrangements and to see Arden dead that very night. He proposes to accept Arden's invitation to sup and to come early, before the other guests arrive. Black Will and Shakebag will have been closeted in the adjoining countinghouse.[64] Mosby will engage Arden in a friendly game at tables before supper; when Mosby signals, "Now I take you" (a phrase similar, in effect, to *checkmate*), then the two assassins will "rush forth"—and take Arden (xiv.104, 102).

Black Will offers further refinements to the plot:

> Place Mosby, being a stranger, in a chair,
> And let your husband sit upon a stool,
> That I may come behind him cunningly
> And with a towel pull him to the ground,
> Then stab him till his flesh be as a sieve.
>
> *(xiv.118–122)*

Raymond Chapman remarks that "even Arden, so proud of his wealth, has such a sparsely furnished house that the guest of honour is placed in the only chair while the host sits on a stool." Wine repeats that this is "an interesting commentary, so it seems, on the sparse furnishings of even a well-to-do Elizabethan gentleman's household." It is, more probably, an interesting commentary on the sparse furnishings of the Elizabethan stage and on the symbolic value and emphasis that props can thereby assume. For Wine also quotes M. Jourdain: "In domestic use the chair was the rightful seat of the master of the house, only given up by courtesy."[65] The significance of the detail is further suggested by its divergence from the source: in Holinshed, "When they came into the parlor, Mosbie sat downe on the benche."[66] The seating arrangement may be a matter of practicality to Black Will, but it is a matter of symbolic staging for author and audience, a realization of Mosby's wish to "sit in Arden's seat." This stage motif of usurpation will be repeated after Arden's murder, when Adam Fowle, Bradshaw, Greene, and Franklin enter and Alice directs their placement: "I pray you be content, I'll have my will.— / Master Mosby, sit you in my husband's seat" (xiv.286–287).

In her nervous social chatter before the murder is committed, Alice somewhat overplays her part. But her feigned objections to Mosby's presence keep our attention relentlessly focused, in these moments of high tension, on Arden's wilfullness in inviting Mosby and on Mosby's invasion of Arden's house. She protests, "Husband, what mean you to bring Mosby home?"; "wherefore do you bring him hither now? / You have given me my supper with his sight"; "You may enforce me to it if you will, / But I had rather die than bid him welcome"; "The doors are open, sir [to Mosby]; you may be gone"; again to Mosby, "henceforth frequent my house no more" (xiv.169, 175–176, 180–181, 197, 212). Arden repeatedly commands her to be hospitable: "Why, Alice, how can I do too much for him / Whose life I have endangered without cause?" (xiv.203–204). She pretends submission, but only for this night, asking Mosby, "henceforth / Be you as strange to me as I to you" (xiv.208). The irony of her stipulation is underscored by the verbal allusion to her first-scene request that he pose as a stranger coming along her door. Mosby answers her with equal irony that "I'll see your husband in despite of you," adding a double-edged vow to Arden: "Thou ne'er shalt see me more after this night" (xiv.213, 215). Alice joins him in this pledge, which is to Arden's death.

The murder is executed as planned. The dying Arden cries, "Mosby! Michael! Alice! What will you do?" (xiv.233), numbering the hierarchy of the violations of his domestic order: the guest, the manservant, the wife of his house. Mosby, in responding, exorcises his old resentment of Arden's early assumption of social superiority: "There's for the pressing iron you told me of" (xiv.235). Alice, in her turn, reiterates her play-long motivation: "Take this for hind'ring Mosby's love and mine" (xiv.238). When she takes up the weapon against her own husband, Michael cries, "O, mistress!" (xiv.239).

Arden's house, for the control of which the conspirators have plotted and committed murder, in the final irony betrays not only Arden but his murderers as well. With Arden's body removed to the Abbey field, Alice is falsely reassured: "Now let the judge and juries do their worst; / My house is clear, and now I fear them not" (xiv.355–356). But when Franklin, the town Mayor, and the Watch are admitted, the house still holds its evidence and witnesses the crime:

> *Franklin.* I fear me he was murdered in this house
>   And carried to the fields, for from that place
>   Backwards and forwards may you see
>   The print of many feet within the snow.
>   And look about this chamber where we are,
>   And you shall find part of his guiltless blood;
>   For in his slipshoe did I find some rushes,
>   Which argueth he was murdered in this room.
> *Mayor.* Look in the place where he was wont to sit.—
>   See, see! His blood! It is too manifest.
>
>   *(xiv.392–401)*

The brief closing scenes satisfy our instinct for justice, but not tidily. Clarke escapes; the innocent Bradshaw, an early foil for Arden, is trapped in the snare of an omniverous civil authority and executed with the murderers. Bradshaw's fate is also detailed in the sources, but it is the playwright who dramatizes Bradshaw's plea to an indifferent Alice to witness his innocence and who thus, reviving the parallel to Arden, heightens the closing scene with an echo of tragic loss. The apprehended criminals, some repentant and some resigned, go to their just executions, but without sentimentality or overt moralizing. The focus does not shift: this is not their tragedy, but Arden's. His death has been motivated but certainly not condoned; he was the figure of order in the little world of his house. What the last scenes thus accomplish is a restitution of order, for *Arden of Feversham* is after all a tragedy about order and the overthrow of order, even if only domestic order.

It would be easy to claim too much for *Arden of Feversham*. Its integrity has been damaged by the fact that it survives to us only in what is evidently a memorially reconstructed text. It may be incompletely realized. And it certainly is not largely conceived: the closing concern with civil justice alone diminishes tragic effect. But the interest of *Arden of Feversham,* to me, is that it documents the struggle of an artist with a form that may have appeared new to him and to his age. My sense of his understanding of his material is that it is the idea of the house that gives substance and significance to his attempt to present the story of Thomas Ardern as a tragedy.

Like the "domestic" tragedies that were to follow, *Arden of Feversham* takes as its protagonist a gentleman, not a member of the middle class, nor a bourgeois hero, nor a citizen-hero, as has often been posited.[67] Rather, the gentle status of the protagonists in such plays should not be underemphasized. And each of these protagonists is given a distinguishing context: his house. He is located in the arena where he has full responsibility for and final authority over family, servants, and guests. It is in his house that the gentleman is king, and that house is seen by the Elizabethan playwright as a little kingdom, a microcosm in which tragic action can ensue. Such action is a violation of what is a powerful ideal of order in the house: this is the nature of "domestic" tragedy. And its tragic action reflects larger challenges to order in the unsettled years of the turn of the sixteenth century and the beginning of the next.

NOTES

1. See, for example, G. R. Hibbard, "The Country House Poem of the Seventeenth Century," *Journal of the Warburg and Courtauld Institutes,* XIX (1956), 159-174; Charles Molesworth, "Property and Virtue: The Genre of the Country-House Poem in the Seventeenth Century," *Genre,* I, No. 2 (April 1968), 141-157; Richard Gill, *Happy Rural Seat: The English Country House and the Literary Imagination* (New Haven, Conn.: Yale University Press, 1972); and William A. McClung, *The Country House in English Renaissance Poetry* (Berkeley: University of California Press, 1977).

2. The report on Semayne's case (decided in 1605), from which I have quoted Coke, was translated into English among *The Reports of Sir Edward Coke Late Lord Chief-Justice of England,* also known as "The King's Bench Reports" (London, 1658, Wing *STC* C4944), sig. Pp3[r]. Coke completed *The Third Part of the Institutes of the Laws of England: Concerning High Treason, and other Pleas of the Crown, and Criminall causes,* or "The Third Institute," in 1628; it was published posthumously (London, 1644, Wing *STC* C4960); see sig. Y3[v].

   William Lambard's *Eirenarcha: Or The Office of the Justices of Peace* was "gathered" in 1579 and "first published" in 1581; I quote from a revised and enlarged edition (London, 1588, *STC* 15165), Bk. II, Ch. 7, sig. S1[r]. Sir William Stanford's *Les Plees Del Coron* was first published in London in 1557; I quote from the second edition of 1560 (*STC* 23220); see Bk. I, Ch. 6, f. 14[v]. The statute of 1478 is recorded in the *Anni Regis Henrici Septimi* (London, 1555, *STC* 9920), Anno xxi. H vii, sig. Nn4[r].

   All the passages quoted concern English criminal law and specifically the issue of justifiable homicide; the law held a man innocent of murder if he killed someone who had broken into his house to commit burglary or assault—because the law held that "a man's house is his castle." In *A History of English Law,* 17 vols. ([London: Methuen, 1903–22], III, 243), W. S. Holdsworth puts this issue in perspective: "The first business of the law, and more especially of the law of crime and tort, is to suppress self-help. And so we find that the further back we go into the history of law the more frequent and detailed are the prohibitions against asserting one's rights by force." The instance of justifiable homicide was largely identified with the legal execution of justice by enforcement officials—even self-defense was a criminal offense—so this early recognition of an exception is all the more significant. The quoted statute of 1478 further clears a servant of any wrongdoing if he protects his master from a housebreaker. A later statute of 1532 clarified that a man who thus defended his house was not only not liable to conviction for homicide but also not subject to the forfeiture of any goods (see Holdsworth, III, 257). The laws testify to English recognition of what Holdsworth calls "the sanctity of the homestead" (III, 293).

   The legal principle was widely familiar, and the central metaphor appears in a variety of literary contexts, including collections of proverbs. See those listed by Morris Palmer Tilley, *A*

Dictionary of the Proverbs in England in the Sixteenth and Seventeenth Centuries (Ann Arbor: University of Michigan Press, 1950), p. 432, M473: "A Man's house is his castle." It was sometimes thought of strictly as a law proverb, but the metaphor was sufficiently commonplace to Richard Mulcaster, writing before 1581, that he extended its meaning to imply the authority of the householder; he limits his advice to a parent supervising a child's education because that parent is "the appointer of his owne circumstance, and his house is his castle" (*Positions Wherein Those Circumstances be Examined Necessarie for the Training of Children* [London, 1581, STC 18253], Ch. 40, sig. Ff1^r). John Donne may have had a similar implication in mind in "Jealosie" (1633), an elegy about a man being cuckolded in his own house, by the narrator:

> Wee must not, as wee us'd . . .
> . . . usurpe his owne bed any more,
> Nor kisse and play in his house, as before.
> Now I see many dangers; for that is
> His realme, his castle, and his diocese.

(from Helen Gardner's edition of *"The Elegies" and "The Songs and Sonnets"* [Oxford: Clarendon Press, 1965], pp. 9–10). By 1642, the metaphor was a dead one that Thomas Fuller turned to fresh significance: "It was wont to be said *A mans house is his Castle,* but if this Castle of late hath proved unable to secure any, let them make their conscience their castle" ("A Fast Sermon Preached on Innocents Day" [London, 1642, Wing STC F2423], sig. D4^v).

3. The Anglo-Norman terms that are traditional in early English legal records reflect, it is worth noting, a significant resource of the English language. Rich as the language generally is in vocabulary and nuance, it may remain specifically suggestive of a cultural investment in spatial identification that the language embraced the French and Latin words *dome, domicile, manor, mansion, habitation, residence,* and *place,* to supplement the Old English *abode, dwelling,* and *house. Home* is a word exclusive to the English, as are all its emotive derivatives, among them *homecoming, homeland, homeless, homesick,* and *homestead.* My source is the *Oxford Dictionary of English Etymology,* which also notes that: "Since literate Englishmen have been acquainted with both French and Latin throughout the Middle Ages and down to our own times, either channel, or both, could be assumed as the means of entry into English, other things being equal" (ed. C. T. Onions, with G. W. S. Friedrichsen and R. W. Burchfield [Oxford: Clarendon Press, 1966], pp. vii–viii).

4. Joyce Youings, *The Dissolution of the Monasteries,* Historical Problems: Studies and Documents, No. 14, ed. G. R. Elton (London: Allen & Unwin, 1971), p. 15. For the following discussion of the Tudor and Stuart land market, I am indebted not only to Youings's *Dissolution* but also to Gordon Batho, "Landlords in England: The Crown," and "Landlords in England: Noblemen, Gentlemen and Yeomen," in *The Agrarian History of England and Wales: Vol. IV, 1500–1640,* ed. Joan Thirsk, gen. ed. H. P. R. Finberg (Cambridge: Cambridge University Press, 1967), pp. 256–306; George C. Brodrick, *English Land and English Landlords* (London: Cassel, Petter, Galpin, 1881); D. R. Denman, *Origins of Ownership* (London: Allen and Unwin, 1958); G. A. Holmes, *The Estates of the Higher Nobility in Fourteenth-Century England* (Cambridge: Cambridge University Press, 1957); Dom David Knowles, *The Religious Orders in England: Vol. III, The Tudor Age* (Cambridge: Cambridge University Press, 1959); S. B. Lilgegren, *The Fall of the Monasteries and the Social Changes in England Leading up to the Great Revolution* (Lund: G. W. K. Gleerup, 1924); R. B. Smith, *Land and Politics in the England of Henry VIII: The West Riding of Yorkshire, 1530–46* (Oxford: Clarendon Press, 1970); B. P. Wolffe, *The Crown Lands 1461 to 1536: An Aspect of Yorkist and Early Tudor Government,* Historical Problems: Studies and Documents, No. 10, ed. G. R. Elton (London: Allen & Unwin, 1970); and Youings, "Landlords in England: The Church," in *The Agrarian History of England and Wales: Vol. IV, 1500–1640,* pp. 306–356.

5. Quoted by Smith, p. 226.

6. From *The Governance of England,* excerpted by Wolffe, p. 91.

7. Batho, "Landlords in England: Noblemen, Gentlemen, and Yeomen," p. 301.

8. Ann Jennalie Cook, *The Privileged Playgoers of Shakespeare's London, 1576–1642* (Princeton, N. J.: Princeton University Press, 1981).

9. Thomas Wilson, *The State of England Anno Dom. 1600,* ed. F. J. Fisher, *Camden Miscellany,* Vol. XVI (London: Camden Society, 1936), p. 23; William Harrison, *The Description of England,* ed. Georges Edelen, Folger Documents of Tudor and Stuart Civilization (Ithaca, N. Y.: Cornell University Press, 1968), p. 94. Edelen bases his text on the 1587 edition.

10. Harrison, pp. 117–118.

11. See Julian Cornwall, "The Early Tudor Gentry," *Economic History Review,* 2nd ser., 17, No. 3 (1965), 456–475.

12. Thomas Gainsford, *The Secretaries Studie* (London, 1616, *STC* 11523), sigs. D3^r and D4^r.

13. M. W. Barley, "Rural Housing in England," in *The Agrarian History of England and Wales: Vol. IV, 1500–1640,* p. 729.

14. Wallace T. MacCaffrey, *Exeter, 1540–1640: The Growth of an English County Town* (Cambridge, Mass.: Harvard University Press, 1958), p. 252.

15. W. G. Hoskins, "The Rebuilding of Rural England, 1570–1640," in *Provincial England: Essays in Social and Economic History* (London: Macmillan, 1963), p. 131. I am also indebted to Peter Eden, *Small Houses in England 1520–1820* (n.p.: Historical Association, 1969); Eric Mercer, *English Art 1553–1625.* The Oxford History of English Art, ed. T. S. R. Boase (Oxford: Clarendon Press, 1962); and Trudy West, *The Timber-frame House in England* (Newton Abbot, Devon: David & Charles, [1971]), among many others.

16. Harrison, p. 277.

17. Harrison, p. 276. Note also page 356.

18. Andrew Borde, *The Boke for to Lerne a man to be wyse in buyldyng of his howse for the helth of body & to holde quyetnes for the helth of his soule, and body* (London, [1540?], *STC* 3373), sig. A2^r.

19. Sir John Oglander, "Commonplace Book," ed. as *A Royalist's Notebook* by Francis Bamford (London: Constable, 1936), pp. 212, 94–95, 82, and 84.

20. Peter Clark, "The Migrant in Kentish Towns 1580–1640," in *Crisis and Order in English Towns 1500–1700: Essays in Urban History,* ed. Peter Clark and Paul Slack (London: Routledge, 1972), p. 149. See also his "Introduction," written with Paul Slack, to the same volume and, among others, Christopher Hill's *Change and Continuity in Seventeenth-Century England* (Cambridge, Mass.: Harvard University Press, 1975) and Joan Thirsk's "Enclosing and Engrossing" and "The Farming Regions of England," in *The Agrarian History of England and Wales,* pp. 200–255 and 1–112.

21. Francis Bacon, quoted by Slack, "Vagrants and Vagrancy in England, 1598–1664," *Economic History Review,* 2nd. ser., 27, No. 3 (1974), 360.

22. Slack, "Vagrants and Vagrancy in England, 1598–1664," in *Crisis and Order,* pp. 360, 377.

23. Thomas Dekker, "O per Se O" (1612), reprinted in A. V. Judges, *The Elizabethan Underworld,* 2nd ed. (New York: Octagon, 1965), pp. 366–381, with the "Articles of their Fraternities," pp. 377–378.

24. Thomas Heywood, *An Apology for Actors* (London, 1612, *STC* 13309), sig. E3^r.

25. Matthew Griffith, *Bethel: Or A Forme for Families* (London, 1633, *STC* 12368), from the Preface entitled "To the Christian Reader." For the following discussion of household government, I have also consulted these contemporary domestic economies and conduct books: Sk. B., *Counsel to the Husband; To the Wife Instruction* (London, 1608, *STC* 1069); W. B., *The Court of good Counsell, Wherein is Set downe the true rules, how a man should choose a good Wife from a bad, and a woman*

a good Husband from a bad (London, 1607, *STC* 5876); Jean Bodin, *The Six Bookes of a Common-weale,* tr. Richard Knolles (London, 1606, *STC* 3193); Richard Brathwait, *The English Gentlewo-man* (London, 1631, *STC* 3565); Robert Cleaver, *A Godly Form of Householde Government* (London, 1598, *STC* 5382); Dudley Fenner, *The Artes of Logike and Rethorike ... with examples from the practice of the same for methode in the gouernment of the famelie* (London, 1584, *STC* 10766); Thomas Gainsford, *The Rich Cabinet* (London, 1616, *STC* 11522), and *The Secretaries Studie;* William Gouge, *Of Domesticall Duties* (London, 1622, *STC* 12119); Christopher Hegendorff, *Domestycal or housholde Sermons,* 2 vols. (Ipswich and Worcester, 1548 and 1549, *STC* 13021 and 13022); Thomas Heywood, *A Curtaine Lecture* (London, 1637, *STC* 13312); Gervase Markham, "The English Huswife," in *Countrey Contentments* (London, 1615, *STC* 17342); Josias Nichols, *An Order of Household Instruction* (London, 1596, *STC* 18540); Dudley North [Fourth Baron North], *Observations and Advices Oeconomical* (London, 1669, Wing *STC* N1286); William Perkins, *Christian Oeconomie* (London, 1609, *STC* 19677); Henry Smith, *A Preparative to Marriage* (London, 1591, *STC* 22685); Robert Snawsel, *A Looking Glasse for Maried Folkes* (London, 1610, *STC* 22886); Torquato Tasso, *The Householders Philosophie,* tr. T. K[yd]. (London, 1588, *STC* 23703); William Vaughan, *The Golden Grove ... A Worke very necessary for all such, as would know how to governe themselues, their houses, or their countrey* (London, 1600, *STC* 24610); William Whately, *A Bride-Bush, Or A Wedding Sermon* (London, 1617, *STC* 25296); George Whetstone, *An Heptameron of Ciuill Discourses* (London, 1582, *STC* 25337); Richard Whitforde, *A werke for housholders* (1530; London, 1533, *STC* 25423).

　　I am also indebted to Carroll Camden, *The Elizabethan Woman* (Houston: Elsevier Press, 1952), especially for the bibliography of contemporary sources; Peter Laslett, *Family Life and Illicit Love in Earlier Generations* (Cambridge: Cambridge University Press, 1977), *The World We Have Lost,* 2nd ed. (London: Methuen, 1971); Laslett and Richard Wall, *Household and Family in Past Time* (Cambridge: Cambridge University Press, 1972); Chilton Latham Powell, *English Domestic Relations 1487–1653* (New York: Columbia University Press, 1917); and Lawrence Stone, *Family, Sex and Marriage in England 1500–1800* (New York: Harper & Row, 1977).

26. Gouge, sigs. Z4^V and S1^V.

27. John Wodroephe, *The Spared Houres of a Souldier in his Travels* (Dort, 1623, *STC* 25939), sig. Tt5^V. See other instances listed by Tilley, p. 411, M132: "Every Man is a king (master) in his own house."

28. See Holdsworth, II, 449–450, where he quotes the statute of treasons.

29. North, pp. 3 and 32.

30. Sk. B., *Counsel to the Husband; To the Wife Instruction,* sigs. C7^V–C8^r.

31. Gouge, sig. H8^r.

32. Laslett, *The World We Have Lost,* p. 94. For more on marital and housing patterns, see also his *Family Life and Illicit Love* and *Household and Family,* and compare Stone, *Family, Sex and Marriage,* especially pp. 46–54.

33. Bodin, Bk. I, Ch. 3, sig. C2^r.

34. Gouge, sig. C1^V.

35. Bodin, Bk. I, Ch. 2, sig. B4^V.

36. Snawsel, sig. A5^V.

37. Nichols, sigs. B3^V–B4^r.

38. Griffith, sigs. B3^V–B4^V.

39. See on this subject Stone, *The Family, Sex and Marriage,* p. 216, and Gordon J. Schochet, *Patriarchalism in Political Thought* (Oxford: Blackwell, 1975).

40. I refer to the domestic tragedies *Arden of Feversham* (published 1592), Thomas Dekker and Ben Jonson's lost "Page of Plymouth" (referred to by Henslowe in 1599), the anonymous *The Yorkshire*

Tragedy (published in 1608), the Jane Shore subplot of Thomas Heywood's *1 and 2 Edward IV* (published 1599), and the anonymous *Warning for Fair Women* (published 1599).

41. *The Lamentable and True Tragedie of M. Arden of Feversham in Kent* (London, 1592, *STC* 733).

42. In all references to the historical persons involved, I follow the spellings of the Wardmote Book of Faversham (ff. 59–60), which was the official account of the murder and which has been reprinted by, for example, Edward Jacob (in *The Lamentable and Trve Tragedie of M. Arden of Feversham, in Kent* . . . [Feversham: Stephen Doorne, 1770], Appendix VIII) and M. L. Wine (in his Revels edition, *The Tragedy of Arden of Faversham* [London: Methuen, 1973] Appendix III). I do so in order to reinforce the distinction between these historical personages and the dramatic characters who will be discussed below.

43. For the information on Sir Edward North, I am indebted to Lionel Cust, "Arden of Feversham," *Archaeologia Cantiana,* 34 (1920), 101–102. For background on Faversham, I have consulted Peter Clark and Paul Slack, "Introduction," in *Crisis and Order in English Towns 1500–1700; Faversham, Kent: The Official Guide* (Faversham Borough Council, [1971]); Frank William Jessup, *A History of Kent* (London: D. Finlayson, 1958); and Anthony Swaine, *Faversham: Its History, Its Present Role and the Pattern for Its Future* (Maidstone: Kent County Council and Faversham Borough Council, 1970).

   Something of Ardern's background may be preserved in two eighteenth-century sources that claim dependence on the oral tradition in Kent. Discovered in the Dolphin Inn in Faversham was a manuscript in an eighteenth-century hand that records that Ardern was from Wye, also in Kent, that he was fifty-six when he first came to Faversham, and that Alyce was twenty-eight (as excerpted in *The Roxburghe Ballads,* ed. J. Woodfall Ebsworth [Hertford: Stephen Austin, 1895], Vol. III, Part 1, p. 47). A William Cook preserved a chapbook (now in the Folger Shakespeare Library, but otherwise unrecorded) that lacks a title-page but probably dates to the early eighteenth century; in it, Ardern is again from Wye, is again fifty-six when he settles in Faversham, and, further, is fifty-nine at marriage and sixty-six at death. As he died in 1550/51, he thus married in 1543 or 1544, according to this account. While both sources testify to continued interest in Ardern's story, neither has any established authority.

44. I quote from "The history of a moste horible murder comytyd at ffevershame in Kente," Harley MSS. 542, f. 34ʳ. This anonymous account is quite similar to Raphael Holinshed's in his *Chronicle of England, Scotland and Ireland* (1577); the section on Ardern has been reprinted by several editors of the play *Arden of Feversham,* including M. L. Wine in his Revels edition; see pp. 148–159. As the manuscript was preserved among Stow's papers, it may have been Holinshed's source. Holinshed edits out all references to North, including that quoted above and the manuscript report that Ardern's wife was "the lord northes wyves dowghtar."

45. Edward Hasted, in *The History and Topographical Survey of the County of Kent,* 4 vols. (Canterbury: Simmons & Kirby, 1778–99), details the grant to Cheyney and its subsequent alienation to Ardern (II, 703–704), and Ardern's other dealings (see I, 199; II, 704, 707, 718; III, 12–13, 550–551; IV, 267). The inquisition post mortem taken at Bexley, Kent on 7 October 1551 is preserved among Chancery Inquisitions Post Mortem in the Public Record Office, ser. II (C. 142), Vol. 93, No. 111. I am grateful to Laetitia Yeandle, the Folger Shakespeare Library's Curator and Cataloguer of Manuscripts, for oral translation of a negative photostat of the manuscript in the Folger's collection.

   According to the Dolphin Inn manuscript, Ardern was "importuned to buy the Abbey-lands by Lord Cheyne"; this description of the transaction may reflect an eagerness, shared by the anonymous author of the chapbook, to clear Ardern of any wrongdoing in acquiring tenanted land and indeed of any evidence of land greed.

46. This description of the North family I again owe to Cust, p. 102 and the *DNB.* Edward Jacob reproduces "The Arms of Sir Edw. North in a Window of Arden's House," in *The History of the Town and Port of Faversham, in the County of Kent* (London: J. March, 1774), plate XV. A. H.

Bullen notes that the arms appeared on the parlor window in his edition of the play *Arden of Feversham* (London: J. W. Jarvis, 1887), p. v.

47. On the construction of gatehouse, guesthouse, and Ardern's house, see Brian Philp, *Excavations at Faversham,* First Research Report of the Kent Archaeological Research Groups' Council (Crawley: W. & J. Jarvis, 1968), pp. 30–31, and Swaine, p. 62. On the relative value of Ardern's house: Thomas Southouse, *Monasticon Favershamiense in Agro Cantiano* (London, 1671, Wing STC S4772), sigs. D6^r–D8^v and sigs. I8^v–K1^r.

48. See Herbert Dane, "The Mayoralty of Faversham," *Faversham Papers,* No. 1 (1964); C. E. Donne, "An Essay on the Tragedy of 'Arden of Feversham'" (1873; rpt. New York: AMS Press, 1972), pp. 1–2; and Jessup, p. 93.

49. Harley MSS. 542, f. 34^r. This account is unique to the manuscript.

50. The discoverers of Ardern's murdered body, "knowing hir euill demeanor in times past, examined" Alyce on the matter, according to Holinshed, p. 157. Similarly, in the Harley manuscript version, "knowynge hir evell behavyowr in tymes past, they examonyd hir" (f. 36^v).

51. Compare Holinshed on Grene (p. 149) and Reade (p. 159), and the Harley manuscript on Grene (f. 34^v) and Reade (ff. 36^r and 37^v).

52. Both Holinshed (p. 157) and the Harley manuscript (f. 36^v) recount the story of Ardern's cheating the town of fair revenue. The record of his disenfranchisement, in the Faversham Wardmote Book (22 December 1550, f. 58), has been fairly frequently reprinted.

53. See Holinshed, p. 154, and the Harley manuscript, f. 36^r.

54. Jacob reports Ardern's civic philanthropy and the subsequent suit. When he wrote in 1770, Ardern's anniversary sermon was still being preached and bread still being distributed, "agreeable to his well intentioned charity, at the expence of the corporation" (*Arden,* Appendix II, p. 135). Bullen records that it was Ardern who gave Faversham the plot of ground where once stood a pillory and where now stands the town pump, p. iv.

55. Again it is the official account of the murder in the Wardmote Book of Faversham that provides the names of all conspirators and details of their punishments. Other surviving records of apprehensions and executions are cited by Wine, pp. 161–163. The chronicle of the many unsuccessful murder-attempts and the story of the miracle in the Abbey grass originate in the Harley manuscript and in Holinshed. Donne emphasizes that Alyce was punished for petit treason.

56. Glenn Blayney notes "immediate popular interest" in Ardern's story, as evidenced by a very brief report of the murder and the executions of the conspirators in the *Breviat Chronicle,* both 1551 and 1552 editions (" 'Arden of Feversham'—An Early Reference," *Notes and Queries,* n.s. II, No. 8 [1955], 336). Stow's account, which is slightly more detailed but in outline quite similar, is in *The Annales of England* (London, 1592, STC 23334), sig. Vvv7^v. The London merchant also focused on the executions; see *The Diary of Henry Machyn ... From A.D. 1550 to A.D. 1563,* ed. John Gough Nichols for the Camden Society, Vol. 42 (London: Camden Society, 1848; rpt. New York: AMS Press, 1968), p. 4. In Thomas Heywood's verse history of England, Ardern's murder in 1551 was the only event of note between 1549 and 1553; that is, between Ket's rebellion and English victory in Boulogne and Sebastian Cabot's trade wth Muscovy (*Troia Britanica, Or, Great Britaines Troy* [London, 1609, STC 13366], sigs. Pp3^r–Pp3^v[Qq3^r–Qq3^v]). Thomas Beard moralizes: "And thus all the murderers had their deserued dewes in this life, and what they endured in the life to come (except they obtaine mercy by true repentance) it is easie to iudge," *The Theatre of Gods judgements* (London, 1597, STC 1659), sigs. S2^v–S3^r). According to John Taylor, the "fearful ends" of the conspirators "will neuer be forgotten," *All the Workes of J. Taylor the Water Poet* (London, 1630, STC 23725), Bk. II, sig. Mm6^v. While Richard Baker records that Ardern "by procurement of his wife was murthered in his owne house," he also tells the story of the blighted grass and emphasizes that "this miraculous accident was not so much for the murther, as for the curses of a widow-woman, out of whose hands the said Master *Arden* had uncharitably

bought the said close, to her undoing. And thus the divine justice even in this world oftentimes works miracles upon offenders, for a mercifull warning to men, if they would be so wise to take it" (*A Chronicle of the Kings of England* [London, 1643, Wing *STC* B501], Bk. III, sigs. Lll3^r–Lll3^v). The ballad "The complaint and lamentation of Mistresse *Arden* of *Feversham* in *Kent*," registered and printed in 1633 (the same year as the third quarto of the play), has been reprinted in *The Roxburghe Ballads* (Vol. VIII, Part 1, pp. 46–53) and by, among others, Wine, pp. 164–170. The chapbook, as noted above, survives without title-page or date in a small volume of related material, including a much condensed version of the play, collected by William Cook and dated by him 1750; internal evidence suggests that he may have copied some pages after 1770.

  For a more thorough stage history of the play in all its versions, see Wine, pp. xlv–lvii. *Arden of Feversham* (London, 1592, *STC* 733) was first attributed to Shakespeare by Jacob in the preface to his 1770 edition of the play; he also noted then that the play was acted in Faversham "at a few Years interval," although from "excessive bad Manuscript Copies." John Payne Collier identified the play as a "domestic tragedy" when he first applied the term to Elizabethan drama in *The History of English Dramatic Poetry to the Time of Shakespeare,* 3 vols. (London: John Murray, 1831), III, 49.

57. I quote from Wine, p. xxxviii. Wine outlines what the playwright may owe to each of these sources, pp. xxxv–xliii, and suggests that he used the second (1587) edition of Holinshed, p. xl.

58. All quotations from the play, unless otherwise indicated, are from Wine's edition for the Revels Plays. I diverge only in using the first-quarto spelling "Feversham" when referring to the play; he has chosen instead to "[follow] the customary spelling of the town" (p. xxxiv). My intent again is to reinforce the distinction between recorded history and dramatic invention.

59. Wine, p. lxxix.

60. There is no other antecedent or prop indicated for the demonstrative pronoun "those" in line twelve than the proffered deeds; Arden calls them "foul objects" and speaks of them not as "these" at hand but as "those" still in Franklin's hands. Franklin can be seen as offering the papers twice, with "Here are the deeds" and again with "Read them." Wine's interpolated stage direction, which I have omitted, is "*He hands over the papers.*" Other editors who have included similar directions are Rev. Ronald Bayne, ed., *Arden of Feversham* (London: J. M. Dent, 1897), p. 1; John Gassner and William Green, eds., *Elizabethan Drama* (New York: Bantam, 1967), p. 5; A. F. Hopkinson, ed., *Arden of Feversham* in *Shakespeare's Doubtful Plays* (London: M. E. Sims, 1907), p. 1; A. K. McIlwraith, ed., *Five Elizabethan Tragedies* (1938; London: Oxford University Press, 1971), p. 245; Arthur H. Nethercot, Charles R. Baskervill, and Virgil B. Heltzel, eds., rev. ed. (orig. 1934), *Elizabethan Plays* (New York: Holt, Rinehart, and Winston, 1971), p. 391; E. H. C. Oliphant, ed., *Shakespeare and his Fellow Dramatists,* 2 vols. (New York: Prentice-Hall, 1929), I, 285; Felix E. Schelling, ed., *Typical Elizabethan Plays* (New York and London: Harper, [1926]), p. 39; and Ashley Thorndike, ed., *Pre-Shakespearean Tragedies,* vol. I of *The Minor Elizabethan Drama,* Everyman's Library (London: J. M. Dent, 1910), p. 57.

61. Harrison, p. 110.

62. Holinshed, as excerpted by Wine, pp. 148–149, and the Harley manuscript, f. 34^r.

63. Whitforde, sig. H1^v.

64. Countinghouse: "a private chamber, closet, or cabinet appropriated to business and correspondence; an office"—*OED*.

65. Chapman, pp. 16–17; Wine, p. 117. The old significance of the "chair" survives in the titles for honored university professors and for the presiding officers of committees.

66. Excerpted by Wine, p. 155.

67. J. P. Collier (in *The History of English Dramatic Poetry to the Time of Shakespeare*) was evidently the first to use the term in connection with Elizabethan drama and probably borrowed it from the French, where "domestic tragedy" was understood to be a bourgeois form. Collier's followers have,

almost without exception, referred to the protagonists of domestic tragedy as middle-class, common, bourgeois, and humble. In what has been accepted as the definitive work on the genre, *English Domestic Or, Homiletic Tragedy 1575 to 1642* (New York: Columbia University Press, 1943), Henry Hitch Adams asserts that "the lowly social station of the tragic protagonist is the one invariable characteristic of the genre" (p. 1).

Of many debts incurred in the writing of this article, two must not go unacknowledged. My gratitude to Alan C. Dessen and to J. Leeds Barroll is great.

"A bed / for woodstock":
A Warning for the Unwary

WILLIAM B. LONG

I HAVE TITLED this paper "A bed / for woodstock" because interpretation of this kind of playbook marginalia is indicative of some of the problems facing textual historians. Who made such notations, when, and why become important questions with far-reaching implications. These few words themselves are unimportant, but scholars' attitudes toward such inscriptions and the inferences that have been drawn from them need much reappraisal.

"A bed / for woodstock" is a marginal inscription in the play usually called *Thomas of Woodstock*. These words were inscribed by the person usually labeled "the prompter" and, when discussed at all, are pigeonholed under the vague rubrics "prompt-directions" or "stage-directions." And I agree to such labeling for some of the theatrical inscriptions; but various kinds of markings were inscribed in play-books, and each kind, in its way, can reveal something of the way theater companies operated. To assume that all markings made in the theater served no other purpose than as prompt-directions is to erase some sharp distinctions and to muddle the processes in which a playwright's manuscript was used in the theater.

The "history" of what happened to a manuscript from playwright to theatrical production has been stitched together chiefly by Sir Walter Greg from many isolated markings that survive in manuscript plays and in other places.[1] Greg's laudable efforts have provided a comprehensive picture out of a morass of details of the processes by which theatrical personnel readied a playwright's manuscript for production; but to do what he did, Greg had to wrench his examples out of the contexts of the plays in which they occur. He drew examples from numerous plays; but as one reads his descriptions of theatrical activity, the impression grows that all of these processes regularly occurred in all plays. This impression is not entirely accidental. Greg (and Sir Edmund Chambers) believed that such patterns of alteration existed, or at least could be shown to have existed if more material had survived. All the steps are thus alleged to be proved by quotations of instances from playbooks. The difficulty comes in presuming that isolated examples of certain changes and miscellaneous markings are an ordered, planned, and regularized pattern of markings—not just occasional notations caused by some exigency and made to aid performance of some passage fraught with difficulty of some sort that today cannot always be identified.

How one approaches those surviving marginalia makes an enormous difference in how one interprets them; for example, are these playhouse marginalia typical of the usual practice, or are they atypical? Greg and others assume that playhouse personnel customarily worked through a play making certain kinds of regulariza-tions, clarifications, and additions to a playwright's manuscript. Extant playbooks contradict such assumptions. The markings in the sixteen surviving manuscript playbooks[2] in no way demonstrate the detailed working-over that Greg hypothesizes. In fact, they demonstrate just the opposite. In these playbooks, there is not even anything approaching a demonstrable pattern of regular marking or adaptation for the stage. One must assume that this is the regular approach of theatrical personnel to a playwright's manuscript. To assume otherwise means relying upon no proof whatsoever—only upon an hypothesis that imaginatively strings together many in-stances of unrelated but interesting, and even colorful, marginal inscriptions.

The temptation to accept this presumably systematic but no less indefensible option is dangerous to the point of being overpowering. In the first place, such an explanation provides a cohesive, universal (and now, because of the magisterial work of Chambers and Greg, authoritatively sanctioned) pattern explaining what would be (or should have been) done to a playwright's manuscript. And secondly, such acceptance allows this facet of exploration of Elizabethan-Jacobean-Caroline theater to be guided by the romantic idealization of the past as a picturesque (although unfortunately somewhat primitive) pageant—just the sort of chasing will-o'-the-wisps that led to so much obfuscation in investigating the nature of the audience and the physical attributes of the playhouses themselves.[3] Scholars posited their presuppositions and then chose evidence to prove them.

Under these assumptions, all too often any markings in playbooks that can be identified as being written by theater personnel (rather than by playwrights, scribes, or censors) are assumed necessarily to be concerned with getting actors and/or properties on stage or with making off-stage noises at the proper times. And most playhouse marginalia do concern such matters. Some few do not. It is with one of these that this paper deals.

Before turning to the notation "A bed / for woodstock" and its relation to the text of the play, it is important to recall the general context of which it is a part and the way textual history usually is handled. Editors of English Renaissance drama find it vital to attempt to determine what kind of copy lay behind the printed texts. Detailed knowledge of what the surviving theater manuscripts reveal is of the greatest importance; yet their evidence is rarely brought to bear; it appears only distantly filtered. Chambers and Greg are invoked and very selectively quoted by many editors who seemingly read them only to search for quotations to bolster their assumptions or to save themselves the bother of research. Chambers and Greg rarely serve as starting points for thoughtful considerations of exceedingly complex prob-lems. Thus it has come to be widely accepted that there was a pattern—a regular series of alterations that a playhouse "prompter" made to a playwright's manuscript in readying it for playhouse use. Several of these alterations were changes made occasionally—even rarely—in the surviving manuscripts, including the emphasizing of authorial calls for music or off-stage noises by adding a notation in the left margin, the noting that certain characters or properties are to be "ready" to come on stage some lines before they are actually needed, and the adding of the names of minor actors to their speech-heads or stage-directions. The difficulty of relying on these alterations as usual playhouse practice is that there is no evidence that they were made with any frequency even approaching regularity; the surviving manuscripts show that such things seldom happened.

But there is another and far more misleading kind of assumption about what happened to plays in the theater. This comes not from any kind of occasional alteration that occurred in Elizabethan-Jacobean-Caroline playhouses but rather from the practices of prompters in eighteenth-, nineteenth-, and even twentieth-century theaters. The very terms "prompter" and "promptbook" tend to foist preconceived notions about the nature of the evidence upon unwary researchers; I prefer the Elizabethan terms "bookkeeper" and "playbook" because they are not encumbered with teleological views.[4] But Greg, in spite of the more than ample evidence that he knew so well, preferred to believe that the "ideal" late sixteenth- and early seventeenth-century "promptbook" should be neat and orderly, containing complete and regular speech-heads, entrances, and exits—with all manner of vaguenesses and ambiguities resolved. Such a state of affairs would indeed be most helpful for both theater and textual historians. Unfortunately, the surviving Elizabethan-Jacobean-Caroline playbooks exhibit no such features, even on an occasional basis; there is no support whatsoever for such expectations.

But the fact that one set of assumptions is highly misleading and that the other is totally without value has not deterred most textual researchers from arming themselves with these tools. Thus when looking at printed texts to attempt to determine what kind of copy lay behind them, even editors with no preconceived notions are woefully ill-equipped. Unfortunately, the pioneering efforts of Chambers and Greg have not been succeeded by a new generation of basic researchers. Instead of re-examining evidence and weighing conclusions again, most textual historians regularly choose either to accept the earlier decisions in their entirety or else to accept much of their general outline and to make changes without offering any evidence for doing so. In both cases, the evidence of the surviving playbooks is ignored.

Thus modern editors commonly refer to "prompters," to "promptbooks," and to theatrical practice as if the reconstructions of Chambers and Greg had been established as proved explanations of what necessarily and invariably happened to manuscripts in playhouses. The text sections of many Arden Shakespeare and Revels Plays editions demonstrate the difficulties that beset editors with such assumptions. Two recent examples will suffice. Brian Morris, commenting on stage-directions in *The Taming of the Shrew,* seems to know of no manuscript examples to guide his judgment as to whether a stage-direction is likely to have been made by a playwright or by theater personnel. Instead of looking at what actually happened in the surviving manuscript plays, Morris merely quotes Greg's statement of what happened occasionally as being what happened regularly.

> We may be reasonably certain that it [the manuscript behind F1 (the First Folio text)] was not prompt-copy. Greg summarizes the features of such a manuscript as follows:
>> Characteristic of prompt-copy are the appearance of actors' names duplicating those of (usually minor) characters, possibly the general appearance of directions a few lines too early, and warnings for actors or properties to be in readiness.[5]

Morris thus has locked himself into a very narrow set of expectations of what an Elizabethan-Jacobean-Caroline "promptbook" might look like. Since his knowledge is so limited, he necessarily has no opportunity to examine *Shrew* in the light of the surviving evidence. Therefore, Morris's discussion of the Folio *Shrew* becomes an exercise in Procrustean bed-making: "None of the stage-directions gives any warning for actors or properties to be in readiness. Indeed, the evidence of the stage-directions works decisively against any theory of prompt-copy. However careless an author may be in this matter, a prompter requires all entries and most exits to be correct and clearly indicated. They are not so in the F text."[6]

But the evidence from the surviving "promptbooks" is by no means so regular and clear-cut as Morris imagines; what editors with modern expectations see as difficulties or even as impossibilities apparently were not regarded as such in late sixteenth- and early seventeenth-century English playhouses. Morris goes on to claim that directions such as *"The Presenters aboue speakes"* [sic], *"They sit and marke,"* *"Pedant lookes out of the window,"* and *"Gremio is out before"* originate in the theater because "they look more like an intervention in the theatres" and "Shakespeare would be less likely than a book-keeper to describe Sly and his entourage as 'Presenters'."[7] Morris then lists another series of directions describing how a character was to look and/or how he was to act, commenting: "All this contrasts sharply with the kind of stage-directions one would expect to encounter in a text set up from prompt-copy."[8]

Morris does not make his readers privy to the sources of information that guide such judgments; but in the surviving manuscript playbooks, stage-directions similar to those in both his lists are always the playwrights', never added by playhouse personnel. Indeed it is these very directions which tell players how or where to do something that I have labeled "playwrights' advisory directions." There is no evidence in the surviving playbooks that theater personnel removed, simplified, or regularized such playwrights' directions in preparing a playwright's manuscript to be a "promptbook." Playwrights' manuscripts probably did not go through the "scribal copy" stage as often as many commentators, including Morris on *Shrew,* postulate. It seems to have been much more common for a play to go directly from the playwright to the players without scribal copying and certainly without much annotation or adding or changing of stage-directions by the personnel—as in *Woodstock.*

Even an editor as learned and as experienced as Harold Jenkins occasionally fails to let his evidence lay where it falls. In the surviving playbooks, bookkeepers have not changed playwrights' entrance directions that leave the numbers of extras indefinite. In comparing the Q2 (Second Quarto) and the F1 texts of *Hamlet,* Jenkins notes several instances of indefinite numbers in Q2 that he is quite willing to call author-ial; but when the numbers in these same instances are reduced but still left vague in F1, Jenkins attributes these alterations to a need for cast reduction. He is unwill-ing to note that these, as well, strongly suggest the hand of a playwright.[9] Notwith-standing the complete lack of precise designation of numbers in the surviving playbooks, Jenkins judges directions in F1 as lacking "the definiteness normally expected of a promptbook."[10] A number of the playwrights' advisory directions—which Greg had called author's directions[11]—Jenkins wishes to see as "the additions of a scribe or editor" because "they more suggest a text prepared for reading than performance."[12]

Hence the "warning" in the title of this essay assuredly needs to be heeded both by those who take for granted that Greg's pronouncements have settled matters and by those who, although more willing to question, are tempted to accept explanations that have no basis in surviving records of theatrical practice. "A bed / for wood-stock" is a test of Greg's categories and assumptions and, more importantly, of the uses that have been made of them.

The notation "A bed / for woodstock" also must be set in its context within the play itself. Greg recorded "A bed / for woodstock" in his list of all "directions," commenting only that it was "required for [the] next scene and discovered about 50 lines later."[13] Thus, by implication, he classified this notation as a "warning direc-tion," analogous to those that warn players to "Be ready" some few lines before their entry is indicated; these occur occasionally in several playbooks; in *Woodstock,* "Shrevs Ready" (f. 179[b], 2208) would seem to be such a direction and is the only such in this play. However, "Shrevs Ready" itself may not be a "warning direction"; only false expectations and readiness to apply labels have made it seem so. If one were to approach this inscription without preconceived notions of its nature and purpose, it very well might be viewed as resulting from the players' noting a need for "Shrevs," *i.e.,* for supplying the persons in these roles with whatever properties or elements of costuming that would indicate their office to the audience.[14] That such an inscription does not occur for the other roles demonstrates exactly the occasional marking and total lack of regularity found throughout the surviving playbooks. Greg viewed all notations made by theatrical personnel as necessarily bearing directly on getting players and/or properties onstage at a particular moment. In the way that he reconstructed the process of annotating a playbook, Greg thus produced a monolithic interpretation of how and why notations were made. The process easily becomes circular, beginning with certain expectations and assumptions, then finding justifica-tion (or "proof") of them in the text.

The First Part of the Reign of King Richard the Second or *Thomas of Woodstock* (British Library [B.L.] MS. Egerton 1994[8], ff. 161–185)[15] apparently was popular, for the manuscript is now thumbed and stained from playhouse use, not merely decayed from several centuries of poor storage. Long prose speeches written into the right margins have suffered considerably, particularly those on the bottom half of the pages where the book most likely would have been held (F, p. v). The play was revived on two occasions after the creation of the original playbook; with each revival, new marginalia were added, so that this manuscript provides insight into theatrical marking practices in three periods.[16] It is probable that composition and original production occurred in the season of 1594–95.[17] Playwright or playwrights, company, and theater of the original performance are unknown.

The writer of the original text may have been a scribe fair-copying (F, pp. vi–vii); but in *Sir Thomas More,* Anthony Munday fair-copied the work of the various original playwrights.[18] It is too often assumed that fair copies of plays were made by scribes as a matter of course. Certainly professional scribes did copy a number of plays, but reliable percentages are impossible to obtain. Scribes cost money; most theatrical companies during most times were in precarious circumstances.[19] Since a number of surviving playbooks are anonymous, it is difficult to determine how many of the sixteen are in the hands of playwrights, but at least five definitely are, and three more are probable; thus half seem to have gone directly from the playwrights to the theatrical companies—and two of these were written for the King's Men in times of prosperity.[20]

Probably all of the speakers' names were added to *Woodstock* after the text was written (a not unusual theatrical practice), most by the writer of the text (Hand S), but many by two others (Hands A and B). Wilhelmina Frijlinck distinguished eight hands in addition to S (F, pp. xiv–xx), and she observed that A (who supplied most of the speech-heads on ff. 176^b and 177^a as well as several other corrections and four directions) and B (who supplied speech heads on ff. 183^b, 184^a, 184^b, and one on 185^b) are "particularly associated with the original scribe" (F, p. xv). It would seem that these three, and possibly also Hand C whose only appearances are the labels for Acts Two through Five, might well have been the playwrights in a collaboration. Hand S thus would have been providing a fair copy;[21] the others would have been correcting his errors or omissions or adding what S could not read in their rough drafts. The availability of these others to supplement S's transcription seems to have been taken for granted by the "Scribe."

A collaboration would seem to be a far more likely explanation of the appearance and functions of S, A, and B (and possibly of C) than the presumption that so many scribes were working over a single playwright's "foul" papers. The probable dating of this play in such financially perilous times would cast doubt on a playwright's or a company's wishing to add the expense of a scribe. If Hand C was not a playwright, he might very well have been one of the acting company recording where they had decided to place the act breaks if, indeed, the players would have had any interest in act breaks. As will be seen with Hands E and F and with Hand G, more than one person concerned with playhouse preparations marked adaptations in the playbook. Freed from the romantic belief that only the "prompter" could alter the text, textual historians have no reason to presume that two or more players could not enter notations that they felt to be needed. The adult companies were cooperative ventures of shared responsibilities; might not their playbooks reflect this mode of organization at least in some measure?

Hand D, whom Frijlinck suggested as the original prompter (F, p. xvi), made various corrections and added a few notes; he probably was a member of the company—perhaps with ready accessability to at least one of the playwrights—who had principal responsibility for seeing the manuscript through its original rehearsals. To avoid presuppositions about the nature of playhouse markings, I substitute for the term "prompter" the less limiting term "bookkeeper"; thus I shall refer to Hand D as "Bookkeeper 1," Hands E and F as "Bookkeeper 2," Hand G as "Bookkeeper 3," and Hand H as "Bookkeeper 4."

The leaves have been folded for margins as is the custom with most other manuscript plays of the period; the basic text is written in a very legible English secretary hand with stage-directions and speech-heads in a finely formed Italian script. Apparently Hand S copied all the dialogue and then went through again to add the speech-heads (F, p. x). If one is copying by columns of a folded page (as is nearly always done in play manuscripts), this is both the most logical and most efficient way of working. Where Hand S could not read the speech-heads or where his copy lacked them, he left blanks to be filled in—presumably by the author of that section.

The addition of speech-heads was not the only instance of a renewed trip through the book in preparation of this final transcript. "There are a great many alterations by the scribe in the same ink as the text and clearly made in the course of writing. But having finished his task he evidently went through it again, for there are a number of corrections likewise in his hand but written in a different ink and with a different pen" (F, p. xi). There are dozens of such instances, a strong corrective to those who expect that playbooks must have started their lives as pristine copies of plays that subsequently were debauched by the "bungling" players. But even with this rash of minor changes, the company deemed the book playable.[22]

What the company evidently did not consider to be playable, however, were the playwright's scene divisions, which survive only at the beginning of the play and at its second scene (f. 162^b, 225); thereafter the "playwright"-scribe recorded none whatsoever although Hand C later marked the beginnings of Acts Two through Five. The scene divisions are the authorial organization appearing in playbooks as vestigial remains of the compositional process, a kind of planning that was no longer needed in the book as it was sold to the players. These divisions function here as an often unheeded reminder that study and stage are two separate if converging worlds, each with its demands and practices. That the players did not delete the scene indications shows again that the annotators of these stagebooks were not interested in producing "scientifically accurate" documents, and furthermore, and even more importantly, that the existence of such non-essential items in the playbooks demonstrates that they themselves were not such repositories of final authority as many would assume they were.

The "playwright"-scribe distributed his text and directions over the four columns provided by the foldings, placing all his directions within rules, often connecting top and bottom rules with braces and favoring the left margin. Except for exits, which are always in the right margin, only one call for music and one entrance

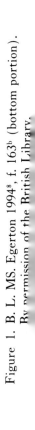

Figure 1. B. L. MS. Egerton 1994^a, f. 163^b (bottom portion).
By permission of the British Library.

Figure 2. B. L. MS. Egerton 1994[8], f. 167[b] (middle portion). By permission of the British Library.

Figure 3. B. L. MS. Egerton 1994[8], f. 169[b] (top portion).
By permission of the British Library.

Figure 4. B. L. MS. Egerton 1994[8], f. 180[b] (bottom portion). By permission of the British Library.

Figure 5. B. L. MS. Egerton 1994[8], f. 184[b] (bottom portion).
By permission of the British Library.

Figure 6. B. L. MS. Egerton 1994[8], f. 185[b] (middle portion). By permission of the British Library.

appear on the right (f. 169^b, 1012 [see Figure 3]; f. 171^b, 1241). All else is entered on the left or as part of this writer's favorite location—centered but beginning far into the left margin, at least as far left as the speech-heads. Only one centered entrance (out of thirty-four) does not begin in the left margin (f. 174^b, 1650). Thus all of S's directions are very easy to spot at a glance. *Woodstock* is a book that has been prepared by professional playwrights for professional players and with which the players apparently felt satisfied.

Even Ben Jonson's numerous complaints about and irritations with players over how they played his creations are not, in fact, typical attitudes of the professional playwright. Jonson no doubt felt that he knew better than the players how to stage his plays.[23] And perhaps he did. But his disparagement of the actors is a theme picked up and much echoed in the supercilious attitudes found in much nineteenth- and twentieth-century criticism—to the considerable detriment of attempts at discovering what went on in Elizabethan-Jacobean-Caroline theaters.

Professional players, needing or wanting to add but few markings to the text, no doubt knew how to play from such a book as *Woodstock*. The manner of inscription of directions and the general handwriting of the playwright-scribe in *Woodstock* thus produced a very readable and easy-to-follow book that has been completed in various details by Hands A, B, and C. In addition to the alterations by A already noted, he certainly has added three stage-directions and probably a fourth. In the left margin of f. 167^b, opposite lines 792–794 (see Figure 2), he has inscribed "Enter the queene / dutches of gloster / Ireland {fflorish}." Lines 795–796 are Hand S's "left-centered" direction: "*Enter Lancaster. (Arondell) Surrye. the queene, woodstock & his Dutches / yorke meetes them In hast.*" The additions of Hand A, except for the flourish, have been deleted in an ink different from the others. Still later, Hand E-Bookkeeper 2 of the first revival has added above Hand A's direction and opposite lines 789–791 "Peticions / [   ]: Mace / fflorish." He apparently was worrying about the properties needed in the scene and has repeated the flourish because the deletions have obscured Hand A's "fflorish."

The dangers of making sweeping generalizations about what playwrights would or would not do is strikingly demonstrated here. It would seem that Hand A as author of this section was checking Hand S's fair copy. The problem is not that Hand A did not know the play, but that as author he knew it too well. He knew what was coming, whereas a scribe would not. Hand A has become slightly confused by anticipating his next scene, and he has erroneously entered the directions for that scene, which had been recorded correctly by Hand S on f. 169^b (see Figure 3):

{ *Trumpetts sounds* }
{ *Exeunt omnes* }

Enter the Queene. the Dutches a Gloster the Dutches of
Ireland and other mayds wth shirts & bands & other lyneing

(*ll. 1012–1015*)

Hand A's lapse has been deleted, probably at rehearsals, by Hand D-Bookkeeper 1. Evidently the book went to the company with this gross playwright's error in it. The players have restored the proper order, avoiding the chaos on stage that would have resulted if they had played as the playwright had indicated. Among the many cautions in dealing with texts must be added that of playwrights' being subject to *lapsus calami* in fair-copying their own work.

Hand A is next seen at f. 170^a, 1072 where he has written "woodstocke" in the left margin. Woodstock does not appear in this scene; and the entire passage in which this word occurs has been marked for omission, apparently during revision after Hand S's fair-copying because the speakers' names have never been filled in. The reason for Hand A's inscribing the name is unknown. Quite discernible, however, are the reasons for his later additions.

In the left margin of f. 179^a, opposite line 2152 he has written "A Drome afare of." Three lines later, Woodstock, hearing this, responds: "ha souldiers. a fore my god, the commons are all vp then." This authorial heightening of dramatic effect resembles his additions on f. 185^b, which is now the final page of the play (see Figure 6). At line 2957, he has added "Drom Collours" in the left margin to embellish further the elaborate triumphal entry.[24] Also in the left margin opposite lines 2969–2970 appears the now partially mutilated "[W]ithin / [fflor]ishe" to announce the entrance at 2972 of "*Nimble wth Trissillian. Bound & Guarded.*" In all three instances, Hand A was concerned with adding to the dramatic impact of the text, possibly to those portions that he authored. In contrast, Hand B, who also has added speech-heads, added no similar sound directions. And such are all the notations of the "playwright"-scribes. The additions of theatrical personnel are another matter.

Hand D-Bookkeeper 1, shepherding the play through readings and rehearsals, has added to the book but seven times in 2989 lines—an average of only once every 427 lines. But averages, too, can be misleading; two sound calls occur within seven lines of each other. Contrary to imagined notions about what kind of changes should be those of a "prompter," two of his alterations were textual and one a speech-head, leaving but four acting changes. Two of the remaining simply amplify authorial "drums." However, the other two introduce much more problematic elements. The first of these textual instances concerns the filling in of a *lacuna* left by the playwright and the changing of a word. Both occasions should make investigators more wary about deciding who made textual alterations.

At f. 163^b, 331, Hand D-Bookkeeper 1 has added the half-line "to be a pleading lawyer" in the space left blank by Hand S (see Figure 1). Presumably Hand S left the space because this portion of the play was not his, and he could not read the rough draft. This half-line was overlooked in re-readings, and it needed to be supplied, presumably by the playwright, when the play went into production. However, in view of Hand D-Bookkeeper 1's next alteration, the change of "cuss" to "my leege"[25] as Woodstock is addressing King Richard (f. 168^a, 832), the gap may have been filled by the players themselves. The change of "cuss" to "leege" is one of discretion and seems to have been done in the course of rehearsal.[26] Five lines after this, "cuss" has been scratched out, but not the attendant adjective, thus leaving a rather strange line for Woodstock: "be yo^u then pleased good [cuss] to heare me speake." It is, apparently, more strange in the study than on the stage, for the playbook remained uncorrected in both the revivals.

In such cases, it always must be remembered that the change that mattered was recorded in the player's part, which he would memorize without reference to the book. The playbook was a matter of record and of convenient reference, not of remembrance. Players' additions and substitutions are likely not only because of the ease of change, but also because of the habit and sanction of embellishing and extemporizing. Guided by content and meter, a player easily could have completed the missing half-line satisfactorily. Tresilian had been recapitulating his career to Nimble:

> ... those dayes tho^u knewst I say
> from whence I did become a plodding clarke
> from wch I bounst as tho^u dost now in buckram̃
> to be a pleading lawyer (& ther I stayd,)
> till by the king I was cheife Iustice mayd.
>
> *(ll. 328–332)*

Such changes by the players themselves are not often considered an aspect of what players may have done with playwrights' manuscripts.

Hand D-Bookkeeper 1's other non-directional addition occurs in a passage of great action that apparently caused playing difficulties. Green is confronted by the avenging Cheney; during the fight, Arundel enters and joins Cheney in killing Green. There is fairly extensive damage to the left margin at this point, but Hand S's "Enter Arondell" is still quite clear. Yet directly under it Hand B has repeated the name, to be followed in two more lines by Hand D-Bookkeeper 1's "Ar:" (see Figure 5).

$A{>}\underline{larum}$ *Ch:*	this shall suffice	
	to free the kingdome from thy villanyes	$<$*Th y F gh*

Enter Arondell	tho^u huntst a noble game right warlick Cheney
Arrondell	cutt but this vlser off, tho^u healst the kingdome
	yeild thee falce Trayto^r, most detested man
Ar:	that setest king Richard gainst his reuerent vncleꝯ
	to shed the royall bloods & make the realme,
	weepe for ther tymless dessolatione

$$(f.\ 184^b,\ 2856\text{--}2863)$$

The speech-heads of Hand B and Hand D-Bookkeeper 1 seem redundant or even pointless; yet evidently some difficulty or confusion moved both the playwright and the player, on different occasions, to make the addition. Since the notations added are abbreviations of the speech-head, the problem is in *noticeability*. It would seem that several times the players encountered problems with this entry and felt the need to make it more legible to the "glancing bookkeeper"—my term for one who does not follow word-for-word, but who only glances at the book when he needs to do so.

Hand D-Bookkeeper 1's calls for "Dromes" on f. 183^b (2741 and 2749) are but amplifications of authorial intention. Hand S had brought on "Drome, and Cullors" in the general entrance at line 2716 and had added other drums off-stage at 2753–2754. This direction is now mutilated to ">s sounds / >in," but the next speech (without speech-head) is "how now what dromeſ are these," fully explaining what is absent. The first notation is in the left margin (Hand S's at 2753–2754), the second in the right (Hand D's at 2749), more than likely because the left at that point is filled with speech-heads. Again, the motivating factor is noticeability.

It is only with Hand D-Bookkeeper 1's remaining two notations that he added what usual expectation would have "prompters" doing. At the top of f. 179^b (2208), Hand D-Bookkeeper 1 has entered "Shrevs Ready" in the left margin, thirteen lines before authorial Hand S's "*Enter Trissilian wth the Shreeues of Kent & Northumberland: wth officers*" (2221). Why this extra notation was made is unknown. It is the sort of warning direction that the theorists would have prompters making continually in order to thrust the actors onto the stage at the proper point.[27] Yet this is the only time in the play that such a notation occurs, and the entrance is not nearly so complicated as many others, nor is there any particular delicacy of timing here. It is possible that for some reason the company had difficulty with this entry and felt the need for the addition. To look for consistency or to expect repetition in similar instances is to pave the way for the questionable assumptions of those who would seek to make a rule of such a rarity as this. But the answer well may lie in the possible explanation proposed above (p. 95) that this is not a "warning direction" at all and that researchers have few greater enemies than their own presuppositions.

Opposite King Richard's speech during which he has a change of heart and rescinds his order to have his uncle murdered, the left margin bears Hand D-Bookkeeper 1's now difficult-to-read inscription: "A bed / for woodstock" (f. 180^b, 2377–2378; see Figure 4). This is but six lines before Hand C's "Actus quint⁹," and at line 2385 authorial Hand S has "*Enter Lapoole wth a light after hime the (2) Murderers.*" There is a discussion among this group; at line 2414, the two murderers exit. Lapoole soliloquizes for eighteen lines (although six of these have been marked for omission); at line 2432, authorial Hand S has in the right margin "*—he drawes the curtaynes<*"; and Lapoole comments, "he sleepeſ vppon his bed. the tyme serueſ fittly / Ile call the murderers in. sound musicke ther / to rocke his sences in eternall slumbers." Evidently Woodstock is in a large curtained Tudor bed.

This bed is ominously present during Lapoole's conversation with the murderers and during his soliloquy. The curtains are then drawn as Lapoole exits, and the ghosts of the Black Prince and Edward III appear to the sleeping Woodstock. It is impossible to be certain if the act breaks were observed. If Hand C's divisions were made at the original performance and not at one of the revivals, bringing on the bed would present no timing problem. If the acting were continuous, the bed would need to be carried on or thrust out at the end of Richard's speech. The bed is the largest property used in the play, and it is understandable that there should be some concern with it; certainly it must be out when Lapoole enters, but both the appearance and the phrasing of this notation are curious.

It is the only mention of any property other than those included by Hand S in his authorial entries. Quite importantly for determining the physical staging used by this company, it is to be noted, and not to be forgotten, that no provision is made in the book for getting this bed onto the stage regardless of whether act breaks were observed. This *notation* (rather than "direction") merely records the presence of the bed. Or rather, I believe that it is the need to obtain such a property that caused Bookkeeper 1 to mark the book so. The bed is "for woodstock"; there is no provision for checking to see if the player is *in* it, although he must be there by the time the curtains are drawn. And the notation says, "A bed." If this bed is—as it certainly seems to be—large enough to have a superstructure with curtains, it is highly unlikely that an acting company in this financially troubled period would possess more than one. Could the players have afforded even one? Such a bed, of course, could have been borrowed, and more than likely was.

This scene is long (287 lines) and vital, involving at least eight players— probably half of the company; no one concerned with this part of the play could have been unaware of this action. Central to it all was the bed and its occupant. In other words, the bed was not something that anyone would need to be reminded about; without it the whole first half of the act would be impossible. Why then this notation? To invoke alleged "rehearsal difficulties" hardly seems sufficient. Other than the supposition that Hand D-Bookkeeper 1 was noting the need for a property that the company had to obtain for this particular play, there simply is no evident reason for the insertion of this notation.

This highly atypical inscription is the kind eagerly grasped and continually cited as a "prompt-direction"; but it patently has nothing to do with "prompting" or even with ensuring the smooth flow of the action of the play. Yet in context, the entry is unusual and reveals more about the workings of the company than generally has been assumed. "A bed / for woodstock" seems to have been written by a member of the acting company while reading through the play to see if it demanded any unusual properties that the company did not possess. Noting them in the margin is a convenience that would make such items easy to find when needed. Assuming that any and all marginalia bear directly upon the literal acting of the play—that every word so inscribed is for the guidance of stage action—is dangerous. Such a regularization and compartmentalization of processes patently is not supported by the surviving evidence. Hand D-Bookkeeper 1 has added, at the most (presuming "my leege" to have been his rather than Sir George Buc's) only seven notations to the very well marked directions of *Woodstock*. Such spare activity by a playhouse "prompter" should itself demonstrate that the players needed to do very little to playwrights' manuscripts.

The disappearance of the final sheet presumably accounts for the lack of license and date. There are several instances of cutting, but these apparently originate with the playwrights rather than with the Revels Office. There are no definite signs of censorial markings in the play as it existed for its original production. Lines 36–42 (f. 161[a]) are marked for omission and crossed off; in the left margin of line 39, the word "out" has been added by authorial Hand S. Similarly, lines 1879–1898 (f. 176^b) have been deleted; Hand S has inscribed "out" in the left margin of lines 1883 and 1895, and the deletion has been made in the same ink in which Hand A entered the speech-heads on this leaf. Since Hand A has not entered the required four speech-heads in this deleted passage, he obviously was copying by columns and thus the cut was made during this completion of the manuscript. Frijlinck suggested that the first cut was made to "forestall criticism" and that the second "probably from a point of view of dramatic criticism by the stage manager" (p. xxii).

However, the second cut contains Richard's comparison of the conquests made by his father the Black Prince in France with his own "farming out" of his English revenues. Richard is encouraged in his wrongdoings by his creature Green. This section is hardly undramatic. The first deleted passage is Lancaster's praise of the Black Prince's carnage in France. If these passages were deleted to "forestall criticism," the common subject is the Black Prince's ravages in France, presented here, of course, as the proper doings of English royalty in marked contrast to Richard's ill-chosen path. What has been removed are anti-French sentiments that have little to do with the invidious comparison of Richard with his father, and their loss does not jar the scenes.

The date of the composition of *Woodstock* is generally set *ca.* 1592–95. Elizabeth's relations with Henri IV were particularly delicate during this period, especially after his public espousal of Catholicism in July, 1593. The playwright's prudence in excising these lines, the reopening of the theaters in December, 1593, and the continuance of playing more or less regularly through 1595 combine with the treatment of theme, verse, and characterization to point to 1594–95 as the date of composition and first production of *Woodstock*.

In preparation for this first production, the "prompter" might be expected to elaborate and to expand upon production factors. The annotations for this production defeat this expectation. Hand D-Bookkeeper 1 is seemingly unconcerned with personnel. There is no identifying of the actors with the roles that they played and no linking of properties to those using them. There are fourteen calls for properties in the 2989 lines, all in the entrance directions; Hand D-Bookkeeper 1 elaborated upon none of them.

Bookkeeper 1 disregarded the exact number of extras. There are fifteen unspecified calls for extras; all remain untouched. Authorial Hand S was quite specific in calling for two murderers for Woodstock, and he always noted this number in their entrances and, atypically, in an exit.[28] On two other occasions, Hand S entered a specific indication of the number of extras.[29] Whether exact or vague, all such directions are left untouched by Bookkeeper 1. The largest number of Hand S's directions (nineteen) are calls for music; fourteen are part of entrances, five are separate additions. The entrances of royal entourages and the clamor of the final battle are the reasons for all these, but in no case has Bookkeeper 1 highlighted them. Similar treatment is accorded Hand S's advisory directions; none are touched. Since all are quite noticeable, nothing additional is necessary.

In the cases of playwrights' directions that pertain to the use of the physical stage rather than only to personnel, Bookkeeper 1 again does not specify. There are but four instances of the need for at least two entrances; the first designates "seuerall doores," the other three merely require two groups to meet. The only playing area needed other than the main stage is "within," and this only three times for horns or drums to sound off-stage (f. 166^a, 584–585; f. 183^a, 2673; f. 183^b, 2753–2754). The only thing that might be classified as a "moveable structure" is Woodstock's bed, which because of its curtained structure is in itself a smaller kind of very portable booth-stage.

Such marking in *Woodstock* is consonant with that found in earlier and later playbooks. The continuity of playing practices hardly can be stressed too strongly. As late as the middle of the final decade of the sixteenth century, new plays were being written to be performed on a playing area essentially unchanged from its medieval antecedents, and players were marking their books in the same very sparse manner so as not to limit their playing to a particular theater; and these practices continued until the closing of the theaters. Even reading through Greg's reprinting in *Dramatic Documents* of the stage-directions in the "promptbooks," one is struck by the reluctance of the theatrical companies to tie plays down to particular stages thereby insuring the general adaptability of the plays for production in different playing areas.

Woodstock apparently was revived *ca.* 1604, approximately ten years after its initial production; and it is significant to note that the players have found nothing either unusable or in need of change. The customs of staging and of marking playbooks have continued unaltered. New notations facilitate smooth presentation but offer no divergences.

For the revivals, Frijlinck isolated four new hands (E, F, G, and H) making alterations in the manuscript. However, the differentiation between Hands E and F rests solely upon their using different colored inks (F, pp. xv–xvi). Frijlinck has assigned eight notations to E, five to F, one possibly to F, and one indeterminable; all occur by line 1629 and are similar in kind: four are amplifications of calls for sound, six are calls for properties, two are the names of players taking minor roles, and three are corrections of words in the text.[30] The entries were made *currente calamo,* probably during rehearsals and are far from being perfectly formed specimens of calligraphy. They are just what hastily noted marginalia might be expected to be. However, the similarities between the letters in the different colored inks make it extremely doubtful that these entries were made by two persons.

The difference in ink color is easily explained in a number of ways: different batches of ink, contamination of the ink, or even use of the same ink on different days. Aside from such commonly similar letters as medial vowels and "l," "m," and "n," the initial "g's" of Hand E (f. 172^b, 1405) and Hand F (f. 162^a, 133) are exceedingly similar, as are their initial "b's," final "s's," and "-ish."[31] In short, the evidence for E and F's being one person is far stronger than for their being two; hence Hands E and F become Bookkeeper 2 in this study. In the last third of the play, however, there appear two more hands that are identifiable later in other playbooks; and it is their presence that dates the revivals of *Woodstock*.

The first is Hand G, who amplified two playwright's calls for flourishes and enunciated a call for "musique" implicit in the dialogue. The first instance occurs at line 820, the others late in the play.[32] It would seem that Bookkeeper 2 ceased marking the book approximately two-thirds of the way through production preparation and that Hand G, now "Bookkeeper 3," took over. His added "florish" here is an amplification of the playwright's "sound" to announce the arrival of the king and is the kind of addition that could be made at any point, here presumably at a later rehearsal. Why Bookkeeper 3 took over from Bookkeeper 2 is impossible to ascertain; since both were members of a company of players who customarily but by no means necessarily performed certain functions other than acting, there can be any number of explanations for this change. That Bookkeeper 3's first addition occurs in territory already covered by Bookkeeper 2 points to the marking of the book by whichever player was covering the function at the time that the addition was deemed necessary. The co-operative effort that I have already noted between playwrights and players in producing a play has a counterpart in the practice of a small group of players holding book on each other. That playwrights and players generally understood and respected each other's professional capabilities and that this basis of association proved eminently adaptable and workable over changes of company and the passage of more than a decade is further testimony to the durability and vitality of the organizational concept. Whatever else Bookkeeper 2 may have done is now lost, but Bookkeeper 3 did other "prompting" because he is identifiable by his annotations in the playbook of the anonymous *Charlemagne* played by the Children of the Queen's Revels *ca.* 1600–04.

The other playhouse person involved here is Hand H, who by virtue of his adding two notations, a name of an actor and an explicit call for music (which also is apparent from the dialogue), becomes "Bookkeeper 4." He also appears as the bookkeeper in Walter Mountfort's *The Launching of the Mary* licensed by Sir Henry Herbert 27 June 1633 and produced by an unidentifiable company in a private theater.[33]

The difficulty at this point in the examination of the *Woodstock* manuscript obviously lies with disentangling the chronology of the additions. Under no circumstances can all the changes to be found in such a manuscript be lumped together in a careless fashion.[34] The original date of the play, 1594–95, is secure enough; Bookkeeper 1 is sufficiently tied to this production. The order of the other additions, their date and provenance, and even the number of revivals itself are rather more tenuous. Frijlinck, following the notion that only one "prompter" would make notations in a manuscript being readied for production, believed that the markings were the result of three revivals: *ca.* 1600, 1623–27, and *ca.* 1635 (F, pp. xxviii–xxix). But it seems more probable that there were only two. I suggest that Bookkeepers 2 and 3 were connected with a first revival *ca.* 1602–04 and that Bookkeeper 4 figured in a second around 1633.

Hands E and F-Bookkeeper 2 made fifteen notations to the text. Three are textual, four are amplifications of flourishes, two are the players' names discussed below, one corrects an earlier, garbled stage-direction and at the same time adds markings for properties and a flourish, and six relate to properties.[35] Four of the last group require a closer look. In the midst of a speech by Tresilian recommending death for the "traitors," Bookkeeper 2 has written "Booke" in the left margin at line 664. At line 682, King Richard asks, "how now what Readst tho^u Busshey." Bushy answers, "the monument of English Chronicleς . . . ." If this entry were to be interpreted as evidence of a "prompter" making certain that a property were in the correct hands when needed—if this were, in other words, what usually has been expected—we should suppose that Bushy should enter during the interchange between the king and Tresilian. Pieces of evidence would fall into place neatly. But a mere glance at the page demolishes such a thesis. All the persons concerned enter together at line 627, the beginning of Act Two. There are neither entrances nor exits until the book is needed. No one else could have brought it in. Bushy must have had the volume with him all the time. Why then the "prompt" notation?

I suggest that this, like "A bed / for woodstock" by Bookkeeper 1, is merely a noting of properties needed for production and that it has nothing whatsoever to do with the actual playing that the "prompter" might be supposed to be concerned with. Exactly the same situation can be seen with Bookkeeper 2's entry of "Paper" (although in the right margin) on f. 168^a, 858. The third act begins with a left-margin inscription of "Blankes" (f. 170^b, 1136), added for the same reason, as is the left-margin "3:B" on f. 174^b, 1629.[36] One of the main impediments to understanding playbooks is the usually tacit assumption that all notations must necessarily be immediate aids to smooth playing. Such is not always the case.

The eighteen markings of Bookkeepers 2 and 3 are similar in kind and complement each other throughout the length of the play, each marking an instance that the players felt needed additional notation. With these added to the four staging directions of Bookkeeper 1, the text is quite full of notices for music and properties to highlight the action; there would have been little more to add unless different kinds of requirements had to be met. Apparently nothing novel presented itself, for Bookkeeper 4 added but two words, one of which is the name of a player in his company. Thus, in terms of what was added and for what reasons, this reordering of revival dates accounts for the extant notations. The highly unlikely alternative would have to place all those who made additions together for a single revival, but the associations of Bookkeepers 3 and 4 with other plays militate against that possibility.

Hand G-Bookkeeper 3 also worked on the anonymous *Charlemagne,* dated by Chambers *ca.* 1600.[37] Frijlinck, noting that George Chapman does not figure in Henslowe's *Diary* after 1599, conjectured that *Charlemagne* is the first of a number of plays that he wrote for the Children of the Chapel, known as the Children of the Queen's Revels after Elizabeth's death (F, p. xviii). They were playing at the second Blackfriars and enjoying a considerable, if short-lived, popularity.[38] Regardless of the possible Chapman connection with *Charlemagne,* this company might well have picked up old manuscript plays from adult companies to supplement the sparkling fare being written for them by Chapman, Marston, and Jonson. If Bookkeeper 3 worked on *Charlemagne* and *Woodstock* at approximately the same time, such a connection between *Woodstock* and the Children of the Chapel is measurably strengthened.

One further element may indicate activity on *Woodstock* at this time. If the hand that changed "cuss" to "leege" on f. 168[a] was not that of Bookkeeper 1 of the original production,[39] then it was that of Sir George Buc.[40] Once again, it is impossible to be precise in dating. Buc was a diplomat in Flanders in 1601 but may have been active in the Revels Office before 1603, and probably was so between 1603 and 1606.[41] (Of course Buc was engaged in licensing plays until shortly before his incapacitation late in 1621,[42] but this *terminus ad quem* is likely too early for the final revival.) It has been claimed[43] that the names entered by Bookkeeper 2, the damaged "G.ad" (f. 162[a], 133) and "George" (f. 172[b], 1405), stand for "Henry Gradwell" and "George Stutfield," whose names appear in the margins of three other manuscript playbooks, *Edmond Ironside, The Two Noble Ladies,* and *The Captives.* Since all four plays are now parts of B.L., MS. Egerton 1994, the identification is both tempting and convenient; but the evidence is far too tenuous to support such equations.[44]

The sixteen additional markings of Bookkeepers 2 and 3 represent considerably more attention to staging than do the seven of Bookkeeper 1, since one of the latter's is the "cuss" to "leege" change, another the addition of speech-head, and a third a change of dialogue. The original production of *Woodstock* was by adult players in an open theater, the first revival presumably by boys in a closed theater. While the popularity of these boys' companies as well as their generally sophisticated repertoire testifies to their considerable skill, three times as many playhouse notations to the same play suggest that the boys needed more help in co-ordinating their backstage activities than did the adult players.

Presuming that Bookkeeper 4 added his two words to *Woodstock* at approximately the same time that he was working on *The Launching of the Mary* (June, 1633), one may date the second revival a generation after the composition of the play. It is a commonplace that audiences' tastes changed rapidly throughout the Elizabethan-Jacobean-Caroline period. That a play so out-of-date could have been deemed worthy of revival would suggest a group playing either to less sophisticated provincial audiences or to those who would patronize the supposedly (by this time) very unfashionable London public theaters.

The precarious fortunes of the lesser companies occasioned rapid changes in their personnel; even the most prominent of these can be seen but fleetingly, usually when mentioned in licenses. With such meager evidence as exists, it is impossible to determine exactly when Bookkeeper 4 used the *Woodstock* book. As in the cases of Bookkeeper 2's "G.ad" and "George," Boas eagerly identified Bookkeeper 4's "Toby" (f. 178[b], 2088) with one Edward Tobye,[45] but such graspings at straws will not suffice to produce the bricks for a firm foundation for dating.

Another matter of concern for this study is the simple observation—and yet no one to date seems to have thought it worthy of mention—that no succeeding "prompter" seems to have found any difficulty in guiding a play with additions made by others in earlier productions. Even the proper names of the players have not been struck out. In preparing an old play, the new companies added a few notations; but they did not delete. What many who are deluded by the fallacy of modernity would no doubt consider as proof of their assumptions about primitive and bungling actors, I should like to suggest is the result of a custom of ease of transmission. Bookkeepers and players deliberately (if unconsciously) left the margins alone because there was no habit of tidying them up. There was no need for such extra work since the book itself was not nearly so important a directional document as it was to become in later centuries.

Often unique texts endorsed with Revels Office licenses, the books were highly valuable to the players in ways no longer important; but much of that value has now been transferred to the director's copy, and by extension, to that of the present-day prompter. Once again, modern habits and customs have determined what ought to appear in a roughly similar document produced by an earlier age. Thus the theater historian is faced either with accepting the "primitive-bungler" explanation or with believing that an early playbook, as it exists, was not merely workable, but desirable. The testimony of three companies of players surely must determine the answer. *Woodstock* is important in documenting the continuity of these dual customs of ease of adaptability and the lack of heavy reliance upon the book in three quite different decades.

"A bed / for woodstock" is but an easily remembered example of theatrical marginalia whose careful contextual examination can aid in elucidating playhouse workings. A tour through the playhouse marginalia of one play can reveal a number of problems and place many caution lights at the pitfalls awaiting anyone seeking glib generalizations about what players did and did not do to manuscripts. "A bed / for woodstock" is an individual example of one kind of marking needing cautious interpretation and can serve as a general warning for many others.

NOTES

1. For the "history" of playhouse manuscripts, see E. K. Chambers, *William Shakespeare: A Study of Facts and Problems,* 2 vols. (Oxford: Clarendon Press, 1930), I, Chapter IV, "The Book of the Play," 92–125; W. W. Greg, *The Editorial Problem in Shakespeare: A Survey of the Foundations of the Text,* 3rd ed. (Oxford: Clarendon Press, 1954), Chapter II, "Theatrical Manuscripts," pp. 22–48; and *The Shakespeare First Folio: Its Bibliographical and Textual History* (Oxford: Clarendon Press, 1955), Chapter IV, "Editorial Problems—2," pp. 105–174. Of course, Greg's most extensive work on manuscripts is his masterful survey, *Dramatic Documents from the Elizabethan Playhouses: Stage Plots: Actors' Parts: Prompt Books,* 2 vols. (Oxford: Clarendon Press, 1931).

2. The sixteen surviving manuscript playbooks are:
Anthony Munday, *John a Kent and John a Cumber,* 1590
Anthony Munday, *et al., Sir Thomas More,* 1592–1593

Anon., *Thomas of Woodstock, ca.* 1594–1595, and revivals *ca.* 1602–1604 and *ca.* 1633
Anon., *Edmond Ironside,* 1590–1600
Anon., *Charlemagne, ca.* 1603–1605
Anon., *The Second Maiden's Tragedy,* 1611
John Fletcher and Philip Massinger, *Sir John van Olden Barnavelt,* 1619
Anon., *The Two Noble Ladies,* 1619–1623
Thomas Dekker, *The Welsh Embassador, ca.* 1623
Thomas Heywood, *The Captives,* 1624
Philip Massinger, *The Parliament of Love,* 1624
John Fletcher, *The Honest Man's Fortune,* 1625
John Clavell, *The Soddered Citizen, ca.* 1630
Philip Massinger, *Believe As You List,* 1631
Walter Mountfort, *The Launching of the Mary,* 1633
Henry Glapthorne, *The Lady Mother,* 1635

3. The views of the audience established principally by Alfred Harbage in *Shakespeare's Audience* (New York: Columbia University Press, 1941) and *Shakespeare and the Rival Traditions* (New York: Macmillan, 1952) now have been radically challenged by Ann Jennalie Cook in *The Privileged Playgoers of Shakespeare's London, 1576–1642* (Princeton, N. J.: Princeton University Press, 1981). The views of Elizabethan theater so widely propounded by, among others, W. J. Lawrence in *The Elizabethan Playhouse and Other Studies* (Stratford-upon-Avon: Shakespeare Head Press, 1913) and *Those Nut-Cracking Elizabethans* (London: Argonaut Press, 1935) and John Cranford Adams in *The Globe Playhouse: Its Design and Equipment* (Cambridge, Mass.: Harvard University Press, 1942) have now been totally supplanted by C. Walter Hodges in *The Globe Restored: A Study of the Elizabethan Theatre,* 2nd ed. (London: Oxford University Press, 1968) and *Shakespeare's Second Globe: The Missing Monument* (London: Oxford University Press, 1973), the monumental series of Glynne Wickham's *Early English Stages 1300–1660,* particularly Volume Two, 1576–1660, Part II (London: Routledge and Kegan Paul; New York: Columbia University Press, 1972), the numerous important articles published over the last several decades by Richard Hosley, and John Orrell in *The Quest for Shakespeare's Globe* (Cambridge: Cambridge University Press, 1983).

4. One must be especially careful in inferring what "prompters" did and did not do, as Bentley warns: "Much of the job description for this position must be inferential." Gerald Eades Bentley, *The Profession of Player in Shakespeare's Time, 1590–1642* (Princeton, N. J.: Princeton University Press, 1984), p. 80.

5. *The Taming of the Shrew,* The Arden Shakespeare (London and New York: Methuen, 1981), p. 2, quoting Greg, *The Shakespeare First Folio,* p. 142.

6. *Ibid.,* p. 4.

7. *Ibid.,* p. 6.

8. *Ibid.,* p. 8.

9. *Hamlet,* The Arden Shakespeare (London and New York: Methuen, 1982), pp. 56–59.

10. *Ibid.,* p. 59.

11. Greg wished to believe that F1 was set from the "prompt-book," but he was bothered by numerous changes that, if he agreed with them, he called "competent and even adroit," and if he disagreed, he blamed on the "book-keeper," whom he dismissed as a "meddlesome bungler." *The Shakespeare First Folio,* pp. 316, 323, and 324.

12. Jenkins, *op.cit.,* p. 57.

13. *Dramatic Documents,* I, 255.

14. This extension of my "warning" I owe to personal conversation with Professor Alan Dessen of the University of North Carolina, Chapel Hill.

15. Anon., *The First Part of the Reign of King Richard the Second or Thomas of Woodstock*, edited by Wilhelmina P. Frijlinck and checked by W. W. Greg, The Malone Society Reprints (Oxford: The Malone Society, 1929). All further references are to this edition. The play is now without cover, title, and (presumably) the final leaf. For convenience, the play will be referred to as *Woodstock* in this study. Page references to Frijlinck's editorial commentary are entered in parentheses in the text, prefaced by "F."

16. Frijlinck believed that there were three revivals (pp. xxvii–xxix), but see below pp. 110–113.

17. Greg, *Dramatic Documents*, I, 251. Chambers (*The Elizabethan Stage*, 4 vols. [Oxford: Clarendon Press, 1923], IV, 42–43) agrees with this date, assigning the handwriting to the late sixteenth or early seventeenth century. A more detailed discussion is provided by F, pp. xxiii–xxx. The arguments for this date are chiefly structural and generic; there are many similarities between *Woodstock* and other histories of the early 1590s. For the 1594–95 date, see below, page 109.

18. For Munday's making a fair copy of *More*, see W. W. Greg, ed., *The Book of Sir Thomas More*, The Malone Society Reprints (Oxford: The Malone Society, 1911), pp. vii and xvi; and Harold Jenkins, "Supplement to the Introduction of Sir Walter Greg's edition of *Sir Thomas More*," in *Collections*, Volume VI, The Malone Society Reprints (Oxford: The Malone Society, 1961 [1962], pp. 180–181, 184–185.

19. Bentley, *The Profession of Player, passim,* esp. pp. 53, 63, and 243.

20. The holograph playbooks are *John a Kent* (1590), *Sir Thomas More* (1592–93), Thomas Heywood's *The Captives* (1624), Philip Massinger's *Believe as You List* (1631) King's Men, and Walter Mountfort's *The Launching of the Mary* (1633) King's Men. Those probably holograph, in addition to *Woodstock,* are the anonymous *Charlemagne* (*ca.* 1603–05) and *Two Noble Ladies* (1619–23).

21. Further substantiation of this view is provided by Frijlinck herself who called the alleged scribe's hand "clearly a literary rather than a professional type" (F, p. viii).

22. So many assumptions are founded on interpretations of evidence viewed from only one perspective. Even if one is not considering quality of production, Shakespeare's pen was a very fertile one; that it also was neat seems always to be romantically distorted. Shakespeare the poet always seems to attract more attention than Shakespeare the man of the theater. "His mind and hand went together: And what he thought, he vttered with that easinesse that wee haue scarse receiued from him a blot in his papers," wrote John Heminge and Henry Condell in "To the great Variety of Readers." (*The First Folio of Shakespeare,* Norton Facsimile [New York: Norton, 1968], sig. A3). This claim by Shakespeare's fellows nearly always sends critics into raptures about natural genius, which was probably of far less importance to the theater people than clean copy. Many "blots" no doubt were acceptable; but the book was much preferable without them, as Shakespeare the player must have known very well.

23. Jonson's fulminations against actors are yet another topic usually not approached in its theatrical contexts. The original production of *Woodstock* is rather too early for Jonson, but the two revivals (*ca.* 1602–04 and *ca.* 1633) correspond to periods of Jonson's dramatic involvement. Perhaps the most famous of his attacks on the way players were doing things are the remarks on the title-page of the 1631 octavo of *The New Inne*: "The | New Inne. | . . . As it was neuer acted, but most | negligently play'd, by some, | the Kings Seruants. | . . ." (as reproduced in *Ben Jonson,* ed. C. H. Herford, Percy and Evelyn Simpson, 11 vols. [Oxford: Clarendon Press, 1925–52], VI, 395).

   Some playwrights may well have followed their creations into production; the Second Child in the "Induction" to *Cynthia's Revels* makes a special point of noting that Jonson is *not* backstage: ". . . wee are not so officiously befriended by him, as to haue his presence in the tiring-house, to prompt vs aloud, stampe at the booke-holder, sweare for our properties, curse the poore tire-man, raile the musicke out of tune, and sweat for euerie veniall trespasse we commit, as some Authour would, if he had such fine engles as we" (Herford and Simpson, IV, 40).

The date is 1600, the company the Children of the Queen's Chapel, and the "author" referred to is singular; hence this may well be a particular thrust, and it is rather dangerous to presume that even though a playwright might act thus with a children's company, an adult company would tolerate even less exaggerated "supervisings." Of such assumptions are errors born.

The reference here to the bookholder has been cited as evidence of the existence at this time of a single functionary doing this job. In actuality, it proves no such thing. We are merely informed that someone held book, hardly a startling piece of information. There is no reason whatsoever to suppose that the holding was not done by more than one person during the course of a performance. Furthermore, practice may well have differed between adult and child companies.

In addition, the various handicaps (or advantages) of youth that kept the boys from being financially and legally responsible also prevented them from performing certain functions in the theater. But surely they were more than capable of holding book on each other. And no matter how many persons might have "prompted" during the course of a play, only one would have done it at any one time. It would have been confusing, pedantic, and totally unnecessary for the boys (and Jonson) to refer to "the bookholders."

24. There is some doubt in establishing this as Hand A. The ink is different, but the "Drom" is formed very much in the same way as his "Drom" at f. 179^a, 2152, and *what* he is doing is the same in all three instances.

25. The cramping of this written-over and interlined addition causes some uncertainty in authorship, but it is in "Ink I" used only by Hand D in but three textual instances: this, the half-line at 331, and the speech head at 2862. His action notations, presumably done at another time, are all in "Ink VII."

26. Greg believed that the similarity in the style of marking identifies the agent to be Sir George Buc (*Dramatic Documents,* I, 252–253). If so, the change would have been made for the first revival. Frijlinck discussed the possibilities in more detail (F, pp. xx–xxi).

27. Greg provided a discussion of "warning directions" (*Dramatic Documents,* I, 216–221).

28. F. 180^b, 2385; f. 181^a, 2414; f. 182^b, 2597–2598.

29. F. 174^b, 1644–1645; f. 178^b, 2119–2120.

30. F. 161^b, 108; f. 162^a, 133; f. 166^a, 628; f. 166^b, 664; f. 167^b, 789, 790, 791; f. 168^a, 823, 858; f. 169^b, 1009; f. 170^b, 1136, 1160; f. 171^a, 1222; f. 172^b, 1405; f. 174^b, 1629.

31. Initial "b's": f. 166^b, 664; f. 170^b, 1136; f. 174^b, 1629. Final "s's": f. 167^b, 789; f. 168^a, 858. Final "-ish": f. 166^a, 628; f. 167^b, 791; f. 169^b, 1009.

32. F. 168^a, 820; f. 178^b, 2093–2094; f. 181^a, 2436.

33. Gerald Eades Bentley, *The Jacobean and Caroline Stage,* 7 vols. (Oxford: Clarendon Press, 1941–1968), IV, 924.

34. As Irving Ribner did in attempting to state the importance of this manuscript: "There are many prompt directions added in different hands, with valuable directions about such things as music and stage noises." *The English History Play in the Age of Shakespeare* (Princeton, N. J.: Princeton University Press, 1957 [rev. 1965]), p. 137. The most complete study of this play, A. P. Rossiter's *Woodstock: A Moral History* (London: Chatto & Windus, 1946), pays very little attention to its life in the theater. Rossiter works out a conjectured sequence for the various hands, but he supposes that all the work was done for *one* production (pp. 172–174).

35. Markings made by Bookkeeper 2: textual, f. 161^b, 108; f. 170^b, 1160; f. 171^a, 1222. Amplifications of flourishes: f. 166^a, 628; f. 167^b, 791; f. 168^a, 823; f. 169^b, 1009. Players' names: f. 162^a, 133; f. 172^b, 1405. Correction of authorial confusion (in addition to markings for properties and flourish): f. 167^b, 789–791. Mentionings of properties: f. 166^b, 664; f. 167^b, 789, 790; f. 168^a, 858; f. 170^b, 1136; f. 174^b, 1629.

36. Frijlinck conjectured that "3:B" may stand either "for *three blankes* or possibly *three billmen* (officers)" (F, p. 57n.). In view of Bookkeeper 2's other notations, the former seems quite probable.

37. *Elizabethan Stage,* IV, 5.

38. *Ibid.,* II, 48–53.

39. See above, pages 105–106 and Notes 25 and 26.

40. Both Frijlinck (F, p. xxi) and Greg (*Dramatic Documents,* I, 252–253) believed this to be Buc's work.

41. Bentley, *op.cit.,* III, 93. A more detailed account is provided by Mark Eccles's "Sir George Buc, Master of the Revels," in *Thomas Lodge and Other Elizabethans,* ed. Charles J. Sisson (Cambridge, Mass.: Harvard University Press, 1933), pp. 434–435.

42. Eccles, *op.cit.,* pp. 481–482.

43. Frederick S. Boas, "A Seventeenth Century Theatrical Repertoire," in *Shakespeare and the Universities and Other Studies in Elizabethan Drama* (New York: D. Appleton and Company, 1923), p. 104. Boas believed that all of the plays now comprising B.L., MS. Egerton 1994 were once owned by William Cartwright the Younger and thus that such identifications are obvious. Boas was far too easily satisfied. He had no evidence as to when these plays came together, and several of the items in the collection have no connection with popular theater. "G.ad" could stand for a number of things other than "Gradwell," and "George" is far too common both as a Christian and as a surname to be in the least conclusive. Bentley notes the possibility that even if this abbreviation does stand for "Gradwell," it well might refer to the almost unknown Richard rather than to Henry (*op.cit.,* II, 450–451).

44. The identifications were denied also by Frijlinck (F, pp. xxviii–xxix); Chambers, *Elizabethan Stage,* IV, 43; Greg, *Dramatic Documents,* I, 253; and Bentley, *op.cit.,* II, 450 and 581.

45. Boas, *loc.cit.* His evidence is no more convincing than for the others; "Toby," like "George," can be a Christian as well as a surname. Both Greg (*Dramatic Documents,* I, 253) and Bentley (*op. cit.,* II, 601) refuse to grant the identification.

Descent Machinery in
the Playhouses

JOHN H. ASTINGTON

> . . . it is rather lyk
> An apparence ymaad by som magyk,
> As jogelours pleyen at thise feestes grete.

> By the benefit likewise of Geometrie, we haue our goodly Shippes, Galleies,
> Bridges, Milles, Charriots and Coaches . . . Pulleies and Cranes of all sorts.[1]

THE earliest irrefutable reference to the presence of flying machinery in the Elizabethan playhouses is Henslowe's famous entry: "Jtm pd for carpenters worke &
mackinge the throne Jn the heuenes the 4 of June 1595 . . . vij^{li} ij^{s}."[2] It has recently
been argued by Glynne Wickham that there is very little evidence to indicate that
the early playhouses had either the throne and its attendant machinery or a cover,
a "heavens," over the stage.[3] In the light of his hypothesis, what we see in the Swan
drawing and also what we see of the Theatre in "The View of the City of London
from the North towards the South" (dated before 1598) are later developments of
playhouse design, which specifically came about as a result of capital investment.
Before the 1590s, Wickham questions "whether any of the builders and financial
underwriters of the three earliest public playhouses would have admitted the construction of so costly an item as heavens as an obligatory feature of these structures
unless they were convinced that this was so common a requirement among all acting
companies of the 1570s and 80s as to justify the expense involved."[4] I think that he
is wrong, and I want in this paper to explain why. As far as theater owners and actors
were able, they would want to share the spectacular traditions of English civic,
academic, and royal entertainments in such things as costumes, scenic emblems, and
"devices." The machinery for flying effects would have been well within reach of
their budgets, as I shall show.

The general weakness of Wickham's argument and of others like it is that it
depends upon the evidence of extant play-texts, and we simply have too few plays
from the earlier period to be able to draw reliable conclusions.[5] Even from the 1590s
onwards, when there certainly were more plays, since there were more theaters and
actors, and when the chances of a play's being published were greater, since publishers had acquired the habit of printing play-texts, we know from Henslowe's lists and
from the Revels records that only a small percentage of the repertory of the companies has come down to us. Again we can use the extant texts to draw certain

conclusions—that the Globe had no descent machinery, for example, or that, as I have myself argued elsewhere, there was a sudden vogue for flying effects that began between 1605 and 1610 and appears to have originated with the Queen's Revels company—but such conclusions are always limited by the incomplete basis upon which they rest.[6] Wickham's assertion that by the 1590s "Stage plays were becoming more spectacular," I find to be extremely dubious both on statistical grounds and because of a number of clear indications of traditions of elaborate spectacle that go back at least as far as the middle of the sixteenth century.[7] Moreover, if the actors had to convince the financial management of the need for the outlay on heavens and throne on the basis of frequency of use, they would have had an extremely weak case at any point up to 1642. Any accountant in his senses would have turned them down, since, as T. J. King has put it, "it can be stated with some certainty that such machinery was not *required* in the vast majority of plays."[8]

We are also dealing, as so often we are, with a chicken-and-egg argument. If the theaters did commit themselves to new spectacular equipment in the nineties, led or followed by Henslowe, where did the initial bright idea arise? When Greene wrote his stage direction at the close of *Alphonsus King of Aragon,* in 1587 or thereabouts, "*Exit* Venus. *Or if you can conueniently, let a chaire come downe from the top of the stage, and draw her vp,*"[9] did the notion suddenly cross his mind, was he thinking of the classical theater, or had he seen the players do something similar in the past? Is the tentative phrasing because he was not sure where the play might be staged, or because he was giving the actors a choice over an effect that he knew they might produce quite easily if they wished to? There seems to me not much doubt that the staging of flying effects in plays, masques, and shows was as well known and understood in 1576 as it was twenty years later, and probably it was as frequently used in relative terms.

Whether Burbage made any provision for the effect when he built his playhouse, we may take it that he knew that it was possible, and not particularly difficult, to fly an actor between the stage and the space above it. On a temporary stage at Greenwich in 1566 the Gentlemen of the Inner Temple made Cupid so descend and ascend from and to heaven in a performance of the play *Gismond of Salerne* before Elizabeth and the court, and although specific references to descent scenes of this sort are few in the years between 1558 and the late 'eighties, there is plenty of evidence of the use of fairly sophisticated staging equipment that could quite easily have produced the effect, were it needed. The Revels Office accounts show constant expenditure on pulleys, ropes, cords, and wire for various kinds of effects, and there is the occasional indication of special machinery to move them. In Mary's reign Robert Trunckwell, master joiner and carver, was paid for "a patron [pattern] of a devyce of a maske and certayne gynnes of woode for the same."[10] In 1564 there is an intriguing reference to "charretts ffor the goodesses & diuers devisses as the heuens & clowds" used in a masque;[11] ten years later there appear payments connected with special performances by Italian players at Windsor and Reading for "Iron woorke for A frame for A seate in A pageant" and "for the woorkmanship of the Seate or Chayer &c."[12] The cost of these, together with "a plank of ffyr & other peeces of sawen wood," was the remarkably high sum of two pounds, ten shillings. I think that the chair, reinforced with iron supports, was probably made to move up and down within a frame. In 1576 payment was made for two "wynches."[13] Perhaps we see payments for machinery so infrequently because what was used was simply part of the common trade-tools of the carpenters, which they were expected to provide for their ordinary wages; I shall have more to say about this matter below.

In any event, the traditions of court staging show that the technology of descent machinery would be well known to the acting troupes, and the effects of flying and moving actors and scenic devices may have been something that they wished to emulate when the gorgeous playing-places began to be built. The effectiveness of the spectacle of the *deus ex machina* is attested to by its use in at least two shows at the universities: John Dee's staging of Aristophanes' *Peace* at Cambridge in 1547 and the performance in Christ Church Hall, Oxford in 1583 of William Gager's play *Dido* for the visiting Pole, Albertus Alasco. The latter play included the effect of "Mercurie and Iris descending and ascending from and to an high place" and of an artificial storm, presumably also managed from the same "high place."[14] In the surviving account for building this part of the temporary theater, the writer uses the term that Henslowe uses fifteen years later: "To Richd. West for felling of 4 timber trees at Chandence for the heaven and othr new building on the stage, 3 othr lesse trees, squaring, dressing and cariage of 2 lods. 6s. 8d."[15] It is interesting that at about the same time John Higins, in producing an English language version of Adrien Junius' *Nomenclator,* renders the Latin phrase "Machina, Supra scenam locus, unde ex improviso deus aliquis apparebat" as "The skies or coūterfet heauen ouer the stage, from whence some god appeared or spake."[16] Although Higins uses the past tense to translate the Latin literally, it is clear from the other theatrical words and phrases which he renders into English that he is thinking of the London playhouses of his own time.[17] By the 1580s *heaven* or *heavens* had already acquired a theatrical sense.

Although the terms that Higins uses seem to me quite specifically to be referring to the public theaters rather than to the court or academic stages, there might be other reasons for entertaining Wickham's hypothesis that the early playhouses were not equipped with heavens and machinery. The center of his argument rests on the cost, although phrasing the question in the way that he does is rather misleading. To build the pillars, the heavens, and the stage roof, the elements that dominate our impression of the playhouse in the Swan drawing, was undoubtedly an expensive and, arguably, an unwise undertaking if they were used only for occasional brief spectacular scenes of descent, as in *Alphonsus* or *Cymbeline*. It remains something of a puzzle that so large and prominent features as the huts and the stage cover were apparently given over to the staging of effects that were very rarely used. On the grounds of cost-effectiveness the superstructure above the stage would never have justified its existence as a working part of the playhouse. Could it not be, and is it not more likely that its first purpose was seen to be a protection for the stage, to save at least some of the planking from rot—in the rebuilt Globe the stage was evidently protected completely—and to shield the tiring-house facade, with its painted decoration, from the weather? The heavens, in other words, were simply an accidental by-product of a stage roof, for which sensible, hard-headed economic arguments could be made, and the area under the roof may indeed have remained unused in certain playhouses. Henslowe therefore had a heavens at the Rose before he chose to hang a throne in it, as the phrasing of the entry suggests.

Were this not so, how expensive would it have been to build a stage heavens, as at Christ Church, solely to stage flying effects? Neither the court nor the university colleges were particularly restrained by considerations of cost in producing their occasional performances, but the evidence of the accounts is that the outlay on this part of the show was not enormous. Christ Church bought all their lumber, squared and dressed, for six and eightpence, although they may have paid only for the work and the transport; Henslowe could buy "a maste" for twelve shillings, or "iiij long peeces of tymber" for six shillings.[18] The Revels Office paid about eightpence each for pulleys and about two shillings each for "greate Ropes"; "Vyces xij and wynches ij" were bought for five shillings.[19] Expenses of this kind, even adding on the wages for carpenters for two or three days to put the frame and platform together, would hardly seem to have been out of the reach of the playhouse builders. The question arises at this point of why Henslowe paid so much for his throne in 1595; I would like to defer it for more extended discussion below. There are other more general considerations. If the actors managed to convince the playhouse owner or builder of the need for some provision for flying effects, would the cheapest or most obvious solution have been to have built an elaborate superstructure over the stage, as was done in the temporary theater built within Christ Church Hall? Surely the firmest footing for the windlass machinery would be within the frame of galleries, presumably on the highest storey above the tiring house, and it would require only a fairly small cantilevered projection, "a juttey forwardes" of some six to eight feet, to act as a small heavens to conceal the throne, to be constructed at this point above the stage. The architectural effect would be similar to the roofed projection for the crane on mills and barns; I see no reason why carpenters, having been asked to provide some expedient for the flying machinery, would produce the massive stage roof that we see in the Swan drawing. Certainly the stage cover would have been expensive to build, but the evidence seems to me to suggest that it was not provided solely or primarily to house the throne. It would also have been possible, at a pinch, to stage descent scenes without any permanent projection over the stage from the plane of the tiring-house wall. The technology of cranes was well enough understood in Elizabethan London for the throne to be worked from a crane arm, which, once the actor was seated, would swivel outwards over the stage and then lower the chair.[20] I consider this unlikely to have been a permanent solution to staging flying scenes, but it could certainly have been done where permanent equipment was not available and when the actors did not want to forgo the spectacular effect of the descent.

The "heavens" then need not have been elaborate or expensive and were not absolutely needed; what of the machinery itself? In this area I think we may risk being somewhat misled by the ingenious reconstructions of descent machinery drawn by C. Walter Hodges, most recently for the Harvard Globe model.[21] Hodges assumes, and he may be right, that the stage technicians in charge of running the throne would do everything that they could to make their work easier. He therefore sketches machinery that is fairly elaborate, although still not particularly expensive, since it is built of wood and common materials. He provides a heavy brake to control the descent of the throne, and a counterweight, made to descend within the tiring-house frame as the throne ascends, so that winching the actor heavenwards again could be done fairly easily by pulling on a rope wound around the large central axle. The result is an efficient, even elegant piece of machinery, but I am not inclined to regard it as typical of what lay in the huts of the Rose or the Swan. The basis of most simple mechanical lifting-devices in the Renaissance was the windlass or capstan: a revolving axle arranged either vertically or horizontally and powered by levers set into it. It was described mechanically both by "Aristotle" and by Vitruvius, and it was one of the main sources of power in the medieval period.[22] Moxon, in describing the carpenters' "crab" at the end of the seventeenth century, gives us another version of the same machine.[23] A simple windlass or capstan, such as those used by James Burbage to build his playhouse, I believe to have been the source of power for the flying machine.

I proceed on G. F. Reynolds's principle "that the simplest explanation is usually to be preferred."[24] There is a good deal of contemporary evidence to support my view, some of it theatrical. That a man could be lowered and lifted by a fairly simple portable device is attested to by a scene from a Caroline play possibly acted at the Blackfriars, Richard Brome's *The Queen's Exchange* (1631).[25] In Act Five a group of characters are engaged in robbing a house; the stage direction reads "*Enter Carpenter, Mason, Smith, in Divels habits; two dark Lanthorns, a Pickaxe and a Rope, with an Engine fastned to a Post, and a bunch of Picklocks.*"[26] The "Engine," whatever it may be, is used to lower and then to lift one of the characters through the trap door to and from the space under the stage, which serves as the cellar that is being robbed. Two men manage the machine while the third gives instructions:

> [*Carp.*]   So, I'l go down;
> And when I shake the rope, then crane me up again
>   . . . So, so, so, let me down handsomely.
>
>   . . . .
> [*Mas.*]   The rope stirs; pull lustily.[27]

Whether or not the scene was actually played as it was written, Brome presumably thought it not impossible as he composed it, and he perhaps took his idea from contemporary burglars' techniques. The verb *crane* might suggest that what was used was a small version of Moxon's "crab," with a crane arm (the "*Post*") and attached windlass. I think that this would have proved fairly awkward for two men to manage, that it is more likely that the "*Engine*" and "*Rope*" are blocks and tackle, and that the *"Post"* is some kind of frame from which the tackle could be made to hang. When the two men "pull," they pull on a rope and raise the weight of their fellow actor fairly easily, although they could of course be pulling on the bars of a windlass.

If such *ad hoc* lifting for a fairly short distance could be managed with a tackle, it is not likely that the throne, which had to cover a distance of between fifteen and twenty-five feet, depending on whether or not the actor was to dismount and move onto the stage, was so equipped. Although multiple pulleys (blocks) give great mechanical advantage, they slow down the rate of movement of the load, and it is important to be able to vary the speed of a flying machine in order to achieve different effects; it would seem particularly desirable to be able to retrieve the god reasonably swiftly, since this is the time, especially during the final moments of ascent, when the trick is at its dramatically weakest. The central mechanical problem of the stage throne was to maintain a reasonable speed of operation while reducing as much as possible the effort required at the source of the power.[28] For this reason the most powerful lifting machine known in Elizabethan London, the tread-wheel, is unlikely to have been used in the huts of the playhouses, although there would have been room even for a fairly large one. Treadwheels were used in the riverside cranes such as those shown as Three Cranes by Visscher and Hollar; the machine uses the leverage of effort applied to a large circumference (the wheel) that bears on a central axle, winding in the rope attached to the load. The disadvantage for theater machinery again is speed: the axle revolves slowly in relation to the movement of the wheel.

We return to what is by far the commonest lifting and pulling machine in the Middle Ages and the Renaissance: the windlass or capstan. It is constantly illustrated in pictures of medieval building, for example, from the twelfth century onwards and in the plates of the Renaissance "Theaters of Machines"; vast ranks of capstans driven by men and horses were engaged in one of the most celebrated of Renaissance feats of engineering, the moving of the Vatican obelisk in 1585–86.[29] Such machinery was in fact so commonly available that it is treated rather dismissively by contemporary writers on mechanics and machinery. Joseph Boillot in 1598 suggests that the best thing that the curious might do is to go and take a look for themselves: "Et d'autant que le dit instrument [the 'molinet,' or capstan] est commun a plusieurs ouvriers, comme charpentiers, maçons, et autres, qui conduisent & manient de gros fardeaux, il n'est de besoin de rapporter les particularitez de la façon d'iceluy, pour le faire, parce que veue la démonstration de la figure le moindre ouvrier ne māquera un semblable, & de telle grosseur que l'on voudra."[30] Windlass machinery then was easily obtainable and unlikely to be expensive if even "le moindre ouvrier" could possess it.

Perhaps the most informative source for the application of similar machinery to the needs of the theater is provided by a book on mining, the celebrated *De Re Metallica* of Georgius Agricola, published in 1556. The mechanical problem in mining was essentially the same as that of the stage technicians: to move weights from a higher level to a lower, and the reverse. The testimony of Agricola's book is that in the middle of the sixteenth century the windlass was the standard tool used in working mines and that it was usually driven by two men turning cranks or levers, one at either end of the central drum around which the rope wound. It was extremely simple and depended upon human energy for its efficiency; Agricola notes that "all windlass workers, whatsoever kind of machine they may turn, are necessarily robust that they can sustain such great toil."[31] Moreover, he makes no mention of any braking device on windlasses of this kind, nor does his illustrator show any. Brakes certainly are shown on some of the larger machines, and they were essential to the operation of mills, for example, but it seems that we should be cautious about assuming that they were used in simpler machines. The following passage, for example, makes clear that the strength of the operators acts as the only brake in descents: "I will explain how heavy bodies, such as axles, iron chains, pipes, and heavy timbers, should be lowered into deep vertical shafts. A windlass is erected whose barrel has on each end four straight levers; it is fixed into upright beams and around it is wound a rope, one end of which is fastened to the barrel and the other to those heavy bodies which are slowly lowered down by workmen. . . . When these bodies are very heavy, then behind this windlass another is erected just like it, that their combined strength may be equal to the load, and that it may be lowered slowly."[32] The accompanying woodcut illustration (see Figure 1) shows exactly what is described: two men lower a bundle of pit props by controlling the movement of the levers—the machine has no mechanical brake.

More importantly from the stage historian's point of view, Agricola also describes how the machines are used to carry men to their work and, presumably, to lift them from the pits afterwards: "miners go down into mines not only by the steps of ladders, but they are also lowered into them while sitting on a stick or a wicker basket, fastened to the rope of one of the three drawing machines which I described at first."[33] The woodcut illustrating these remarks shows what I believe must be the basis for reconstructions of descent machinery in the playhouses: a miner descends a mine shaft sitting on a T bar, holding the rope with one hand and his lamp in the other (see Figure 2). Above him, on the surface, two men work the cranks of a windlass that is driven entirely by their own strength—it has no brake. There is no question that such machinery would have been extremely difficult to manage, yet there is not much evidence from contemporary sources that it would have been radically adapted when used in a theater. The use of a counterweight, which Hodges provides for his machinery, would have relieved the stress on the bars of the windlass; it was not appropriate to the narrow mine shafts that Agricola describes, although he does show counterwound buckets, for example, for lifting ore. But there is very little medieval or Renaissance evidence elsewhere for the use of counterweights on cranes or other lifting devices: it seems, for some reason, to have been rare. In any event, counterweights in the playhouse were no easier to manage than they were in the mine. They could hardly descend in front of the tiring house, and to assume that a shaft for a counterweight was provided within the tiring-house frame, as Hodges

Figure 1. Lowering heavy weights with a windlass. Georgius Agricola, *De Re Metallica,*
1556.

Figure 2. Lowering a man with a miner's windlass. Georgius Agricola, *De Re Metallica,* 1556.

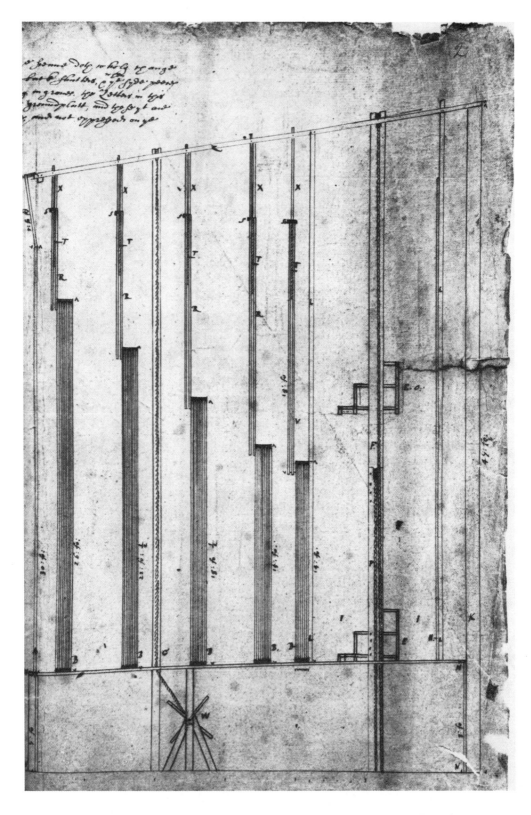

Figure 3. Elevation of the stage for *Salmacida Spolia*, 1640. (Detail).
By permission of the British Library.

does, is to be entirely speculative. A brake of some kind would have been needed when the throne stopped above the stage for the god to speak from on high; the laborers could hardly be expected to sustain the weight while the actor delivered a twenty-line speech, as in *Cymbeline*. A fairly simple expedient—a loop of rope fastened to a beam, for example, simply to hold one of the windlass levers back—could have been provided for this purpose. The strap brake may have been used, as may the ratchet system used on ships' capstans.[34]

Such evidence as remains of machinery specifically to do with the theater also points in the direction of simplicity rather than elaboration and further suggests to me that the technology was not much altered between the date of Dee's flying dung beetle in 1547 and the closing of the theaters. We might be tempted, on the basis of the greater frequency of flying effects in later plays and of the evidently enlarged roof over the stage of the Globe after 1613, to infer that the machinery in the playhouses became more sophisticated as time went on. Although this may have been the case, there is little evidence of it in Webb's drawings for the court masque *Salmacida Spolia* in 1640, when no lesser actors than the King and Queen moved on Inigo Jones's flying machines.[35] What Webb draws of course is a temporary stage, but certainly one that was not constrained by matters of expense. One assumes that Jones would have provided the safest and most effective machinery that he knew: what he did provide were windlasses with four bars, exactly of the type shown in Agricola's woodcuts (see Figure 3). There were two positions on the stage where flying effects were worked: a machine slightly downstage of center "by which ye Deityes were lett vpp & Downe," and an "Engyne" upstage in which flying chairs holding several characters moved. The motive power for the former was a windlass, labeled a "Capstall" in the notes, placed under the stage, and from which ropes ran to the full height of the scene and over pulleys to hoist the various effects attached to the other end. To power the heavier seats upstage Jones evidently ganged a number of windlasses together, in the manner recommended by Agricola; there was no room for them under the stage, and the note explains that "The Capstalls for these Engynes were placed in ye vault under ye floore of ye roome." There is no evidence in the drawing, although of course it is a simplified plan, either of brakes or of counterweights and no mention of them in the explanatory notes.

The Italian staging practice that, in part, was Jones's model in the masques reveals a similar dependence upon the simple machines of capstan and windlass, at least as that practice is set forth in Sabbatini's *Practica di Fabricar Scene e Machine ne'Teatri* (1638). His forty-fifth device, a moving cloud, is powered in exactly the same way as were the flying machines at Whitehall in 1640. "When this operation is to be done, four or eight men will be placed at the handles of the capstan, *who will slowly turn the capstan while the cloud descends* [italics mine], until it rests above the level of the stage. To make it ascend, they should reverse the capstan until the cloud has returned to its original place."[36] Here is as clear a statement as any that the weight of the descending machine was borne directly by the men on the bars of the capstan or windlass.

We can never be sure of exactly what Henslowe paid for in 1595, since so much technical knowledge in the Middle Ages and the Renaissance was never written down, but we can define the area of probability. If we set aside the question of the roof and heavens over the stage, which I do not regard as a part of the playhouse solely designed or provided for the staging of descent scenes, the equipment needed to create flying effects was neither uncommon nor expensive. I find it extremely unlikely that the playhouse owners would hesitate long over authorizing the money for the machinery itself: the throne chair, two long sturdy ropes, pulleys through which to lead the ropes from the windlass to a point directly over the stage, and the windlass itself, of a standard type available, as Boillot says, from any builder's or carpenter's yard. The only other expense would be wages for the men to turn the windlass, who did require certain special qualities in that they had to be both physically strong and intelligent enough to be able to respond to the demands of the scene below them on the stage: as Sabbattini puts it in discussing the management of another stage effect, "It is necessary in these actions to take great care since very often mishaps result, and fools and thick-witted persons should not be allowed to participate."[37] I take it that two stagehands could probably operate the windlass, unless the throne was very heavy indeed.[38] On the evidence of the plays, their work in the huts would not be required very often, and either they would have had other jobs around the theater or else they were hired as laborers by the day when needed.

It is precisely in connection with this kind of organization that we might say that the establishment of permanent playhouses helped the development of the companies and allowed them both to widen their repertory and to use a broader range of techniques of staging. It is not exactly, to take the case of machinery, that the playhouse management were able to provide expensive facilities that the actors themselves could not otherwise afford, but that the machine was simply there if it was needed and did not have to be set up for a given performance and then taken down again as happened on the temporary stages at court. The acting troupes themselves were unlikely to have either the time or money to make the kind of preparations paid for by the universities or the Revels Office, and the more they had to rely on the revenue of public performances in temporary conditions and on touring, the more elementary, in terms of staging, was their repertory likely to be. The descent throne was nothing new in 1576, or 1595—miraculous flights, after all, were a favorite spectacle in medieval performances—but to have the equipment ready when it was needed, when either a new play called for the effect or when the company decided that it could fund an extravagant production in the hope of its being a getpenny, that situation was new and offered a new freedom to the actors. For a relatively small outlay of capital, the builders of the theaters could provide the machinery over the stage; the expense of running it was then borne by the companies, if they chose to use it.

The question remains of why the evidently cautious Henslowe paid over seven pounds for his throne, when he ought to have been able to buy all his materials for under a pound, unless I am misreading contemporary account lists badly. The remaining six pounds would have paid for a great deal of labor: in 1592 he paid what seems to have been a large number of workmen of various kinds six pounds for a whole week's work.[39] Yet the 1595 entry, read in one way, indicates that the work was done on one day, the fourth of June. What exactly was he paying for? Seven years later he paid only fourteen pence for arrangements for a specific effect in a play on the same theme as Peele's *The Love of King David and Fair Bethsabe*—one which evidently showed the spectacular end of Absalom: "pd for poleyes & worckmanshipp for to hange absolo*me*."[40] What more than pulleys and workmanship was he getting for a further seven pounds? I can offer no direct explanation, but I certainly do not think that the carpenters are likely to have provided him with equipment that differed markedly from that described by Agricola, Sabbattini, Webb, and Moxon. One answer might be that on the fourth of June he paid the carpenters the balance of what he owed them for the major work on the playhouse in the preceding Lent and subsequently, which included, possibly as the latest item, the fixing up of the throne machine. That is, "Jtm pd [1] for carpenters worke & [2] mackinge the throne Jn the heuenes. . . ."

The larger question is why the Rose was not provided with a throne when it was built, which returns us to Wickham's hypothesis. Henslowe's entry is not prescriptive, however; there is no need to assume that the theater was without machinery before 1595. In Lent of that year the playhouse underwent "Repracyones," which perhaps included repairs to the stage cover and the consequent temporary removal of the throne and machinery. Equally, the throne that was made in 1595 could have been a replacement for a well-used, battered veteran. The *deus ex machina* was popular enough and the essential machinery that drove it cheap enough for it to have been standard equipment in any permanent playhouse.

NOTES

1. Geoffrey Chaucer, *The Squire's Tale*, 11. 217–219: *The Complete Works of Geoffrey Chaucer*, ed. F. N. Robinson, 2nd ed., (London: Oxford University Press, 1957), p. 130. Henry Peacham, *The Compleat Gentleman* (London, 1622; Amsterdam: Theatrum Orbis Terrarum, 1968), p. 73.

2. *Henslowe's Diary*, ed. R. A. Foakes and R. T. Rickert (Cambridge: Cambridge University Press, 1961), p. 7. (The author wishes to thank the Social Sciences and Humanities Research Council of Canada for financial support during the period of study that led to this paper.)

3. " 'Heavens,' Machinery, and Pillars in the Theatre and Other Early Playhouses," in *The First Public Playhouse: The Theatre in Shoreditch, 1576–1598*, ed. Herbert Berry (Montreal: McGill-Queens University Press, 1979), pp. 1–15.

4. *Ibid.*, p. 12.

5. See, for example, the new evidence recently discovered by R. M. Benbow about playwrighting in the early 1570s: "Dutton and Goffe versus Broughton: a disputed contract for plays in the 1570s," *Records of Early English Drama Newsletter*, 1981:2, 3–9.

6. "The Popularity of *Cupid's Revenge*," *SEL: Studies in English Literature*, 19 (1979), 215–227.

7. Wickham, p. 12.

8. *Shakespearean Staging, 1599–1642* (Cambridge, Mass.: Harvard University Press, 1971), p. 148.

9. Ed. W. W. Greg, Malone Society Reprints (Oxford: The Malone Society, 1926), ll. 2109–2110.

10. *Documents Relating to the Revels Office at Court in the Time of King Edward VI and Queen Mary,* ed. A. Feuillerat, Materialien zur Kunde des älteren Englischen Dramas, vol. 44, gen. ed., W. Bang (Louvain: Uystpruyst, 1914), p. 220. Christmas, 1556–57.

11. *Documents Relating to the Office of the Revels in the Time of Queen Elizabeth,* ed. A. Feuillerat, Materialien zur Kunde des älteren Englischen Dramas, vol. 21, gen. ed., W. Bang (Louvain: Uystpruyst, 1908), p. 117.

12. *Ibid.,* p. 227.

13. *Ibid.,* p. 262.

14. Holinshed's *Chronicles* (London, 1587), sig. 6D4^V. Cited in *The Life and Minor Works of George Peele,* ed. C. T. Prouty (New Haven: Yale University Press, 1952), p. 61.

15. Christ Church Disbursement Book, as cited by Prouty, p. 61.

16. *The Nomenclator or Remembrancer of Adrianus Iunius,* trans. J. Higins (London, 1585), sig. N7^V. See L. B. Campbell, *Scenes and Machines on the English Stage during the Renaissance* (Cambridge: Cambridge University Press, 1923), *passim.*

17. So, for instance, he renders "Scena" as "The frunt of the theatre: the place where the players make them ready, being trimmed with hangings, and out of which they enter upon the stage." "Fori" becomes "The galleries or standings for the beholders of plaies: the scaffolds" (N7^V).

18. *Henslowe's Diary,* pp. 10, 14.

19. Feuillerat, *Elizabeth,* pp. 338, 262, 240. "Vyce" could also mean windlass. Higins, translating *Exostra,* has "A vice or gin of wood, wherewith such things as are done within out of sight, are shewed to the beholders by the turning about of wheeles" (N7^V).

20. C. Walter Hodges draws a throne worked by a crane in his hypothetical reconstruction of the second Globe, although not of the type that I am suggesting here; see *Shakespeare's Second Globe* (London: Oxford University Press, 1973), pp. 84–91.

21. See *Shakespeare's First Globe Theatre* (Cambridge, Mass.: Harvard University Press, 1980).

22. *Mechanica,* Vol. VI of *The Works of Aristotle,* trans. E. S. Forster (Oxford: Clarendon Press, 1913); Vitruvius, *De Architectura,* trans. M. H. Morgan (Cambridge, Mass.: Harvard University Press, 1914).

23. Joseph Moxon, *Mechanick Exercises,* 1678–1703 (New York: Praeger, 1970), p. 159, plate 9.

24. *The Staging of Elizabethan Plays at the Red Bull Theater 1605–1625* (New York: Modern Language Association, 1940; rpt. New York: Kraus, 1966), p. 53.

25. *The Dramatic Works of Richard Brome,* [ed. R. H. Shepherd] 3 vols. (1873; rpt. New York: AMS Press, 1966), III, 453–550. See G. E. Bentley, *The Jacobean and Caroline Stage,* 7 vols. (Oxford: Clarendon Press, 1941–68), III, 86–87.

26. *Brome,* III, 535.

27. *Brome,* III, 536.

28. "It is also evident that the more easily the weight is (to be) moved, the greater will be the time (required); and the greater the difficulty with which the weight is moved, the shorter the time; and conversely" (Guido Ubaldo, *Mechanicorum liber,* in *Mechanics in Sixteenth Century Italy,* ed. and trans. S. Drake and I. E. Drabkin [Madison: University of Wisconsin Press, 1969], p. 317).

29. See L. F. Salzmann, *Building in England down to 1540* (Oxford: Clarendon Press, 1952); Jacques Besson, *Théâtre des Instrumens Mathematiques et Mechaniques* (Lyons, 1579); Agostino Ramelli, *Le Diverse et Artificiose Machine* (Paris, 1558); Heinrich Zeising, *Theatri Machinarum* (Altenburg, 1614–21); Domenico Fontana, *Della Transportatione dell'Obelisco Vaticano* (Rome, 1590); W. B. Parsons, *Engineers and Engineering in the Renaissance* (Baltimore: Williams and Wilkins, 1939).

30. *Modelles, Artifices de Feu, et Divers Instrumẽs du Guerre* (Chaumont, 1598), p. 19.

31. *De Re Metallica,* trans. H. C. and L. H. Hoover (London: Mining Magazine, 1912), p. 162.

32. *Ibid.,* p. 171.

33. *Ibid.,* p. 212. The three machines referred to are two versions of the windlass (the second with a flywheel) and a variety of treadwheel.

34. See Sir Henry Manwayring, *The Sea Man's Dictionary* (London, 1644). The book was written some twenty years before it was published. "Paule ye Capsten, that is to stay it wh the iron Paule, wch beareing against the whelpes keepes the Capsten from turning backe." Manuscript copy of 1633, B.L., Additional MS. 48157.

35. B.L., MS. Lansdowne 1171. Reproduced in *Inigo Jones. The Theatre of the Stuart Court,* Stephen Orgel and Roy Strong, 2 vols. (London: Sotheby Parke Bernet, 1973), II, 736–741.

36. *The Renaissance Stage,* ed. Barnard Hewitt (Coral Gables, Fla.: University of Miami Press, 1958), pp. 159–160.

37. *Ibid.,* pp. 126–127.

38. For a reasoned calculation of the time and effort required to work a theatrical windlass and for much other information on machinery, see John Ronayne, "Decorative and Mechanical Effects Relevant to the Theatre of Shakespeare," in *The Third Globe,* ed. C. Walter Hodges, S. Schoenbaum, and L. Leone (Detroit: Wayne State University Press, 1981), pp. 216–217. I am grateful to Mr. Ronayne for allowing me to see his paper before its appearance in print and for discussing it with me.

39. *Henslowe's Diary,* p. 10.

40. *Ibid.,* p. 217.

Chapman's *Caesar and Pompey* and the Fortunes of Prince Henry

ROLF SOELLNER

THE *TRAGEDY OF CAESAR AND POMPEY* is the most puzzling and disputed of George Chapman's dramas. Its date, its place among his tragedies, and its meaning are in doubt, and critics have quarreled about who is its hero: Caesar, Pompey, or Cato.[1] We should, I think, ask the question what Chapman's purpose was in writing this problematic play—Chapman generally was a writer with a purpose. The answer, I believe, is that he composed it very much with an eye on Prince Henry, the major patron of his life, from whom he expected so much and by whose early death he was so bitterly disappointed. *Caesar and Pompey,* I intend to show, breathes Chapman's hopes for and anxieties about this young man of large, perhaps unlimited, aspirations.

Henry and his father were diametrically opposed personalities.[2] While James saw himself as a *rex pacificus,* a universal peacemaker, his son delighted in military exercises and dreamed of glory and chivalry. Henry was a charismatic figure, as contemporaries were quick to note; he was the glass of fashion and the mold of form compared to James, who was a king of shreds and patches with his ungainly physique, his coarse manners, and the homosexual tendency that led him to chose handsome young men as his favorites, who were resented as upstarts. But Henry also was and has remained an ambiguous character: possessed of great gifts and a powerful personality, he was full of promise; yet his burning zeal, stirred by fulsome flattery, might have spelled trouble for England and the world had he succeeded his peaceful, if limited, father. His death in 1612 at the age of eighteen has left these ambiguities unresolved.

From an early age Henry was considered to be a profitable patron for writers, and in the process he was soon made the recipient of advice, wanted and unwanted, Chapman becoming a notable provider. But Chapman was a poet and dramatist who shunned simplistic moral and political prescriptions. The character of Caesar in the play, on whom Henry was conditioned to orient himself, bears witness to Chapman's humanistic probing of the evolution of this conqueror and ruler and to Chapman's awareness of the complex interplay between human motives and politico-military opportunities; factors impervious to calculation—the Renaissance liked to call them "fortune"—play a large role in these processes. Some of the play's problems that have plagued critics stem from the tentativeness and hesitation that insinuated themselves into Chapman's mind as he thought of conquest and statecraft and the nature of the prince, ancient and modern. Chapman, I think, did not finish his thoughts and therefore could never quite pull the play together into a unified whole. Provocative and, in places, brilliant as *Caesar and Pompey* is, it is a troubling and vexing drama.

I

The present text of *Caesar and Pompey* may have had a long gestation. At any rate, a long time—probably about twenty-five years—passed between its composition and its first printing in the Quarto of 1631. Scholars have generally placed the date of composition at either around 1605 or around 1612. The later date was preferred by Thomas Marc Parrott, the first modern editor of Chapman's plays, because of "the somewhat intangible evidence of style and rhythm," and it has been accepted by others who like Parrott see in the drama a climax of Chapman's growth toward Stoicism.[3] External evidence, however, points to a date sometime before 1605. As Frederick Fleay first suggested and E. E. Stoll reaffirmed with detailed arguments, the character of Bellamont in Dekker and Webster's *Northward Ho* (1605/06) is an unmistakable parody of Chapman. To quote Stoll, "Bellamont is a poet, a dramatic poet associated with one of the companies. He is old, and is repeatedly called white and hoary. He has classical tastes and acquirements, is the author of a *Caesar and Pompey,* and also is fond of laying his scene in the modern court of France. He writes both comedies and tragedies. He is a respectable and dignified person, with a leaning toward high-flown diction. All this fits Chapman and no one else."[4] It is surely to Chapman's *Caesar and Pompey* that Bellamont alludes when he boasts: "I can in the wryting of a tragedy, make *Caesar* speak better than ever his ambition could: when I write of *Pompey* I have *Pompeies* soule within me, and when I personate a worthy poet, I am then truly my selfe, a poor unpreferd scholler."[5] This remark does not prove that the play was actually finished by the time of the first performance of *Northward Ho;* in fact, it sounds to me as if it meant that Chapman was in the process of writing it. Such news would have traveled fast in the circle of Jacobean playwrights, without there necessarily being much information on the nature of the play; that Caesar was to be "ambitious" hardly required inside knowledge.

If the play was begun or written before 1606, as appears to be the case, it would have been early among Chapman's tragedies, preceded, if at all, only by *Bussy d'Ambois,* which (although on slender evidence) is generally thought to stem from 1604. A consideration that has not previously been adduced argues for *Caesar and Pompey* preceding the Byron plays, which (on better evidence) are dated 1606–08. One of Chapman's sources for the former play is Plutarch's *De Fortuna Romanorum,* and two passages deriving from it (II.iv.129–42 and III.i.119–32) are paralleled in *The Tragedy of Byron* (I.i.141–43 and V.ii.234–71). It stands to reason that Chapman drew on Plutarch's essay again for *Byron* because he had studied it for his Roman play, and at least the former passage in *Byron* gives the impression of being remembered rather than, as in *Caesar and Pompey,* directly copied. (Compare *De Fortuna Romanorum* 4.) If so, *Byron* probably did not precede our play—or at least did not precede it by very much. 1605–06 is a good guess for *Caesar and Pompey*'s composition. Chapman would then have been for some time in the service of Prince Henry as "sewer-in-ordinary," a court position that he seems to have assumed soon after the accession of James to the English throne.

Graham Parry suggests that Chapman may have initially attracted Henry's attention by his *Bussy d'Ambois,* for Henry was particularly interested in French affairs and began entering into correspondence with Henri IV as early as 1606.[6] A play about Caesar would have been apt to stimulate Henry's interest in Chapman further because the Prince was from various sides urged to study Caesar's military accomplishments and even encouraged to think of himself as a future Caesar, absurd as this may appear to us. As J. W. Williamson says, Henry was subjected to a powerful mythologizing force from birth, and the myth of the conqueror accompanied him into England in 1603: "The Scots bade farewell to their Hercules, their Achilles, their Alexander and Caesar and lectured England concerning the anointed presence that was coming."[7] Robert Peake the Elder's portrait of Henry at the Hunt, painted in the same year, shows the nine-year-old boy in the strutting martial pose of Henry VIII. For the analogies with Caesar, King James had unwittingly pointed the way when in his *Basilikon Doron or his Majesty's Instructions to his Dearest Son* (1599) he recommended to him the study of Caesar's *Commentaries on the Gallic War.* Sir Clement Edmondes promptly dedicated to Henry his *Observations upon the Five First Books of the Commentaries* (1604), saying to him that "Your high understanding in this your tenderness of years is admired by the world."[8] By the time Chapman wrote *Caesar and Pompey,* the Prince was certainly looked upon as old enough to profit by Caesarian precepts. A play on Caesar in 1605 or 1606 by a writer employed at Henry's court could hardly have failed to be thought in some sense also about Henry and intended for him.

Parry (without noting *Caesar and Pompey*) assigns Chapman, rightly I think, to those who were troubled about the encouragement given to Henry to make himself into a future conqueror. The most outspoken of the objectors was Samuel Daniel, who dedicated to him *The Tragedy of Philotas* (1604), a drama about Alexander's overweening general, and urged him that he could find here a lesson in statecraft for the future. He could see "With what encounters greatest fortunes close, / What dangers, what attempts, what manifolde / Incumbrances ambition undergoes."[9]

But unlike *Philotas, Caesar and Pompey* is not a closet tragedy although it was eventually dedicated to a patron, as closet tragedies generally were. Rather, it has all the appearance of being written for the theater. Parrott noted the numerous and unusually detailed stage directions in the 1631 quarto and opined that the text was printed from a theater copy that had been carefully marked for performance.[10] John Russell Brown, while objecting that these directions may just as well have been authorial, is convinced that Chapman had the stage in mind while composing it and that he wrote in the tradition of the commercial theater.[11] Fleay interestingly suggested that an anonymous *Caesar and Pompey* performed by the Lord Admiral's Men in 1594 was by Chapman and that a few fragments of it survive in the 1631 text.[12] E. K. Chambers thought Fleay's speculation "not worth pursuing" in view of the many Caesar plays of the time.[13] But the possibility of an association of Chapman's play with the Admiral's Men is intriguing. Not that it was ever performed by them; we may trust Chapman's assertion that it never touched the stage.[14] But it is possible that originally Chapman set out to revise a play in their possession; if so, it was very likely not his own; the present play is too sophisticated to be apprentice work and to date from 1594. But if Chapman had a company and a theater in mind for his *Caesar and Pompey,* it must have been the Admiral's Men and their theater, the Fortune, since Prince Henry had become the patron of this troupe in 1604. It is true that Chapman usually wrote for the children's companies, but here was a difficult classical play that made unusual rhetorical demands; most of all, here was a play apt to appeal to Henry. And the Fortune would have been an appropriate arena for this martial drama with its incessant evocation of the fortunes of war. There is no way to give a definite answer to the question why it never reached this or any other stage; but I shall suggest that the reason may have been connected with Henry's Caesarian aspirations.

The dedication of the 1631 quarto to Lionel Cranfield, Earl of Middlesex, is a chapter in Chapman's frustrating and frustrated search for patrons and sources of income. No poet was ever so unlucky in his choice of patrons.[15] His Homer translation is the most conspicuous case in point. Chapman presented the first installment of the *Iliad* (1598) to the unfortunate Earl of Essex, whose subsequent rash adventure and execution left the poet no time to reap much profit. He then dedicated the first twelve books to Henry (1609) and followed them up with the entire *Iliad* (1611) only to see the promised munificence vanish with the Prince's death. Finally, he stubbornly persisted in dedicating the *Odyssey* to his latest patron, Robert Carr, Earl of Somerset, the former favorite of the King, who by this time had fallen into disgrace after being tried and convicted as an accomplice in his wife's murder of Sir Thomas Overbury—a foolish if magnanimous gesture by Chapman, who believed in Carr's innocence. The dedication of the quarto of *Caesar and Pompey* was again to a fallen grandee, and it has all the appearance of an act of despair by the impecunious poet, now in his early seventies. Cranfield was a man in eclipse, after having had one of the most spectacular careers of the age.[16] From an apprentice, he had slowly risen to become Lord Chancellor in 1621 and was created Earl of Middlesex in 1622. In trying to bring order into James's chaotic finances, he ran afoul of the King's favorite, the Duke of Buckingham. Cranfield was tried and convicted in 1624 on largely unsubstantiated charges of corruption in office. While laboring to restore the King's finances, he had not neglected to enlarge his own wealth; but after his fall, he was mainly concerned with defending his shrinking property— hardly a patron of even second rank. The torturous dedication indicates Chapman's embarrassment about offering an old and unperformed play. But he evidently thought that *Caesar and Pompey* might have some attraction for the Earl and hoped it would "fall under no exception in your lordship's better judging estimation" for its "scenical representation"—Chapman's way of saying that it was stageworthy and that Cranfield was a connoisseur of the theater (he was an inveterate playgoer).[17] Chapman must also have thought that the Earl, who in Fuller's words had "tasted of both breasts of fortune,"[18] would be interested in a play, the plot of which turned on the reaction of its major characters to Fortune, the double-faced goddess who is invoked repeatedly. Most of all, I think, Chapman believed that a play which insisted on justice in political action and did so through a notable figure, the philosopher Cato, would appeal to a man who prided himself on the justice of his actions and felt he had been harshly treated. In Cranfield's defense at his trial, he had pleaded that "though he had been a judge eight years not a single charge of corruption in the exercise of his judicial office had been brought against him."[19] In smarting from the injustice of the world, Chapman and Cranfield were brothers in spirit.

Even if the Earl merely "vouchsafed in his idle minutes" to throw "some slight glances" at the book, as Chapman invited him to do, he could not have helped being impressed by the play's championship of justice. The title page proclaimed it: "Caesar and Pompey. A Roman Tragedy, declaring their Warres. Out of whose events is evicted this Proposition. *Only a just man is a freeman.*" (The italics are those of the text.) This "proposition" appears again as an epigraph in bold capitals just before the beginning of the play proper. We may assume that it was put in these prominent places to strike Cranfield's eyes, and we should be wary of taking it as the theme for which Chapman designed the play, as earlier critics did. Parrott thought there was no doubt that the motto stated "the central and dominant idea," that Cato was the "personification" of this idea, and that Chapman identified himself with Cato, making the philosopher his mouthpiece.[20] It is for this reason that the play has been thought to be the culmination of Chapman's Stoical thought.

It is true that Cato dies with the Stoic paradox on his lips, "Just men are only free, the rest are slaves" (V.ii.177), and that variations of the idea occur as he prepares himself for suicide (IV.v.65–66; V.ii.1–21)—Chapman took the *sententia* literally from Plutarch's "Life of Cato," one of the three Plutarchian *Lives* that were his main sources. But the play as a whole does not push the Stoic thesis (and, even if it did, *Caesar and Pompey* would not necessarily be a later play since we do not know that Chapman became more Stoical in later life). Cato, far from being the central figure, appears in only five of its sixteen scenes; he is altogether absent in the long middle stretch from II.v to V.ii; to explain his absence, Parrott had to assume a weakness in the dramatic structure.

As Suzanne Kistler, in what I think is the best critical discussion of *Caesar and Pompey*, has pointed out, the play has three main characters and Cato is third in importance.[21] We should trust the title page to the degree that the play primarily treats the wars of its two titular heroes; the tragedy turns about these "two suns of our Roman heaven," as Cato's opening line has it; in the Argument prefixed to the drama, it is called "a martial history," and Cato is barely mentioned. Cato establishes at the beginning of the play the standards of political decency. He opposes Caesar's Machiavellian maneuver in the Senate to obtain permission for Pompey's army to enter Rome, a pretext to have his own army do likewise. Cato here and later voices some of Chapman's favorite ideas, such as the need for justice, the desirability of virtue and religion in politics, and the freedom of the soul to choose its heavenly destiny on the basis of its immortality. But Cato is not simply Chapman's mouthpiece. As Kistler points out, Cato's judgment of Pompey is quite faulty. He errs in believing that his protégé does not seek personal power and glory, and since he is blind to Pompey's shortcomings, does not see that Pompey's indecision and ambition bear a heavy guilt in his defeat. So Cato comes to wonder why Pompey loses even while acting on ethical principles:

> When Pompey
> Did all things out of course, past right, past reason,
> He stood invincible against the world:
> Yet now his cares grew pious, and his powers
> Set all up for his country, he is conquered.
> (*V.ii.65–69*)

Wrong as Cato is about Pompey, he is right in acknowledging here the element of fortune, of chance, in politics, of which he took no cognizance before. But it is sad to find the man who sought to make ethics a branch of practical politics abandoning all activity and withdrawing into a solipsism that puts his private salvation above the welfare of the state. He advises his son to withdraw from action in public life because "the time's corruption / Will never bear it" (V.ii.112–113). Surely Chapman did not at any time subscribe to such utter defeatism. Rather, I think, Cato's life and death demonstrate the difficulty—perhaps the impossibility—of reconciling the demands of the contemplative life with the business of government. Cato cannot rule Rome; only Caesar can.

At any rate, Cato is not a mere choric figure; he is a dramatic character, certainly by and large admirable, a man of principles, but human enough to make errors and to suffer from depression in misfortune. He is a strong man, who yet loses his political nerve and energy in defeat even while retaining his private courage. His *sententia* that only a just man is a free man is an apology for his suicide and must be understood in its dramatic context. Put on the title page of the play and as an epigraph for the plot, it creates a false impression.

It is even possible that Chapman revised and augmented somewhat the final appearance of Cato for the purpose of strengthening its support of his motto; as Parrott noted, these scenes are the most polished of the play. The text of the quarto as a whole is quite troublesome, apparently set up from Chapman's foul papers, which may have become even fouler through revisions over the years. But certainly Chapman undertook no general revision of the text for printing. There is a considerable confusion of names and speech assignments, and there are omissions, rough passages, and, even for Chapman, unusually tortured phrasings.[22] By contrast, the fifth scene of Act Four with Cato is practically perfect, and the concluding episode of Cato's death (V.ii.1–178) is hardly less so. This smoothness is the more notable as both passages contain difficult philosophical speeches. Notable also is that after Cato's death, the play comes to a rather hurried conclusion.

If the destitute old dramatist devised an obtrusive motto and touched up the final Cato scenes in order to appeal to Cranfield's generosity, blurring the focus of the play somewhat in the process, we will readily forgive him. We do not know whether the appeal worked; there is no record of any remuneration, which, in any case, could not have been princely. Gone were the days when Chapman could hope for such rewards.

II

Caesar and Pompey relates clearly to the tendency in Prince Henry's environment to see him as a budding Caesar. Chapman, like others, was aware of James's desire to see his son study Caesar's military science. As James said in the *Basilikon Doron,*

> But by reading authenticke histories and Chronicles, yee shall learne experience by Theoricke, applying the bypast things to the present estate, *quia nihil novum sub sole* [Eccl. 1:9] such is the continuall volubilitie of things earthly, according to the roundnesse of the world, and revolutions of the heavenly circles: which is expressed by the wheeles in Ezechiels visions, and counterfeited by the poets *in rota Fortunae.* And likewise by the knowledge of histories, yee shall knowe how to behave your selfe to all Embassadours and strangers; being able to discourse with them upon the estate of their owne countrey. And among al prophane histories, I must not omit most specially to recommend unto you the Commentaries of *Caesar*; both for the sweete flowing of the stile, as also for the worthinesse of the matter it self: For I have ever beene of that opinion, that of all the Ethnick Emperors, or great Captains that ever were, he hath farthest excelled, both in his practise, and in his precepts in martiall affaires.[23]

It was this passage that stimulated Sir Clement Edmondes to dedicate his *Observations upon ... the Commentaries* to Henry, "Emboldened specially because it carrieth *Caesar* and his Fortunes, as they come related from the same Author: which, in the deepe Iudgement of his most excellent Maiesty, is preferd above all other profane histories; and, so commended, by his sacred Authoritie to your reading, as the chiefe paterne and Maister-peece of the Art of Warre."[24] Chapman's dramatic "martial history" would have brought Caesar and his fortunes even more vividly to Henry's attention, and, on one level at least, it could teach him the kind of lessons that James believed his son should learn from histories: Chapman's Caesar demonstrates a general's excellence in the theory and practice of war, a leader's coping with good and bad fortune, and a diplomat's tact in the treatment of friends and enemies.

It is obvious that Chapman, a belated Christian humanist in a court where his philosophy of life was becoming *démodé,* had much sympathy with the general aims of James's old-fashioned conduct book. He would have approved of the King's insistence that a ruler should be a good, god-fearing man; in view of Chapman's belief in heroic supermen, he may even have agreed that a king should be like a little god. Certainly he would have applauded the sovereign's obligation to prevent and heal factionalism, to be just, and to suppress his tyrannical urges. The Caesar of Chapman's play is very much concerned with his image as a tyrant and seeks to erase it from people's minds. But for such commonplaces, which agreed with Chapman's Christian humanism, he did not have to read the *Basilikon Doron*. There is, however, one passage that Chapman appears to have had directly in mind when he composed *Caesar and Pompey*. Demanding that Henry observe his obligation to God, James urged his son to piety by asking him to consider the golden chain that linked his soul to heaven:

> Now as to Faith, which is the nourisher and quickner of Religion, as I have alreadie said, It is a sure persuasion and apprehension of the promises of God, applying them to your soule: and therefore may it be iustly called the golden chaine that linketh the faithfull soule to Christ: And because it groweth not in our garden, but is *the free gift of God*, as the same Apostle saith, it must be nourished by prayer, Which is nothing else, but a friendly talking with God.[25]

Chapman gave this image to Cato in a long theological discourse with the philosopher Athenodorus in which Cato bases his claim for the freedom of the just man on his free soul with which he can reach toward heaven:

> Past doubt, though others
> Think heaven a world too high for our low reaches,
> Not knowing the sacred sense of him that sings:
> "Jove can let down a golden chain from heaven,
> Which, tied to earth, shall fetch up earth and seas."
> And what's that golden chain but our pure souls?
> A golden beam of him, let down by him,
> That govern'd with his grace, and drawn by him,
> Can hoist this earthy body up to him,
> The sea and air, and all the elements
> Compress'd in it; not while 'tis thus concrete,
> But fin'd by death, and then given heavenly heat.
> *(IV.v.125–136)*

Although Chapman had Cato supply the Homeric source for the image of the golden chain from the *Iliad* (VIII.18–26), Chapman provided it with an interpretation that draws on Christian ideas about the resurrection of the flesh and the ascension of the soul into heaven. These are astonishing ideas for a pagan philosopher, and they jar with the classical matrix of the play. When Henry read them, he could hardly help being reminded of his father's words and image, admonishing him to piety.

Like Daniel, Chapman must have seen a danger in the admonitions rampant in Henry's environment to steel himself for future martial glories. By 1605, the Prince took an increasing interest in political affairs and was being told that he would sometime have to play an even stronger and more vital role in the theater of world history. Those in particular who were anti-Spanish and saw in his father's politics of accommodation mainly the weakness hoped that Henry would become a strong and victorious king and change the course of England toward a belligerent championship of the Protestant cause. The danger became more apparent later in identifications of Henry with Caesar—"mon jeun Caesar et G. Alexandre," George Marcelline called him in *Les Trophées du roi Jacques I* (1609).[26] In the English edition, *The Triumphs of King James* (1610), Marcelline emblematized Henry as "one figured Caesar, aloft, deposing or treading [the] Globe under him, holding a book in one hand, and a sword in the other, so that it may be said of you, . . . you are Caesar."[27]

Henry's temperament made him susceptible to challenges of his martial spirit. Contemporaries observed his ardent soul, his urge to transcend limitations, his burning zeal. He himself once remarked to John Harington: "I have pleasure in overreaching difficult matters."[28] It is significant that Chapman gave his Caesar the kind of fiery spirit and exertions beyond his strength that were Henry's hallmark, exertions that may have been responsible for his early death. It is in fact as a disease that Chapman's Pompey describes this spirit in Caesar, making it the cause of his epilepsy:

> And your disease the gods ne'er gave to man
> But such a one as has a spirit too great
> For all his body's passage to serve it;
> Which notes the excess of your ambition,
> The malady chancing where the pores and passages
> Through which the spirit of man is borne
> So narrow are, and strait, that oftentimes
> They intercept it quite, and choke it up.
>
> *(I.ii.246–253)*

This diagnosis has no warrant in Chapman's sources. Since Pompey is Caesar's foe, it may be thought to be biased; and Chapman's Caesar is indeed quite rational and controlled in general. But once, at least, before he boards the fateful ship that is to take him to Brundisium, we catch a glimpse of the heroic, quasi-demonic spirit that drives him beyond the limits of nature (II.v).

We will later analyze the revealing soliloquy Caesar utters on this occasion. For the moment it will suffice to note that Chapman was conditioned by his humanistic background to find a spirit that funneled ambition into the human mind dangerous. This bias is indicated by the way he lectured Henry in the dedication to the *Twelve Books of the Iliads* (1609) on the need of the prince to turn inward and to subdue his emotions:

> Since perfect happinesse, by Princes sought,
> Is not with birth, borne, nor Exchequers bought;
> Nor followes in great Traines; nor is possest
> With any outward State; but makes him blest
> That governs inward; and beholdeth theare,
> All his affections stand about him bare;
> That by his power can send to Towre, and death,

> All traitrous passions; marshalling beneath
> His justice, his meere will; and in his minde
> Holds such a scepter, as can keepe confinde
> His whole lifes actions in the royal bounds
> Of Vertue and Religion.[29]

This virtuous discipline and self-control, Chapman continued, were to be learned by "Princely presidents," such as Homer provided, and reading the *Iliad* would make Henry see "one Godlike man create / All sorts of worthiest men." Chapman's Caesar, interestingly, uses a very similar phrase before his crossing to Brundisium when he speaks of having "ransack'd all the world for worth / To form in man the image of the gods" (II.v.12–13). But the fiery images of his speech show that Caesar is not free from "traitrous passions" when he utters these words.

Chapman's Caesar, we shall see, is not a clear-cut model of imitation for Henry; Chapman was no propagandist like Marcelline. And although he was ideologically closer to Daniel, he did not fashion his Caesar to personify the simple warning that Daniel offered to the Prince in his *Philotas*. Chapman's attitude toward Henry's aspirations was somewhere between Marcelline's and Daniel's: he sought to encourage the young man's energy and enthusiasm but also to purify them and to steer him away from thoughts of conquest and military glory.

III

Caesar was in the Renaissance the prime example of a *fortunatus*, a man signally favored by Fortune.[30] In this respect too, the character of Chapman's hero and the play relate to Prince Henry as contemporaries saw him before his early death, a man whom they hoped, and whom many expected, to be blessed by good fortune. *Caesar and Pompey* is a *fortunatus* play that sets Caesar, the favorite of Fortune, against Pompey, who is rejected by her, and contrasts their actions and attitudes.

Structurally and thematically, the play resembles Thomas Lodge's *The Wounds of Civil War* (*ca.* 1588), a crude conqueror play and story of internecine strife that pits the younger and more energetic Sulla, a *fortunatus,* against the older Marius in a struggle for rule in Rome. Marius goes down heroically in the end and, by his example, inspires Sulla, who until now has swum in the sea of all his fortune, to turn inward, renounce his dependence on fortune, and exchange the gifts of the world for the promise of eternity—none too soon since he promptly dies afterward. In thought and execution, *Caesar and Pompey* is a much subtler drama. It poses the claims of the contemplative life, the alternative to the life of political action, primarily through the philosopher Cato and the influence that he seeks to exert on Pompey—with dubious results—rather than through the protagonists themselves.

Pompey, although characterized in detail, serves mainly as Caesar's foil. He is a man whose self-confidence is weakening, who reacts rather than acts, and who relies more on his friends and on Cato than on himself. By contrast, Caesar becomes increasingly independent of others. In the early Senate scene (I.ii), he conspires with

Metellus and supports himself by sycophants and the mob; but from his defeat at Dyrrachium onward, nobody is counsel to his thoughts, and he becomes a self-assured and uncontested leader.

Much as in Lodge's play, the contrast between the two protagonists is clearly shown by their attitudes toward the goddess Fortuna. Caesar demonstrates the truth of Pompey's axiom that he who wants to gain the empire "must have fortune / That goes beyond man" (I.i.181–182). But Caesar does not slavishly depend on Fortune nor attribute his mistakes to her influence. When a lieutenant suggests blaming her for the defeat at Dyrrachium, Caesar answers peremptorily: "It was not fortune's fault but mine, Acilius" (II.iii.10). Caesar, like Machiavelli, believes that while Fortune may rule a considerable part of men's actions, she also allows a large part of their fate to be governed by men themselves. The gods help those who help themselves, or as Caesar puts the case reversely, "Secure and idle spirits never thrive / When most the gods for their advancement strive" (III.ii.73–74). Thus Pompey is wrong when he accuses Caesar of being a mere minion of the fickle Fortuna and disingenuous in denying his own reliance on her (I.ii.165–184). Even while decrying her aid, Pompey is very much dependent on her and anxious for her help. After his initial victory, he invokes her in an elaborate emblem and claims to have subdued her; but it is clear that he very much seeks her future aid (II.iv.129–144). Before the battle of Pharsalia, he asks for reassurance from his followers that they will blame fortune, rather than himself, if he loses (III.i.25–27)—a marked contrast to Caesar's stance after Dyrrachium. And Pompey succumbs to fear of fortune just before the battle of Pharsalia begins, indicating his weakening of nerves.

When, after his fatal loss, he flees in disguise to Lesbos to join his wife, first he has to test her reaction to his changed fortunes before revealing himself to her. It is she who instructs him in scorning his fate and in seeing himself as "great" only now—significantly he again requires an outside stimulus to rise above his fortune. His promise of total reformation, of turning inward, is therefore suspect:

> I will stand no more
> On others' legs, nor build one joy without me.
> If ever I be worth a house again
> I'll build all inward.
>
> *(V.i.203–206)*

His resolution collapses promptly as his murderers close in upon him:

> See, heavens, your sufferings! Is my country's love,
> The justice of an empire, piety,
> Worth this end in their leader? Last yet, life,
> And bring the gods off fairer: after this
> Who will adore their deities?
>
> *(V.i.259–263)*

One sympathizes with Pompey's outcry under the brutal attack; but his "last yet, life," betrays his desire to cling to life in spite of his despair that it can be lived meaningfully. Pompey lacks Cato's courage and dies, as he lived, weakly. For Prince Henry, Pompey's attitude toward fortune would have constituted a negative example, just as Caesar's was a positive one.

At that same time, Pompey's and even more Cato's deaths pose the question whether a political leader in the world that Chapman paints can really afford the luxury of an inward life. This is the question Chapman also posed through his stoical hero Clermont in *The Revenge of Bussy d'Ambois.* In *Caesar and Pompey,* not even Caesar escapes this dilemma since what makes him successful is not his contemplative morality. In fact, ethically Caesar is a most ambiguous character. The earlier Caesar is quite clearly "ambitious" in the derogatory Renaissance sense of the word; he stirs up factionalism in Rome and appeals to sycophants and the mob. After his loss at Dyrrachium he changes markedly. But the question is whether he improves morally or merely puts on a façade. Critics differ on this question: for one he remains a Machiavellian whose every action is merely a tactical move in his campaign for the empire; for another, he grows less selfish and gains in decency and stature.[31] The problem is that Chapman provides no insight into Caesar's soul in the later parts of the play, presenting merely his public gestures and actions, inviting speculations about the motives behind them without satisfying our curiosity. Robert Ornstein calls him an "empty colossus."[32]

Only at one moment in the play does Caesar allow a glimpse into his thinking and feeling separate from a public gesture, in the one soliloquy he has before boarding the ship that will carry him and his fortunes across the stormy Adriatic Sea to muster his reinforcements at Brundisium (II.v.1–37). We must scan it closely.

Caesar begins by addressing the stormy night that imperils and seeks to spite his endeavor. As he scorns the elements, his spirit strikes the spark of madness that Pompey says a man who seeks to rule the Roman empire needs—"the one is mad that undergoes it" (I.ii.183–184). Caesar is now a *fortunatus* supremely confident of "the necessity of fate for Caesar." Pride, arrogance, and an iron determination ring in his words when he speaks of himself as "I, that have ransack'd all the world for worth / To form in man the image of the gods"—the phrase that resembles closely what Chapman told Henry was Homer's achievement. With all this egotistical ambition, Caesar sees himself (and presumably Chapman saw him) as a creative spirit who out of chaos forges a new fate for Rome as the civilizer of the world. Plutarch's *De Fortuna Romanorum,* on which Chapman drew for this play, pointed the way in this direction. Chapman merged this idea with the Nietzschean hope for the evolution of supermen that was his favorite vision. He admired the heroic fervor of overreaching heroes like Achilles, which he bestowed on two other of his tragic heroes, Bussy and Byron. But, as the tragic falls of these heroes show, he was also keenly aware of the potentially dehumanizing force of this spirit.[33] And Caesar's spirit is ambivalent; his vision for Rome poses the question whether he aims at engendering an ethical and cultural elite or a race of military robots.

There are further ambivalences. Caesar claims that he "Must like them [that is, the gods] have power to check the worst / Of all things under their celestial empire"—one is gratified that he seeks to curb merely the "worst," whatever that may be. He obviously feels already a king here—he calls himself so by a slip of the tongue a little earlier (II.iii.109)—and kings, as James told his son, are little gods. But Caesar's imagination reaches into boundless realms; he sets himself above the elements and the turbulence of nations. His passionate ambition will not let him rest

> till the crown be set
> On all my actions, that the hand of Nature,
> In all her worst works aiming at an end,
> May in a master-piece of hers be serv'd
> With tops and state fit for a virtuous crown.
> (*II.v.18–21*)

Caesar's overweening ambition aims at ruling Rome masterfully. The question is whether the "virtuous crown" to which he aspires indicates his desire to govern ethically or expresses his fascination with the Machiavellian *vertù,* with which Chapman elsewhere associates the word *virtue.*[34] Will Caesar strive for the moral improvement of the world or for the display of his power and strength? This, of course, is also the kind of question that must have gone through Chapman's mind as he watched Henry develop toward manhood.

The ending of the play leaves the question up in the air what kind of ruler Caesar will be or was, except that he was efficient. It is true that Caesar's gestures and actions in the play become increasingly noble and magnanimous, but his thoughts remain hidden, and it is possible to suspect Machiavellian motivations even in his most generous acts. The audience—one of readers, as it has turned out—is relegated to making up their own minds. After Dyrrachium, Caesar is gracious to the captured Vibius, sending him back to Pompey with an offer of peace. Antony suggests that Caesar is maneuvering to bring about a change of fortune by making Pompey refuse an offer apparently so gently proffered, a suggestion that Caesar rejects peremptorily: "I try no such conclusion, but desire / Directly peace" (II.iii.83–84). But this may be political posturing, and the result of the offer is in any case that predicted by Antony. Before, during, and after the battle of Pharsalia, Caesar is at the crest of his fortune and at his best. Pompey's weakness makes Caesar's strength even more apparent. Instead of fearing fortune like his adversary, Caesar confidently looks toward and beyond victory. In a lengthy speech, he prays that the gods will give him victory and that "my use of it / May wipe the hateful and unworthy stain of tyrant from my temples, and exchange it / For fautor of my country" (III.ii.113–116). He conjures up a vision of a future Rome, radiant, full of riches, a treasure of art, and a center of world civilization. But again, one might say that he speaks for public consumption. And this speech is similar to his subsequent magnanimous and compassionate gestures. He laments his slain officer Crassinius and devises an epitaph that links him (and himself) to the welfare of Rome: Crassinius "fought for Rome and died for Rome, / Whose public weal springs from his private tomb" (IV.ii.28–29). Caesar deplores the shedding of Roman blood and hopes that Brutus, who fought on Pompey's side, has escaped death. When Brutus turns up alive, Caesar welcomes him graciously. Caesar is a man of magnificent gestures: the reader is at liberty to ascribe them to a generous heart or a calculating mind.

Yet gestures account for much in the theater, and an audience, generally less skeptical than a reader, would presumably feel that Caesar is not merely upgrading himself publicly but that he is also strengthening himself morally. But Chapman has Caesar disappear after Pharsalia for two long scenes and most of a third, and these bring Cato to the fore as a counterforce. Cato is given the most devastating assessment of Caesar possible, one that leaves nothing good in him and evokes all too painfully the Machiavellian Caesar of the beginning. Cato impugns Caesar's justice, recalls his illegal raising of an army, and declares him guilty of all the bloodshed of the civil war. Cato rejects the notion that he should accept mercy from Caesar, "when death / Is tenfold due to his most tyrannous self" (IV.v.25–44). And, to quote Parrott's paraphrase of the subsequent, somewhat difficult lines: "Caesar's parts, which are so much admired, are outward shows, *tongue, show, falsehood,* which lead to bloody death; they are vainglory, villainy, and, rated at their best, they could be maintained with what a truly worthy man would cast away as insignificant, *parings.*"[35] The audience as well as the readers have the option to credit or discount Cato's character analysis: they may see here the true picture of Caesar underneath the varnish, or they may find Cato embittered and out of step with Caesar's change because of the philosopher's withdrawal to Utica.

The ambiguities of Caesar's character remain unresolved in the end. Caesar continues compassionate. He is horrified at Pompey's murder and punishes the murderers. He commands a sumptuous tomb and impressive statue to be erected for Cato in Utica, a change that Chapman made from his source, in which the citizens of Utica commemorated Cato in this manner on their own. But Caesar's motivations remain subject to doubt. He explains the punishment of Pompey's murderers by an aversion to seeing Roman blood spilled and by a desire not to "confirm the false brand of my tyranny / With being fautor to his murderer / Whom my dear country chose to fight for her" (V.ii.207–209). He is pushing generosity rather far by calling Pompey a fighter for Rome—Pompey triumphed indeed over some of Rome's enemies, but his last battles were against Caesar. One wonders whether Caesar hates tyranny or hates to be thought a tyrant—his concern about this "false" image is obsessive. And his nobility appears overstated. True, one expects noblesse by the victor in his final speeches; but is it not hypocritical for him to say that he "envies" Cato's death? Whatever Caesar may do or say, his besetting problem remains: he has not cleared his reputation and he has not come to terms with the Cato legend. The questions about his character are not resolved, and the play is open-ended.

Chapman may have been uncertain about the true nature of Caesar. In drawing an ambiguous portrait, he was quite in agreement with the contradictory and conflicting tradition of the Renaissance; Shakespeare's Caesar came from the same background.[36] One might wish though that Chapman had focused on the Caesarian dilemma a little more clearly in the end and that instead of the conventional (if problematic) necrologue for Cato by Caesar, the play would pose once more the question about which direction Caesar will go: will he become a Machiavellian conqueror-tyrant or a benevolent humanistic monarch of the kind that James envisioned in the *Basilikon Doron*?

By a dramatic design of fate, the legend of Prince Henry, that potential English Caesar, has also remained open-ended. We do not know how he would have borne himself as a king and whether he would have brought peace to England or war and ruin. Surely Chapman, like Daniel, hoped for the former and feared the latter. If my reading of the play and the times is accepted, Chapman aimed at creating a parallel between Henry and Caesar, but unlike the jingoists around the Prince, Chapman was reluctant to contribute to Henry's Caesarism. He saw in Henry's burning zeal, much as in Caesar's, a promise of greatness and a danger for world peace. With his sense of history and artistic and moral integrity, Chapman realized that a career like Caesar's should not be made a simple inspirational or cautionary tale. And he must have felt something of a malaise, the malaise of an old humanist faced with Machiavellian absolutism.

This malaise may finally be the reason why this provocative play never reached the stage; even if imperfect, it is certainly better than many plays that did. Surely the current associations of Prince Henry with Caesar made this a difficult play to perform, and Chapman's ambiguous characterization of Caesar increased the difficulty. Perhaps Chapman himself was dissatisfied with the portrait and with its application to Henry. Or perhaps those who were stirring the Prince's Caesarian ambitions were displeased with this puzzling and ambivalent Caesar. More likely, Chapman feared potential trouble and therefore withheld the play. The sewer-in-ordinary of Prince Henry could hardly afford to lose the favor of his employer.

NOTES

1. Cato was the choice of hero by Thomas Marc Parrott in his influential edition of *The Plays of George Chapman*, 4 vols. (1910; rpt. New York: Russell and Russell, 1961). References in this article are to this edition. For recent critics, Pompey is the choice of Elias Schwartz, "A Neglected Play by Chapman," *Studies in Philology*, 58 (1961), 140–159; Caesar is seen as the hero-villain by James F. O'Callaghan, "Chapman's Caesar," *SEL: Studies in English Literature, 1500–1900*, 16 (1976), 319–331.

2. For Henry's life and influence on literature, see J. W. Williamson, *The Myth of the Conqueror. Prince Henry Stuart: A Study of 17th Century Personation* (New York: AMS Press, 1978), and Elkin C. Wilson, *Prince Henry and English Literature* (Ithaca: Cornell University Press, 1946).

3. Parrott, *The Tragedies*, II, 655.

4. E. E. Stoll, *John Webster* (Boston: Mudge, 1903), p. 66. See also Ennis Rees, *The Tragedies of George Chapman* (Cambridge, Mass.: Harvard University Press, 1954), pp. 126–130, and Elias Schwartz, "The Dates and Order of Chapman's Tragedies," *Modern Philology*, 57 (1959–60), 80–82. The earlier dating is disputed by Robert Ornstein, "The Dates of Chapman's Tragedies Once More," *Modern Philology*, 59 (1962–63), 61–64.

5. Thomas Dekker and John Webster, *Northward Ho* (London, 1607), IV.ii, sig. E2^v.

6. *The Golden Age restor'd: The Culture of the Stuart Court* (Manchester: Manchester University Press, 1981), p. 67.

7. Williamson, p. 22.

8. *Observations upon the five first bookes of the Commentaries* (London, 1604), sig. f3^v. Compare Wilkins, p. 30.

9. *The Tragedy of Philotas* (1605), ed. Laurence Michel (New Haven: Yale University Press, 1949), p. 97.

10. Parrott, p. 656.

11. "Chapman's *Caesar and Pompey:* An Unperformed Play," *Modern Language Review,* 49 (1954), 467.

12. Frederick R. Fleay, *A Biographical Chronicle of the English Drama 1559–1642*, 2 vols. (London: Reeves and Turner, 1891), I, 65.

13. E. K. Chambers, *The Elizabethan Stage,* 4 vols. (Oxford: Clarendon Press, 1923), III, 259.

14. The title page of the second quarto of 1653 proclaims that the play was acted at Blackfriars. This is probably a bookseller's invention; in any case, the reference would have to be to the period after 1631.

15. For Chapman's problems with his patrons, see Charlotte Spivack, *George Chapman* (New York: Twayne, 1967), and Millar MacLure, *George Chapman: A Critical Study* (Toronto: University of Toronto Press, 1966).

16. On Cranfield, see Menna Prestwich, *Cranfield: Politics and Profit under the Early Stuarts* (Oxford: Clarendon Press, 1966) and R. H. Tawney, *Business and Politics under James I: Lionel Cranfield as Merchant and Minister* (Cambridge: Cambridge University Press, 1958).

17. Tawney, p. 276.

18. Thomas Fuller, *Worthies of England* (London, 1662), ed. John Nichols (London, 1811), p. 72.

19. See *DNB* and G. E. C., *The Complete Peerage,* ed. H. A. Doubleday and Hayward de Walden (London, 1937), pp. 683–690.

20. Parrott, pp. 658–662.

21. Suzanne F. Kistler, "The Significance of the Missing Hero in Chapman's *Caesar and Pompey,*" *Modern Language Quarterly,* 40 (1979), 339–357.

22. See Parrott's textual notes. The most conspicuous instance of roughness is II.i, the one farcical scene of the play. Except for ll. 83–95, which are in blank verse, the scene is in prose, the only one of this kind in the play. But the text approaches blank verse sporadically, and it is set up as verse, giving a general impression of doggerel. Fleay thought the scene a fragment of the old Caesar play of 1594, which he attributed to Chapman. Parrott surmised that the scene constituted Chapman's revision of some old scene either by Chapman or somebody else. It is presumably not by somebody else since it has the earmarks of Chapman's style and since it skillfully parodies a major theme of the play, the pursuit of fortune. I suspect that its "blank verse in the rough" represents Chapman's first draft. If Chapman looked upon it as embryonic poetry, he may not have thought his assertion in the Dedication contradictory that his style avoided "hasty prose." Jonson claimed that he wrote his poems first in prose, and a process of composition by mixing prose and poetry is quite likely for Chapman.

23. *Basilikon Doron* (1599; ed. 1616), in *The Political Works of King James* (Cambridge, Mass.: Harvard University Press, 1918), p. 40.

24. *Observations upon Caesars Commentaries* (London, 1609), sig. A2^v.

25. *Basilikon Doron,* p. 15.

26. (London, 1609), sig. 2^v. Compare Williamson, p. 35.

27. (London, 1610), f. 66.

28. Sir John Harington, *Nugae Antiquae,* 2 vols. (London, 1804), I, 390, quoted by Williamson, p. 33.

29. "Epistle Dedicatory: The *Iliads,*" in *The Poems of George Chapman,* ed. Phillis B. Bartlett (London: Oxford University Press, 1941), p. 385. In *Euthymiae Raptus or the Tears of Peace,* Chapman, again addressing Prince Henry, sees man as transformed into God's image through learning (*Poems,* p. 181).

30. Caesar was designated as a *fortunatus* by Plutarch in *De Fortuna Romanorum* (4 and 6), one of Chapman's sources. So was Sulla. Both are among the *fortunati* in Giovanni Pontano's *De Fortuna,* in *Opera,* I (Venice, 1518), f. 287.

31. Compare O'Callaghan versus Kistler.

32. *The Moral Vision of Jacobean Tragedy* (1960; rpt., Madison: University of Wisconsin Press, 1965), p. 80.

33. See Richard Ide, *Possessed with Greatness: The Heroic Tragedies of Chapman and Shakespeare* (Chapel Hill: University of North Carolina Press, 1980), p. 77.

34. See Richard Corballis, "Some Machiavellian Moments in English Renaissance Drama," in *Elizabethan Miscellany 2,* Elizabethan and Renaissance Studies, No. 71 (Salzburg: Inst. für eng. Sprache & Lit. Univ. Salzburg, 1978), pp. 16–17.

35. Parrott, p. 673.

36. See Ernest Schanzer, *The Problem Plays of Shakespeare* (New York: Schocken Books, 1963), pp. 16–23. Compare Kistler, p. 342.

Three Plays in One:
Shakespeare and *Philaster*

LEE BLISS

In ADDITION to a room and a wench, Beaumont and Fletcher shared an interest in literary romance, distinguished social pedigrees, and a close connection with Jonson and his circle. Yet Beaumont and Fletcher entered the Jacobean theatrical scene as more than literary gentry intent on dramatizing Sidney and Spenser for a sophisticated, coterie audience. Their plays owe as much to the immediate theatrical milieu as they owe to the late sixteenth-century aristocratic romances that critics have claimed as their sources.[1] From the beginning, Beaumont and Fletcher were both self-consciously interested in dramatic form, in its potential as an artistic medium, and also pragmatically concerned with the work of contemporary playwrights. For example, Beaumont's *Knight of the Burning Pestle* (1607) takes plays and audiences as its subject, while direct borrowings appear with his first play, *The Woman Hater* (1606).[2] Most interesting, perhaps, is the extent of Shakespeare's influence on both young men, even while they were still writing for the children's companies. *The Woman Hater* alludes throughout to numerous Shakespearean plays, both comedies and tragedies, and in *The Faithful Shepherdess* (1608) Fletcher employed a Shakespearean dramatic model to orchestrate the shifting amatory patterns borrowed from Spenser and Sidney.

Beaumont and Fletcher's debt to Shakespeare has of course long been recognized, their allusions and borrowings carefully tracked down and annotated. In larger matters, *Hamlet* is frequently seen as the primary source for *The Maid's Tragedy* as well as for *Philaster,* and Fletcher, throughout his long career, continued to use Shakespearean characters and situations and even to rewrite entire Shakespearean plays.[3] If such evidence of appropriation leads us simply to dismiss the younger dramatists as plot-starved plagiarists who debased their sources,[4] we will never inquire whether in their own work they achieved anything artistically independent and valuable. But perhaps Shakespeare should be seen neither as the yardstick against which his contemporaries' achievement must be measured nor, in a newer formulation, as the towering presence whose work must necessarily be deconstructed by subsequent dramatists.[5] Most probably, to his younger contemporaries Shakespeare was both good and successful, therefore influential (though perhaps no more so in his time than Jonson or Marston, both of whom also influenced Beaumont and Fletcher). Shakespeare's plays entered the realm of dramatic resources, just as Kyd's, Lyly's, and Marlowe's had for Shakespeare himself; he was available for witty allusion (and lines from *Hamlet* soon enjoyed the status of Marlowe's pampered jades or Kyd's *pocas palabras* and ocular fountains) as well as for more substantial pilfering. Setting aside minor borrowings or later major reworking of single plays, I want to explore the possibility that Beaumont and Fletcher finally found their distinctive tragicomic voice by aligning and rearticulating Shakespearean comedy and tragedy.

The early influence of Shakespeare is clear, both in the use of *Much Ado About Nothing* in *The Woman Hater* and in the inventive adaptation of *A Midsummer Night's Dream* for *The Faithful Sheperdess*.[6] Yet individually and in the first collaborations, Beaumont and Fletcher also favored dramatic experiment. Although *The Knight of the Burning Pestle* and *The Faithful Shepherdess* initially proved unsuccessful on the stage, Beaumont and Fletcher boldly shaped borrowed materials into wholly new kinds of comedy and tragicomedy. In their first and most completely source-bound joint effort, *Cupid's Revenge* (1608), they attempted to make tragedy out of Sidneian pastiche. Neither right comedy nor tragedy, *Cupid's Revenge* also misses the balance among generic elements that distinguishes the popular tragicomedies to come. Whether through inexperience as collaborators, recalcitrant and insufficiently transformed romance material, or a temperamental incapacity for tragedy, Beaumont and Fletcher could not satisfactorily integrate comic dramatic structures and characters with the fatal punishments of an angry god.[7] The young playwrights seem to have shared this modern critical judgment: although *Cupid's Revenge* was apparently a commercial success, they did not recapitulate its form in *Philaster* (1609).[8] *Philaster* reveals continued generic experimentation. Beaumont and Fletcher turned not to Sidney again but to the contemporary drama that had inspired their earliest plays. Although *Cymbeline* may have pointed Beaumont and Fletcher towards a new kind of tragicomedy,[9] the primary Shakespearean influences on *Philaster* predate Shakespeare's own final turn to romance.

That Beaumont and Fletcher set out intentionally to transform their Shakespearean heritage seems unlikely. A predilection for allusion and borrowing—in lines, situations, plots—is clear in their earlier practice; both young men liked building on other playwrights' work. That in beginning to write for the King's Men, Beaumont and Fletcher should revert to dramatic models—and especially to plays by their new employer's senior dramatist—should not be surprising. For whatever reason, Shakespearean allusions reappear in *Philaster*: the plays most frequently cited by annotators are *Hamlet, Othello,* and *Twelfth Night*. I shall argue, although I cannot prove, that these three plays also stand in more fundamental ways behind this first achievement of the Beaumont-and-Fletcher phenomenon. *Cupid's Revenge* is not forgotten, for Sidneian prose romance helped establish the cast of characters and typical relationships of the dramatists' later plays. A successful tragicomic structure emerges only when Beaumont and Fletcher adjust these characters to a more daring, yet also more specifically theatrical, generic mixture. Shakespeare provided convenient and familiar dramatic models for both genres. Filtering characters and situations through the prism of Shakespearean comedy and tragedy, Beaumont and Fletcher discovered an effective shape for the concerns and structure of feeling that we consider their hallmark. If specific earlier plays did help Beaumont and Fletcher to find their distinctive tragicomic blend, then investigating the ways in which they altered their Shakespearean points of departure will help to differentiate and define the younger playwrights' own subject and technique. It may enable us to see both what they were interested in dramatizing and how they finally evolved a dramatic form for their own romance-derived tragicomic vision.

The most immediately obvious dramatic source for *Philaster* is of course *Hamlet*. Itself a redaction of an earlier (now lost) revenge tragedy, *Hamlet* exerted an undoubted influence on Shakespeare's contemporaries. As a storyline, it may have seemed a sure thing to the budding dramatists; but I think we also sense in Beaumont and Fletcher a special affinity for this play and its themes, an attraction deeper than the promise of commercial success. Danby perhaps overestimates *Hamlet*'s determining effect, but he rightly sees that its mood and subject (its "moral bewilderment and confusion") clearly approximate *Philaster*'s; indeed the problem of piercing false appearances to discover truth plagues all of Beaumont and Fletcher's heroes.[10] Yet the isolated figure, cut off from his social and political identity and forced to maintain himself in the new King's court, had become a Jacobean commonplace, and such characters no longer required revenge motives, or their plots tragic outcomes. Contemporary playwrights had explored the situation's possibilities and discovered a romantic resolution—in both tragicomedy (Marston's *Malcontent* and, as it stands, the First Part of *Antonio and Mellida*) and comedy (Sharpham's *Fleer* and Day's *Humour Out of Breath*). Sidney's *Arcadia* is of course also pertinent here.

Both dramatic and nondramatic precedents suggest that the basic story, which found its most famous and compelling dramatic form in *Hamlet*, came to Beaumont and Fletcher associated with a variety of alternative developments and generic permutations. The younger playwrights have not simply taken Shakespeare's story and inadvertently, or perversely, gutted it of tragic force. *Cupid's Revenge* proved to be a salutary experiment. Aware now of the transformations necessary to turn tragedy to tragicomedy, they offered in *Philaster* their own redaction of the *Hamlet* model. Eschewing the example of other dispossessed-prince tragicomedies, Beaumont and Fletcher used Shakespeare himself to alter fundamentally the initial political conflict.

They start their modifications early. Philaster has no murdered father to avenge, since the Calabrian coup was apparently bloodless, and the usurper is also the true king of a country to which he can return. While the King's rule is more openly tyrannical than Claudius's, his sense of guilt is also more frequently on show. Shakespeare's Claudius has been demoted in *Philaster* to a flat, uninteresting (and unnamed) character, a paper tyrant swinging between remorse for past deeds and bombastic delusions of godhead. Yet the King's apparently genuine concern for his daughter partially prepares us for his acceptance of the true prince once Philaster has become *de facto* son-in-law and political savior. Arethusa herself assures us that she intends to be heaven's means of righting her father's political injustice, and her resemblance to Shakespeare's plucky romantic heroines encourages our belief in her ability to effect her will. Philaster shares Hamlet's moody indecisiveness, but little else. He is no disillusioned scholar come home to find his world collapsed, and neither the burden of an heroic past nor the moral imperative to redeem a fallen present presses heavily upon him. Loyal citizens and courtiers ensure Philaster's physical safety, and this absence of personal danger prolongs and emphasizes his vacillation between opposed commitments. Political concerns exist, but without the urgency that attends them in *Hamlet*. The issue at hand is a politic marriage, but there are no ghosts demanding blood revenge and no foreign military threats. The protagonist's youth also helps explain his hesitation and inaction: Philaster's tongue-tied, idealistic love for the usurper's daughter more easily balances the contrary private claims of family honor and personal rights. We are prepared for the (possibly complex) intrigue whereby Arethusa, alone or abetted by a comic providence, will manage to evade her father's wishes and substitute proper bridegroom for comic braggart-suitor. In short, the play mutes metaphysical or political questions and relegates them to backdrop status as vaguely elevating, generically appropriate, "high concerns."

If in *Philaster* Beaumont and Fletcher nod at *Hamlet* only to depart on their own course, if they are at some pains to tell us that their play will not be centrally preoccupied with politics or tragedy, why have they so persistently been accused of undermining their source and trivializing its Shakespearean premises? Part of what disturbs the play's surface lies in the particularity with which *Hamlet* itself, rather than the displaced-prince *topos,* is invoked, and the decision to use Shakespearean allusions as dramatic shorthand may indeed have been ill-advised. Moreover, despite preparations for a happy ending, Beaumont and Fletcher do not entirely suppress the potentially tragic (and eminently Jacobean) concerns that *Philaster* shares with *Hamlet* and contemporary satiric drama by Marston, Chapman, and Tourneur. Such questions remain, and they govern Beaumont and Fletcher's search for other Shakespearean models.

Evoking Shakespeare's *Hamlet* without supplying an analogous complexity in their own prince or in the situation—political or metaphysical—that he faces must make Philaster seem shallow. Eliot's strictures on inadequate objective correlatives really fit Philaster, and the extravagantly heroic intensity of his response, better than Hamlet. Moreover, Philaster does not enjoy Hamlet's dramatic preeminence. Beaumont and Fletcher do not share Shakespeare's earlier interest in tragedy of character. Yet while such distinctions may highlight different areas of emphasis in the two plays, the younger playwrights cannot be wholly absolved of having paid a rather high price for allusive, "Shakespearean" characterization. They have made comparisons inevitable as well as invidious.

Of more substantial structural importance, however, is the effect of *Hamlet* and contemporary satiric drama on the way that Beaumont and Fletcher bracket their central romantic complication with a contrasting frame. The play's initial dialogue establishes a socio-political setting, one whose force derives less from its links with the specific realities of James I's court than from its quasi-allegorical and convention-al assertion that the public world has corrupted the private one, that political relations have distorted sexual ones.[11] *Philaster*'s court may be less venal and sexually corrupt than that of *The Malcontent* or *The Revenger's Tragedy*, but it is still not the fully remediable world of romantic comedy. Like Hamlet, Philaster must operate in a capacious but also distinctly trivial and mundane society. Arethusa's waiting women span the gamut from virtue to vice, but the bawdy, cynical repartee that marks all courtly encounters compromises the loyal nobles, including Dion, from the very beginning of the play. A certain satiric rigor both sets off the Petrarchan extremism of Arethusa, Philaster, and Bellario and also qualifies the wish-fulfillment ending.

State concerns may not dominate *Philaster*, but they do affect all personal relationships, and they redefine the possibilities for romantic love. Braggart and sensualist, Pharamond proves undesirable as prince or husband. An opportunist in both politics and love, he finds his appropriate match in the unprincipled Megra. Political and domestic tyranny unite in the King, who sees in a well-calculated dynastic marriage the means to secure his uneasy throne. Even Philaster's apparent rejection of politics cannot free his romantic devotion of its taint. Arethusa wittily rationalizes her wooing with the idea of political restitution; her supposed sexual betrayal becomes Dion's clinching justification for political revolt.

Even as the play seems to turn away from *Hamlet*—away from politics and a court milieu—toward the apolitical solitude of the idealized countryside of romance, the lovers are never allowed fully to escape the world they flee. Political and social concerns can be defused, tamed to both the love theme and the final happy ending: thus Pharamond's political ambition is temporarily outmaneuvered in a sexual in-trigue straight out of city comedy. Yet even when the play moves outside the city, Beaumont and Fletcher do not allow it to become conventionally pastoral.[12] The court, too, hunts in the forest, and the gentry's smutty speculations reappear in the Woodmen's hearty appreciation of Megra's heroic sexual capacity and in their per-sonal knowledge that the best use of leafy brakes lies in "tumbling" errant court wenches (IV.ii.20-31).[13] What has often been taken as the romantic core of *Philaster* —the isolated display of its principals' exquisite sensibility in the face of the most sophisticated psychological pressures—remains shadowed by a cynical, earthy, and materialistic world that would find the lovers' "private sports" as unintelligible as does the Country Fellow.

Philaster cannot escape the political world or its challenge to his youthful idealism, but the altered *Hamlet* situation offers a way out of the hopelessly dead-locked loyalties that otherwise might bring on tragic catastrophe. Unlike Gertrude's betrayal of both son and first husband—the marriage to Claudius that is a given of Hamlet's world—Arethusa's defection is only imputed, the unforeseen result of her successful stratagem to expose Pharamond. In turn, Pharamond's prominence means that in *Philaster* the main political opponents are also romantic rivals. Through the willful marriage of his child, the triumph of true love can finally redeem a father's sins and return a kingdom to its rightful prince.

Although Hamlet's political quandary is soon left behind, his obsession with the problem of false appearances, of differentiating seeming from being, is not. One of the central concerns in *Philaster* is the way in which a loved woman's apparent disloyalty, a betrayal of love at the most private and fundamental level, can spread to poison all relationships and shatter the protagonist's sense of self. *Hamlet* offered Beaumont and Fletcher one dramatic model: it presents a vulnerable idealist who suffers imprisonment in a seemingly endless circle of suspicion and self-accusation as a consequence of his doubt and despair. Having transformed a political dilemma into a primarily amatory one, Beaumont and Fletcher find in other Shakespearean plays the way to pursue, yet also finally to resolve, a similarly anguished disillusionment.

In *Philaster* the woman upon whose faith the world's stability depends is now the romantic heroine, her guilt apparent, not real. The play shifts from *Hamlet* to romantic intrigue comedy in Act Two and then back to a tragic model, this time *Othello*. The slandered-beloved plot requires of Arethusa a new passivity. The challenge is Philaster's, and given Dion's willingness to lie, this test demands not clever intrigue but the lover's faith that should distinguish Philaster's devotion from the King's and courtiers' instant assumption of Arethusa's guilt. It is not a test that Philaster immediately passes. Nor is he equipped to suspend judgment while pursuing truth; like Othello, Philaster lacks Hamlet's ironic, if intermittent, detachment.

Philaster is a naif in love as well as politics, and the play's romantic emphasis makes the movement from *Hamlet* to *Othello* appropriate. Though in a manner more foreshortened and clumsily explicit than Shakespeare's, Beaumont and Fletcher establish in Act One the grounds of Philaster's mistrust: the romantic hero understands himself and the nature of passion as little as he understands women. In the wooing scene Philaster expresses considerable uneasiness with Arethusa's forthright declaration of love, for "how this passion should proceed from you, / So violently, would amaze a man / That would be jealous" (I.ii.94–96). Arethusa's and Bellario's later bold defenses of each other, like Desdemona's of Cassio, serve only to confirm their guilt before the lover who judges them.

In the shifting confrontations of Act Three of *Philaster,* allusions to *Othello* replace those to *Hamlet*. Such echoes suggest that *Othello* came naturally to mind as Beaumont and Fletcher developed their own protagonist's situation; they also, however, call attention to the lack of a substantial tempter-figure in *Philaster,* since Dion plays "honest Iago" for only a few lines.[14] *Othello* stands behind Beaumont and Fletcher's emotional orchestration in Act Three, but less in plot detail than as a master example for the tragic progress of a rash, unfounded jealousy. Beneath obvious differences the plays share a fundamental concern with the nature of romantic love and with its potential for psychological annihilation as well as for the re-creation of the self central to romantic comedy.

Beaumont and Fletcher typically suppress or ignore their characters' individual psychological complexity. Here they do not examine the process by which Philaster's love is overturned. Instead they emphasize a fundamental and disturbing similarity between the hero's romantic and idealistic response and the court's. The King shares his courtiers' cynicism, so that the mere existence of Bellario confirms Megra's accusation; yet Philaster too instantly convicts both page and mistress. Even before Dion swears, "I took them; I myself," Philaster demonstrates his readiness to believe the worst: to Dion's question whether he knows the "boy," Philaster mutters "Hell and sin know him!" (III.i.114, 104). Philaster's doubt is later confirmed when he learns that the King himself suspects his daughter—"O my misfortune! / Then 'tis no idle jealousy" (III.ii.71–72)—but in fact the corroboration afforded by a father's mistrust is not really needed. For Philaster, as for Othello, doubt itself constitutes proof. Faced with the ocular evidence of Bellario's "smooth . . . brow" and unchanged appearance, Philaster, like Othello, wavers: seeing that "the face you [gods] let him wear / When he was innocent is still the same, / Not blasted," Philaster "cannot now / Think he is guilty" (III.i.153–158).[15] The two knowledges confound each other, and such bifold authority splits the psyche and annihilates the bases for distinction, choice, even life itself. The lie with which Dion hoped to precipitate political revolt instead destroys the motive for any action whatever. Philaster flings at "False Arethusa" any "little right I have / To this poor kingdom" and seeks only a solitary wasteland in which to curse all women "Till my last hour" (III.ii.119–120,141). His friend banished, his lady become "A mere confusion, and so dead a chaos, / That love cannot distinguish," Philaster finds his sense of himself—and hence his world—betrayed at the very source of its meaning (III.ii.139–140). His "occupation" too is gone, but Philaster is a romantic young lover, not a warrior; his primary response to chaos is suicidal despair.

Following *Othello, Philaster* now focuses on its principal characters' obsession with private bonds and with the betrayals that obliterate public responsibilities and call in question the possibility of human truth and commitment. This movement also invokes the Shakespearean model that will ultimately provide a happy resolution and save the characters from their own mistakes. Philaster berating Bellario and Arethusa echoes not only Othello with Desdemona but also Orsino with Viola-Cesario at the point of utmost confusion in *Twelfth Night* (V.i). Shakespeare's late romantic comedy provides the least obvious and least analyzed of Beaumont and Fletcher's major "borrowings" for *Philaster*. Indeed, rather than consider the relation between *Philaster* and *Twelfth Night,* critics have preferred to complain about the major difference between the plays at this point: the spectacular surprise at the denouement when Bellario's secret identity is finally revealed to the characters and audience.[16] Yet the shift that combines *Othello* and *Twelfth Night* in Act Three also changes the play's emphasis and structure. It brings Bellario into almost equal prominence with Arethusa and Philaster, again diffusing character interest and discouraging tragic intimacy or empathy. It points to the way in which Beaumont and Fletcher find a structure appropriate to their concerns, a structure that abandons both Shakespearean tragic models.

In part, we discount Shakespeare's influence and at the same time castigate Beaumont and Fletcher as failed Shakespeares because we still think of Shakespeare primarily in terms of rich characterization rather than the structure of his plotting. However tied to a post-Renaissance exaltation of character, the general critical dismissal of Beaumont and Fletcher's efforts as at best flat and perfunctory, at worst inconsistent, may indeed be justified. Certainly one senses at times an arbitrary rhetorical heightening or a too evident manipulation of plot. Yet psychological depth and complexity, the gradual anatomizing of one heroic character's response to the discovery of evil and betrayal, do not engage Beaumont and Fletcher as goal or dramatic method. The younger dramatists have—and turn their sources to—their own interests. The concern with emotional design, within scenes or sequences of scenes, provides more than purely rhetorical or esthetic effects. Beaumont and Fletcher's focus lies in the pattern of experience illustrated by their characters' individual plights, not in the characters themselves. The diffusion of our attention among several characters and the repetition of experience or situation accomplish more than a recycling of effective scenes; they define a world in which such replication is inevitable.

That world is one in which appearance and reality remain indistinguishable, even as the gap between them threatens to assume tragic proportions. Both the public and the private worlds stand in desperate need of trust and communal unity, yet the play is peopled by men unable to trust others because unable to believe in themselves. Dion characterizes the situation early, in conventional Jacobean terms, as one in which "Every man ... has not a soul of crystal, for all men to read their actions through; men's hearts and faces are so far asunder that they hold no intelligence" (I.i.247–250). In such an atmosphere Dion (quite mistakenly) distrusts the citizens' loyalty and constancy, and Philaster has learned (rather bookishly and, as it turns out, ineffectually) that "Our ears may be corrupted; 'tis an age / We dare not trust our wills to" (I.i.316–317). Like Iago certain that "knowing what I am, I know what she shall be," the play's cynics judge others by themselves. And although the King extols Arethusa's silence and modesty as more movingly expressive than the "offered language" of those "whose eye / Speaks common loves," his own guilty hypocrisy destroys any real faith in the veracity of his daughter's eloquent appearances (I.i.105–107). Belief in Megra's accusation is, perhaps not surprisingly, immediate and widespread.

Philaster is not pure romantic comedy: love offers no separate, parallel but redeemed, world. Philaster credits Dion's allegation as quickly and naively as he had believed Arethusa's declaration of love and probably on the same grounds: "to suspect / Were base, where I deserve no ill" (I.ii.91–92). Philaster is not simply injured innocence, however. If Dion casually perjures himself in the public interest—"I'll say I know it; nay, I'll swear I saw it" (III.i.34)—Philaster does no less in his private pursuit of truth: in trying to trap Bellario, he defames both himself and Arethusa. His lie cannot uncover "truth"; it only provokes Bellario's anguished and convincing self-declaration. Left to believe and disbelieve the words and features that "look so truly ... though I know 'em false," Philaster is distracted, "mad," before a visible world that will not yield up its secret truths (III.i.280–281). As the courtiers make clear in later describing Pharamond and Megra, even the most guilty can "look" repentant, "like a mortified member," or so "modest" that no man can "see in her face but that she's honest" (IV.i.21–22, 29).

In such a world all are helpless, potential victims or initiators of mistrust. The long, frequently lovely arias of bewilderment and desertion may float free of any naturalistic moorings in character or situation, yet they create more than a typical Beaumont-and-Fletcher sentimentalism. They voice the condition in which all the play's characters, even the most decisive, act and have their being. Arethusa prays for a "breast / Transparent as pure crystal, that the world . . . may see the foulest thought / My heart holds" (III.ii.144–147), but in a fallen world she—and Bellario—can only repeatedly act out their constancy and hope one day to be believed. Time and circumstance must arbitrate what men cannot untangle; fear of deception prohibits simple faith.

With such dilemmas, *Philaster* touches *Twelfth Night* and blends it with *Hamlet* and *Othello*. Verbal parallels are few; the chief apparent link is the Bellario-Viola likeness (although Beaumont and Fletcher's figure is often traced instead to another Shakespearean "page," Julia in *Two Gentlemen of Verona,* or to Palna in Perez's continuation of Montemayor's *Diana*). Yet despite *Philaster*'s political frame and the perhaps deceptive invocations of *Hamlet,* the play moves to create a world and mood shared by Shakespeare's bittersweet romantic comedy. *Twelfth Night* employs the never-never-land setting of romance, its twins and shipwrecks. Yet its happy ending leaves intact our sense of its fragility; it reminds us that passion has proved an overmastering force and that the characters could not achieve the final saving reconciliations on their own.

Bellario, like Viola, must depend on "hasty time" to "reveal the truth to your [Arethusa's] abused lord / And mine" (III.ii.172–174; compare *TN,* II.ii.39–40). Trust may—perhaps must—be given arbitrarily. In *Twelfth Night* Viola and Antonio choose to believe of the sea captain and Sebastian that the mind will reflect the "fair and outward character" (*TN,* I.ii.51); Philaster accepts the "pretty helpless innocence" and apparent devotion of the page met at a forest well (I.ii.123). Yet in *Twelfth Night,* too, knowledge of a deceitful world sustains the lurking fear of betrayal that later explodes in hatred. Antonio's violent condemnation of the Viola whom he believes to be Sebastian—"O how vile an idol proves this god! / Thou hast . . . done good feature shame" (*TN,* III.iv.374–375)—would not be out of place in *Philaster.* In wildly variable temperament, Philaster certainly resembles Orsino, whose mind Feste calls "a very opal," and Orsino's repudiation of his trusted betrayers, both page and mistress, finds its echo in Philaster's denunciations of Bellario and Arethusa. Both masters threaten to kill the pages whom they loved out of, in Orsino's words, "a savage jealousy / That sometimes savours nobly" (*TN,* V.i.117–118). Each is surprised by his servant's prompt and devoted acquiescence. Cesario, "most jocund, apt, and willingly, / To do [Orsino] rest, a thousand deaths would die" (*TN,* V.i.130–131); Bellario, more sensationally, offers to be hewn "asunder, and whilst I can think / I'll love those pieces you have cut away . . . and kiss those limbs /

Because you made 'em so" (*Phil.,* III.i.255–258). Later, both Philaster and Orsino renounce their vengeance, award their mistresses to the traitorous servants, and, embittered, seek a total separation. The world of *Philaster* is darker, more uncertain, because the personal crisis has expanded to occupy the play's central action, not just a portion of the final act's resolution.

It is perhaps not fully demonstrable whether at this level *Twelfth Night* influenced *Philaster,* or whether Beamont and Fletcher's own handling of related romance materials led them to a final unmasking that could then play off *Twelfth Night*'s. More interesting is the fact that in establishing their own blend of the traditional dramatic kinds, Beaumont and Fletcher seemed to think in terms of specific earlier plays, not just abstract generic qualities. *Twelfth Night* proved particularly congenial, although *Philaster* does not simply jump from the desperate rush towards violent annihilation in *Othello* to the muted threats and fortunate revelations of comedy. The borrowed elements that had been self-consciously left discrete in their juxtaposition finally meld into a structure expressing the collaborators' particular voice. In Acts Four and Five, *Philaster* becomes Beaumont and Fletcher's own.

The stabbing in Act Four, before which Arethusa is allowed her prayers, nominally administers "a piece of justice" reminiscent of *Othello* (*Phil.,* IV.v.72). Yet changed dramatic circumstances belie the Shakespearean echo: Beaumont and Fletcher have radically transformed the situation's possibilities for heroism as well as for tragedy. By way of Juvenal's Sixth Satire, Philaster has just expressed an overriding impulse to escape his dilemma (although his pastoral vision of a chaste "mountain girl" to bear his "large coarse issue" is hardly idyllic). As is usual with Philaster, rage gives way to the desire for retreat and relinquishment. He asks Arethusa for his own death before he undertakes to punish her. Indeed each of the romantic principals begs death at the hands of his beloved, and this propensity for self-sacrifice changes the whole tone of what seem to be climactic confrontations. The impulse to obliteration is not projected but internalized. The struggle becomes a matter of who will kill whom, where all seek the release of death. All reach an abnormally heightened emotional state: if Philaster, claiming a "temperate ... heart," has a pulse that "keeps madman's time," the same diagnosis must apply to Arethusa and Bellario's eager submission to death at Philaster's hand (IV.v.46, 55).

Even as we watch a skewed reenactment of *Othello*'s finale, Beaumont and Fletcher's version isolates and distances its lovers' passionate self-abandon. Our detachment stems not merely from the substitution of superficial wounds for ritualized murder—the danger not the death—but from the treatment of the lovers themselves and the imposition of a frame that sets off the lovers' behavior.[17] First, Philaster's jealous fury is not allowed to build steadily and inexorably, and his desertion of rational concerns thus appears both undignified and implausible. In Act Four Philaster's characteristic emotional oscillation is both intensified and compressed: he swings now from passivity to rage within a few lines. Moreover, he draws attention not only to his intemperateness but also to the sensible response that his situation demands: "I am to blame to be so much in rage. / I'll tell her coolly when and where I heard / This killing truth" (IV.v.18–20). His immediately rekindled wrath, upon seeing Bellario with Arethusa (the perfect opportunity to confront them both), and his lapse into fatalistic "temperateness" within twenty lines are now marked off as extreme and inadequate, not tragically inevitable, responses. Even Bellario, willing to play the scene by Philaster's rules, observes that his master's "tongue" too "keeps madman's time."

Any tragic sense of relentless fatality is again subverted in Beaumont and Fletcher's treatment of the scene's emotional and rhetorical climax. A willing Arethusa, on the point of receiving "peace in death" from Philaster, is interrupted by the Country Fellow's comic turn. Critics focus on the Country Fellow for good reasons. The juxtaposition of styles and interpretations can hardly be accidental; the play's subtitle suggests the scene's popularity, and a woodcut of it decorated the first quarto's title-page. However critically disputed the effect, the Country Fellow's entrance changes our relation to the play's world, and Arethusa's surprising description of the potential tragedy that he has disturbed—"our private sports, our recreations" (IV.v.91)—ensures our sudden detachment. The wandering yokel's initial soliloquy brings to the scene of strained and ultimately suicidal passion a whole world of normal, stolid, but good-hearted folk, tragedy's asp-bearers who "hunt" only the occasional "gay sight" to round out a life that they find eminently worth living. He offers both a rhetorical contrast and the common sense that "sees" literally and hence explodes our acceptance of the action as, for dramatic purposes, both plausible and affecting. Philaster is driven off by more than a sword stroke.

The play balances delicately between two opposed views of its action. (And for this balance to hold it is necessary that we, as well as Philaster, remain ignorant of Bellario's sex. Beaumont and Fletcher's irony here is not that of *Twelfth Night*'s where an informed audience watches with amusement the characters' misunderstandings of people and events; Bellario must not be known for what she is if the *Othello* action is to have a potentially tragic weight.) The central misapprehension, with its attendant emotional crisis, is all-important to its sufferers, capable of overturning their world and annihilating the will to live; at the same time it is unreal, incomprehensible to the ordinary man and to the courtiers who arrive soon after him. Even to the play's audience, which knows Arethusa's innocence and thus at least half the truth masked by appearances, it is a mistake become nightmare through Philaster's own disoriented imagination, the product of a mind spinning helplessly in a void that it has itself created. Neither view cancels the other. The play makes us participate in both.

This balance is, by and large, maintained until the end of the play, and from it arises that peculiar esthetic distance and structure of feeling which we associate with Beaumont-and-Fletcher tragicomedy. The rustic humorist need not return (although the comic Citizens do). The play has grounded us in its own version of a normal world—unromantic and itself conventional, but also distinct from the stereotyped "corrupt court" of the political frame. The shift in perspective releases us from the demands of Philaster's claustrophobic hysteria and reminds us of our own status as spectators; through it the play exposes its own artifice as well as Philaster's emotional distortions. Sharing with the authors an amused awareness of their protagonists' limitations, we find the distance from action appropriate to nontragic experience. We can accept Philaster as romantic hero in a new sense, for we are not asked wholly to adopt the young lovers' estimate of themselves or their predicament.[18] We can now fit the hyperbolic praise of Philaster to its proper function as the guarantee, often provided in comedy, that the extravagantly emotional young man, whom we see apparently committed to misguided extremism in the pursuit of virtue, will prove salvable as both husband and ruler. Shakespeare was not above hedging his bets with the same device, with Orsino as well as other young rulers overthrown by first love. And as in Shakespearean comedy, learning how to behave in one role teaches the maturity needed in other, ostensibly unrelated, roles.

We can now watch with some detachment Philaster's psychological disintegration as he confronts Bellario. Despite the development of such potentially tragic situations, Beaumont and Fletcher have also assured us from the outset that the gods are just and that in some unforeseen manner things will work out. In immediate terms, Philaster's frantic oscillations—the stabbing and repentance, the creeping in and out of bushes—provide unexpected theatrical excitement while also tracing the possible progress of an abnormality that has already been acknowledged and placed by the dramatists. At the same time, self-destruction provides the opportunity for re-creation. Philaster discovers the grounds for belief in his lovers' loyalty, for Bellario repeats and confirms Arethusa's behavior. Through their faith, Philaster finds himself. He can now move out of the private world of his own fantasies, the nightmare wood in which all the lovers have wandered. The play's two worlds join on the comic note of Philaster and Bellario's wonderfully hyperbolic tussle over the honor of taking blame for Arethusa's wounds. In this verbal contest, each fabricates publicly acceptable explanations—a servant's revenge, a prince's political ambition—quite foreign to the actual, and in some sense much more serious, psychological dislocations that we have witnessed.

Philaster's transformation is neither immediate nor complete. When he defends Bellario's worth and seeks to expire in his friend's embrace, Philaster continues his adolescent self-dramatizing, his desperate clinging to heroic absolutism in language and gesture (IV.vi). It recurs later when he offers to kill himself in shame at having been tricked into allowing Bellario's torture. At Dion's ambiguous assertion that "All's discovered," Arethusa quite sensibly demands, "What is discovered?" (V.v.130, 132). In contrast, Philaster's immediate offer to stab himself hints at a readiness to retreat from adult responsibilities. Still, the emergence of a new, more mature Philaster is sketched, and more important, this development allows Beaumont and Fletcher to bring into the comic resolution their concern with problems of identity and love's proper nature.

In prison, reunited with both Arethusa and Bellario, Philaster discovers the catharsis of asking and receiving forgiveness. Whether adapted from *Lear* or no, a new plain style seems to mark Philaster's change: "Take me in tears betwixt you, /

For my heart will break with shame and sorrow" (V.ii.34–35). With this new accent (even granting its emphasis on the pathetic) and the wedding masque in which Bellario as Hymen solemnly recounts his "glad story" of the twined cedar branches, reconciliations and resolved impossibilities associated with romance enter the political world. Arethusa strikes an appropriately wondrous final note as she introduces her "plain truth" that

> this gentleman,
> The prisoner that you gave me, is become
> My keeper, and through all the bitter throes
> Your jealousies and his ill fate have wrought him,
> Thus nobly hath he struggled, and at length
> Arrived here my dear husband.
>
> *(V.iii.46–51)*

The ending is not unalloyed romance, however, and the inaccurate (albeit lovely) imagery of shipwreck and tested innocence reminds us of its differences from as well as its likeness to romance. Not all the generic expectations of romance will be fulfilled. Private reconciliations remain separate from public ones: the King still plays political tyrant as well as heavy father, and his conversion depends upon the external threat presented by Pharamond's capture and the Citizens' revolt.

Philaster's personal integration seems complete when the King suddenly restores the Prince's political identity ("Be yourself"). Philaster demonstrates a new poise and self-command with the Citizens: "I am what I do desire to be, your friend; / I am what I was born to be, your Prince" (V.iv.97–98). When Megra repeats her accusation, Philaster refuses to share the King's rekindled belief in Arethusa's sexual misconduct. Beaumont and Fletcher frame the challenge to Philaster's love in terms that recall this world's pervasive distrust and its corrosion of love and friendship. With no apparent means to clear her name, Arethusa is in exactly the position she was at the end of Act Two. As she says, for her audience either her guilt or innocence "lies in your belief" (V.v.43). The King's reply proves him, in this regard, unchanged. Philaster's experience of the loyalty of both his lady and his page leads him to the proper response, although the note of rising tension in his answer might prepare us for a relapse.

That his faith can yet be shaken, that he makes himself the butt of our laughter at the final discovery, neither negates the dramatists' treatment of their serious concerns nor cancels utterly Philaster's own status as prince and husband. However less than ideal, he will not be the first young man in a comedy to bring immaturity and even irresponsible egotism to the altar. *Othello* becomes joined to the comic conventions of *Twelfth Night,* and to encourage our acceptance, we are offered Arethusa. At the beginning as "yet / No woman," she has found "herself" in marriage, even though disowned by her father (I.i.103–104;V.iii.68). More important, she has demonstrated both the wit and the constancy to prove her husband's Viola.

In this blend of genres lies the formal solution to *Philaster* and also, to modern critics, the root of its failure. The apparent trajectory of the action is towards death; the world of the play destroys the possibility of love, trust, or commitment. Pressures set up by the cues for tragedy in *Philaster* threaten to explode Beaumont and Fletcher's final demand that we accept another genre—one allowing for compromise and manipulated endings. Allusion to specific Shakespearean plays as potential patterns for the action of *Philaster* only compounds the problem. The opening political frame of *Philaster* leads us to expect Hamlet—or, shifting gears, at least Orlando—but we are given Orsino.

To be fair to Beaumont and Fletcher, they do not promise the consolations provided in their final generic model quite so abruptly or cynically as critics have implied. The dramatists maintain the balance established in Act Four. Even more than the ending of *Twelfth Night,* that of *Philaster* is poised delicately between the celebration of romance and the acknowledgment that the satisfactions of romance belong to the world of fairy-tales and art. Without a wise clown to remind us of a world resistant to happy endings, Beaumont and Fletcher preserve the distinctive tragicomic tone of *Philaster* to the end by focusing on Bellario. In one sense, with such a conclusion the dramatists sustain the return to romantic idealism: we end with a lyric description of love that emphasizes selfless and total service, and with Arethusa's serene confidence in welcoming Bellario into the marital arrangement. Yet only Arethusa, not Bellario, ideally belongs to romantic comedy. Indeed the disguised page resembles Viola-Cesario less than she does the fictional "sister" described to Orsino, that forlorn maiden whose "history" is a "blank" because "she never told her love" (*TN,* II.iv.110–111). The last lines of *Philaster* stress the static pathos and accepted frustration of desire that limit Bellario's character.[19] The drive toward union, regeneration, and society's future typical of comedy is halted. In the equivocal nature of Bellario's final identity, we are recalled to Beaumont and Fletcher's central preoccupation with feelings of abandonment, with helpless immobility and the annihilation of self. Even as the skewed comic conclusion provides the properly wonderful conversions and recognitions, it marks the dramatists' attenuation of the sense of openness and fresh possibilities aroused at the end of a romance.[20] Despite an early emphasis on intrigue, only through the introduction of fortunate chance, in both the political and private realms, can the plot be untangled—Pharamond's sudden interest in the city's marvels and Bellario's secret identity. Given the play's world and the extent to which its inhabitants remain untransformed (Pharamond, Megra, the courtiers), the muted assurances are appropriate.

A certain detachment from the resolution of the play suits Beaumont and Fletcher's dramatic method throughout. Theatrically successful within its own terms, *Philaster* offers at least part of its audience the esthetic pleasure of further recognitions. Literary allusiveness ensures our awareness of the play as art, indeed its special status at a double remove from life. If the present argument is at all persuasive, Beaumont and Fletcher insist not only on the fictionality of their play but also on its evolution from earlier plays in each of the genres combined in it. Evocations of *Hamlet* and

Othello help characterize the world of *Philaster* as a potentially tragic one; its dangers are real, although in this case they can be averted by proving that Bellario has not betrayed Philaster. The allusions themselves, and the transformations by which Shakespearean tragedy slides toward romance, also underline the characters' inadequacy, their inability to handle a tragic world. They require the benevolent Providence of romance, because even discovering the old truths does not ensure the capacity—in either the King or Philaster—to act on them.

At the end Bellario both emblematizes this fundamental helplessness and provides the means by which, in a final allusion, Beaumont and Fletcher ask us to acknowledge and participate in their self-conscious art. The confrontation between Dion and his daughter halts the action at just the point where romance and tragedy seem hopelessly deadlocked; through it the authors provide the final, wished-for surprise in precisely the form to elicit the audience's own sophisticated recognition. In the final reunion, the conventional, patterned exchange of information places *Philaster* not only in the line of its dramatic models but also within a long history of idealistic, gracious, and artificial entertainments, a tradition stretching back from *Twelfth Night,* through Sidney's *Arcadia,* to the origins of romance. With it, the specific and generic "parts" from which *Philaster* is constructed fall into place. Their unity constitutes Beaumont and Fletcher's claim to a distinctively Jacobean maturity. Successfully, if allusively, they create an artful, partly patchwork, imitation of our fallen world. Frankly exercising the artist's prerogative to correct creation, they then redeem it with the sleight of hand that simultaneously fills and acknowledges the confines of their art.

NOTES

1. In the Revels edition of *Philaster* (London: Methuen, 1969), Andrew Gurr argues for Sidney's *Arcadia* as the playwrights' primary inspiration and for the play itself as "no less than the translation of [Sidney's] high literary and educational designs" into the form of "commercial drama" (p. xxv; compare also pp. lix-lxxi). Gurr extends in purely literary terms the sociological analysis of John F. Danby's influential *Poets on Fortune's Hill: Studies in Sidney, Shakespeare, Beaumont and Fletcher* (London: Faber and Faber, 1952), although Gurr also argues, convincingly I think, against charges of royalist absolutism stemming from Coleridge but upheld in subtler form by Danby (compare Gurr's Introduction, pp. lii-lviii). Both of these fine studies insist on Sidney and nondramatic romance as the most illuminating approach to Beaumont and Fletcher's plays, however, and my own essay seeks to explore a different, though largely complementary approach.

2. Dating the Beaumont and Fletcher plays must remain conjectural, but I have assumed the sequence that is, with a few notable exceptions, generally accepted: Beaumont's *The Woman-Hater,* 1606, and *Knight of the Burning Pestle,* 1607; Fletcher's *Faithful Shepherdess* and, probably, the joint *Cupid's Revenge,* 1608; *Philaster,* 1609; *The Maid's Tragedy* and, perhaps, *The Coxcomb,* 1610; *A King and No King,* 1611. For the collaborative plays, I do not try to distinguish Beaumont's or Fletcher's individual contribution. I would extend to all the collaborative works Gurr's conclusion about *Philaster*: discussing these plays according to the portions assigned each dramatist—whether by Cyrus Hoy's seven articles on "The Shares of Fletcher and his Collaborators in the Beaumont

and Fletcher Canon" (*Studies in Bibliography*, 8–9, 11–15 [1956–62]) or others—would "stretch the available evidence [for scene division] beyond its breaking-point" and prove an unproductive exercise in disintegrating what seems so evidently a joint effort (compare Gurr, p. xxiv).

3. In *The Debt to Shakespeare in the Beaumont and Fletcher Plays* (1938; rpt. Folcroft, Pa.: Folcroft Press, 1969), D. M. McKeithan exhaustively collects certain and possible borrowings (see Chap. II for Beaumont's earlier plays and Chap. III for *Philaster, Cupid's Revenge,* and other collaborative dramas). Both Danby (pp. 202–204) and Robert Ornstein (*The Moral Vision of Jacobean Tragedy* [Madison: University of Wisconsin Press, 1965], pp. 171–178) stress *Hamlet* as the primary Shakespearean influence on *Philaster* and *The Maid's Tragedy.* Clifford Leech, too, investigates the indebtedness of *Philastar* to this Shakespearean tragedy, in *The John Fletcher Plays* (Cambridge, Mass.: Harvard University Press, 1962), pp. 83–86; Leech goes on to discuss not only the obvious dependency of *The Woman's Prize* on *The Taming of the Shrew* but also that of *Thierry and Theodoret* on *King Lear* and of *Bonduca* on *Cymbeline,* as well as a more restricted Shakespearean inspiration behind *The False One* and *A Wife for a Month.*

4. For example, David L. Frost's *The School of Shakespeare: The Influence of Shakespeare on English Drama 1600–42* (Cambridge: Cambridge University Press, 1968), Chap. 6: "Beaumont and Fletcher: 'Crows and Daws.' "

5. See, for example, Howard Felperin's *Shakespearean Representation: Mimesis and Modernity in Elizabethan Tragedy* (Princeton, N. J.: Princeton University Press, 1977).

6. For a more extended discussion of Fletcher's structural as well as thematic uses of *Midsummer Night's Dream* in *The Faithful Shepherdess,* see this author's "Defending Fletcher's Shepherds," *SEL: Studies in English Literature,* 23 (1983), 295–310.

7. As Eugene M. Waith says in *The Pattern of Tragicomedy in Beaumont and Fletcher* (New Haven, Conn.: Yale University Press, 1952), "If all the characters were saved from death and if the play ended in repentance and reconciliation, its total effect would be very little different. Even as it stands, with five deaths, *Cupid's Revenge* is more like tragicomedy than tragedy" (p. 14).

8. In "The Popularity of *Cupid's Revenge*" (*SEL: Studies in English Literature,* 19 [1979], 215–227), John H. Astington suggests that this commercial triumph may explain the King's Men's eagerness to acquire the young authors' services (p. 218).

9. In *The Influence of Beaumont and Fletcher on Shakespere* (Worcester, Mass.: Oliver B. Wood, 1901), Ashley H. Thorndike argues for Beaumont and Fletcher's priority, but his thesis has not been generally accepted. The possibility that either play might somehow explain the other must remain open until the problems in dating both are resolved. *Cymbeline* and *Philaster* may also have appeared at the same time. Gurr sensibly reviews the arguments in his Introduction, pp. xlv–l, and establishes the plausibility of simultaneous production in 1609, when the theaters reopened.

10. Danby, p. 203; see also note 3.

11. Countering aspersions of escapism, Peter Davison, in "The Serious Concerns of *Philaster*" (*ELH,* 30 [1963], 1–15), argues for a preoccupation in the play with a serious contemporary political concern, the split between King and Parliament. Davison here extends and develops the work of M. G. M. Adkins in "The Citizens in *Philaster*: Their Function and Significance," *Studies in Philology,* 43 (1946), 203–212. Despite such claims, specific political concerns (as opposed to more generalized and conventional ones related to "corrupt courts"), in Philaster's Sicily or James's London, do not seem to press very seriously on the play's action. Gurr takes up the matter with more restraint in his Introduction, pp. li–lviii, and sensibly concludes the likelihood of Beaumont and Fletcher's sympathy with Dion's rather generalized criticism of the King in IV.iv.

12. Waith notes that the two apparently contrasting worlds—the sixteenth-century historical and political Sicily and the idyllic pastoral Sicily of Theocritus, whose spring gives its name to Princess Arethusa—are related in the play, "one implying the other. The world of the play is not entirely the world of pastoral romance, nor is it a true reflection of the world of actuality. The woods echo

Philaster's worldly disillusionment, and the court is, after all, only pseudohistorical" (p. 17). Indeed the court is less historical than it is the product of Jacobean dramatic conventions.

13. All quotations from *Philaster* will be taken from Gurr's Revels edition, cited in note 1. Quotations from Shakespeare's plays will be to the Arden editions: *Othello,* ed. M. R. Ridley, 7th ed., rev. (London: Methuen, 1958) and *Twelfth Night,* ed. J. M. Lothian and T. W. Craik, 2nd ed., rev. (London: Methuen, 1975).

14. In the confrontations in Act Three, the most interesting verbal recollections of *Othello* in *Philaster* are associated with Bellario. When Bellario tells Philaster, "You are abused; / Some villain has abused you" (III.i.216–217), he echoes Shakespeare's Emilia. In the "brothel scene" of *Othello,* Emilia twice uses the word *abused,* once to Othello (*Oth.,* IV.ii.14–16) and once, in language more nearly repeated in *Philaster,* to Desdemona and Iago: "The Moor's abus'd by some most villainous knave" (*Oth.,* IV.ii.141). Asked by Philaster to testify against Arethusa, Bellario also briefly stands in for Iago. When Othello demands of Iago, "Show me thy thought. . . . By heaven I'll know thy thought," Iago replies, "You cannot, if my heart were in your hand; / Nor shall not, whilst 'tis in my custody" (*Oth.,* III.iii.120, 166–168); Philaster collapses this dialogue into a single plea to Bellario: "Tell me thy thoughts; for I will . . . rip thy heart / To know it; I will see thy thoughts as plain / As I do now thy face" (*Phil.,* III.i.235–238). Although these seem genuine verbal echoes and suggest that *Othello* had come to mind as a potentially useful design for this portion of *Philaster,* it is worth noting that the lines are memorable in their Shakespearean context because of the dramatic irony's shock value; this is lost in Beaumont and Fletcher's transposition of speakers.

15. Philaster here echoes a doubting Othello's anguished response to Desdemona's innocent appearance: "If she be false, O, then heaven mocks itself, / I'll not believe it" (*Oth.,* III.iii.282–283).

16. Once the "surprise" is revealed, however, Beaumont and Fletcher share their joke with the audience, and at Philaster's (as well as Dion's) expense. As Gurr notes, Philaster's "joyful hysteria" at discovering his page to be female mixes comedy with pathos (p. lxiv); I would say that, along with Dion's interview with Euphrasia-Bellario, it tips the balance. My own criticism of *Philaster*'s ending would be that stopping the play to develop the new situation (including Euphrasia's lengthy account of her love's history) destroys the dramatic rhythm; Beaumont and Fletcher awkwardly (though I think intentionally) seek a final change in the play's mood while insisting on a last-minute *coup de théâtre.*

17. The term, though not the argument, is Arthur C. Kirsch's; see *Jacobean Dramatic Perspectives* (Charlottesville: University Press of Virginia, 1972), pp. 43–44.

18. Although I think Clifford Leech's general argument mistaken, his description of this double effect is apt: "They are telling a romantic story, it is true, and will bid us rejoice in the lovers' final happiness, but they are under no illusions about the nature of their romantic hero" (p. 89). In suggesting that *Philaster* was designed merely as a tidier version of *Hamlet* (p. 84), Leech moves away from the play's real emphasis, but the idea of a delicate and complex response (however "simple" the characters and their story) is important and nearer the play's balance than Philip J. Finkelpearl's dismissal of Philaster as simply "a comic fool in the tradition of . . . unsure husbands and lovers . . . obsessed by cuckoldry" ("Beaumont, Fletcher, and 'Beaumont & Fletcher': Some Distinctions," *English Literary Renaissance,* 1 [1971], 155).

19. Describing the origin of her devotion to Philaster, Bellario both recalls Othello's unself-conscious wooing of Desdemona and emphasizes the loneliness to which altered circumstances have consigned her. Bellario reports that her father "oft would speak / Your worth and virtue, and . . . I did thirst / To see the man so raised" (V.v.158–161; compare *Oth.,* I.iii.128–129: "Her father lov'd me, oft invited me, / Still question'd me the story of my life"). Like Desdemona, Bellario fell in love with the hero through his language, for she says, "I did hear you talk / Far above singing" (*Phil.,* V.v.173–174). While Desdemona can, like Arethusa, lead her suitor to declare his passion,

Bellario's love isolates and silences her, since "for I knew / My birth no match for you I was past hope / Of having you" (*Phil.*, V.v.181–183). The use of reminiscences of Desdemona to rationalize Bellario-Euphrasia's disguise underlines Beaumont and Fletcher's very different conception of their character.

20. Whoever is responsible for the First Quarto (Q1)—either Beaumont and Fletcher or, more probably, another hand (compare Gurr, pp. lxxii–lxxix)—the author of its truncated final section tidies up the comic conclusion and stresses its resemblance to romantic comedy and to *Twelfth Night*. In Q1, Pharamond's parting vow of revenge recalls Malvolio's. More important, Bellario comes forward immediately after Megra's accusation, to "reveal her hair" to her father (as the stage direction has it); a husband is provided for her (Thrasiline, whom we are now told she once loved); and Galatea's match to Cleremont rounds off the story with a triple wedding worthy of Shakespeare at his least probable. The Second Quarto offers two major changes. It recasts the Dion-Euphrasia recognition to resemble more closely that of Viola and Sebastian in *Twelfth Night*. Dialogue replaces Bellario's silent removal of her cap, and while a patterned exchange is conventional in such scenes, the additional speeches are markedly closer to those of *Twelfth Night* than to those of, for instance, *The Comedy of Errors* or *Pericles*. In the Second Quarto's conclusion then, Beaumont and Fletcher pointedly refuse to reproduce the multiple couplings of either *Twelfth Night* or Q1. Q2's "impaired" comic ending thus expresses in little Beaumont and Fletcher's originality; it exemplifies the transformation of specific and generic antecedents that produced their distinctive tragicomic structure and tone.

Jonson's Alchemists, Epicures, and Puritans

ROBERT M. SCHULER

THE DEBATE over Jonson's satirical purpose and dramatic method in *The Alchemist* has tended to shift between two poles of emphasis: was his primary aim to satirize two "social pests" of his day, Puritans and the professors of alchemy, or to ridicule "human greed and credulity" through the vehicle of alchemy?[1] The more we have come to understand his erudite use of the metaphor of alchemy to articulate themes, to effect characterization, and simply to make elaborate jokes, however, the less simple has this question become. Thus one critic argues that Jonson identifies himself with Subtle, as "symbolic comic alchemist, who brings to perfection the intentions of nature," another that he is the detached artist-alchemist who comically/ chemically "distills" his characters so as to reveal their ultimate baseness.[2] These suggestions, while not always consonant with each other, seem at least generally right, especially when considered in light of Jonson's witty address "To the Reader," which, although neglected by most critics, nicely anticipates the analogy between poetry/drama and alchemy. If the reader is but a "Pretender" to understanding, Jonson warns, the reader is "never more fair in the way to be cozened (than in this Age) in Poetry, especially in Plays"; for the supposed "professors" of art, "by simple mocking at the terms, when they understand not the things, think to get off wittily with their ignorance. Nay, they are esteemed the more learned and sufficient for this, by the many, through their excellent vice of judgement."[3] Thus Jonson hints that the poetasters are just like the wordy Subtle himself, that "smoky persecutor of nature" (I.iii.100); and the undiscerning member of the audience or the mere "Reader" (that is, not an "Understander") is no more than the fool taken in by the verbal dexterity of sham alchemists who also "(to gain the opinion of copy) utter all they can, however unfitly" ("To the Reader," p. 228). Credulity is credulity, whether its object is false alchemy or bad poetry.[4] Jonson, it is implied, is the true artist-alchemist: he does not "cozen" or "run away from Nature," but uses language justly and (as the "Prologue" has it) *tries* to "cure" us—transform us into something better, if we will but own our follies, as we see them reflected in the actions of his characters.

These kinds of insights regarding the metaphor of alchemy as art seem to be central to the play's themes and even to Jonson's general conception of himself as a morally significant dramatist. In reading *The Alchemist,* one must, however, maintain a balance between the metaphorical and the literal, the abstract and the

171

concrete. Herford and Simpson characterize Jonson's interest in the subject of alchemy itself in this way: "The alchemist stood with one foot in the region of the
prodigious, which allured Jonson's burly and vehement imagination, while the other
was planted firmly on that ground of current human nature and everyday experience
which satisfied his Humanist taste."[5] This comment suggests that against the thematic and imaginative uses of alchemy we must always place the concrete, the "everyday," the factual and historical. The present essay attempts to extend our understanding
of Jonson's complex dramatic art by singling out a very specific, historical aspect of
alchemy that, I think, serves as an object of ridicule in itself and at the same time
provides Jonson with the dramatic and figurative means of integrating various
strands of his satire. I am referring to the historical links between alchemy, Puritanism, and millenarianism. In brief, my argument is this: (1) in *The Alchemist* Jonson
presents alchemy and Puritanism (specifically, Anabaptism) as similar kinds of
frauds, and in this analogy he was both responding to an actual nexus of ideas and
analyzing that nexus with profound psychological insight; (2) while the Anabaptist
Brethren's pursuit of the philosophers' stone for the sake of the "glorious discipline"
provides the dramatist with a *means* of satirizing pride and greed hypocritically
posing as piety, it also reflects accurately the actual political millenarianism
of the radical Puritan sects that is one of the *objects* of Jonson's satire: "Verily,
'tis true," Tribulation blatantly claims, "We may be temporal lords ourselves, I take
it" (III.ii.51–52); (3) the best way to understand Jonson's figurative and dramatic
use of these topical materials is through a reconsideration of the pivotal character,
Sir Epicure Mammon; for as different as he appears to be from the Brethren, his is
the fun-house mirror's image of the Anabaptists that, through distortion and exagger-
ation, shows most clearly their specific follies; (4) a recognition of Jonson's dramatic
method of mirroring aids in our understanding of the play's morally ambiguous
dénouement.

I

The historical links between alchemy and Puritanism, first of all, have by now been
well established. Especially among the radical sectaries of the mid-seventeenth century have scholars been able to demonstrate affinities with Paracelsian medicine and
alchemy,[6] but Harold Fisch has shown that even the moderate virtuosi of the seventeenth century considered themselves *adepti;* moreover, their conception of the
"priesthood of Nature" had been anticipated a century earlier by the highly influential Paracelsus (d. 1541):

> They form a body of the elect rather after the manner of the predestined few in Calvinism
> and perhaps the same false and narrow application of the Hebraic Covenant-doctrine is
> here at work. The idea of the naturalists as an elect and exclusive priesthood had been
> powerfully expressed by Paracelsus in the sixteenth century; he had thought of himself
> especially as having been divinely elected to bring to light the great *arcana* of Nature, and

from this brooding illusion of special tasks and exclusive revelations, issued many of the eccentric aspects, the strange obsessions of alchemy and iatrochemistry in the period we are considering.[7]

In England as early as the 1570s we have an example of an English Puritan preacher who identified himself as both a Calvinist *electus* and an alchemical *adeptus*,[8] and from about the time Jonson was writing *The Alchemist* we have a remarkable document that makes an explicit parallel between the Calvinist doctrines of grace and election and the tenets and processes of alchemy.[9] Given Jonson's extensive knowledge of alchemy, it is virtually certain that he knew of Paracelsus's exalted view of himself or of cases like these, but the astuteness of Jonson's satirical analysis depends not so much upon his knowledge of particular cases as upon his penetrating understanding of the prideful impulse lying behind the exclusivity of both alchemy and Calvinism: the need to see oneself as chosen, selected above all others, for a special grace or knowledge. The smugness of the Puritan elect was a commonplace of anti-Puritan satire,[10] but in identifying Puritanism with alchemy—and thereby revealing what Fisch calls "the same false and narrow application of the Hebraic Covenant-doctrine" as the *basis* of that identification—Jonson was able to make his satirical vision more encompassing, more complex, and much more trenchant.

Herford and Simpson pointed out long ago that "when Ananias introduces himself as 'a faithful Brother' (II.v.7), and Subtle affects to understand by this a devotee of alchemy, the two professions at once assume the air of parallel fraternities" (H & S, II, 104). In light of the extensive criticism that has developed this general point, I need not belabor it here, but I do want to show how some hitherto unnoticed or unexplored details go far to establish the explicit parallels between Puritanism and alchemy, not merely as "parallel fraternities" but as manifestations of the same moral and psychological weakness that I have just described. A good example of the unexplored detail, incidentally, is the way that Subtle's reply to Ananias's self-introduction as "a faithful Brother" specifically alludes to the sectarian nature of Puritanism, wherein each splinter group claimed an exclusive *gnosis* and election. As if to suggest that the same contentious sectarianism exists among alchemists, Subtle belligerently responds, "What's that? / A Lullianist? A Ripley? *Filius artis?*" (II.v.7–8).[11] Details such as these indicate that Jonson was up to more than a general satire of "parallel fraternities."

While neither the "Argument" nor the "Prologue" to the play refers to the Puritans as an object of satire (as does, for example, the "Prologue to the King's Majesty" of *Bartholomew Fair*), the "Puritan context" is firmly established in the opening scene. The setting in Blackfriars (initially mentioned at I.i.17), first of all, places the action in a residential area inhabited largely by Puritans. Dol Common's immediate concern (beginning at line 10), as she tries to quiet the uproar of Face and Subtle's argument, is the presumed threat posed by these "sober, scruffy, precise neighbours, / (That scarce have smiled twice, sin' the king came in)," who "Would run themselves from breath, to see me ride, / Or you to have but a hole to thrust your heads in, / For which you should pay ear-rent" (I.i.164–169).[12] At this point, the Puritan neighbors are the feared representatives of normalcy or at least of the law-abiding element in society that would expose or punish the three rogues who are presently in a state of civil war. As it turns out, of course, these "scruffy, precise neighbours" prove only to be fools when they do in fact materialize in V.i, at exactly the same moment that Lovewit—the other presumed representative of normalcy and order—unexpectedly returns. Neighbour 3, perhaps the dullest of the lot, admits for example that had Jeremy "hung out . . . banners / Of a strange calf, with five legs . . . Or a huge lobster, with six claws," "We had gone in then, sir" (V.i. 7–10). Lovewit's own impatience with his precise neighbours becomes explicit a few lines later, when Jeremy outfaces them and they become so befuddled as not to know what they in fact did see; Lovewit's next comment is said musingly to himself but refers to those half-dozen dimwits surrounding him: "He [Jeremy] has no gift / Of teaching i' the nose, that e'er I knew of!" (V.i.10–11). This reference to the characteristic nasal twang of the Puritan preacher brings us back, near the climax of the play, to Dol's initial characterization of the "precise" denizens of Blackfriars and completes a complex pattern of reference begun in scene one.[13]

One purpose of this first scene, then, is to take the audience in, momentarily at least, with Dol's belief that the Blackfriars Puritans will (like Lovewit) function as a social, if not moral, norm. The "Understander," however, will perhaps be wary of this assumption, if he attends to Dol's jibe that "not a puritan in Blackfriars will trust" Face, "So much as for a feather!" (I.i.128–129). For this topical allusion to Puritan merchants who deal in such frippery as feathers, despite the professed Puritan abhorrence of such frills (see Ananias's horror at starch and Spanish ruffs), is barbed: we are warned from the outset that Puritans are hypocrites and that whatever judgments they might make have to be seen in light of that fundamental weakness.

Such is the complexity of Jonson's satirical vision, however, that at the same time he has Dol see the Puritans as a threat from the outside respectable world, he begins showing us how the practiced rogues on the inside are in fact like the Brethren. For example, Subtle—whose very name has obvious connections with *precisian*[14]—uses alchemical terms to describe his transformation of Jeremy from impoverished butler into a cozener *par excellence,* but some of his words—like Nathan Field's—connect alchemy with Puritanism. Has he not, Subtle asks,

> Sublimed thee, and exalted thee, and fixed thee
> I' the third region, called *our state of grace?*
> Wrought thee to spirit, to quintessence, with pains
> Would twice have won me the philosophers' work?
> Put thee in words and fashion? *Made thee fit*
> *For more than ordinary fellowships?*
> (I.i.68–73; italics mine)

This initiation into the elect of roguery introduces a theme that Jonson develops carefully throughout: the identification of Puritans as cozeners. This was a frequent accusation in Elizabethan and Jacobean drama that satirized the Puritans,[15] but in making the specific connection between Puritans and alchemical cozeners, Jonson opened a rich vein of satire.

Another commonplace theme of anti-Puritan satire was the charge of sedition or treason, because of the civil disorder attributed to the dissension of nonconformists.[16] This notion Jonson also introduces in Scene One and proceeds to develop in his own masterful way, for the dissent between Subtle and Face, as each cheater claims superiority in cozenage, is a comic version of this civil disorder. As Dol says, the very "republic" (I.i.110) of rogues is in danger; if her accomplices do not promise to "cozen kindly," she "shall grow factious too" (I.i.137, 140).[17] Her final admonition to Subtle is "leave your factions, sir. / And labour, kindly, in the common work" (I.i.155–156). Add to these hints the fact that Blackfriars itself is located in the "liberties," outside the jurisdiction of the London municipal authorities, and we have neat parallels between these cheats who have set up shop there, the actual London Puritans who also live there, and the "exiled Brethren," who have fled the ecclesiastical and civil authorities of England in order to practice their (cozening) religion. These political references also anticipate Sir Epicure Mammon's "free state" (IV.i.156), which, as we shall see, is also associated with both alchemy and Puritanism.

In sum, then, while the Puritans of Blackfriars would like to be seen as representatives of order, morality, and decorum, their hypocrisy, greed, and self-interest are no different from the motives of these factious con-artists who now momentarily patch up their differences in an unholy covenant, to be broken as soon as one achieves a decisive advantage over the other.

If this first scene lays the groundwork for the Puritanism-alchemy nexus that is to be developed more fully as the plot moves forward, we must also recognize, as my reference to the "exiled Brethren" has just intimated, that Jonson explicitly distinguishes between the English Puritans as described by Dol (and as they briefly appear in V.i–iii) and the two major representatives of sectarianism in the play, Ananias and Tribulation Wholesome. For while much of Jonson's satire throughout applies to the doctrines and idiosyncracies of English Puritanism generally, the dramatist has chosen to identify Ananias and Tribulation specifically as Anabaptists— members, that is, of one of the most radical and rabid of the sects. This fact is crucial to our understanding of some of Jonson's specific satirical attacks and, more important, to our understanding of his themes of millennialism and anarchy.

Like many of the sects of the mid-seventeenth century (such as the Family of Love, with which Anabaptism has affinities, and to which Jonson alludes in V.v.117), Anabaptism has its roots in the Reformation of the sixteenth. In fact, Anabaptism was among the very earliest of the radical sects to achieve prominence after the Reformation, and as early as 1521 it was condemned by Catholics and Protestants alike.[18] The main theological departures from orthodoxy were a rejection of infant baptism, the belief that Christ took no bodily substance from Mary, a denial of the real presence in the Lord's Supper, and teaching that sin after adult baptism cannot be forgiven by penance and that repeating sinners were to be excommunicated to preserve a pure and united church. To these were added a code of behavior that, as well as endorsing community property, included "Separation from the world, by which is meant 'all popish and anti-popish works and Church services, meetings and church attendance, drinking-houses, civic affairs, the commitments made in unbelief and other things of that kind' "; a refusal to bear arms or undertake civil offices; and a refusal to take oaths, following Matthew 5:34 and James 5:12.[19] While these beliefs were formulated by the Anabaptists themselves and therefore defined a fairly specific group, the term *Anabaptist,* as given early currency by Zwingli, became one of general abuse and was "charged with an emotional content in which fear played a considerable part."[20] Professor Holden's comment that for Elizabethans and Jacobeans the term had become "a synonym for riot and rebellion" (*Anti-Puritan Satire,* p. 92) explains the response of fear: the anti-social, anti-government, and communistic attitudes of the Anabaptists made them a threat not only to the theological but to the political order as well. That this fear was well founded, history seemed to demonstrate all too clearly, and the social disruption generally associated with Puritanism looked pale when compared to the millenarian anarchy of radical Anabaptism.

Among the radical groups generally called "millenarian" were two main schools of thought: the apocalyptic, which pessimistically saw no hope for mankind before the end of the world, which was imminent, the last thousand years of the fifth and last monarchy (predicted in the Book of Daniel 7) having already expired; and the truly millenarian, which interpreted the Book of Revelations optimistically and which usually expected "a reign of the saints on earth before the end of all things."[21] One group of Anabaptists, who anticipated the militant and anarchic Fifth Monarchy Men of the 1640s and later, were of the latter sort, and early in the sixteenth century some of the saved Brethren attempted to implement their beliefs:

> The first millenarian development after the Reformation was in Germany and at a popular level. As early as 1520 a vagrant priest, Thomas Müntzer, established himself at Zwickau near the Bohemian border, and declared that the elect must rise up and annihilate the godless to prepare for Christ's coming and the millennium. He won a considerable following among the local weavers, mine-workers and peasants. The most important movement was in 1534–5 when the Anabaptists won control of the city of Münster and proclaimed it as the New Jerusalem. Its programme included polygamy, a ferocious legal code based on the statutes laid down in the Old Testament, and the abolition of the private ownership of money and many other goods; the social order was inverted completely. In June 1535 the New Jerusalem was captured by an army of mercenaries raised by the bishop of Münster, and the saints were put to the sword.   (Capp, *p.* 27)

For theologians, these uprisings in Germany served only to discredit millenarian thought, until the mid-seventeenth century when the study of millennialism among the early Church Fathers (for example, Tertullian and Irenaeus) made these ideas seem much less revolutionary.[22] Nevertheless, for "a century or more [after 1534–35] a brief reference to the ill-omened name of Münster was enough to destroy arguments in favour of religious toleration and enough to prove that all Anabaptists, even the pacific, should be suppressed."[23] There is little doubt, then, that in the popular imagination the association of riot and rebellion with the Anabaptists remained firm, despite the fact that, historically, the early Anabaptists in England—some of whom were actually survivors of Münster—were perceived by Church and State authorities as heretics, not as purveyors of sedition.[24]

The seditious element in Anabaptism was nevertheless emphasized by polemicists,[25] and the satirists could turn this into either an impulse toward anarchy or merely antisocial behavior. Jonson, it appears, chose the former tack, but he went even further in associating the anarchic millenarianism of Münster with the Anabaptist Brethren in England. That Jonson had the notorious Münster episode in mind, first of all, is clear from Subtle's reference to Ananias, in his third speech to him, as "you Knipper-Doling" (II.v.13) and from Subtle's later reference to Ananias and Tribulation as "my brace of little John Leydens" (III.iii.23). Bernt Knipperdollinck and Jan Bockelson (alias John of Leyden) were the chief instigators of the anarchic "millennium" of Münster: Bockelson was the fanatical leader, Knipperdollinck a cloth merchant, important figure in the Münster guilds, and patron of Anabaptists, whose daughter Bockelson married.[26] The Münster affair had already served Thomas Nashe in *The Unfortunate Traveller* (1594) as a vehicle for anti-Puritan invective,[27] and the mass hysteria that Knipperdollinck and Bockelson inspired among the some 10,000 inhabitants of Münster is conceivably an analogue for the plague of madness and greed in the Blackfriars of Jonson's play, the shaky "republic" over which Subtle, Face, and Dol temporarily rule. If we recall the parallels already drawn between the fraudulent alchemists and the hypocritical cozening Brethren, we can now see another comic parallel, in that the confidence artists are, as it were, awaiting in fear and trembling the Last Judgment—the coming of Lovewit—at the same time that they are enjoying their (short-lived) "millennium" in Blackfriars.[28]

This tempting suggestion seems to be supported by the framework of contextual reference in the play and by the currency of millennialist speculation in Jonson's time that, I believe, contributed to more than the characterization of Ananias and Tribulation. It is, however, to the latter, whose sectarian affiliation would already reek of the anarchy of Münster, that millenarian thought is most immediately applicable. The scriptural basis of Christian millennialism—from earliest times through the seventeenth century—is found only in the Book of Daniel and the Book of Revelation.[29] The former gives a vision of the rise and fall of four successive world-empires, after which would follow a kingdom, the fifth monarchy, that would last forever (Daniel 7). The latter describes the thousand-year reign of Christ and the saints, predicts the overthrow of Satan that makes this possible, and describes—via symbolic beasts, seals, and vials—the coming of the final apocalypse (see especially Revelation 20).[30] Various interpretations of these enigmatic works were, of course, possible, and they stimulated much speculation during the Reformation. Some of it was

scholarly and passive. Catholics could claim, for example, that the fifth monarchy—
the papacy—was already in being and would remain dominant until the end of time
(Capp, p. 21). Calculating events differently, Protestant theorists obtained different
results:

> The exiled Italian Protestant, Jacobus Brocard, argued [in a London publication of 1582]
> that the seventh and last vial was already in progress. As early as 1597 one writer had fixed
> on 1666 as the date when Antichristian Rome would fall, a prophecy which later found
> widespread support, and there was general agreement that Christ's coming was imminent.
> The most important of these writers was John Napier of Merchistoun, the Scottish laird
> who invented logarithms, who reconciled for the first time all the prophetic numbers and
> identified all the seals, trumpets, woes and vials. [Writing in 1597,] Napier concluded that
> Rome and her allies would fall by 1639, and that the world would end about 1688.
>
> (Capp, *pp. 26–27*)

In addition to these armchair millennialists, however, were the more flamboyant
Elizabethan zealots. One of these was William Hacket, who was executed on 28 July
1590 for having, in the course of his preaching of the imminent second coming,
spoken "divers most false and traiterous words" against Queen Elizabeth.[31] Although
Hacket was the most notorious, there were many other latter-day prophets and
proclaimers of the millennium with whom Jonson would have been familiar.[32] As we
shall see, a strange blend of apocalyptic and millenarian ideas pervades the thinking
of the Anabaptist Brethren in *The Alchemist,* and it is largely the Books of Daniel
and Revelation that provide them with a wealth of biblical reference to this end.
Hence, while the excesses of Thomas Müntzer and the militant Anabaptists of the
early sixteenth century caused the Reformers to reject the idea of an earthly paradise,
and while millenarianism became "respectable" only in the seventeenth century
(Toon, p. 19), the Elizabethans and early Jacobeans well knew what it was; indeed,
they could find it in their bookstalls or on their very street corners. They also had
a vivid conception of Anabaptism, with which extreme millenarianism was associated. What, then, can we now say that Jonson generally gains by numbering Ananias
and Tribulation among the "exiled" Anabaptist Brethren? First, it gives him a
license to treat these characters, as radical Separatists, with even greater contempt
and hostility than he could the more moderate Puritans who tried to integrate
themselves into the Anglican church and English society. Second, his choice allowed
him to exaggerate any vice or idiosyncracy associated with Puritans generally.
Finally, Anabaptism, with its fundamental doctrines of election and the millennium,
provided Jonson with a metaphorical vehicle that meshed perfectly with that of
alchemy, whose adepts claimed to perfect both matter and spirit. With these tools
to hand, Jonson created not only the memorable characters of Ananias and Tribulation, but a complex mirror figure, Sir Epicure Mammon, to anatomize both the follies
of his age and the fundamental weaknesses of mankind.

II

While Sir Epicure is by himself a rich image of ridiculous self-deception and perverted imagination, he also provides a dramatic and thematic context for Ananias and Tribulation, whom we see only after Mammon has graced the stage. In his own gross way, Mammon embodies both the "religious alchemy" of Subtle and the "alchemical millennialism" of the Anabaptist Brethern, and by anticipating these themes he renders Jonson's satire of the latter characters all the more incisive.

Sir Epicure's first entrance in II.i shows him to be not only a confident *adeptus* who can expound to Surly "The manner of *our* [the alchemists'] work" and explain that classical myths are "All abstract riddles of *our* stone" (II.i.94, 104; italics mine) but also a grave member of an elect who sermonizes Surly in the terms and rhetoric of a Puritan preacher. His manner is aptly described by Dol, who has espied his approach: "Coming along . . . Slow of his feet, but earnest of his tongue, / To one that's with him" (I.iv.7–9).[33] Sir Epicure evangelizes thus:

> You shall no more deal with the hollow die,
> Or the frail card. No more be at charge of keeping
> The livery-punk, for the young heir, that must
> Seal, at all hours, in his shirt. No more,
> If he deny, ha' him beaten to't, as he is
> That brings him the commodity. No more
> Shall thirst of satin, or the covetous hunger
> Of velvet entrails, for a rude-spun cloak,
> To be displayed at Madam Augusta's, make
> The sons of sword and hazard fall before
> The golden calf, and on their knees, whole nights,
> Commit idolatry with wine and trumpets:
> Or go a-feasting, after drum and ensign.
> No more of this.
>
> (*II.i.9–22*)

In the hectoring repetition of "no more. . . . No more. . . . No more. . . . No more of this" and in such phrases as "thirst of satin," "covetous hunger," "sons of sword and hazard," and "commit idolatry," we hear the fervent tone of the convert, the enthusiast who has already received the inner illumination and who must now proselytize: "You are not faithful, sir," he says to his sceptical interlocutor (II.i.29). Moreover, if analyzed rhetorically, this speech, although in verse, conforms remarkably to the description that Jonas Barish gives of the excesses of Puritan prose, as Jonson's contemporaries perceived them: a reliance on repetition, apposition, clichés, anaphora, and genitive phrases leading to "a narcotic doze . . . a trancelike rhythm that conceals the vacancy of meaning beneath."[34]

If there are any doubts about the intended flavor of these words, one need only attend to the many biblical references here and in Mammon's other early speeches;

not only do we encounter the "golden calf" and "Solomon," but later Surly is assured that the "ancient patriarchs" had the stone and that Mammon has "a book, where Moses, and his sister, / And Solomon have written of the art; / Aye, and a treatise penned by Adam / . . . O' the philosophers' stone, and in high Dutch / . . . Which proves it was the primitive tongue" (II.i.81–86).[35] Tracing the secret of alchemy back to the patriarchs and even to Adam was an alchemical commonplace, but Jonson's addition of the notion of the "primitive tongue" is a deliberate anticipation of Ananias's hatred of all "heathen languages" except Hebrew, which of course he considers to be the primitive tongue of the Bible.

The following scene (II.ii), in which Face now appears as Subtle's half-demented "firedrake" or "lungs," allows Mammon to expatiate upon the luxury and lust that he will enjoy with the stone, but it also continues the theme of religion and alchemy and thus prepares the audience for the calculated entrance of the supposed "*homo frugi*" in the next scene. Face tells Mammon that "master" is "At's prayers, sir, he, / Good man, he's doing his devotions, / For the success" (II.ii.28–31). And immediately before Subtle's appearance, when Surly objects that he who achieves the philosophers' stone must be "A pious, holy, and religious man, / One free from mortal sin, a very virgin," Mammon replies, using the same kind of sophistry by which Ananias and Tribulation are to distinguish between "coining" and "casting" of Dutch dollars (III.ii.150–156):

> That *makes* it, sir, he is so. But I *buy* it.
> My venture brings it me. He, honest wretch,
> A notable, superstitious, good soul,
> Has worn his knees bare, and his slippers bald,
> With prayer and fasting for it: and, sir, let him
> Do it alone, for me, still. Here he comes,
> Not a profane word afore him: 'tis poison.
>   (*II.ii.98–106; italics mine*)

Thus are we prepared for the entrance of the crafty Subtle: soft-spoken, pious, full of biblical phraseology and Puritan cant—an image, in short, of deceit and hypocrisy that we recognize at this point in the drama as a wonderful joke on the greedy Mammon who thinks it is he who is exploiting this "pious drudge." Subtle's language is a clever blend of religious cant and the solicitous advice of an alchemical "father" speaking to his initiated alchemical "son" (Mammon frequently alludes to his alchemical kinship with Subtle). The religious element is set up by Mammon himself who introduces Surly as "An heretic, that I did bring along, / In hope, sir, to convert him" (II.iii.304). By this time we are used to the idea that avarice-and-lust-through-alchemy is Mammon's religion, but Subtle carries this through with a vengeance in his first long speech, the earnestness of which parallels that of Mammon's first long speech quoted above:

Son, I doubt
You're covetous, that thus you meet your time
I' the just point: prevent your day, at morning.
This argues something, worthy of a fear
Of importune and carnal appetite.
Take heed you do not cause the blessing leave you,
With your ungoverned haste. I should be sorry
To see my labours, now, e'en at perfection,
Got by long watching and large patience,
Not prosper, where my love and zeal hath placed 'em.
Which (heaven I call to witness, with yourself,
To whom I have poured my thoughts) in all my ends,
Have looked no way, but unto public good,
To pious uses, and dear charity,
Now grown a prodigy with men. Wherein
If you, my son, should now prevaricate,
And to your own particular lusts employ
So great and catholic a bliss: be sure,
A curse will follow, yea, and overtake
Your subtle and most secret ways.

(II.iii.4–23)

Again the sermonizing tone, the use of words and phrases like "my son," "zeal," and "yea . . . your subtle and most secret ways" recall the hectoring Puritan preacher. One can see the arch-pretender Subtle playing his part to the full, beginning even here to work himself up to the pitch of those enthusiastic "exercises" and "prophesyings" that he himself directly mocks later in the play (III.ii.54; see below).

The real evidence of Subtle's illuminated adeptship comes, however, in the next 150 lines (II.iii.53–210). Framed as a debate with Surly, this section is another of Subtle's virtuoso performances. Cheered on from the side lines by Mammon ("Aye, now it heats: stand, father. / Pound him to dust—"; "Well said, father! / Nay, if he take you in hand, sir, with an argument, / He'll bray you in a mortar"), Subtle attempts to overwhelm Surly with the intricacies of alchemical theory (especially the idea that art perfects nature) and terminology. But Surly's terse comment, even before Subtle hits his stride, forges the link between the adept's obfuscation of "things" by "terms" that do not signify, and the overwrought phraseology of the Puritans: "What a brave language here is? Next to canting?" (II.iii.42). For *canting,* in addition to the usual gloss of "thieves' jargon or private language," also means a whining manner of speaking (*OED*) and therefore brings to mind the Puritan preacher's sucking up, as Subtle says, his " 'ha' and 'hum' in a tune" (III.ii.55), that characteristic nasal intonation alluded to by Lovewit and noted above.[36] With the entrance of Dol, however, the discussion—and the plot—takes a turn. Sir Epicure has only one tantalizing glimpse of this "lord's sister," and despite Surly's exclamation, "Heart, this is a bawdy house!" he wishes "to have conference with her" (II.iii.226, 243). Face whets Mammon's appetite with this description:

                                she is a most rare scholar;
                  And is gone mad with studying Broughton's works.
                  If you but name a word, touching the Hebrew,
                  She falls into her fit, and will discourse
                  So learnedly of genealogies,
                  As you would run mad, too, to hear her, sir.
                                . . .
Mammon: What is she, when she's out of her fit?
Face: Oh, the most affablest creature, sir! So merry!
                  So pleasant! She'll mount you up, like quick-silver,
                  Over the helm; and circulate, like oil,
                  A very vegetal: discourse of state,
                  Of mathematics, bawdry, anything—
                              (*II.iii.237–242; 252–257*)

These temptations are, naturally, more than Mammon can resist; the scene concludes with Sir Epicure looking forward to his interview with Dol, and Surly to his
own plan of unravelling the "subtleties of this dark labyrinth" (II.iii.308). What is
important about the introduction of Dol at precisely this moment, however, is that
this hardened punk, who in Scene One had scornfully lampooned the "precise neighbours" and the supposed alchemical adeptship of Subtle (whose alchemical "glass"
she breaks), is now identified with both these enterprises so as to reflect first on
Mammon and then on the Anabaptist Brethren. While Dol only later tells Sir
Epicure that she studies with Subtle "the mathematics, / And distillation" (IV.i.83–
84), the language of alchemy provides the sexual innuendo of Face's descriptive
speech,[37] and so she is associated with the canting, "pious" alchemy of Subtle and
the voluptuous life that Mammon assumes the philosophers' stone will make possible.
Just as important at this point in the play, however (since the next character to enter
is Ananias), is Dol's connection with the radical Puritanism, rabid Hebraicism, and
the apocalyptic millennialism of Hugh Broughton; for this anticipates the definitive
linking of Mammon and the Anabaptists.

    Numerous critics have noted that Sir Epicure, like the Anabaptists, hopes to
remake the world in his own image and that his rhapsodies "of life and lust"
(IV.i.166) body forth his perverted imagination, but no serious effort has been made
to examine fully the complex interrelationships among alchemy, the millenarian
vision of Sir Epicure, and that of the Anabaptists,[38] or to show by what dramatic
means these connections are made. An important step in such a consideration is to
note that Mammon, in the two scenes just discussed, presents himself not only as a
would-be pious Puritan-alchemist, but also as a Messianic figure (likening himself
to Solomon) about to inaugurate his own millennium. Thus he tells Surly in their
first scene that with the stone he will be able to "renew" an old man "To the fifth
age" (II.i.55–56) and that he will restore the sick and even "fright the plague / Out
o' the kingdom, in three months" (69–70). While at times Sir Epicure almost seems
to believe that he will put the stone to such altruistic uses—just as Subtle's crazed
imagination sometimes makes him forget that he is only a con-artist and not a

genuine alchemist (for example at I.i.63–80)—Sir Epicure's true role as Messianic figure, when not self-deceived, is to establish an earthly paradise for his own pleasure.[39]

These chiliastic ravings reach their height only later (IV.i), when Mammon is courting Dol, after we have been introduced to the Anabaptists. Here, Mammon's dramatic function is to prepare us for their entrance: Jonson's technique is to anticipate one set of characters and their attendant themes by way of a distorted image of similar obsessions and themes in another set of characters. Hence, before Ananias enters in II.v, we have seen the corpulent knight's Puritan-millenarian-alchemical fervor regarding his adeptship, his self-appointed Messianic role of bringing health, safety, and pleasure into the world, and his pseudo-religious sermonizing of Surly. We have also seen the "pious drudge" Subtle, his true motives of avarice and lust hidden behind a similar but more clever mask of piety, alchemy, and adeptship, sermonize Surly in a vocabulary and fervor matching Sir Epicure's. Dramatically, then, Jonson has carefully prepared us for Ananias's entrance; for Ananias, too, pretends piety; he too seeks the benefits of alchemy in order to bring about the millennium; and, of course, he is the genuine article when it comes to radical zeal and canting language.

III

As with Mammon's first appearance, Ananias's is signaled by Dol, who describes him as he approaches; her caricature again focuses our attention: "He looks like a gold-end-man" (II.iv.21). Thus Ananias's ambiguous position as a Deacon—one who deals with the secular affairs of a "spiritual brotherhood"—is satirically prefigured, and we are almost ready to meet the hypocrite who so shrewdly will "deal / For Mammon's jack and andirons" (II.iv.23–24). Note that the Brethren are connected with Mammon from the outset; "gold-end-man" hints, too, that Ananias is a would-be alchemist, although we learn what kind only as the action develops. For his entrance to have the desired effect, however, Jonson must complete our preparation, and in this he demonstrates a consummate skill as comic dramatist and satirist.

Subtle, with his own cozening imagination stirred by this new challenge, ponders his strategy of adopting a new persona; at the same time, he suggests that it is really the same "old" confidence game:

> Now,
> In a new tune, new gesture, but old language.
> This fellow is sent, from one negotiates with me
> About the stone, too; for the holy Brethren
> Of Amsterdam, the exiled Saints: that hope
> To raise their discipline by it. I must use him
> In some strange fashion now, to make him admire me.
> (II.iv.26–32)

Thus we have the rationale for Subtle's change in tone from the quiet, pious alchemist to the pugnacious, argumentative character presented to Ananias and later to Tribulation; this makes sense as a gulling strategy. But there seems to be more to it. If Subtle is still appearing as an alchemist—as he has just done to Mammon—why, in the lines just before this speech, does he say to Face, "Let him in. / Stay, help me off, first, with my gown"? It is understandable that Subtle wishes to use "a new tune, new gesture" to suit a new dupe, but why must he hastily change his alchemist's gown, his very garb, for the earnest brother? Could it not be that, just as Ananias represents the genuine article when it comes to the Puritan cant that Epicure and Subtle have both been mimicking in order to sanctify alchemy, he is also the genuine article when it comes to the figure of the "pious drudge" that Subtle has just been presenting to Mammon? Is it not possible, that is, that Subtle's disguise to Mammon has been the very appearance of a non-conformist preacher, not only in "tune," "gesture," and "language" but also in physical appearance, in the very Geneva gown and bands worn by the approaching Ananias? Such a ploy would make for a brilliant *coup de théâtre*: the con-man Subtle, posing as a holy alchemist, takes off his gown, only to be met by the hypocritical "sanctified" Deacon, come to deal for Mammon's jack and irons as base metal for the philosophers' stone—dressed, as it were, in the very disguise of falsehood that Subtle has just removed. Here is a literal use of the distorted mirror-image technique that we have been seeing through metaphor, theme, and dramatic action. The comic effect of Ananias's first appearance (II.v) is not unlike that of the perfectly timed entrances of Shakespeare's Dromios or Olivia/ Sebastian; the satiric effect is unsurpassed.

With this shock of recognition still reverberating in the audience's visual imagination, Jonson now proceeds to make his point verbally. Subtle's references to Ananias as "A Lullianist ... A Ripley ... *Filius artis*" are only the beginning of Jonson's technique of using the "old language" of alchemy (that is, the same used with Mammon) to reveal the connections between the exiled Brethren and the brothers of the art. Here, for example, Subtle demands of Ananias, "Can you sublime, and dulcify? Calcine? / Know you the *sapor pontic*? *Sapor stiptic*? / Or what is homogene, or heterogene?" (II.v.9–11). When Ananias says this is "heathen language," Subtle calls him a "Knipper-Doling" and proceeds to put Face through the alchemical catechism of which Ananias is ignorant. While Ananias smugly asserts that "All's heathen, but the Hebrew," Subtle assumes the position of a "sanctified Elder" of alchemy questioning his disciple in the arcane terms of the truly "primitive language." The stichomythic rapidity of this dialogue—punctuated repeatedly by Subtle's "This is heathen Greek, to you, now?"—is more than comic, however, as some of the specific terms smack of Puritan vocabulary and demonstrate that alchemy and "canting" are fundamentally similar. When, for example, Subtle demands that Face "answer i'the language" and "Name the vexations, and the martyrizations / Of metals in the work" (II.v.19–21), we are reminded of what Tribulation is to call the "chastisements" and "rebukes we of the Separation / Must bear, with willing shoulders" (III.i.1–3)—the persecutions, that is, of the exiled Anabaptists.

Consider also the blend of paradox (which here recalls Puritan casuistry) and biblical echoes in Face's description of the philosophers' stone:

'Tis a stone, and not
A stone; a spirit, a soul, and a body:
Which, if you do dissolve, it is dissolved,
If you coagulate, it is coagulated,
If you make it to fly, it flieth.
(*II.v.40–44*)[40]

No sooner is the equation made between the "heathen Greek" of alchemy and Puritan cant than Jonson demonstrates the Brethren's hypocrisy and casuistry. Ananias, when asked what he wants, reveals that he is but "a servant of the exiled Brethren, / That deal with widows', and with orphans' goods; . . . / A deacon," and that he intends "to deal justly, and give (in truth) / Their utmost value" only if the orphans' parents were "Sincere professors" of Anabaptism (46–49, 57–59). Subtle indignantly responds, " 'Slid, you'd cozen, else," and discovering Ananias's name, exclaims, "Out, the varlet / That cozened the Apostles! Hence, away . . . wicked Ananias" (72–76). In making Ananias the re-incarnation of the biblical figure who was struck dead for withholding the rightful price of land from the apostles (Acts 5:1–10) and whose name became synonymous with *liar,* Jonson shows that this cozening religionist resembles not only Subtle himself but also the cheating poetasters of "To the Reader" who misuse language so abominably. This theme becomes even more explicit in Ananias's acceptance of Subtle's distinction between "coining" and "casting" (III.ii.151–153), activities that were frequently associated with would-be alchemists.[41] To end the present interview, however, Subtle sends Ananias packing with the warning that the "Elders" must come

Hither to make atonement for you quickly.
And gi' me satisfaction; or out goes
The fire: and down the alembics and the furnace
. . . .
. . . All hope of rooting out the Bishops,
Or the Antichristian Hierarchy shall perish,
If they stay threescore minutes. The Aqueity,
Terreity, and Sulphureity
Shall run together again, and all be annulled. . . .
(76–86)

If this brief scene with Ananias elucidates the parallels between Anabaptist election and alchemical adeptship, as well as those between alchemical language and the hypocritical Anabaptist canting, it ends by introducing the "millenary dream" of the exiled Brethren ("rooting out the Bishops," and so on) and links that dream with the making of the philosophers' stone. This linkage is the basic joke underlying the whole pathetic enterprise of the Anabaptists, as it is developed in the two scenes involving Tribulation Wholesome, III.i and III.ii. It is apt that Tribulation is the unwitting satirist of his own pursuit: "the restoring of the silenced Saints . . . ne'er will be, but by the philosophers' stone" (III.i.38–39). For as ignorant, dishonest, and zealous as Ananias is, he lacks the larger vision, political ambition, and utter worldliness of his pastor.

The relationship between the two is clearly worked out in the opening lines of III.i, where Wholesome attempts to convince the fanatical tailor that it is "Not always necessary" that "the sanctified cause / Should have a sanctified course" (III.i.13–14) and that it is permissible for the Brethren to employ alchemy for their own purposes. This little scene neatly parallels II.i, where Mammon attempts to convince Surly of the truth of alchemy. Hence the worldliness of Tribulation is directly compared to that of Mammon; moreover, the scepticism of Surly and the scrupulosity of Ananias—although vastly different in some ways—are shown to be similar. In each case the doubter is overpowered by a "wiser" initiate: Mammon rationalizes his pursuit of alchemy by trying to "convert" Surly through a display of alchemical jargon, while Wholesome initiates Ananias into the subtle sophistries of Anabaptist logic. But while Surly calls upon common sense and his wide experience among the London demimonde to temper Mammon's enthusiasm, Ananias provides a counterpoint of prophetic biblical utterance to his pastor's hypocritical chop-logic (both Anabaptists, however, exploit the pseudo-biblical phraseology of Puritan cant to the full). Hence the Deacon invokes the prophecy of Isaiah 19:18, "In that day shall five cities in the land of Egypt speak the language of Canaan . . . one shall be called, the City of destruction," when he accuses Subtle of "speak[ing] the language of Canaan" (III.i.6). And, associating Subtle with one of the apocalyptic beasts that must be overcome before the millennium can be instituted, Ananias claims that Subtle "bears / The visible mark of the Beast in his forehead" (III.i.7–8; see Revelations 16:2, 19:20). Similarly, Ananias's claim that Subtle's "philosophy blinds the eyes of man" (III.i.10) suggests St. Paul's admonition "lest any man spoil you through philosophy and vain deceit, after the tradition of men, after the rudiments of the world, and not after Christ" (Colossians 2:8).[42] But Wholesome seems all too eager to follow the "rudiments of the world" and goes so far as to argue that Subtle himself may be converted to Anabaptism:

> It may be so,
> When as the work is done, the stone is made,
> This heat of his may turn into a zeal,
> And stand up for the beauteous discipline
> Against the menstruous cloth and rag of Rome.
> We must await his calling, and the coming
> Of the good spirit.
>
> *(III.i.29–35)*

Here again Jonson has Tribulation unwittingly make a direct analogy between the ravings of alchemy and radical enthusiasm—between Subtle's "heat" (his "passion" or irascible nature, brought on, Tribulation explains, by "The place he lives in, still about the fire, / And fume of metals, that intoxicate / The brain of man, and make him prone to passion" [III.i.18–20]) and Puritan "zeal."[43] But if at this point we recall Subtle's earlier pose (for Mammon's benefit) as "pious drudge" in sober Puritan costume, speaking in the very intonation and heady zeal of the "sanctified Elder" himself, Tribulation's lines become even more humorous and resounding, for Subtle has, in this guise, already received his "calling" and seen the "beautiful light" (as Ananias calls it a few moments later), both as alchemist and as illuminated brother.

It is important to note, however, that Tribulation's primary interest here is the establishment of an earthly kingdom. Just as Mammon will supposedly "heal" the literally ill with the stone, Tribulation will use the sovereign cordial of gold (as a bribe) to cure the "disease" of the magistrate who enforces the law against nonconformists, thereby "restoring . . . the silenced Saints":

> And so a learned Elder, one of Scotland,
> Assured me; *aurum potabile* being
> The only medicine, for the civil magistrate,
> To incline him to a feeling of the cause:
> And must be daily used, in the disease.
> (*III.i.40–44*)

This reasoning is apparently irresistible to Ananias, for he replies, "The motion's good, / And of the spirit; I will knock first. Peace be within" (III.i.47–48).

As III.ii begins, Subtle is all too aware of the Brethren's political aspirations, and he neatly plays up to them while accepting the unctuous apologies of Tribulation, who continues to treat his worldly goal as a good "motion" and "of the spirit" (he says, for example, that the Brethren "are ready / To lend their willing hands to any project / The spirit and you [Subtle] direct"). Leading up to a pitch for yet more funds, Subtle points out that here in England the stone will enable the Brethren to "make friends" among the great by effecting fantastic cures of their myriad loathsome diseases, "that even the medicinal use shall make you a faction, / And party in the realm" (III.ii.25–26). Abroad they can hire mercenaries or simply "buy / The king of France out of his realms; or Spain, / Out of his Indies"; in fact, they will be able to do anything that they desire "Against lords spiritual, or temporal." To these suggestions comes Tribulation's self-damning reply, "Verily, 'tis true. / We may be temporal lords ourselves, I take it" (III.ii.48–52). The Brethren's millenarianism is again referred to near the end of the scene when, with reference to the legality of coining Dutch dollars, Ananias says, "We know no magistrate. Or, if we did, / This's foreign coin" (III.ii.150–151). Thus are we shown the political ambitions of the Anabaptists—which Jonson's audience would see as an attempt to duplicate the notorious anarchic "millennium" of Münster.[44] Jonson's intricate paralleling of alchemy, radical Puritanism, and millenarianism can now be seen as a deliberate satirical and dramatic strategy. Just as he perceived that the same pride

and egotism underlay the claims of Puritans to election and the claims of alchemists
to adeptship, Jonson also saw that each of these systems (both of thought and of
language) gave rise to an even wilder flight of perverted imagination and pride: the
notion that the *electus/adeptus* could take it upon himself to reform the whole world,
bring about the millennium, and restore humanity to an Edenic state.

Before Jonson can complete the development of this theme by way of the further
comparison between the Anabaptists and Sir Epicure, he must remind his audience
of that connection before this scene is over—lest it be forgotten while the interven-
ing action concerning Surly and other minor characters takes place. This he does in
a substantial passage (III.ii.53–97) of vitriolic attack on the mannerisms and hypocrisies of the Brethren, put in the mouth of Subtle. At first, this seems to be a
gratuitous polemic that Jonson could not resist, and one that interrupts the dramatic
action. On the contrary, however, this direct attack—while it is a summation of
many of the common elements in anti-Puritan invective—is perfectly in keeping with
the quarrelsome persona that Subtle has adopted. Moreover, it is triggered by Tribulation's comment, "We may be temporal lords ourselves," and it is meant to point
out that Tribulation's admission of political aspiration is only one example of the
fundamental worldliness that underlies the Anabaptists' hypocrisy, and that they—
no less than Sir Epicure—serve the god Mammon. They cheat widows of their
legacies, they have "zealous wives" rob their husbands "for the common cause," they
claim providential guidance in demanding forfeited bonds. If these activities (not to
mention their seeking the philosophers' stone) match Sir Epicure's in greed, the
Anabaptists also appreciate the table and the bed:

> Nor shall you need, o'er night to eat huge meals,
> To celebrate your next day's fast the better:
> The whilst the Brethren, and the Sisters, humbled,
> Abate the stiffness of the flesh.
>
> (*III.ii.74–77*)[45]

In order to point out again that the Brethren are cozeners, Subtle sums up all
their hypocrisies by saying that "Not one / Of these so singular *arts*" (III.ii.91–92,
italics mine) will be necessary once they have the stone. Like Subtle himself, the
Anabaptists have more than one "art" or scam behind which to hide their actual
desires; like Sir Epicure's pretended altruism and beneficence, these pretenses will
no longer be necessary once they implement their own millennium with the stone.

The verbal comedy in this part of the scene is itself an illustration of the very
hypocrisy so savagely satirized: for the sake of greed and a lust for power, Tribulation
desperately attempts to keep a lid on the zealous interruptions of Ananias, lest Subtle
destroy the whole alchemical apparatus and with it the Brethren's considerable
investment. The comic irony is intensified by the fact that Ananias's outbursts are
all in response to the trivial *bêtes noires* of stiff-necked scrupulosity (Subtle's use of
Christmas instead of *Christ-tide,* his references to bells, starch, "Popish" traditions),
not to any of Subtle's morally significant accusations. Furthermore, Tribulation

himself is so eager to placate Subtle's ire that, in the midst of the latter's diatribe, he cries out, "Let me find grace, sir, in your eyes" and, as if to acknowledge Subtle's defamations,

> Mind him [Ananias] not, sir.
> I do command thee, spirit (of zeal, but trouble)
> To peace with him. Pray you, sir, go on.
> (*III.ii.65, 83–85*)

When Tribulation mildly interposes a single demurral—to justify the Brethren's adopting of names like Tribulation or Persecution—he reveals the venal motive behind the practice:

> Truly, sir, they are
> Ways that the godly Brethren have invented
> For propagation of the glorious cause,
> As very notable means, and whereby also
> Themselves grow soon, and profitably famous.
> (*III.ii.97–101*)

As if to focus the themes of hypocrisy and greed on a particular case, Jonson concludes the scene by having the Anabaptists show their true colors in agreeing to the counterfeiting scheme. This nicely complements the earlier revelation, at the end of II.v, of their scrupulous duplicity in Ananias's resolve to "deal justly" for the orphans' goods only if their parents were "of the faithful." The two actions are related too because the Dutch dollars are to be made from the orphans' pewter, which the Brethren are now buying. This episode is also important because it directly introduces the theme of counterfeiting, to be developed with regard to Sir Epicure. These scenes with the Anabaptists serve then to identify even more closely the alchemical millennialism of both the Anabaptists and of Sir Epicure and to show the fundamental worldliness of all these sons of Mammon.

IV

Just as Sir Epicure's initial scenes (where the alchemy-religion-sensuality-millennium nexus is introduced) prepare us for the satiric exposition of Ananias and Tribulation, now their scenes make possible the further development of these themes as the wealthy knight returns. The courting scene with Dol Common (IV.i) is carefully constructed to lead up to Sir Epicure's comic downfall in IV.iv (culminating in the "explosion" off-stage of the alchemical laboratory). Dol therefore becomes increasingly important, but not only as the agent of Mammon's overthrow. Dol the prostitute is also Jonson's figure for the counterfeit, the perversion of nature; as such, she is the dramatist's ideal means of re-introducing his theme of true alchemy/true art versus charlatanry/false art and relating it to those I have been pursuing.

Dol's immediate function is to provide a focus for Mammon's fantasies of sensuality, which are now to be recognized as the disguised gluttony and carnality of the Anabaptists given shameless celebration. This speech, uttered just before Dol's entrance, sums up the pleasures that he so rapturously expatiates upon later in the scene:

> Now, Epicure,
> Heighten thyself, talk to her, all in gold;
> Rain her as many showers, as Jove did drops
> Unto his Danae: show the god a miser,
> Compared with Mammon. What? The stone will do't.
> She shall feel gold, taste gold, hear gold, sleep gold:
> Nay, we will *concumbere* gold. I will be puissant,
> And mighty in my talk to her! Here she comes.
>
> (*IV.i.24–31*)

As the scene progresses, however, Mammon's fantasies take on more and more the color of Anabaptist millenarianism, and in this too Dol's role is crucial. This "lord's sister" was described earlier, in II.iii, as

> a most rare scholar;
> And is gone mad with studying Broughton's works.
> If you but name a word, touching the Hebrew,
> She falls into her fit, and will discourse
> So learnedly of genealogies,
> As you would run mad, too, to hear her, sir.
>
> (*237–242*)

In *Volpone* (1606), Jonson had already associated the philological, textual, and rabbinical studies of Hugh Broughton (1549–1612) with alchemy and jargon-ridden jibberish. After hearing one of Volpone's virtuoso speeches (in his disguise as the mountebank Scoto of Mantua) on the curative virtues of his "blessed *unguento*," the gullible Sir Politic Would-be exclaims, "Is not his language rare?" The sceptical Peregrine replies, "But alchemy, / I never heard the like: or Broughton's books" (II.ii.109–111; compare Surly's "What a brave language here is? Next to canting?" II.iii.42). As if on cue, Volpone then sings a song which claims that his "*oglio del Scoto*" surpasses Raymond Lully's "great Elixir" (that is, the philosophers' stone), and in his next protracted speech, while using the very linguistic obfuscation employed by Subtle, Volpone mocks the fruitless labors of the alchemists who "blow, blow, puff, puff, and all flies in *fumo*: ha, ha, ha, Poor wretches!" (144–145).

In both plays, Jonson is satirizing the abuse of language through meaningless jargon, but in *The Alchemist* the connections between Broughton and alchemy are extended to embrace the millennial anarchy of the Anabaptists. First, Broughton claimed to understand abstruse terms and enigmatic passages in the Bible (he is mainly remembered for his part in a dispute over the meaning and translation of the terms *Hades/hell/Sheol*; see *DNB*); to Jonson these claims would recall those of the adepts who alone "understood" the obscure terms and allegories of alchemy, as well as the "preciseness" of the Brethren like Ananias, for whom "All's heathen, but the Hebrew" (see II.v.17 and Mammon's "high Dutch" as "the primitive tongue" of Adam). Secondly, Broughton's notorious obsession with biblical genealogy and the apocalyptic interpretation of history links him to both alchemy (wherein the secret of transmutation was handed down from Adam to the patriarchs—p. 180, above) and Anabaptism; Broughton claimed, for example, to have predicted in a sermon the Spanish Armada (*DNB*), a political event of supreme importance to the chronologies of apocalyptic and millenarian exegetes alike, where it was frequently identified with specific allegorical events in Daniel or Revelation.[46] Thirdly, while in fact this pugnacious rabbinical scholar was an anti-Separatist and while his beliefs were, strictly speaking, apocalyptic rather than millenarian,[47] Jonson clearly associates his brand of radical Puritanism with the Anabaptists. This was not hard to do, because Broughton's chief preoccupation in later life—which he vociferously reiterated in speech and in print between 1599 and 1610—was a scheme for converting the Jews of Constantinople, by means of his own Hebraistic skills. This aspiration would have struck Jonson as yet another outlandish "millenary dream," especially since it was generally believed that the conversion of the Jews would take place only just before the end of the world or just before the institution of the millennium.[48]

All these associations with Broughton's name, to receive full development only in IV.v, are introduced here in IV.i, as Face prepares Mammon for Dol's entrance. Thus, when Face leeringly tells Mammon near the beginning of the scene that "she is almost in her fit to see you" (8), not only do we see the connection between sectarian enthusiasm and libertinism, but also we are prepared for the Broughton-like millenarian ravings of Dol's actual "fit" in IV.v. These in turn may be likened to the Anabaptist "exercises" and "prophesyings"—those spontaneous utterances associated with "speaking in tongues"—which Subtle has already openly mocked. Face manages to insinuate this point with a good deal of irony, while at the same time setting up the ultimate "cause" of Mammon's downfall:

> But, good sir, no divinity i' your conference,
> For fear of putting her in rage. . . .
> Six men will not hold her down. And then,
> If the old man should hear, or see you . . .
> The very house, sir, would run mad. You know it
> How scrupulous he is, and violent,
> 'Gainst the least act of sin. Physic, or mathematics,
> Poetry, state, or bawdry (as I told you)
> She will endure, and never startle: but
> No word of controversy.
>
> (*IV.i.9–18*)

Once Dol herself is onstage, she both continues this line of thought and broadens it. The coy banter on the "art" versus "Nature" *topos*, which had been introduced in Subtle's explanation to Surly about how alchemy perfects nature (II.iii.125–176), is particularly important in this regard, and it has a special significance in light of Jonson's "To the Reader," where the would-be "professors" of art "run away from Nature" and "cozen" the unwary. Here, Dol herself is first and foremost a counterfeit, not only in that she is a whore disguised as a noblewoman, but also in that she is, ironically, a false "compound," although Mammon does not recognize this: "I do see / The old ingredient, virtue, was not lost, / Nor the drug, money, used to make your compound" (IV.i.51–53). This is said in reply to Dol's doubly ironic claim, "Sir, although / We may be said to want the gilt and trappings, / The dress of honour; yet we strive to keep / The seeds, the materials" (48–51). Mammon's praise is so excessive, though, that Dol affects to fear he is "play[ing] the courtier" (66); demurely she protests, "This art, sir, i' your words, / Calls your whole faith in question" (71–72). Undeterred, Mammon picks up his cue:

> Nature
> Never bestowed upon mortality,
> A more unblamed, a more harmonious feature:
> She played the stepdame in all faces, else.
> Sweet madam, let me be particular.
>
> (73–77)

Thus the hypocritical lecher courts the painted whore, whose appearance is anything but natural; like the false alchemists and the poetasters, Mammon, "by simple mocking at the terms, when [he] understand[s] not the things, think[s] to get off wittily with [his] ignorance." If we have not already made the connection between this little parody and the way that false alchemy mocks Nature, Jonson has Mammon question this "lord's sister" about her pursuits:

> I see
> You're lodged here, i'the house of a rare man,
> An excellent artist: but what's that to you?
> *Dol:* Yes, sir. I study here the mathematics,
> And distillation.
> *Mammon:*   Oh, I cry you pardon.
> He's a divine instructor! Can extract
> The souls of all things, by his art; call all
> The virtues, and the miracles of the sun,
> Into a temperate furnace: teach dull nature
> What her own forces are. . . .
> *Dol:* Aye, and for his physic, sir—
> *Mammon:* Above the art of Aesculapius,
> That drew the envy of the Thunderer!
> I know all this, and more.

Dol:	Troth, I am taken, sir,

Whole, with these studies, that contemplate nature.
(80–95)

This is Jonson's intellectual comedy at its best, as these two abusers of nature try to pull the wool over each other's eyes while extolling the "art" of the arch-cozener Subtle.

Mammon cannot resist, of course, revealing his great "secret," but as he does so, Dol plays on his fantasies and guides the conversation toward the dangerous topic of "controversy"—specifically the topic of the latter-day millennium. Proclaiming it a "mere solecism" that "such a feature / That might stand up the glory of a kingdom" should live "recluse" in a "cloister," Sir Epicure magnanimously addresses this "Daughter of honour":

I have cast mine eye
Upon thy form, and I will rear this beauty,
Above all styles.

Dol:	You mean no treason, sir!
Mammon:	No, I will take away that jealousy.

I am the lord of the philosophers' stone,
And thou the lady.

(116–121)

Dol's pretended maidenly shock and his own conception of the two of them as monarchs of the stone (both nicely encapsulated in "treason") lead to his fantasy regarding the kingdom he will establish. Picking up his earlier references to Jove and "his Danae" and to "Nay, we will *concumbere* gold," and perhaps mingling with these the roles of both Messiah and patriarch, Mammon declares that the "good old wretch" is at this moment making projection:

Think therefore, thy first wish, now; let me hear it:
And it shall rain into thy lap, no shower,
But floods of gold, whole cataracts, a deluge,
To get a nation on thee!

(125–128, italics mine)

Now Dol, "the glory of her sex," shall be taken out of this obscure "nook, here, of the Friars" to "taste the air of palaces; eat, drink / The toils of emp'rics, and their boasted practice"; she will wear "the jewels / Of twenty states," and at her name "Queens may look pale" (130–144). These anarchic visions provide Dol with her cue, and so she asks directly, "But, in a monarchy, how will this be? / The prince will soon take notice; and both seize / You and your stone: it being a wealth unfit / For any private subject" (147–149). After some consideration, Mammon hits upon the solution—one that anticipates his downfall. " 'Tis no idle fear!" he says,

> We'll therefore go with all, my girl, and live
> In a free state; . . .
> . . . .
> . . . set ourselves high for pleasure,
> And take us down again, and then renew
> Our youth, and strength, with drinking the elixir,
> And so enjoy a perpetuity
> Of life and lust. And thou shalt ha' thy wardrobe,
> Richer than Nature's, still, to change thyself,
> And vary oftener, for thy pride, than she:
> Or Art, her wise, and almost-equal servant.
>   (*155–156, 161–169*)

With his "millenary dream" reaching its height, Mammon himself is approaching a fit of ecstasy; Face has to warn him, in fact, "Sir, you are too loud" and gets him off to "Some fitter place," with the final admonition, "Good, sir, beware, no mention of the Rabbins." Mammon, his mind on other things, assures him, "We think not on 'em," but his fate is sealed: not only will his alchemical vision of going off to a "free state," like a utopian Separatist or exiled Brother, to establish his own realm of sensuality, never be realized, but that very dream—interpreted, as it were, by Hugh Broughton through Dol—brings about his ruin.

The plot of the play gains momentum from this point onward, and in the three following scenes Kastril returns with his sister, Face and Subtle square off in their vying for Dame Pliant, and Surly makes his entrance as Don Diego. These scenes, which develop the bawdy-house theme most clearly, perhaps serve also to throw Mammon's self-delusion and self-gulling into a clearer light, for these unwitting victims of Subtle and Face lack Mammon's "heroic" humor. At any rate, IV.v shows us the results of Mammon's millennarian fantasies:

> Alas I talked
> Of a fifth monarchy I would erect,
> With the philosophers' stone (by chance) and she
> Falls on the other four, straight.
>   (*33–36*)

While Dol's babble from Broughton's *Concent of Scripture* (1590) would have a comic effect even if chosen at random, Jonson's garbling of the learned biblical scholar has been selective and deliberate, just as his quotations or adaptations from alchemical writings suit particular dramatic and thematic purposes. First of all, the occasion for Dol's fit—the reference to one of the key millenarian texts, the four monarchies of Daniel 7—recalls not only the radical eschatology of the Anabaptists but also the whole tradition of alchemical allegoresis. For, just as Broughton's jumbled commentary on the hidden meaning of the monarchies in Daniel and on the beasts, legs, and horns of Revelation (see IV.v.1–11) assumes an absolute ability to understand divine wisdom through allegory, so the secret wisdom of alchemy is understood only by the adept-interpreter.[49] As Subtle had demanded of Surly,

> Was not all the knowledge
> Of the Egyptians writ in mystic symbols?
> Speak not the Scriptures oft in parables?
> Are not the choicest fables of the Poets,
> That were the fountains, and first springs of wisdom,
> Wrapped in perplexed allegories?
>
> (*II.iii.202–207*)

Related to allegoresis is Broughton's obsession with biblical etymology and the problems of translation, noted above and here articulated by Dol:

> For, as he says, except
> We call the Rabbins, and the heathen Greeks—
> . . . To come from Salem, and from Athens,
> And teach the people of great Britain— . . .
> To speak the tongue of Eber, and Javan— . . .
> . . . We shall know nothing—
> . . . Where, then, a learned Linguist
> Shall see the ancient used communion
> Of vowels, and consonants— . . .
> A wisdom, which Pythagoras held most high—
> . . . To comprise
> All sounds of voices, in few marks of letters—
> . . . .
> And so we may arrive by Talmud skill,
> And profane Greek, to raise the building up
> Of Helen's house, against the Ismaelite,
> King of Thogarma, and his Habergions
> Brimstony, blue, and fiery; and the force
> Of King Abaddon, and the Beast of Cittim;
> Which Rabbi David Kimchi, Onkelos,
> And Aben-Ezra do interpret Rome.
>
> (*IV.v.12–32*)

Again the concern for language, the references to "heathen" and "profane" Greek, and the glosses on the Apocalypse (for example, Brimstony, King Abaddon, Beast of Cittim) have all been selected to link Broughton's nice biblical studies with the scrupulous hypocrisies and millenarian dreams of both the Anabaptists and Sir Epicure.[50] Moreover, the biblical genealogies, Broughton's main concern in the *Concent* and the garbled subject of the first part of Dol's ravings, recall the alchemists' tracing of the secrets of the stone back through Solomon and the patriarchs to Adam, as Epicure does in II.i. As if to clinch all these interconnected themes, Subtle himself now reappears, presumably having resumed his Puritan gown. Again the point is made both visually and verbally, as he also resumes a decidedly Puritan self-righteousness: "How! What sight is here! / Close deeds of darkness, and that shun the light!" (41–42). After being rebuked, Mammon feebly claims, "Our purposes were honest." Subtle responds, "As they were, / So the reward will prove" (62–63);

at this cue *"A great crack and noise within"* is heard, and Face rushes to report the destruction of the whole operation, *"in fumo, . . .* As if a bolt / Of thunder had been driven through the house" (67–68). This last reference recalls Mammon's own earlier reference to "the art of Aesculapius, / That drew the envy of the Thunderer," as well as the notion of divine retribution providentially ordained, since Subtle reports a moment before that the "great work within" "has stood still this half hour": "No marvel, . . . When such affairs as these were managing!" (47–50). The scene ends with Face making a last few arrangements to bilk Mammon of even more money, as a "penance" for his "voluptuous mind," and, after Sir Epicure's sorry retreat, with Face and Subtle rejoicing in their triumph.

V

If, in the end, the fantastic dreams of the Anabaptists prove to be as empty as those of Sir Epicure, Jonson nevertheless makes sure that we see their defeat in similar terms, in order to complete the pattern of mutual reflection through distortion and parallel. Moreover, the fall of Subtle and Dol is also brought within this same frame of reference.

The bedlam of Act Five begins with the appearance of those Blackfriars Puritans whose presence, along with the return of Lovewit himself, recalls the fears expressed by Dol in the opening scene. Furthermore, the "indenture tripartite," the actual subject of that first scene, is again referred to, as Subtle and Dol attempt to cut Face out of the winnings because of his supposed liaison with Dame Pliant:

> *Subtle:*   Now he is gone about his project, Dol,
>   I told you of, for the widow.
> *Dol:*   'Tis direct
>   Against our articles.
> *Subtle:*   Well, we'll fit him, wench.
>   . . . .
>
>   Thou'st cause, when the slave will run a-wiving, Dol,
>   Against the instrument, that was drawn between us.
>   . . . .
>
>   . . . To deceive him
>   Is no deceit, but justice, that would break
>   Such an inextricable tie as ours was.
>   *(V.iv.70–72, 80–81, 102–104)*

Like the cozening Anabaptists, Subtle "distinguishes well" here. When it is Face, rather than Subtle and Dol, who "Determines the indenture tripartite" (130) a few lines later, the "republic" of thieves falls, and their triumvirate is dissolved: thus the first "state" within the liberties—based as it was on greed and dishonesty—crumbles, paralleling the demise of the other "millenary dreams" in the play.

By this time, Mammon and the Brethren have come for revenge and gone off again to fetch the officers and a warrant. As it turns out, Mammon, who thought himself above the law and who dreamed of going off to a "free state" to erect his own kingdom, is foiled by Lovewit's invocation of the common law of the land. Nor can Tribulation and Ananias, who "know no magistrate," hope to be championed by the very civil authorities they reject. To these ironies Jonson adds direct reminders of the absurd millennialism of all these characters. Just before Mammon is finally dismissed, he is exposed, as he abashedly tries to keep up a front of good intentions (he has already had to suffer Surly's mockery at V.iii.1–7). He will get his andirons and jacks back, says Lovewit, only

> by public means.
> If you can bring certificate, that you were gulled of 'em,
> Or any formal writ, out of a court,
> That you did cozen yourself: I will not hold them.
> . . . Upon these terms they're yours.
> . . . .
>
> What should they ha' been, sir, turned into gold all?
> *Mammon:*   No.
> I cannot tell. It may be they should. What then?
> *Lovewit:* What a great loss in hope have you sustained?
> *Mammon:* Not I, the commonwealth has.
> *Face:*   Aye, he would ha' built
> The city new; and made a ditch about it
> Of silver, should have run with cream from Hoxton:
> That, every Sunday in Moorfields, the younkers,
> And tits, and tomboys should have fed on, *gratis*.
>   (*V.v.67–70, 73–80*)

This interjection by Face—who has now reverted to the innocent butler, Jeremy—is wholly out of character here, but Jonson allows him this last jibe at Sir Epicure for our benefit, to underscore the absurdity of Mammon's millennialism. Characteristically, Jonson goes one step further. In II.iii, Face had predicted that were Sir Epicure to hear Dol "in her fit," he "would run mad, too" (240, 242). By now the corpulent knight is so overwrought that he is in fact transformed from a temporal or optimistic alchemical millennialist, who would have set up his own kingdom of life and lust with Dol, to a raving apocalyptic, or pessimistic, millennialist:

> I will go mount a turnip-cart, and preach
> The end o' the world, within these two months. Surly,
> What! In a dream?
>   (*V.v.81–83*)

Rather than enjoying the "fifth monarchy" that he "would erect with the stone," Sir Epicure will now preach the end of the world, like the most desperate of apocalyptic preachers.[51]

The image of Mammon preaching in a turnip-cart is another of Jonson's devices for superimposing theme, character, and action. Back in Scene One, Dol had referred to those "sober, scruffy, precise neighbours . . . Rascals, / [who] Would run themselves from breath, to see me ride" (I.i.164, 166–167)—that is, to be carted as a whore. This common punishment for criminals is also referred to by Surly, when he unmasks himself and pounces on Subtle, who is trying to pick his Spanish Don's pockets, and threatens him with "A good cart, / And a clean whip" (IV.vi.29–30). Moreover, Surly hopes that Subtle, like a common criminal or obnoxious Puritan, will "answer, by the ears" (54). Thus Mammon's mounting a cart as a crazed enthusiast aptly associates him with the prostitute and the cozening alchemist, both of whom deceive others and abuse nature.

When the Anabaptists return to the scene, they bring the Apocalypse with them, as it were, both in their ranting babble and in their imagery. The scarlet woman of Revelations is present in the various denunciations of the whores Dol and, by association, Dame Pliant. A few examples:

> *Kastril:* . . . Punk, device, my suster!
> *Ananias:* Call her not sister. She is a harlot, verily.
> (*V.iii.50–51*);
>
> *Mammon:* Madam Suppository.
> . . . .
> *Kastril:* The nun my suster.
> *Mammon:*   Madam Rabbi.
> (*V.v.13, 20*)

Tribulation, no longer eager to justify the Brethren's use of alchemy, now calls Subtle and Face "Profane as Bel, and the Dragon" (V.v.14), alluding to an apochryphal story added to Daniel 12.[52] These exclamations mesh perfectly with Ananias's apocalyptic language: the "stench" of Subtle's house is "broke forth: abomination / Is in the house," which "is become a cage of unclean birds" (V.iii.45–47; compare Revelation 17:4–5, 18:2). Ananias cannot resist comparing the scoundrels to the plagues of Pharoah: "Worse than the grasshoppers, or the lice of Egypt" (V.v.15; compare Exodus 7–11), but mainly he sees them as the apocalyptic "Locusts / Of the foul pit," or "Scorpions, / And caterpillars" (13–14, 20–21), from which those who "have the seal" will be protected as doomsday unfolds. Here is the scene that he has in mind, complete with an apocalyptic alchemical furnace:

And the fifth angel sounded, and I saw a star fall from heaven unto the earth; and to him
was given the key of the bottomless pit. And he opened the bottomless pit, and there arose
a smoke out of the pit, like the smoke of a great furnace; and the sun and the air were
darkened by reason of the same pit. And there came out of the smoke locusts upon the earth,
and unto them was given power, as the scorpions of the earth have power. And it was
commanded them that they should not hurt the grass of the earth, neither any green thing,
neither any tree, but only those men who have not the seal of God in their foreheads.

(*Revelation 9:1-4*)

To cap all this imprecation, Ananias proclaims Subtle and Face to be "the vessels /
Of pride, lust, and the cart" (V.v.23–24), thereby unwittingly anticipating Mammon's wheeled pulpit and identifying the most appropriate vehicle for the Anabaptists themselves. Nor has Jonson finished with this useful conveyance. The brazen-
faced Lovewit now invites the Brethren to enter the house to see for themselves how
they were deceived. No sooner has Mammon left the stage—calling for his "turnip-
cart"—than the Anabaptists, having surveyed the contents of the house, reenter:

Tribulation: 'Tis well, the Saints shall not lose all yet. Go,
    And get some carts—
Lovewit: For what, my zealous friends?
Ananias: To bear away the portion of the righteous,
    Out of this den of thieves.
Lovewit: What is that portion?
Ananias: The goods, sometimes the orphans', that the Brethren
    Bought with their silver pence.
Lovewit: What, those i'the cellar,
    The knight Sir Mammon claims?
Ananias: I do defy
    The wicked Mammon, so do all the Brethren,
    Thou profane man. I ask thee, with what conscience
    Thou canst advance that idol against us,
    That have the seal? Were not the shillings numbered,
    That made the pounds? Were not the pounds told out,
    Upon the second day of the fourth week,
    In the eight month, upon the table dormant,
    The year, of the last patience of the Saints,
    Six hundred and ten?
Lovewit: Mine earnest vehement botcher,
    And deacon also, I cannot dispute with you,
    But, if you get you not away the sooner,
    I shall confute you with a cudgel.
Ananias: Sir.
Tribulation: Be patient Ananias.
Ananias: I am strong,
    And will stand up, well girt, against an host,
    That threaten Gad in exile.
Lovewit: I shall send you
    To Amsterdam, to your cellar.

> *Ananias:*   I will pray there,
> Against thy house: may dogs defile thy walls,
> And wasps, and hornets breed beneath thy roof,
> This seat of falsehood, and this cave of cozenage.
>   (*V.v.90–115*)

Given the providential ruin of the Brethren, the "seal of God in their foreheads" claimed by Ananias now has to be seen as the same "visible mark of the Beast" that Ananias saw in Subtle's forehead (III.i.8). At any rate, Ananias's pseudo-biblical chronology and his desperate reference to the "last patience of the Saints" (that is, the millennium; see Revelation 14:12 and *passim*) are but his last futile efforts to cling to the Brethren's dream of "restoring ... the silenced Saints" (III.i.38), of being "temporal lords" (III.ii.52): like other fantasies in the play, these too have gone up *in fumo*. As Tribulation sadly understands, the Anabaptists' only hope lies in patience; the zealous Ananias sees himself as "Gad in exile," who will eventually conquer: "Gad, a troop shall overcome him; but he shall overcome at the last" (Genesis 49:19). His last prayer will be for a providential and apocalyptic plague to destroy Lovewit's house—an event with all the likelihood of Mammon's "end o'the world."[53] As no cart will save Mammon's soul, no carts will come to save the Brethren's investment. Were they to stay in England, Tribulation and Ananias would perhaps also be in danger of "riding," like the whores and cozeners whom they pretend to denounce. As it is, they must make the best of retreating to the "free state" of Holland, but without the preposterous luxury that Mammon had hoped for in his imagined "free state" and without the license to impose on others, as they and the alchemists alike have done "i'the liberties" of Blackfriars.

Jonson, however, cannot resist one last thrust at the millenary dreamers. As the timid Drugger—who himself aspires to making the philosophers' stone (see I.iii.74–80)—appears for the last time, Lovewit mistakes him for another Anabaptist, an action that recalls Subtle's deliberate mistaking of Ananias as *filius artis,* upon his first entrance:

> *Lovewit:*   Another too?
> *Drugger:*   Not I sir, I am no Brother.
> *Lovewit:*   Away you Harry Nicholas, do you talk?
>   (*He beats him away*)
>   (*V.v.116–118*)

Henry Nicholas (Henrick Niclase, 1502?–1580?), originally an Anabaptist, founded another radical sect that became perhaps just as notorious as the Anabaptists themselves, the Family of Love. Lovewit's epithet suggests that anyone who conceives of grandiose schemes of self-aggrandizement—even on the relatively moderate scale of the bourgeois Drugger—is as insane as the millennialists and visionaries of radical Puritanism.[54] Combined with Drugger's own reference to "Brother," it also completes the larger pattern of mirror images and parallels among millenarians, epicures, and alchemists.

The resolution of the play, which has evoked so much conflicting critical response, is accomplished within fifty lines of the Brethren's dejected exit (only Kastril's brief dismissal intervenes). While attractive arguments have been made endorsing Lovewit's indulgence toward Face and ours toward Lovewit, the foregoing analysis of satirical purpose and dramatic methods suggests a more uncompromising judgment. If Lovewit's genial capitalism is at first appealing, it is nevertheless no better, say, than Drugger's: that Lovewit is allowed to bully this small businessman off the stage does not grant Lovewit moral superiority. Furthermore, despite the urbanity of Lovewit's own apology, it must—especially in light of the hypocrisies of Mammon and the Anabaptists—fail to convince:

> That master
> That had received such happiness by a servant,
> In such a widow, and with so much wealth,
> Were very ungrateful, if he would not be
> A little indulgent to that servant's wit,
> And help his fortune, though with some small strain
> Of his own candour. Therefore, gentlemen,
> And kind spectators, if I have outstripped
> An old man's gravity, or strict canon, think
> What a young wife, and a good brain may do:
> Stretch age's truth sometimes, and crack it too.
> (V.v.146–156)

Lovewit's opportunism is not to be classed with the ridiculous millennial fantasies of Tribulation, Ananias, and Sir Epicure or with the insatiable greed of Subtle—or is it?

Like white-collar crime, Lovewit's rationalizing and cozy resettling into the life of Blackfriars simply has the appearance of greater respectability and is therefore even more insidious than the exaggerated obsessions of those whom he (or rather Face) has outwitted. If Dol could mock the smugness of Lovewit's "precise" and hypocritical neighbors, Lovewit himself is a worthy denizen of the "liberties." Besides all this, Lovewit has, if not a millenary dream, a "glorious future" planned for himself that is just as absurd: "think / What a young wife, and a good brain may do." Not only has this "old man's gravity" been outstripped in that he has foolishly made a January-May marriage (has Face completely overcome his lust for Dame Pliant? And whose brain is "good" but Face's?), but also his "candour" (honor, morality) has undergone more than "some small strain." He has too readily donned his Spanish cloak (how different is this from the gown of falsehood worn by alchemist and Anabaptist alike?), and by legal sophistry he has laid claim to property and money obtained through fraud (again, how different is this from the profitable casuistries of Subtle and Ananias/Tribulation?). We must not, in other words, fail to see in Lovewit yet another mirror image of greed and foolishness, although one with less apparent grotesqueness than those seen earlier.

Nor must we fail to see—prepared as we have been by the previous action—that the end of the play mirrors its beginning. For what else is the Face-Lovewit-Dame Pliant arrangement but another "venture tripartite" (the "old man" Lovewit replacing the aging Subtle, and a pliant widow replacing the common whore), based on trickery and blackmail? Ironically, it is also the play's ultimate "republic" (or "country," as Face is to call it), for while the "republics" or "free states" or "temporal lordships" of Subtle-Face-Dol, Mammon, and the Anabaptists were all outside or above the law, Lovewit's tidy establishment in the Liberties runs smoothly, "By order of law" (V.v.65): sanctioned, that is, by the sheer possession of property and by a "marriage" that is "Perfect" (V.v.6) insofar as the external forms have been observed. But like the "articles" or would-be legal "instrument" by which Subtle, Face, and Dol were bound to each other, the tenuous threads of deceit that make up the fabric of this new Blackfriars commonwealth can hardly prove "an inextricable tie."

There is something in most of us, nevertheless, that resists this clear-sightedness. Most people have some "millenary dream" and, like Philip Larkin's Toad, want "the fame and the girl and the money / All at one sitting."[55] Having observed the excesses of Sir Epicure, the Anabaptists, and Subtle himself, we also need to find something positive in Lovewit's triumphing over both the dupes and the con-artists, even if he is yet a greater con-artist who, like the laborers in the vineyard hired last, is paid out of all proportion. The original Blackfriars audience of the play must have been severely challenged in this regard, for they would have had the added pleasure of laughing at their own "sober, scruffy, precise neighbours" at the beginning of Act Five, as well as the nearly irresistible urge to applaud the urbane and apparently superior Lovewit as one of their own. But Jonson has anticipated that difficulty from the start, and while I believe he has deliberately put his audience in this awkward position, he has also shown us the way out. For not only has he warned us to look closely at the "terms" to see if they correspond to the "things" they represent (as in the last speeches by Face and Lovewit), but also he has pointed out that his play presents various mirrors—some more distorted than others, some presenting pleasing but absolutely false images—in which we must try to see ourselves:

> If there be any, that will sit so nigh
> Unto the stream, to look what it doth run,
>   They shall find things they'd think, or wish, were done;
> They are so natural follies, but so shown,
>   As even the doers may see, and yet not own.
>   ("Prologue," 20–24)

The final clue lies in Face's getting the last word, a fact that should give us pause. If he wishes us to be his "country" (as the jury was addressed by one pleading "not guilty"), we must nevertheless insist on being (as the "Prologue" exhorts us) "judging spectators": not only of the esthetic merits of the play but also of its analysis of human weakness. If we succumb to Lovewit's invitation to be only "*kind* spectators" (italics mine) and to Face's final invitation—which is really no more than a bribe—we become like those other corrupt judges, the "civil magistrate[s]" whom Tribulation hopes to cure with *aurum potabile,* "the only medicine" (p. 187 above):

> And though I am clean
> Got off, from Subtle, Surly, Mammon, Dol,
> Hot Ananias, Dapper, Drugger, all
> With whom I traded; yet I put myself
> On you, that are my country: and this pelf,
> Which I have got, if you do quit me, rests
> To feast you often, and invite new guests.
>   (*V.v.159–165*)

To be true "understanders," that is, we must read these speeches with the attention demanded by Jonson's epigrams. Nor should this mirror of art show us only the minor foibles of the likes of Dapper, Drugger, or Kastril on the one hand and the monstrous reflections of alchemy, epicureanism, and perverted religiosity, on the other. If we become smug in our mockery of one group of characters or self-righteous in denouncing the other, while at the same time applauding Lovewit, we neither "see" nor "own" our natural follies. What makes such moral judgment both difficult and rewarding is Jonson's perfect blending of the particular (the outrages of Anabaptism, grotesque libertinism, and fraudulent alchemy) and the general (the human weaknesses of pride, sensuality, and greed found in ourselves no less than in Lovewit). *The Alchemist* requires us to see both. Jonson's own "millenary dream" is that, by seeing such "fair correctives," we will be genuinely "cured," not merely bought off with entertainment, and thus prove his alchemy true.

NOTES

1. The first view, that of R. J. L. Kingsford, ed., *The Alchemist* (Cambridge: Cambridge University Press, 1952), p. ix, is attacked by the Revels Plays editor, F. H. Mares (London: Methuen, 1967), p. xxxi.

2. Michael Flachmann, "Ben Jonson and the Alchemy of Satire," *SEL: Studies in English Literature,* 17 (1977), 279; C. G. Thayer, *Ben Jonson: Studies in the Plays* (Norman: University of Oklahoma Press, 1963), p. 102. See also Judd Arnold, "Lovewit's Triumph and Jonsonian Morality: A Reading of *The Alchemist,*" *Criticism,* 11 (1969), 151–166, especially 155–157. These readings assume, rightly I think, that Jonson, like Shakespeare or Donne, saw alchemy as both a legitimate pursuit (and therefore as a source of "positive" metaphor) and as a vehicle for charlatans (and therefore as a source of "negative" metaphor and as an object of ridicule).

3. *The Alchemist,* "To the Reader," in *The Complete Plays of Ben Jonson,* 4 vols., ed. G. A. Wilkes, based on the edition of C. H. Herford and Percy and Evelyn Simpson. (Oxford: Clarendon Press, 1982), III, 228. Unless otherwise indicated, all citations from Jonson's plays are from this edition.

4. Douglas Duncan, in *Ben Jonson and the Lucianic Tradition* (Cambridge: Cambridge University Press, 1979), pp. 200ff., sees Jonson himself questioning the validity of his own analogy between poet and alchemist.

5. *Ben Jonson,* 11 vols., ed. C. H. Herford and Percy Simpson, (Oxford: Clarendon Press, 1925), 11

vols., II, 89. Subsequent references to this edition, henceforward H & S, will be given in the text by volume and page number.

6. See, for example, Keith Thomas, *Religion and the Decline of Magic* (London: Weidenfeld and Nicholson, 1971), pp. 270–271; Christopher Hill, *Intellectual Origins of the English Revolution* (Oxford: Clarendon Press, 1965) pp. 122–123; Ronald S. Wilkinson, "The Alchemical Library of John Winthrop, Jr. (1606–1676) and his Descendants in Colonial America," *Ambix*, 11 (1963), 33–51, *Ambix*, 13 (1966) 139–186; P. M. Rattansi, "Paracelsus and the Puritan Revolution," *Ambix*, 11 (1963), 24–32; Charles Webster, "English Medical Reformers of the Puritan Revolution: A Background to the 'Society of Chymical Physicians'," *Ambix*, 14 (1967), 16–41.

7. Harold Fisch, *Jerusalem and Albion: The Hebraic Factor in Seventeenth-Century Literature* (New York: Schocken, 1964), p. 205. It is also worth noting that certain of Paracelsus's social and theological ideas were consonant with the beliefs of the Anabaptists, the chief sect of Puritanism with which Jonson is concerned in *The Alchemist* (see below); see Walter Pagel, *Paracelsus: An Introduction to the Philosophical Medicine of the Renaissance* (New York: Karger, 1958), pp. 17, 43, 114.

8. Robert M. Schuler, "William Blomfild, Elizabethan Alchemist," *Ambix*, 20 (1973), 75–87.

9. Schuler, "Some Spiritual Alchemies of Seventeenth-Century England," *Journal of the History of Ideas*, 41 (1980), especially 303–308.

10. William P. Holden, *Anti-Puritan Satire 1572–1642*, Yale Studies in English, No. 126 (New Haven, Conn.: Yale University Press, 1954), pp. 118, 126.

11. Bertil Johanson, *Religion and Superstition in the Plays of Ben Jonson and Thomas Middleton* (Cambridge, Mass.: Harvard University Press, 1950), p. 220, n. 2, notes how this idea is suggested in the references to the Anabaptists as the "company of the Separation" and "we of the Separation" (IV.vii.85; III.i.2), as *separation* (of the pure from the gross) refers to one of the chief alchemical operations.

12. It is no accident that the reference to "ear-rent" would recall precisely the kind of punishments endured by radical Puritans themselves in this period: even in this Jonson anticipates the association between cozeners (fraudulent alchemists) and Puritans. See below and note that Subtle refers to the "shorte[ning] of ears" for "libel 'gainst the prelates" (III.ii.86–87); see also Aaron Michael Myers, *Representation and Misrepresentation of the Puritan in Elizabethan Drama* (Philadelphia: University of Pennsylvania Press, 1931), p. 37. The reference to the whore's cart is the first of several, whose cumulative effect is discussed below.

13. It is worth noting in this context that Jonson's contemporary, Nathan Field, not only alludes to Blackfriars as a district where one could hear such preaching but also associates this "teaching i' the nose" with alchemy:

> *Widow.* Precise and learned *Princox,* dost not thou go to *Black-fryers.*
> *Bould.* Most frequently Madame, vnworthy vessell that I am to partake
>   or retaine any of the delicious dew, that is there distilled.

The play on "vessel," in its religious and alchemical sense, is worthy of Jonson himself; see *Amends for Ladies* (1611), III.iii.29–33, in *The Plays of Nathan Field*, ed. William Peery (Austin: University of Texas Press, 1950).

14. For the terms *precise* and *precision* see Myers, pp. 19–20, 22.

15. Holden, p. 115.

16. As G. R. Elton notes, the Reformation was an age of uniformity, "an age which held at all times and everywhere that one unit could not comprehend within itself two forms of belief or worship. The tenet rested on a single fact: as long as membership of a secular polity involved membership of an ecclesiastical organization, religious dissent stood equal to political disaffection and even

treason." "The Age of the Reformation," in *The New Cambridge Modern History* (Cambridge: Cambridge University Press, 1958), II, 5.

17. The hubbub of this scene also anticipates the hysterical babble of Dol "in her fit" in IV.v, which (see below) is another image of radical Puritan anarchy.

18. Ernest A. Payne, "The Anabaptists," in *The New Cambridge Modern History,* II, 119, 129.

19. These points of doctrine were formulated in 1527 at Schlätt, near Schaffhausen, and they circulated widely in the sixteenth century; quotations are from Payne, "The Anabaptists," p. 125. For lists of Anabaptist heresies that correspond to these beliefs and that appear in the Proclamations of Henry VIII, Edward VI, and Mary, see Irvin Buckwalter Horst, *The Radical Brethren: Anabaptism and the English Reformation to 1558* (Nieuwkoop: De Graaf, 1972), pp. 50, 61, 91–92.

20. Payne, "The Anabaptists," p. 119.

21. B. S. Capp, *The Fifth Monarchy Men: A Study in Seventeenth-Century English Millenarianism* (London: Faber, 1972), p. 27. For the sixteenth-century backgrounds of millenarianism, see all of Ch. 2. See also below, p. 197–198.

22. Ironically, in this period millenarian ideas combined with radical politics to create a genuine revolution, to the extent that in 1649 the Commonwealth could be referred to satirically as "New-Munster" (Horst, p. 28).

23. Peter Toon, "Introduction," *Puritans, The Millennium and the Future of Israel: Puritan Eschatology 1600–1660,* ed. Peter Toon (London: Clarke, 1970), p. 19.

24. Horst, pp. 61, 137, and *passim.* For a discussion of apocalyptic militarism, see Michael Walzer, *The Revolution of the Saints: A Study in the Origins of Radical Politics* (Cambridge, Mass.: Harvard University Press, 1965), pp. 291–293; 297–298.

25. See, for example, Heinrich Bullinger, *An Holsome Antidotus . . . agaynst the . . . Anabaptistes,* trans. John Veron (London, 1548), sigs. H1^r, I4^r, and *passim.* See also Myers, p. 96, and note 16 above.

26. For the Anabaptists at Münster, see Payne, "The Anabaptists" and Norman Cohn, *The Pursuit of the Millennium: Revolutionary Millenarians and Anarchists of the Middle Ages,* 3rd ed. (London: Paladin, 1970), pp. 252–328. P. G. Rogers, in *The Fifth Monarchy Men* (London: Oxford University Press, 1966), gives this account of the movement: "John Buckhold and his followers were called Anabaptists by their contemporaries because they rejected infant baptism, and therefore required their followers to be re-baptised. It was, however, their other doctrines, bound up with their belief in the imminence of the millennium, which caused the greatest scandal and horror. Indeed, for many years to come the word Anabaptist was to be used loosely to describe religious fanatics and desperadoes of all kinds, and it conjured up in the mind of the law-abiding the most terrible images of excess and disorder" (p. 8).

27. See *The Works of Thomas Nashe,* ed. Ronald B. McKerrow, rev. F. P. Wilson, 5 vols. (Oxford: Blackwell, 1958), II, 232–241. Nashe refers to *"Iohn Leiden* and all the crue of Cnipperdolings" (p. 239), as if to indicate that the latter term was a commonplace in Jonson's time.

28. Gerald H. Cox, in "Apocalyptic Projection and the Comic Plot of *The Alchemist,"English Literary Renaissance,* 13 (1983), 70–87, sees Lovewit's return as an apocalyptic "second coming," blended with the parables of the talents and the unexpected return of an absent master (for example, Matthew 24:45–51, 25:14–30; Luke 19:11–27). Cox's excellent article, which I encountered only after the present essay was in its final form, fully explores the play's apocalyptic elements, but from another point of view and without reference to millenarianism as such.

29. To these were added, when available, the Sibylline Oracles, a collection of prophecies compiled by Jewish and Christian writers in imitation of the pagan "Sibylline Books" (Toon, *Puritan Eschatology,* p. 17) and, in a writer like John Foxe, "any [other] prophecy which was conceivably relevant" (Capp, p. 26).

30. Toon, Ch. 1; Capp, p. 20.

31. See Rogers, *The Fifth Monarchy Men*, pp. 8–10.

32. See, for example, Capp. pp. 29, 33–34.

33. Duncan, in *Ben Jonson and the Lucianic Tradition*, sees in this description "a comic allusion to Aristotle's remark that 'traits generally attributed to the great-souled man are a slow gait, a deep voice, and a deliberate utterance' " (p. 196).

34. Jonas A. Barish, *Ben Jonson and the Language of Prose Comedy* (Cambridge, Mass.: Harvard University Press, 1960), pp. 198–199.

35. For a close examination of Mammon's language as based on biblical texts and for the resulting parody of religion (especially the parody of Solomon in Sir Epicure), see Myrddin Jones, "Sir Epicure Mammon: A Study in 'Spiritual Fornication'," *Renaissance Quarterly*, 22 (1969), 233–242.

36. For the nasal twang of the enthusiastic preachers, see Holden, *Anti-Puritan Satire*, pp. 103, 117–118; Myers, pp. 36, 85 (where it is associated with lust), and this passage from Randolph's *News from the New World:* "lunatic persons, walkers only: that have leave only to *Hum* and *Ha*, not daring to prophecy, or start up upon stools to raise doctrine" (quoted in Myers, p. 16).

37. This point is developed by Flachmann, "The Alchemy of Satire," pp. 268, 272–274.

38. A minor exception is Paul A. Trout's unpublished paper of more than ten years ago, "The Millenary Dream of Alchemy," given at the 88th Annual Convention of the Modern Language Association, 29 December 1973 (11 pp.), which touches on this point incidentally. Trout's main concern is with alchemy and millenarianism of the Commonwealth period; he sees Jonson's vision as an "uncanny prescience" and suggests that the dramatist "foreshadowed" the historical convergence of alchemy and millenarianism (for example, among the Fifth Monarchy Men) of the interregnum (pp. 5, 8–9). We have already seen, however, that the historical connections between alchemy and Puritanism easily antedate the year 1610; millennialism in alchemy was not a peculiarly seventeenth-century phenomenon, as the example of Paracelsus shows. See, for example, Fisch, *Jerusalem and Albion,* pp. 218–219, and Trout's own dissertation, "Magic and the Millennium: A Study of the Millenary Motifs in the Occult Milieu of Puritan England, 1640–1660," University of British Columbia, 1974, pp. 64–68. Neither here nor in his short paper does Trout examine *The Alchemist* in detail.

39. Trout says, mistakenly, I believe, that a "philanthropic ideal also motivates Mammon" and that his supposed projects to relieve suffering, cure disease, and make friends wealthy anticipated the philanthropic enterprises of Samual Hartlib ("Millenary Dream," p. 6). I doubt that Hartlib would like the comparison.

40. Compare John 20:23, "Whose soever sins ye remit, they are remitted unto them; and whose soever sins ye retain, they are retained."

41. See, for example, the association of one Martin Pery, accused of "false clipping or false coyning of money" under Henry VIII, with fraudulent alchemists in William Blomfild's peom, "The Compendiary of the Noble Science of Alchemy" (1557), ed. Robert M. Schuler, *Three Renaissance Scientific Poems, Studies in Philology,* Texts and Studies, 75 (1978), 25, 47. In I.i.113–114, Face threatens Subtle under the statute of 1541, "for laundering gold, and barbing [that is, clipping] it," anticipating Ananias as a "gold-end-man."

42. Jonson's attitude toward Ananias's prophecies is unwittingly summed up in the next scene by Tribulation:

> It is an *ignorant* zeal that haunts him, sir.
> But truly, else, a very faithful Brother,
> A botcher: and a man, by *revelation,*
> That hath a competent *knowledge* of the truth.
>   (*III.ii.111–114, italics mine*)

43. In this and in his following explanation that "We must give, I say, / Unto the motives, and the stirrers up / Of humours in the blood" (III.i.27–29) is the psychological basis, as it were, of Jonson's moral analysis of the human failings of pride and egotism that underlie the notion of adeptship/election.

44. F. H. Mares notes that Subtle's reference to "drawing the Hollanders, your friends, / From the Indies, to serve you, with all their fleet" (III.ii.23–24) recalls the attempts of the followers of John of Leiden to take control of the Dutch towns of Amsterdam, Deventer, and Wesel, which led to their persecution and flight to England in the 1530s and later (ed. cit., pp. 81n., 97n.). Subtle introduces Dutch alchemy in his comparison of Dapper to "dead Holland, living Isaac" (I.ii.109), which Herford and Simpson gloss as "John and John Isaac, surnamed Holland, reputed to have been the first Dutch alchemists in the first half of the fifteenth century" (X, 63). The geographical range of the Anabaptist-alchemical nexus is extended to Germany first when Ananias complains to Subtle that "one, at Heidelberg, made it [the philosophers' stone], of an egg, / And a small paper of pin-dust" (II.v.70–71) and later when Tribulation admonishes the Deacon: "You did fault, to upbraid him [Subtle] / With the Brethren's blessing of Heidelberg" (III.i.35–36). *The Mennonite Encyclopedia* (Scotsdale, Pennsylvania: Mennonite Publishing House, 1956), II, 691 indicates that "the Anabaptist movement was widespread in the Heidelberg area in the late 16th century."

45. Libertinism was a common accusation aimed at the Anabaptists, deriving probably from the polygamy at Münster and from rumors of licentiousness regarding many of the sects (see, for example, Myers, pp. 96ff.). Throughout this diatribe, as with the references to "Brethren" and "Sisters" in the passage quoted, Subtle turns Puritan cant upon the Anabaptists themselves. See, for example, his use of *exercises, graced, vizard, idol,* and so on; these and other terms are explained in detail by M. van Beek, *An Enquiry into Puritan Vocabulary* (Groningen, The Netherlands: Wolters-Noordhoff, 1969).

46. See Paul Christianson, *Reformers and Babylon: English Apocalyptic Visions from the Reformation to the Eve of the Civil War* (Toronto: University of Toronto Press, 1978), index, s.v. *Armada;* Katharine F. Firth, *The Apocalyptic Tradition in Reformation Britain 1530–1645* (London: Oxford University Press, 1979), *passim;* Toon, *Puritan Eschatology,* p. 77. Both Christianson and Firth have substantial discussions of Broughton's career, as does G. Lloyd Jones, *The Discovery of Hebrew in Tudor England: A Third Language* (Manchester: Manchester University Press, 1983), who notes that for Broughton and others, "the motives for studying Hebrew were implicit in the study of apocalyptic" (p. 166).

    Dame Pliant's reference to the Armada, as she explains her dislike for Spaniards (IV.iv. 29–30), as well as the "defeat" of this formidable Spanish threat in the form of Surly's Don Diego, makes for an amusing jab at the apocalyptic significance of Surly's near overthrow of the "republic" of thieves, but the eventual success of Lovewit—in the same Spanish costume—suggests to me the conquest not only of the thieves but of ordered society as a whole. See my conclusion below, and compare the positive interpretation of Lovewit's apocalyptic return in Cox, "Apocalyptic Projection," pp. 84–87.

47. He actually began the apocalyptic teaching among the exiled Puritans in Holland; see Keith L. Sprunger, *Dutch Puritanism: A History of English and Scottish Churches of the Netherlands in the Sixteenth and Seventeenth Centuries,* Studies in the History of Christian Thought, No. XXXI (Leiden: Brill, 1982), p. 331; see also Ch. 3, "The Amsterdam Separatists and Anabaptists." For Broughton's egotistical debate with another Hebraist, one who embraced Separatism, see his *Certayne Questions ... Handled Between Mr Hugh Broughton ... and Mr Henry Ainsworth* (Amsterdam? 1605); and Michael E. Moody, " 'A Man of a Thousand': The Reputation and Character of Henry Ainsworth,1569/70–1622," *Huntington Library Quarterly,* 45 (1982), 203.

48. Firth, *Apocalyptic Tradition,* pp. 159–160, 163; Christianson, *Reformers and Babylon,* pp. 107–109, 129; Toon, *Puritan Eschatology,* p. 24.

49. Broughton himself published *A Revelation of the Apocalyps* in the same year that *The Alchemist* was first performed. One might add that Dol's reference to a "fourth chain" (10) has to do with biblical chronology too and that Broughton recapitulates his theory of the "fiue chaines whiche drawe from Adams fal vnto our Lords resurrection" in *An Epistle to the Learned Nobilitie of England* (1597), pp. 27–29; in concluding this account, he refers obliquely to the millennium: "The fyfte chayne reacheth from Babels fall to our Lordes death. This was knowen in the Apostles time to all Iewes: and commeth infinitely to be regarded in the newe Testament. And this one poinct is enough to stoppe all Antichristian mouthes: that the sonnes labours haue a better story than that of *Bitias Atlas* scholler in Didoes court: euen his labours through all ages till Christ shewed a newe worlde: where all that marke it, shalbe as the sunne in the kingdome of the Father" (p. 29). Interestingly, Broughton goes on, in the next page, to compare the true translator to the goldsmith, the bad translator to "counterfaiters, and forgers of metalles."

50. The original passages from the *Concent of Scripture* from which Jonson selected these details are printed in Herford and Simpson, X, 104-106.

51. See the distinction above between the millenarian and apocalyptic (p. 176). For this last image of Sir Epicure, Jonson probably had in mind some of the more crazy apocalyptic prophets of the recent past, like William Hacket (above, p. 178).

52. See *Dictionary of the Bible,* ed. James Hastings, rev. Frederick C. Grant and H. H. Rowley (New York: Scribners, 1963), p. 41.

53. Professor Capp's comment is pleasingly apt: "Despite the pleasure with which it anticipated the punishment of God's enemies, the apocalyptic school was definitely pessimistic in outlook. There was no real hope of improvement before the end of the world" (*The Fifth Monarchy Men,* p. 27).

54. On the Family of Love, see Middleton's play of that name and, for a brief survey and introduction to a mass of scholarship, Horst, *The Radical Brethren,* pp. 152–154. In the 1570s, the heyday of the Familists in Elizabethan England, they objected to being associated with the Anabaptists, but Jonson and other satirists tended to group the radical sects together. Myers notes that, among satirists, the Familists were most noted for "turning Scriptures into meaningless jargon and [for their] many preposterous prophecies of coming political events" (p. 17). By the middle of the seventeenth century, the Behmenists were frequently called Familists and thus the Familists were linked with "the alchemical movement"; see the major study by Jean Dietz Moss, *"Godded with God": Hendrik Niclaes and His Family of Love, Transactions of the American Philosophical Society,* Vol. 71, part 8 (Philadelphia, 1981), p. 63.

55. "Toads," in *The Less Deceived* (London: Marvell Press, 1955), p. 31. The moral seriousness of the play is well argued in a recent study by Richard Dutton, *Ben Jonson: To the First Folio* (Cambridge: Cambridge University Press, 1983), pp. 113–124. This fine overview examines *The Alchemist* in light of the social and moral concerns of *The Forest* and *Cataline* and, from this perspective, considers the play's various "republics" as well as the problem of audience entrapment, which results from a willingness "to suppress our moral judgement in the interests of comic entertainment" (p. 117).

The Playhouse as an Investment, 1607–1614; Thomas Woodford and Whitefriars

WILLIAM INGRAM

THIRTY YEARS ago G. E. Bentley summed up contemporary scholarship on the "obscure private playhouse in Whitefriars" with the succinct if wry observation that the playhouse had "a rather shadowy existence before 1613" and that it was probably "not . . . used at all after that date".[1] Our knowledge has not advanced much beyond this minimum in the three decades since Bentley's remark. We still do not know where the playhouse was, or when it began to be used as a playhouse, or by whom, in other than the most general terms.

We know of only two companies that certainly occupied the playhouse. They were both companies of children, and they both seem to have had royal patents, although only the second company's patent has been found. The first company, the Children of the King's Revels, seems to have played at Whitefriars only in 1607 and 1608. They were followed by the Children of the Queen's Revels from 1609 until 1613 or 1614. Possibly the Lady Elizabeth's players also used the playhouse for one year in 1613–14, but this is only conjecture. It seems likely that the playhouse was intended from the outset to capitalize on a fashionable trend; its promoters surely felt that there was money to be made in such an enterprise, for the expenses of the undertaking could hardly be justified on grounds other than the expectation of profit.

The main source of our information about the playhouse and its tenants is still the lawsuit commonly referred to as Andrews vs. Slater, first transcribed in 1888 by James Greenstreet and published in the *Transactions of the New Shakspere Society* for that year.[2] More information has been made available to us since Greenstreet's day by the publications of C. W. Wallace, H. N. Hillebrand, and others, but we still have nothing resembling clarity; it would be fairer to emend Bentley's term and claim that we have come out of obscurity into mere murkiness.

In the present essay I want to explore the current state of our knowledge, add a few new facts, and essay a few conjectures. The paper is organized topically and begins with a brief historical survey.

I. Brief Historical Survey

Lording Barry turned twenty-seven in mid-April 1607, but the occasion was marred by his father's death. Nicholas Barry had made his will just ten days earlier, and before the month was out the father was dead and buried and the will had passed through probate. Lording Barry probably received his legacy by the early summer;

his biographer C. L. Ewen estimates that it may not have amounted to more than about £10.[3]

By late summer of the same year, however, Barry was involved in a project that necessitated larger sums of money. No doubt his inheritance disappeared quickly enough. On 4 August 1607 he borrowed £20 for six months from John Keale, with William Trevell and Edward Sibthorpe as surety.[4] A week later, on 12 August, he engaged himself in three more loans. He borrowed £20 from Thomas Woodford, probably for six months, with Trevell as surety, and on the same date he and Trevell borrowed another £60 from Woodford on a separate note, due on 25 November, with Sibthorpe and Michael Drayton as surety.[5] On yet a third bond bearing the same date, he borrowed £5 more from Woodford, to be repaid on 9 October.[6] Three days later, on 15 August 1607, Barry borrowed £7 from Anthony Wilkins, to be repaid £1 a week commencing 3 October, and on the same date he borrowed £4.6.9 on a second bond to Wilkins to be repaid on 1 November.[7]

Barry's indebtedness from these bonds alone—there may have been others of which we are ignorant—was close to £120. A prudent man could have supported his family for ten years on such a sum. By the middle of the following summer Barry had defaulted on all of these loans and had been sued, along with his co-signer William Trevell, in various courts of law. The pattern of borrowing suggests a capital investment of some magnitude taking place in the summer or autumn of 1607 involving primarily Barry, but also in some measure Trevell, Sibthorpe, and Drayton, with much of the money being advanced or, more probably, arranged for by Thomas Woodford. The pattern of due dates (the loans are all for periods of six months or less) suggests a general expectation on the part of the borrowers that income from the investment—and thus for the repayment of the loans—would not be long in materializing. And the pattern of defaults and lawsuits in 1608 equally attests to the failure of the venture by the following summer.

There are further signs of activity between the summer of 1607 and the summer of 1608, to fill in the borders of this financial frame. Some time before 30 August 1607 Richard Edwards, a tailor dwelling in the parish of St. Dunstan's in the West between Ram Alley and Chancery Lane, advanced four felt hats with hatbands to Edmund Sharpham. Sharpham's play *Cupid's Whirligig,* which we know to have been performed by the Children of the King's Revels at Whitefriars, had been entered in the Stationers' Register just two months earlier, on 29 June, and the hats may have been intended for a production of the play. On 30 August Edward Sibthorpe came to Richard Edwards with a request for another hat and band; but since Sharpham had not yet paid for the earlier hats, Edwards required bonds of both Sibthorpe and Sharpham before complying. Some months later, on 23 December 1607, Thomas Woodford approached Edwards with a request for yet another hat, a felt hat embroidered with silver and with a pearl hatband, to be used for a play later that same day ("utend*um* pro se vel s*ervientes* suos in quodam int*er*ludio postea eodem vicesimo t*er*cio die Decembris . . . in quadam domo in le White ffryers lon-don"). But Edwards had still not been paid by Sharpham or Sibthorpe. Woodford offered to take on their debts along with his own and to sign a bond to Edwards in the Court of Arches. With that, Edwards acquiesced. Woodford later defaulted on the bond.[8]

Thomas Woodford may himself have been resident in Whitefriars at this time. The precinct, although a liberty and therefore extra-parochial, was nevertheless considered a part of the parish of St. Dunstan's in the West, and the baptisms, marriages, and burials of the precinct's inhabitants appear in the St. Dunstan records in the same way that the records of the poor prisoners in the Fleet appear in the registers of St. Bride's Church. The parish clerk of St. Dunstan's recorded in his register that on 8 September 1607 "Jeffry Daveys servant to Mr Woodford out of the ffryers" was buried in the churchyard. When the receipts for ground, pit, and knell were recorded in the churchwardens' account book for that date, the "servant" was somehow misrecorded as "Mr Woodford*es* Infant"; the error is a careless one, even considering the vague similarity between the two words in secretary hand, but it does not weaken the basic evidence about "Mr" Woodford's residence in Whitefriars.[9]

Later that month the playhouse itself was mentioned in the register, with the burial on 29 September 1607 of one "[blank] Gerry out of the playe howse in ye ffryers." This entry has been known for some sixty years and was reproduced by Chambers, but its cognate entries have curiously never been mentioned: the burial also on 29 September of "ffrauncis sonne of the saide Gerry" and on 30 September of "[blank] Wife of the saide Gerrey." With these new citations before us, we may no longer presume, with Nungezer, that "Gerry" was one of the children in the company.

By the middle of October, still more loans were in train. William Cooke, a haberdasher of St. Lawrence Pountney Parish (the parish where Lording Barry lived), lent £20 on 16 October to Barry, Trevell, and Sibthorpe, with John Mason and John Cooke as surety. Mason is of course the playwright, whose play *The Turk* would later be published as having been played by the Children of the King's Revels at Whitefriars. He had probably joined the syndicate by this time. I do not know who John Cooke was; he does not reappear. William Cooke proved a shrewd lender; for his money, he required and got "An assureaunce of twoe twelue *partes* of the Lease of the Whyte ffryars playe house, And of A *parte* of the Shares as maye appeare by the wrightinge*s* therof made by Barrey and Sybthorpe," which Cooke kept "for his better securytye" in the transaction. William Cooke thus joined Lording Barry, William Trevell, Edward Sibthorpe, John Mason, and Michael Drayton as a shareholder in the enterprise.[10]

Although the loan from Cooke was formalized on 16 October 1607, at the shop of Randall Hanmer, a scrivener in Friday Street, Cooke did not simply hand over the £20. The borrowers wanted him to hold it for them and to advance it in stages. Barry and Sibthorpe were in charge of the parceling out, and they requested £2.3.0 to Mason at once. Further, Sibthorpe was to have £3 "for the boyes of the playe house there boorde and dyett," and Cooke noted that "the three pound*es* then payed" was "for there weekes dyett aforehand." Barry and Sibthorpe asked Cooke to hold the remainder of the money until they should ask for it "from tyme to tyme to paye for the boyes dyett*es*" in subsequent weeks; Cooke conjectured that this novel method of disbursing a loan was due to the plague, for it was then "in the Sycknes tyme when no p*er*son would trust them." A week later, on 22 October, Cooke paid Sibthorpe another £3 "for the said Playe boyes diet," and by 27 October he had paid the balance to Mason, thus clearing the books.[11]

Like the other loans that form the basis of this summary, this loan from Cooke was defaulted. So were some of Cooke's further loans to his new colleagues, and eventually he had to go to law to recover. In his plea he claimed that "he hadd" out of all this trouble "halfe a Share of the whyt ffryars playehouse assigned vnto him wch Coste him about ffyve and ffortye pound*es* wch he hath loste Amongeste them."[12]

Cooke's comment about "Sycknes tyme" is borne out by the records.[13] The plague was indeed alive in the City in the autumn of 1607, at its worst in September and October (177 plague deaths in the week of 24 September), and the pestilence may have been one factor in the playhouse's ill fortune; playing must surely have been prohibited for most of that period. Cooke's loan in October was soon gone; by mid-November Barry was borrowing money from Nicholas Carrier and yet more money from Thomas Woodford.[14] Then, in December, the Great Frost descended upon the City, freezing the Thames until January. The plague abated, but the syndicate's need for capital did not. The syndicate may also have sensed a need for better management; perhaps Edward Sibthorpe's performance as master of the boys was found wanting. Martin Slater, a seasoned player then in his late forties, began negotiations with the syndicate at about this time with the aim of bringing his professional skills to the management of the group. To finance this move Barry, apparently with the help of Slater himself, persuaded one George Andrews, a silk-weaver, to buy into the syndicate. William Cooke had estimated that his half-share had cost him £45, and this may well have been the going rate, for Andrews was asked for £90 for his full share. He balked, and the syndicate settled for £70.[15]

Andrews joined the syndicate in February 1608, and by early March 1608 the group was ready to enter into formal agreement with Slater about the terms and conditions of his employment. We are fortunate in having the text of this document, for it was reproduced in full by George Andrews as a part of the pleadings in his suit against Slater in Chancery in February 1609. The Articles of Agreement were dated 10 March 1608 and were between Slater on the one part and the syndicate— "Lordinge Barry, George Androwes, Michaell Drayton, Willyam Trevell, Willyam Cooke, Edward Sibthorpe and John Mason of the Cittie of London gentlemen"—on the other.[16] The terms of the agreement are businesslike and no doubt represent Slater's considered notions of what the operation required in order to survive financially.

But it may already have been too late. Trevell had been forced, even as Andrews was buying into the group, to borrow yet more money; this time it was £50 from one Elizabeth Brown. The loan was due in six months, and, like all the others, it was not repaid.[17] By Easter Term 1608 the chickens were coming home to roost. John

Keale sued Barry, Trevell, and Sibthorpe in the Court of Common Pleas and was awarded the judgment.[18] Thomas Woodford sued Barry and Trevell in three separate suits in the Court of King's Bench and was awarded all three judgments.[19] Barry and Trevell were in especial jeopardy because they had been the principal borrowers of the past summer. Barry had the foresight to disappear at about this time, and by late summer of 1608 he had commenced his astonishing new career as a pirate on the high seas.[20] William Trevell was left holding the bag, and he was pursued by lawsuits to the end of his life and even beyond; in 1643 his widow Susan sued in the Court of Requests for relief from the continued persecutions of Thomas Woodford.[21]

At some point during the spring or summer of 1608, the syndicate must have given over the operation. It may well have been in April, shortly after the performance of *Byron* by the Children of Blackfriars that caused the King to close that playhouse and apparently the other playhouses in London as well. At some later point, probably in the summer, the syndicate entered into negotiations with Robert Keysar and Phillip Rosseter with the object of assigning the lease to them. Rosseter was a lutanist and composer in the King's service, a senior colleague of John Dowland's, and a musician of the first rank who has not yet received adequate attention from theater historians. He lived in St. Dunstan's Parish, on the edge of Whitefriars, in a house in Fleet Street near Fetter Lane.[22] No evidence has yet turned up about the details of the negotiations between Rosseter and the Barry-Drayton syndicate, or to suggest when they took place; but since Barry would have had to be a party to such a transfer, and as he was not in London after the summer of 1608, the range of possibility is limited. Rosseter and his colleagues in due course transferred to the Whitefriars playhouse the company of offending children from Blackfriars, and on 4 January 1610 they received a renewal of their patent under the name of the Children of the Queen's Revels.[23]

The sale of the lease to Rosseter and his colleagues was accompanied by two events that may or may not be related to it. The first is the claim by William Trevell, as recalled by his widow in 1643, that the Barry-Drayton group was evicted from the playhouse by Sir Anthony Ashley on the pretext that half a year's rent was unpaid.[24] The second is Martin Slater's complaint, in his answer to Andrews, that he and his family had been ejected from their rooms over the playhouse even though by the terms of the Articles of Agreement he was to occupy the rooms without molestation "duringe the continewance of the said lease." Since we know from other sources that Rosseter and his colleagues occupied the Whitefriars playhouse without incident from their purchase of the lease until it expired in 1614, we must assume that the Barry-Drayton syndicate effected a legal transfer to them. This being so, Slater may well have had a just claim to continued tenancy under the lease, although there is no record of his pursuing such a claim at law.

Similarly, Sir Anthony Ashley may have thought that the syndicate had defaulted on the rent, not realizing that they had instead sold the lease, and he may therefore have evicted them—and Slater as well—in error. Trevell's widow Susan claimed that Ashley, "beinge Landlord of the Playhouse," had made his move "by combina-

cion with" Thomas Woodford "vppon *pre*tence that halfe a yeares Rent for the Playhouse was unpaid"; that is, he "entred into the Playhouse & turned the Players out of doors & tooke the fforfeiture of the Lease."[25] If the lease had been transferred in the summer of 1608, as I have suggested, then the alleged missed payment would have been the one due at Michaelmas (29 September) 1608. The Blackfriars children apparently continued to play at Blackfriars through the Christmas season of 1608–09, and it is possible that Rosseter was not concerned about the Whitefriars tenants being slow to move out in the autumn. They may well have been still in the playhouse in September and October. More likely, however, the eviction was not an "error" at all but was the result of a request from Rosseter that Ashley bring some force to bear to hasten them along, and in particular to evict Slater, who might otherwise have tried to stay on. Susan Trevell's notion that the eviction was contrived may thus be correct.

But even this simple summary has its problems. Is it possible that William Trevell did not know that the lease had been sold? Or was he too embarrassed by the failure of the enterprise to tell his wife the truth? She, in any event, seems to have believed that the syndicate was evicted by collusion between Ashley and Woodford, and she nowhere mentions the sale of the lease. We know too much about Ashley and Woodford to be able to dismiss her claims out of hand—there may well have been collusion, and with Rosseter as well, and the entire matter may be much more complex than I have suggested. Nor is it entirely clear by what means Ashley had come to be the landlord of the playhouse—assuming that here, as elsewhere, Susan Trevell's statement is to be trusted.

The new tenants were destined to have better luck than the old, but, like the old syndicate, they needed cash. Richard Hunt, a speculator operating on the shady side of the law, met "one Emanuell Read a Player" at about this time. We know of Reade as a player with Lady Elizabeth's company in 1613, and with Queen Anne's Men in 1616, but Hunt's encounter predates both of these. Chambers conjectured that Reade was one of Phillip Rosseter's players before joining the Lady Elizabeth's company, and Chambers appears to have been right; at least Reade's encounter with Richard Hunt in 1610 supports the conjecture, for Reade—no longer apparently a child even by 1610—urged Hunt to purchase a share in Rosseter's playhouse. Hunt was persuaded; as Thomas Woodford recalled some ten years later, Hunt "did buy of one Phillip Rossester or some other a part of a Playe house then lying and being in y[e] *precinct*es of the white ffryres London."[26] Hunt seems to have given his new associates the impression that his funds were limitless, and Rosseter or his colleagues importuned Hunt to undertake a special task for them. The "Lease of y[e] said Play house was w[th]in some fower yeares of Expiring," they explained; but they had heard that one John Babington of Worcester, gentleman, "had a Concurrant Lease for yeares from his ffather Late Bishopp of Worcester deceased of the whole house."[27]

The "Late Bishopp of Worcester" would have been Gervase Babington, who had died on 17 May 1610; Hunt's conversation with the Rosseter group may have taken place in the summer or autumn of that year. A "Concurrant Lease" is a quite proper legal notion, meaning in simplest terms a second lease to the same property, granted by the same lessor, in force during years which overlapped some or all of the years of the first lease. In our own age this would be an anomaly of sorts; less so perhaps in 1610, for the parties involved in the matter in that year did not seem to find the situation unusual or deserving of comment or explanation.

Rival claimants to tenure, and claims about rival leases, would of course be nothing new in the history of the English theater. Herbert Berry has shown how Robert Browne and his company found themselves caught at the Boar's Head playhouse by the rival demands of Richard Samwell, Oliver Woodliffe, and Francis Langley, each claiming to be the rightful landlord and receiver of rents.[28] The situation at the Whitefriars playhouse is not so well attested as the conflict at the Boar's Head; from the documents at hand we learn only that in some fashion not made clear, Lord Buckhurst[29] claimed to hold title to that part of Whitefriars that included the playhouse; and so, in an equally unclear fashion, did the Bishop of Worcester. The "lease" that John Babington was rumored to have must have descended to him, with other of his father's goods, when the Bishop's estate went through probate in the summer of 1610.

Richard Hunt sought the advice of Thomas Woodford about the purchase of the lease. Hunt knew that Woodford "had ye said house long before in his sole possession" but that some years previous he had "solde his Lease and tytle thereof vnto y^e ... M^{rs} of the Children of ye Kings Revells," that is, to Drayton and Barry.[30] Woodford agreed to ride to Worcester with Hunt to visit John Babington and sound him out about the concurrent lease. They found Babington willing to sell, but his price was five hundred marks (£333.6.8); Woodford and Hunt thought the price "too deare."

Business affairs then took Woodford to Germany, probably in midwinter 1610–11. When he returned to London he found that Hunt had been "in ye interim further incourraged by ye said Players ... to goe through wth ye said Bargaine." Hunt once more sought Woodford's aid, offering Woodford £160—or so Woodford later recalled—to "get him ye said Lease," and further offering that, if successful, Woodford "should enioye one half of ye profits thereof during his naturall Life." Woodford was apparently attracted by the offer, for he assayed Babington again, this time through the intermediary of Babington's legal counsel, one Thomas Woodward of Lincoln's Inn, an old acquaintance and coeval of Thomas Woodford's. Woodford crossed his colleague Woodward's palm with the requisite silver ("Tenn poundes for a gratuity"), and the lease was soon forthcoming, at a cost of £80 for the lease and £10 to Woodward.[31]

Hunt, "well likeing" the issue, completed his profit-sharing negotiations with Woodford, and the lease was assigned to one Thomas Otwood of London, a comfit maker, who was then "the monye keeper to ye said Hunt." All of this was accomplished by October 1611, according to Woodford's own recollection. Since the main object of the exercise was to secure the second lease for the use of the players, one wonders if Otwood in turn made some sort of assignment to Rosseter; but on this matter the documents are silent. As Rosseter and his colleagues still held the play-house under the terms of the lease from Lord Buckhurst, they may have had no immediate need for the protection of the Bishop's lease and may well have deferred buying it. Hunt and Woodford may therefore have contented themselves with hold-ing the lease until a later date, a service on behalf of the players for which the players would have been expected to show some financial gratitude. Hunt and Woodford may not have expected any real profit from the Bishop's lease until 1614, when the Buckhurst lease would expire.

The activity at Whitefriars from 1611 on has left little in the way of documenta-tion. We know that by July 1613 Phillip Rosseter had joined with Philip Kingman to lease a plot of garden ground in Whitefriars and to build a new playhouse there, against the day when they might have to vacate the old one. Kingman was a former player (if indeed they are the same man) who since 1607 had been the proprietor of the Black Bell Inn "next vnto Temple Barr" and therefore a near neighbor of Rosseter's.[32] Work on their project was stopped, however, on 29 July 1613 by a directive from the Privy Council.[33]

We also know that in March 1613 Rosseter arranged to join his company with the Lady Elizabeth's company under Henslowe—the plans for a new playhouse may have been connected with this merger—but that in March 1614 Henslowe renego-tiated the relationship. Chambers speculated that the major feature of the renegotia-tion involved Henslowe's buying out of Rosseter's interest in March 1614 and running the two companies himself. Such a transaction may well have been just what Rosseter wanted, for he was without a new playhouse and on the verge of losing his lease to the old one. He may have had the shrewdness to foresee that the Bishop's lease by itself provided shaky grounds for continued occupancy once the Buckhurst lease expired. Indeed, he may have deferred buying the Bishop's lease from Hunt because of just such concerns.

Events proved him right. Lord Buckhurst, who had made the lease to Woodford and Drayton, had died on 27 February 1609, just two weeks after Andrews and Slater had fired their first legal shots at one another. With his death the possibility of renewing the lease may have vanished. In none of the surviving documents do any of the parties speak of renewal as an option open to them. There is no clue in Lord Buckhurst's will about the disposition of his interest in Whitefriars, nor is any transfer enrolled in Chancery. Nevertheless, with the expiration in 1614 of the lease made by him to the playhouse, its rights seem to have reverted to Sir Anthony Ashley. Ashley, pressing what he took to be his legitimate claims of landlordship, fell into conflict with Hunt and Woodford and their claims under the concurrent lease from the Bishop. Hunt being "blowen and driven into great misery" by this turn of events, "ye old Lease of ye said house being expired," it fell to Thomas Woodford to stand against Ashley's claims "till he [Woodford] had expended one hundreth markes besides his great Losse of tyme in gaineing and keepeing the possession of ye said house against Sr Anthony Ashley knight and others defending ye Tytle thereof against ye Bishopp of Worcester then being." Hunt would not bear his share of the costs, and eventually Woodford, "being tyred with expence," was forced to drop his claims.[34]

The playhouse may well have stood empty during the course of this skirmishing. In any event, Ashley's victory over Woodford seems to have marked the end of its career.

We have then a playhouse with a documentable life of seven years, from 1607 to 1614. Of the two companies that occupied the playhouse, the first must have been a classic example of incompetence coupled with ill luck; I find this set of tenants by far the more interesting and wish that I could better document their enterprise. Most of them were unlikely participants in such an undertaking; I would like to know what tempted a tallow-chandler, a silk-weaver, a haberdasher, and other assorted types—some of them apparently frustrated playwrights—to think that they could make a quick profit in such a venture. My own bias, implicit in the title of this paper, is that such ideas about the theater's being a source of easy wealth were common-place at the time. But I would like to know more. I wonder where they recruited their children, and what Sibthorpe's qualifications were that he should have been put in charge of the board and lodging for the boys. I wonder what kind of competence Drayton brought to the mounting of the plays—assuming that such work fell to him. I wonder what features of the enterprise—or what troubles in Slater's own life—prompted him to leave off playing with Queen Anne's company in the provinces to take on the managership. And I wonder what happened to the children when the operation folded.

More is known generally of the second company. It played several times at Court, and some of the boys became adult players of note. Although it underwent reorganization in 1614 with the expiration of the lease, it cannot be said to have "failed" in the spectacular manner of its predecessor. After 1614 there is no further record of the Whitefriars as a playhouse, apart from a well-known fabrication of John Payne Collier's.[35]

II. The Leases, Part One

[Note. This and the following section are frankly tedious. Readers with no taste for such minutiae may skip over them with an easy conscience.]

The surviving records are not especially clear on the matter of the leases to the Whitefriars playhouse. Both Andrews and Slater stated in their lawsuit that the lease from Lord Buckhurst to Woodford and Drayton was for a period of six years, eight months, and twenty days. It is an odd figure, and the likeliest explanation is that it was computed so that the lease would terminate on a quarter day, and more likely on one of the two traditional quarter days for leases, Michaelmas in September or Lady Day in March.

J. Q. Adams argued in *Shakespearean Playhouses*[36] that the lease must have expired at Christmas 1614. In his view "the original lease of the building, it seems, expired on March 5, 1608. But before the expiration—in the latter part of 1607 or in the early part of 1608—Drayton and Woodford secured a new lease on the property for six years, eight months, and twenty days, or until December 25 (one of the four regular feasts of the year), 1614."

This hypothesis is not without its faults, but it does serve to make sense of a puzzling comment made by Andrews in his lawsuit. Andrews claimed that in February 1608 Lording Barry represented himself as holding a moiety of a lease "made . . . about Marche then next followeinge." The phrase is curious. Adams treated it literally, as meaning about March 1608, one month into the future. He further conjectured that "in February, 1608, after having secured this renewal of the lease"— but a month before the renewed lease was to come into force—"Thomas Woodford suddenly determined to retire from the enterprise" and sold his interest in the renewed lease to Lording Barry. Barry could thus represent himself to Andrews in that month of February as having an interest in a lease due to commence in March.

This is a compact supposition, but there are problems. First, while it is true that Andrews remembered Barry's claiming in February to have an interest in the lease, it does not follow that Barry necessarily acquired his interest in the lease in that month. Barry might have bought his interest some months previous—in the previous August, for example, when he was borrowing so heavily.

Second, Adams has got his arithmetic wrong. Eight months from his preferred date of March 5th does not get us to Christmas but only to November, a possible though not probable time for a Jacobean lease to expire. The figure of six years, eight months, and twenty days is repeated three times in the lawsuit; so the eight months is unlikely to be an error for nine months. To terminate at Christmas the lease would have had to begin in April, a consideration which in turn would make suspect Andrews's recollection about March. The matter is far from clear.

A typical lease of the period would run for a definite number of whole years beginning and terminating on the same quarter day. Rents were normally payable quarterly on the quarter days, or half yearly; if the latter, the more common days for payment were Lady Day and Michaelmas. In leases made at leisure, where the lessee was in no haste to occupy the premises, the quarter days in the spring and autumn were likelier to serve as beginning and terminating days than the winter or summer days. James Burbage's lease from Giles Allen to the Theater site in Shoreditch, although signed on 13 April 1576, was framed to run "from the feaste of the Annunciacion of our Ladie then last paste before the date of the saide Indenture for the Tearme of one and Twentie yeares from thence nexte followinge."[37] Leases made for reasons of urgency, on the other hand, might well begin on one of the other quarter days, or indeed on any day at all. The lease from Nicholas Brend to the Globe site in St. Saviour's, arranged by the parties almost two years after the expiration of the Shoreditch lease, and in the face of threatened legal action by Giles Allen, was signed on 21 February 1599 and framed to run from Christmas 1598 for thirty-one years.[38]

A lease terminating at Christmas might be troublesome for a playing company, especially a company with hopes of playing at Court, for in its final year it would disrupt their activity in mid-season. A lease with only a few years remaining would be even more problematical on this point. Alternatively, a lease terminating at Michaelmas might well leave the players, in their final months, with an empty house, if the year of termination should happen to be a plague year with playing suspended in the summer. For a playing company, vacating a playhouse in the spring might seem the most preferable of the choices available—assuming that choice is an option, for it must be remembered that the termination date of the lease might have been for the convenience of the landlord rather than of the players.

If, however, we can allow ourselves the presumption that the lease made by Lord Buckhurst to Whitefriars was made at leisure—which is by no means certain—and if we then hypothesize that the lease might have been designed to terminate on 25 March 1614, we may reckon backwards six years, eight months, and twenty days to a commencing date of 5 July 1607. If Woodford and Drayton had negotiated a new lease to begin on this date, then Barry's flurry of borrowing activity in the following month begins to make sense. Woodford and Drayton would have had their new lease at just the time that documentable activity in and about the playhouse begins. Barry's big loans in August may well have been intended to buy out Woodford; the largest of them, for £60, was for only three months, so Barry must have been expecting to receive income from his investment in the fall of 1607, not half a year later in March 1608.

Perhaps Sibthorpe and Trevell were caught up in the enterprise even before Barry. Woodford and Drayton may well have been negotiating with them even as the new lease was being arranged. Trevell recalled in 1610, and his widow recalled even in 1643, that he had been persuaded to invest in the playhouse not only by Woodford but also by a Mr. Smith and by Sir Anthony Ashley. I have no clue about the identity of Mr. Smith. Ashley's relation to the various leases to the premises is not yet clear to me; he may indeed have had an interest in the property, as Woodford found in 1614, and that interest may have existed as early as 1607. Perhaps Ashley was instrumental in assisting Woodford and Drayton to their new lease. I simply do not know. Of Edward Sibthorpe I know even less; but it is clear that both Sibthorpe and Trevell were willing to second Barry in his borrowings in August 1607, and I believe that this readiness on their part indicates that they were already involved in the project to some degree.

One also needs to accommodate the possibility that Woodford—as he claimed in 1620—did indeed have a sole lease to the premises at one point and that circumstances prompted him to renegotiate it to include Drayton. This original lease may well have been for ten years, that is, to have taken effect in March 1604. The plague of 1603 was abated by then, the King had arrived in London, and Aaron Holland was probably busy furnishing out the Red Bull at about this same time. Having leased the Whitefriars building in March 1604, Woodford may have been unable to make much headway with it. One wonders if he approached his uncle Thomas Lodge the poet.[39] In any event, Woodford seems to have struck a bargain with Michael Drayton, but Drayton's terms may have included a redrawing of the lease. If this is what happened, then the peculiar figure of six years, eight months, and twenty days is accounted for; it is simply a reckoning from the date of the renegotiation forward to the original date of expiration.

All of this is of course conjecture, and one would happily trade it all in for a few more hard facts. My own sense is that Woodford renegotiated the lease in July 1607 to include Drayton and that Barry bought out Woodford in August 1607. I am also tempted to see a relationship between the supposed expiration of the lease in March 1614 and Rosseter's conjectured readiness to be bought out by Henslowe in that same month. These conjectures leave me with two problems. The first is Andrews's remark about the lease commencing in March. This remark does not square with my hypothesis, and I take comfort only in the realization that it does not square with anyone else's either. Andrews may simply have been wrong. The second problem is Woodford's need for a fancy hat in December 1607 for a play. If he had sold out in August, why was he buying part of a costume four months later? Even if he had not sold out, I cannot imagine why he needed to be running errands of this nature.

III. The Leases, Part Two

The lease made by Lord Buckhurst, a lease held successively by Thomas Woodford, by Lording Barry and the rest of the syndicate, and finally by Phillip Rosseter, must also be seen as a particular lease in the larger problem of the concurrent leases to the playhouse. On this latter topic, while we have the guidance of legal tradition, we have tantalizingly little evidence to go on, and any attempt at reconstructing the circumstances will be as fraught with uncertainty as are the various attempts in our own age to reconstruct exemplars of primitive man from a few fragments of bone. Nevertheless, someone must sooner or later venture an initial hypothesis; I do so here, and I apologize in advance for the legal complexities of the next four paragraphs.

A concurrent lease is not necessarily the product of confusion or ignorance. The concept is legitimate; a concurrent lease is said to exist when a lessor, having demised certain premises to a lessee, subsequently makes a second lease of the same premises to a second lessee. What is not always clear is the reason that a lessor might have for choosing this course of action. Normally a lessor holds the reversion of his lease; that is, when the term of the lease expires, the interest in the property reverts to the lessor. So the legal interest in the Shoreditch property reverted to Giles Allen upon the termination of James Burbage's lease on 25 March 1597. But a second, or concurrent, lease has the effect of an assignment of the reversion, so that upon the expiration of the first lease the interest in the property reverts not to the lessor but to the holder of the second lease—assuming that the second lease has not also expired.

The further effect of the second lease may take one or two forms, depending upon whether the second lease was assigned by a properly executed deed or by some other means such as a lease parole. If the assignment was by deed, then the holder of the second lease is, immediately upon the date of commencement of his lease, interposed between the lessor and the first lessee. It may be convenient to use shorthand symbols for these three parties; let us call the lessor L, the first lessee F, and the second lessee S. With the execution of the first lease, F becomes L's tenant and L becomes F's landlord. With the interposition of the second lease, that relationship between F and L ceases; S then holds the intermediary position of lessee to L and landlord to F. L thenceforth collects rent and enforces covenants against S, not against F, while S assumes the role of landlord in relation to F.

In the event that the second lease has a term extending beyond that of the first lease, S will succeed to the property when F vacates. The relationship between S and L will remain unchanged at that point, except that S may now occupy the premises formerly held by F and thus be tenant as well as lessee. In addition, and this is an important point, S may exert his right of tenancy as soon as F's lease terminates, even if it terminates prematurely, such as by forfeiture.

A different relationship obtains when the second, or concurrent, lease is assigned in some manner other than by deed. In such a case, the second lease is wholly void at the common law during the full term of the first lease; even if the first lease terminates prematurely, as by forfeiture, the claims to tenancy by S are not thereby moved forward. Upon the expiration of the full term of the first lease, the second lease (if it has not itself expired) takes effect as a lease of the property, but at no time during its life would a second lease made in this fashion have any legal status as an assignment of the reversion. Only a concurrent lease assigned by deed can have such status. The holder of a second lease not assigned by deed would thus stand in a legally ambiguous relation to the lessor, and in no clear relation to the holder of the first lease, during the entire period of the first lessee's tenancy under the first lease. Let us emend the shorthand symbols to reflect this distinction; let us have SD indicate the holder of a second lease assigned by deed, and SP the holder of a second lease assigned by some other means.

Having made our way through that thicket, we must now consider how our scraps of evidence fit the various paradigms. We know, from Thomas Woodford's testimony, that Anthony Ashley claimed a reversionary interest in the playhouse upon the expiration of Rosseter's lease in 1614. We also know, from the testimony of Trevell's widow, that Ashley attempted to claim his reversionary interest in 1608 on the grounds of an alleged failure by the syndicate to pay the rent. These incidents are consistent with the behavior that one might expect of the holder of a second lease assigned by deed. To continue the use of our shorthand symbols, then, this hypothesis would have Lord Buckhurst as L, Woodford and his successors through Rosseter as F, and Ashley as SD. Susan Trevell's notion that Ashley was "Landlord of the Playhouse" in 1608 would thus be correct.

Carrying this assumption further, we might even propose that Ashley's second lease was made before 1607, so that Ashley would have seen himself as having some future interest in the premises that Woodford, the holder of the first lease, was renegotiating with Drayton in that year. William Trevell recalled more than once that Ashley was among those urging him in 1607 to buy into the Barry-Drayton syndicate.

But if Ashley had been SP instead of SD—that is, if his lease was not conveyed by deed—then he would have had no claim in 1608. Not that Ashley would necessarily have been deterred by such a consideration; so out of fairness to that side of his nature, let us venture for a moment a contrary set of assumptions. Let us assume that Ashley was SP, and further let us assume that the failure to pay the rent at Michaelmas 1608 was a genuine failure, signaling the forfeiture of the lease and providing Ashley with a legitimate pretext for his intervention. But Ashley would have been wasting his time; as SP he would have had no rights until 1614, forfeiture or no; the result of a forfeiture would have been that the interest in the property reverted to Lord Buckhurst, who was still alive in the autumn of 1608 and who might then have made a new lease to Rosseter, or not, as he chose. But we know that Rosseter did not have a new lease but had Woodford's old lease, with its same expiration date; Woodford said in 1620 that he had once owned the lease that Rosseter subsequently owned. So I think we must assume that the lease was not forfeited in 1608 as Ashley professed to claim. Even if it had been, there would have been little profit, and therefore little point, in Ashley as SP attempting to foreclose on the premises, for he would have been prevented from exploiting his advantage under the terms of his lease. It is therefore likely that Ashley held his lease by deed and was SD.

But there is another concurrent lease, the Bishop's lease, the one held in 1610 by John Babington. We know little of this lease, only that Thomas Woodford purchased it in 1611 and that in 1614 he found it of insufficient force to overthrow the claims of Sir Anthony Ashley. We may be reasonably certain that the Bishop's lease was not, like Ashley's, a concurrent lease made by Lord Buckhurst; for in that case the Bishop would have been Ashley's lessor even as Ashley was lessor to Rosseter. There is no indication that the Bishop played such a role. It is likelier, if we are to deal in suppositions, that the Bishop had a second lease to Lord Buckhurst's first lease; that is, that Buckhurst was F and the Bishop S in their relation to some unknown first landlord L.

Further research will confirm or shatter this supposition; in the interim, it serves as a possible explanation of the few facts that we know. The Bishop's concurrent lease would entitle him to tenancy upon the termination of Lord Buckhurst's lease; in the interim, if the Bishop was SD, he would have been Buckhurst's landlord. Buckhurst died in February 1609 and the Bishop in May 1610. The Bishop's lease passed to his son John Babington; I do not know who inherited Buckhurst's lease. Whoever it was, he would have been obligated to pay rent to the holder of the Bishop's lease, and after 1611 Hunt and Woodford held this lease. The rental may not have been much; we may guess that Rosseter paid more to Ashley than Ashley paid to Burkhurst and his heirs, and they in turn paid even less to the Bishop and his successors. Woodford's fight with Ashley in 1614 would then have been not for possession of the lease, but for tenancy of the playhouse, and on that head Ashley's claim would have been the better one.

There is one disturbing problem connected with my assumption that the second leases—Ashley's and the Bishop's—were conveyed by deed. The problem is that I have found no enrollments of any of the deeds in question, including Babington's sale to Woodford in 1611. It is true that a deed did not have to be enrolled; but it would be a comfort to find such confirmation in the records. The alternative, that the leases were conveyed by means other than by deed, is not, I think, tenable, as I have tried to show.

IV. The Shares

The first syndicate seems eventually to have divided its operation into shares worth one-sixth of the enterprise or half-shares worth one-twelfth; but it is not entirely clear how these shares were calculated or whether they were intended from the outset to be sixths. The syndicate, in its earliest manifestation, numbered only four: Barry, Trevell, Sibthorpe, and Drayton. Later Mason was added, then Cooke, then Andrews, finally Slater. The earliest notice of "shares" is by William Cooke, the sixth person to join the group, who asserted that in October 1607 he had, as security for his loan to Barry and Sibthorpe, an assurance of two-twelfths of the lease to White-friars and of "A parte of the Shares" of Barry and Sibthorpe. In Cooke's lawsuit in 1609 he specified his portion as "halfe a Share of the whyt ffryars playehowse," which cost him £45.[40]

It is difficult to understand the distinction that Cooke was making between his one-sixth, or "twoe twelue partes of the Lease," and his one-twelfth, or half-share, in the venture. Perhaps a share of the enterprise and a share of the lease were distinct, although it is hard to imagine the rationale for such a disjunction. George Andrews, the seventh person to join the group, described his share as "a Sixth parte of the messuage premisses and profittes,"[41] and Martin Slater, the eighth person to join the group, had his share spelled out in some detail in the Articles of Agreement as "the sixt parte ... of all such profitt benefitt gettinges and commoditie as shall at any tyme arrise come and growe by reason of any playes showes interludes musique or such like exercises to be vsed and performed aswell in the said playehowse as elsewhere."[42] Susan Trevell claimed in her suit against Thomas Woodford that her late husband William Trevell, one of the four original members, had "a sixt parte of the Lease of a Playehouse."[43] One can notice these discrepancies—that Andrews spoke of a share of the messuage while Slater did not, or that Susan Trevell recalled only a share of a lease, or that William Cooke spoke of "shares" as distinct from a share of the lease, but that they all spoke of the shares as sixths, even after the number of sharers had risen from six to eight—one can notice all this and still be unable to elucidate or clarify.

J. Q. Adams theorized that the six shares were divided unequally among the eight members of the syndicate with Drayton, Barry, Andrews, and Slater holding full shares and Trevell, Cooke, Sibthorpe, and Mason holding half-shares. But Adams did not know about the documents in which Trevell's share is described as a sixth or in which Cooke spoke to our confusion about his sixth of the lease and twelfth of the operation. I think we are forced to conclude, in the absence of better information, that we do not know just what a "share" in the enterprise entailed.

V. Thomas Woodford as Financier

The "businessmen" in the playhouses during the final decade of Elizabeth's reign were the familiar names of the theater: Philip Henslowe for the Rose, the Burbages for the Theatre and later for the Curtain and the Globe, Francis Langley for the Swan and later with Oliver Woodliffe for the Boar's Head, Edward Alleyn with Henslowe for the Fortune. For the first decade of James's reign the names are somewhat less familiar. Henslowe, Alleyn, and the Burbages continue, of course, but they are joined by Robert Keysar, the lessee of Blackfriars, Thomas Woodford, the lessee of Whitefriars, and Aaron Holland, the owner and builder of the Red Bull. Much less is known of the later businessmen than of the earlier ones. Our knowledge of their relation to their playhouses is more tenuous, of their relations with playing companies more puzzling.

James Greenstreet was the first scholar to find a reference to Thomas Woodford, in the Andrews vs. Slater suit discussed earlier. The readers of Greenstreet's transcriptions noted the presence of Woodford and Drayton as leaseholders and assumed quite naturally that Drayton must have been the artistic presence in the operation. Thomas Woodford, otherwise unknown, was cast as the financier.

C. W. Wallace, who later found Woodford's name in a lawsuit involving a dispute over shares in the Red Bull playhouse, announced in 1909 that Woodford was "a man little known to historians of the stage, but connected, I find, with nearly every theatre in London."[44] Such a remark was irresponsible, but coming from Wallace it was bound to carry conviction, despite the absence of corroborating evidence. By 1917 J. Q. Adams, with no additional facts at his disposal, could nevertheless describe Woodford as "a wealthy London merchant . . . whom we know as having been interested in various theatrical investments. . . . [W]hat connection, if any, he had with the Globe does not appear."[45] This last comment was a gratuitous red herring, but it soon developed a staying power of its own; G. E. Bentley felt constrained to describe Woodford in 1941 as "a well-to-do London merchant who was interested in theatrical investments. He was concerned with the Children of Paul's in 1600 and with the Whitefriars theatre, the Red Bull, and perhaps even the Globe."[46]

H. N. Hillebrand, whose survey of the Whitefriars playhouse in his book on the child actors remains the best work on the subject, managed to avoid the hyperbole in 1926 while endorsing the general enthusiasm: "This Woodford", he wrote, "is a man hitherto almost unknown in theatrical annals, and yet he promises to take an important place in the future, when we have unearthed more facts about his activities; for he was fond of dabbling in theatrical affairs, and had his finger in more than one pie."[47]

It is a curious achievement for a man to be so elevated to a position of prominence in the history of theatrical affairs on the basis of a contagious enthusiasm
rather than on hard facts. In the early 1930s C. J. Sisson found the enormous bundle
of documents comprising the "Old Joiner of Aldgate" suit and discovered that
Thomas Woodford was one of the peripheral figures in that dispute. Woodford had
bought the play from George Chapman and had arranged for its production by the
Children of Paul's. Not much more than that emerges from the testimony of the
various parties, including Woodford himself; but Sisson's enthusiasm knew no bounds.
"It is certain," he claimed in 1936, "that Woodford was not merely the financier of
a company, like Henslowe, but that he was the manager and, in a measure, the
proprietor of the Children of Paul's, doubtless by negotiation with [Edward] Peers
and in partnership with him. . . . We must therefore add Woodford to our list of
theatrical managers at this period."[48]

One cannot fail to be impressed by this rising tide of certitude about Thomas
Woodford. Nagging doubts, if any of us are so afflicted, will likely center upon the
paucity of evidence to substantiate what seem to be reasonable claims. One would
like more facts. But alas: the facts, when they are finally dug out, fail unaccountably
to support the claims. They tell us nothing about a shadowy figure of wealth and
influence, a proprietor and manager, controlling the destinies of players and playhouses out of a fondness for dabbling in theatrical affairs. Fond of dabbling he may
have been, but the rest of the picture is a distortion. The "wealthy City merchant"
is instead revealed to us as a financially troubled young man, just finding his feet in
the marsh of City investment and speculation, in his twenties when he engaged
himself in the Whitefriars venture and still in his twenties when he abandoned it.
So we might begin any new study of the Whitefriars playhouse with a closer look
at Thomas Woodford.

VI. Thomas Woodford: A Revisionist Biography

Thomas Woodford was in his nineteenth year when the family fortunes collapsed.
On Thomas's nineteenth birthday his father had been a prosperous City businessman
with a splendid shop in Cornhill and a number of important connections. By Thomas's
twentieth birthday his father was bankrupt and imprisoned in the King's Bench
Prison, where he remained for more than a decade. It was a startling turn of events
for a man whose life had been filled with auspicious signs. Gamaliel Woodford had
early become a protegé of Sir Thomas Lodge, grocer, alderman, and Lord Mayor.
The elder Woodford served in Lodge's Cornhill shop, eventually taking over the
lease as his own as he advanced to the livery of the Company; he married Lodge's
daughter Joan, a girl of eighteen, and a few years later Sir Thomas Lodge stood
godfather at the christening of his grandson Thomas Woodford. Joan Lodge Woodford died in 1583, at the age of twenty-eight, and by the end of that year Sir Thomas
Lodge made his own peace with God, naming Gamaliel Woodford as one of the
executors of his will and leaving a "standinge cupp of silver all guilt weing twentie

and seaven ounces" to his "godsonne Thomas Wodforde the sonne of the saide Gamaliell."[49]

By 1592 Gamaliel Woodford had remarried and had risen in his Company to the posts of renter warden and third warden. He had also begun to set his sights on some larger business venture, for in that year he renegotiated the lease to the "mansion house and shop" in Cornhill for a fifty-year term at a cost to him of £200 above and beyond the annual rent.[50] The extent of the new venture is unclear, but one of its activities was the importing of woven goods from Italy. It also seems to have involved—and may even have been the inspiration of—one Anthony Warren, a young man who had just earned his freedom in the Grocers' Company in that same year and who seems to have been gifted with an unrestrained entrepreneurial imagination. It was no doubt at Warren's urging that young Thomas Woodford, still in his teens, became an agent for the enterprise, armed with commissions that took him to Italy on assignments to purchase cloth.

From its inception in 1592 the enterprise seems to have grown for some five years before the bubble burst, during Thomas Woodford's nineteenth year in 1597. Gamaliel Woodford seems to have been out of his depth by this point and curiously at the mercy of the wheeling and dealing of young Warren and of a third partner, a haberdasher named William Bowser. To meet the need for capital, these three had borrowed money in the City; but to cover their tracks they had also set up an elaborate network of borrowings from one another, so that they might all appear to be much more greatly in debt than was actually the case. This collusion obligated them to appear publicly as antagonists, lending money to one another and then, after the inevitable default, proceeding at law against one another. Bowser, at one stage in this chicanery, found himself suing himself.[51] These maneuvers were all intended to stand off the genuine creditors when the crunch came. The intricacies of the game are of no consequence—except as they may have served the young Thomas Woodford as an apprenticeship in the ways of playing the London money market—but it is clear that by 1597 the Masters in Chancery had grown suspicious of these fraudulent lawsuits and had ordered a set of interrogatories to explore the extent of collusion among the three principals.[52]

These interrogatories, with their depositions and indeed the lawsuits that prompted them, seem all to have perished, making the task of reconstruction more difficult; all that remains is an occasional summation in the books of Decrees and Orders in Chancery.[53] But the news that the three men were having troubles in Chancery promptly brought the real creditors to their doors. Warren seems to have been the first to sense the inevitable and to declare bankruptcy; the creditors hastened to fasten upon Bowser and Woodford, who promptly sued one another for relief. Woodford's other debts came pressing in upon him at the same time, and when William Sebright, the Town Clerk of London, sued him for default on a loan, Woodford saw no recourse but to insulate himself from further litigation by committing himself to prison.[54]

While the last act of this drama was taking place, young Thomas Woodford was in Venice purchasing a quantity of "Italian silke Cipers" on commission for Warren. There he "heard of the ffall of Warren and Bowser" into bankruptcy.[55] He commenced his journey home with the cipers (more properly *cypress,* a lawn-like fabric with a ready market in London), but at the Staple town of Staden downriver from Hamburg his merchandise was confiscated by one of Warren's creditors. At Staden Thomas Woodford heard the news of his own father's "faylinge, breache, & betakinge himself to prison in the king*es* benche."[56] He returned home to find the family economy in a shambles and numerous lawsuits in train.

Over the next several months young Thomas was summoned to testify in litigation that could have damaged his father yet more. Sensing this, he lied to the examiners about his father's business dealings, and about his own activities, and was charged with perjury; he refused to answer the interrogatories of the court and placed himself in further jeopardy.[57] It must have been a very trying twentieth year. In the midst of this ordeal the Company of Grocers awarded Thomas Woodford his freedom by patrimony (twenty is a somewhat early age for this), and the Company later voted to exempt Gamaliel Woodford from the mandatory payment of corn money on the grounds that he was "in some decay."[58] The Cornhill shop was leased out, first to Simon Harvey, then to Anthony Payne (who was to figure later in Woodford's suit against Aaron Holland). And it fell to Thomas Woodford to find a means of extricating his father from debt and from prison.

How the wheel had turned in five years! All seemed to be rising in 1592 with the new lease, the new partnership, the new business venture; but after five years of enthusiasm came the apogee, and after 1597 there followed five years of hardship, in which young Thomas coped with lawsuits and creditors, sustained his father in prison, and sought for various means to raise cash. He began to play the money-lending game, as had many a financially straitened young man before him, serving as a middleman or conduit between investors and borrowers. Under the right circumstances, and if one developed the right contacts, this activity could prove remunerative. Woodford seems to have found his métier in this line of activity and to have developed an eye for investment, perhaps not unlike young Francis Quicksilver in *Eastward Ho.*

Then in 1602, in his twenty-fourth year, he found himself the middleman in another kind of venture. Someone wanted a play written and staged, but anonymously. A writer had already been found. Woodford was to buy the play from the writer, as though on his own initiative, and arrange for its production. Woodford must have found the terms attractive, for in 1602 he arranged to purchase from George Chapman a play called "The Old Joiner of Aldgate," and further, "by [his own] meanes & appointment"—as he insisted in his deposition before the court—arranged with Edward Pearce for the play to be performed by the Children of Paul's. The history of this curious enterprise has been told in detail by C. J. Sisson,[59] although Sisson could not accept as correct the cumulative evidence of the depositions that Woodford was merely a casual participant in the affair. And it remains to observe that Woodford may have discovered in this escapade a new venue for raising capital, as well as a new predilection for things theatrical. But the undertaking was unsatisfactory in certain other ways; some time after the event Edward Pearce quarreled with young Woodford and beat him up.[60]

By this point the crisis may have been easing for the Woodford family. Gamaliel Woodford seems to have made himself tolerably comfortable in the King's Bench Prison and was said to have had his family resident with him on numerous occasions. With some of the profit from his son's ventures, he had recommenced investments of his own. But he wanted more money. Although the rent on the Cornhill shop provided a steady if minimal income for him, he could perhaps sell the lease outright and have a goodly sum to speculate with. In the year after the "Old Joiner" venture the Woodfords petitioned the Grocers' Company for permission to sell their lease; with some reluctance, the Company finally assented.[61]

The vision of Gamaliel Woodford conducting his business from prison, where he was insulated from the claims of his legitimate creditors of old, proved irksome. One of the creditors complained in the Court of Star Chamber in 1607 that Gamaliel Woodford went voluntarily to prison in 1597 "and there hathe hetherto remayned" as a "contynueinge prisoner" for these ten years and more, but still doing business in the City by means of his godson Gamaliel Warren, son of the infamous Anthony Warren. All lies, countered Gamaliel Woodford; he had wrongly "suffered and indured above tenne yeares imprisonment" for the debts of William Bowser and still remained close confined. He had no money; let his tormentors sue Bowser.[62] In that very year, however, young Thomas was negotiating, or renegotiating, his lease with Michael Drayton to the Whitefriars playhouse, the activity with which this essay began.

There are further curiosities to relate about our powerful theater-manager; Woodford was before the Justices of the Middlesex Sessions in 1614 for passing counterfeit coin; he was before the High Court of Admiralty in 1616 on a well-documented charge of piracy "super alto mare"—perhaps inspired by the example of Lording Barry before him; and, like his father, he was himself the object of a Grocers' Company benevolence in 1628 when he was imprisoned for a long term in the Counter for debt. The details of these matters—if I may use that frustrating phrase of C. W. Wallace's—"must await another time."

NOTES

1. *The Jacobean and Caroline Stage,* 7 vols. (Oxford: Clarendon Press, 1941–1968), II, 625.

2. "The Whitefriars Theatre in the Time of Shakspere," *Transactions of the New Shakspere Society 1887–1892,* III (13), pp. 269–284.

3. C. L'Estrange Ewen, *Lording Barry, Poet and Pirate* (London: the author, 1938), p. 6.

4. P.R.O. (Public Record Office), C.P.40/1800, mb. 1834.

5. P.R.O., K.B.27/1410, mb. 1312[v]; see H. N. Hillebrand, *The Child Actors: a chapter in Elizabethan stage history,* Illinois Studies in Language and Literature, 11 (Urbana: University of Illinois Press, 1926; rpt. New York: Russell and Russell, 1964), p. 229.

6. *Ibid.*

7. P.R.O., K.B.27/1408, mb. 483; K.B. 27/1410, mb. 1311^V; see Hillebrand, p. 229.

8. P.R.O., K.B.27/1410, mb. 1032; see Hillebrand, p. 232.

9. Guildhall Library, MS. 10,342, the Parish Register of St. Dunstan's in the West.

10. P.R.O., REQ.2/414/139.

11. *Ibid.*

12. *Ibid.*

13. E. K. Chambers, *The Elizabethan Stage,* 4 vols. (Oxford: Clarendon Press, 1923), IV, 350.

14. For Carrier, see P.R.O., REQ.2/414/139 and PROB.11/111, f. 269; for Woodford, see P.R.O., K.B.27/1410, mb. 1312.

15. P.R.O., C.2.Jas I/A.6/21.

16. *Ibid.* The entire document is printed by Greenstreet; the Articles of Agreement are also in Hillebrand, pp. 223–225.

17. See M. J. Dickson's essay "William Trevell and the Whitefriars Theatre" and Margaret Dowling's corrective essay "Further Notes on William Trevell" in *Review of English Studies,* 6(1930), 309–312 and 443–446. The document under discussion is P.R.O., REQ.2/392/90, Trevell vs. Methold.

18. P.R.O., C.P.40/1800, mb. 1834.

19. P.R.O., K.B.27/1410, mb. 1312.

20. Ewen, *Barry,* pp. 10–16.

21. P.R.O., REQ.1/37, f. 247, for Susan Trevell's suit. Thomas Woodford countersued in Chancery in 1643 (P.R.O., C.8/75/160) in an effort to defeat Susan Trevell's plea but was apparently unsuccessful.

22. For his residence, see the entry of his burial on 23 May 1607 in the Parish Register of St. Dunstan in the West, Guildhall Library, MS. 10,342.

23. Chambers, II, 56; Hillebrand, p. 237.

24. P.R.O., REQ.1/37/247.

25. *Ibid.*

26. These and subsequent details are from Thomas Woodford's bill of complaint in Chancery on 25 October 1620 (P.R.O., C.2.Jas I/W.11/21).

27. *Ibid.*

28. "The Playhouse in the Boar's Head Inn, Whitechapel," in *The Elizabethan Theatre* I, ed. David Galloway (Toronto: Macmillan, 1969), pp. 45–73.

29. Lord Buckhurst was, of course, Thomas Sackville the poet, author of the best parts of the *Mirror for Magistrates* and co-author of *Gorboduc.* He was also the late Queen's cousin and Lord Burghley's successor as Lord Treasurer; James created him Earl of Dorset in 1604. He had extensive holdings in Whitefriars; the wardmote inquest book for the Parish of St. Dunstan's in the West (Guildhall Library, MS. 3018/1) speaks of the precinct as "the Lo: Burkhursts libertie" (f. 69^V). The same book records, on 21 December 1609 (f. 86), the presence of "one playhouse in the same precinct not fitting there to be nor tolerable."

30. P.R.O., C.2.Jas I/W.11/21.

31. *Ibid.*

32. For his residence, see the wardmote inquest book for the Parish of St. Dunstan's in the West (Guildhall Library, MS. 3018/1), *passim*; also P.R.O., REQ.2/396/56.

33. *Collections,* Volume IV, Malone Society Reprints (Oxford: The Malone Society, 1956), pp. 58–59.

34. P.R.O., C.2.Jas I/W.11/21.

35. Joseph Quincy Adams, *Shakespearean Playhouses* (1917; rpt. Gloucester, Mass.: Peter Smith, 1960), p. 322.
36. Adams, p. 313.
37. P.R.O., REQ.2/87/74; reproduced in C. W. Wallace, "The First London Theatre: Materials for a History," *Nebraska University Studies,* 13(1913), 181.
38. Chambers, II, 415 and 417.
39. Thomas Woodford's mother was Joan Lodge, daughter of Sir Thomas Lodge, grocer and Lord Mayor.
40. P.R.O., REQ.2/414/139.
41. P.R.O., C.2.Jas I/A.6/21.
42. *Ibid.*
43. P.R.O., REQ.1/37, f. 247.
44. C. W. Wallace, "Three London Theatres of Shakespeare's Time," *Nebraska University Studies,* 9 (1909), 294.
45. Adams, p. 311.
46. Bentley, II, 624.
47. Hillebrand, p. 230.
48. C. J. Sisson, *Lost Plays of Shakespeare's Age* (Cambridge: Cambridge University Press, 1936), p. 71.
49. Sir Thomas Lodge's will is P.R.O., PROB. 11/68, ff. 230^r–231^v.
50. Guildhall Library, Minutes of the Court of Assistants of the Company of Grocers, MS. 11,588/2, p. 7.
51. P.R.O., C.33/93 "A" f. 172^v; C.33/94 "B" f. 168.
52. P.R.O., C.33/93 "A" f. 183; C.33/94 "B" f. 181^v.
53. P.R.O., C.33/93 "A" ff. 168^v, 172^v, 173^v, 177, 183; C.33/94 "B" ff. 167, 168, 168^v, 174^v, 181^v.
54. P.R.O., STAC.8/289/12.
55. P.R.O., STAC.5/D.8/2.
56. *Ibid.*
57. P.R.O., STAC.5/D.8/2; STAC.5/D.1/25.
58. Guildhall Library, Minutes of the Court of Assistants of the Company of Grocers, MS. 11,588/2, p. 211.
59. Sisson, *Lost Plays;* Woodford's deposition is P.R.O., STAC.8/8/2, ff. 163–164.
60. Hillebrand, pp. 213, 230.
61. Guildhall Library, Records of the Court of Assistants of the Company of Grocers, MS. 11,588/12, pp. 418, 427, 430, 431.
62. P.R.O., STAC.8/289/12.

The "Business" of Shareholding, the Fortune Playhouses, and Francis Grace's Will

S. P. CERASANO

PHILIP HENSLOWE, owner of the Rose playhouse and part-owner of the first Fortune playhouse, simplified matters greatly when he referred to the players who rented one of his houses as "the company." Actually, the financial relationships maintained by a playhouse lessor and a group of players were complex, and in Henslowe's case they were complicated additionally by his diverse involvement as the players' accountant, investor, and occasional financier. Most unfortunately, however, we cannot gain a clearer definition of Henslowe's position from our present understanding of the company's finances. The nature of the partnerships among players seems equally confused. The men with whom Henslowe conducted business have been described variously as "shareholders," "managers," and "householders," without explanation of the differences suggested by those labels.

In terms of traditional scholarship, the subtle distinctions in company finance have been passed over as unimportant. Instead, generalizations about shareholding and playhouse management prevail. Accepted wisdom holds that all companies adopted similar financial structures and that landlords were forced to adopt a defensive posture in dealing with their players. Yet convincing evidence points up contradictions to these views: financial arrangements changed during the histories of several major companies, and landlords probably differed in the ways that they controlled their leases. Therefore, it is no longer safe to assume that what was customary at Henslowe's Rose was also workable at the Theatre or the Red Bull. Nor is it sufficient to adduce, as E. K. Chambers did, that "withal the players, or the most discreet of them, prospered."[1]

Under these circumstances, then, the newly discovered will of actor Francis Grace urges a detailed reexamination of the most basic premises underlying company finance. Written and proved in 1623, the document indicates that substantial financial alterations were made in the transition of the Lord Palsgrave's Men from the first to the second Fortune playhouse, the period around 1620 when an old style of shareholding underwent significant innovations. Furthermore, Grace's will helps to illustrate a trend in shifting authority that resulted in the players moving to a central position (over the landlord's) in the Henslowe-Alleyn entrepreneurship. (By 1622, in fact, the Fortune's players were their own landlords, a development that temporarily ensured them greater control over their enterprise.) Moreover, the financial developments exemplified by Grace's testament were manifested in analogous contexts, in the Second Globe for instance. Consequently, the issues that it raises are far-reaching, and they require an interpretation within the fullest scope allowed by extant documentary sources. In order to understand the ramifications of Grace's will we must, in effect, redetermine the implications of the shareholding system and related company finances as they continued to evolve.

At the instigation of Grace's last will and testament, I intend to initiate a revisionist view of financial considerations that touched the companies throughout the period from 1576 to 1635. The copious detail that we need to consider as background for discussion is more manageable if it is organized topically. Therefore, this paper is presented in four sections, arranged in roughly chronological order, that lead up to Grace's will as the last segment in my history of shareholding. Part I explores the development of the concept of shareholding, along with the influences of company size, composition, and the sharers' status within a company. Part II concentrates on the value of shares and the conditions attendant on what Hamlet termed "a fellowship in a cry of players." Here I am interested primarily in the availability and market value of shares and the means by which they were gained, maintained, and given over. In Part III, I examine the relationship of shareholding to inheritance, commencing with Francis Grace's will. The document is significant in providing an explanation for the phenomenon by which the players came to own their own playhouse in 1622 and later lost that prerogative altogether. Part IV summarizes the whole.

I

Discussions of theatrical shareholding accept, without hesitation, that all playing companies adopted common financial arrangements, ones modeled on the practices of the Lord Chamberlain's-King's Men at the Globe. According to Chambers, whose work best indicates the state of present thinking on the topic, each company created a fixed number of shares. A player would purchase his share, or part of a share, for a set fee. As long as the company remained a lucrative proposition, he would retain that share, being returned on a regular basis a percentage of the profits and gaining also the right and responsibility to participate in decision-making. Should he decide to leave the troupe, he would sell the share back to the company, provided, that is, he left with the good will of his fellow sharers.[2] Concurrently, Chambers suggested that in an exceptionally rare situation a player might hold a "privileged share" for which he was free of any liability to contribute toward everyday maintenance costs or the expenses incurred in the ongoing acquisition of playbooks, costumes, or other properties held in common by the sharers.[3] Simply conceived, the process seems mechanical, almost benign in its implications. Underlying these tenets, however, are several significant, though unverified, assumptions: first, that shareholding was most thoroughly a commercial transaction, a matter of shuffling credits and debits in which the profit motive predominated; second, that the acquisition of shares, together with the prerogative it brought, was granted only to those who could afford the initial investment; third, that the system guaranteed some players a secure and sizable income, not to mention an elevated professional standing, perhaps heedless of talent or experience. Therefore one reads in work influenced by Chambers's that a sharer "would be expected to buy his way into a company," or that "players aspired to the condition of merchants."[4]

Yet the very language of shareholding, which styled a man "adventurer, storer and sharer,"[5] suggests more precisely the diverse associations intrinsic to the special relationship between the sharer and his investment. It emphasizes the importance of protection, cooperation, and even trust (financial and otherwise) in the agreements, along with the spirit of nurtured risk inherent in the whole tenuous business. The sense of tidy security conveyed by Chambers's explanation of the sharers' arrangements disregards the fact that theater entrepreneurship was perilous. Although the system would seem impervious to abject failure, there was always the chance that a company could be broken, even beyond economic retrieval. Losses could not always be regained. However, in a theatrical enterprise, the willingness of a player to "venture" was engendered both by economic necessity and creative force. It reaffirmed to the companies time and again that they were the ones who could best secure their own living.

From the outset it is important to understand that the players' livings were never completely within their control, the profits to be shared never wholly predeterminable. The earliest traceable arrangements, well before the construction of the public playhouses, portray shareholding as the simple division of income among company members or as payment made according to a determined fee-schedule. For instance, during the reign of Henry VIII, the Lord Chamberlain's accounts show that payments were made to a company's leader and his fellows on a sliding scale from the most senior to the most junior. Thus a standing troupe of eight to ten men was accommodated within a fixed allocation in the Exchequer allowance.[6] Benefits for companies visiting at Court were similarly evenhanded; most were confined to token gratuities of about £10 (whether in 1582 or 1613).[7] The sums paid actors on provincial tour were also restricted, regardless of the number of players who shared the profits, the distance that they had traveled, or annual increases in living costs. At Canterbury in 1568/69, the "Qwenes maiesties players" received 20s. for an unnamed performance. In 1570/71 the payment to the company was 15s.; in 1585/86, 30s.; in 1593/94, 20s. The higher rates might have been compensation for multiple performances; but as a rule each entry coordinates with an individual performance. Other companies that visited the town during the same period were paid as much as 30s. (Lord Strange's Men) or as little as 6s. 8d. (those known as "Pembroke's Players," 1575/76). Most importantly, there was no correlation between a company's size and its receipts. In the 1570s the Earl of Leicester's Men (with six full-time members) received 18-20s. at Canterbury, while the Queen's Men (with as many as twelve players) received 15s.[8] No consistent fee-schedule emerges from the accounts, although one fact does stand out: there were fixed upper limits to the fees that Lord Mayors were willing to lay out for entertainment. Consequently, and not totally apart from the conditions that attended the later companies, the size of a troupe was restricted by external limitations on available income.

Unexpectedly, the tendency for companies to be controlled by what they could be paid and the number of performances that they could reasonably mount seems to have set a long-term precedent in terms of their size and financial structure. The larger of the early companies were composed of between six men (the Earl of Leicester's Men, 1572) and twelve men (as Queen Elizabeth's Men, 1583).[9] By 1600, despite growing popularity and the gradual establishment of a ready audience, the average number of members in any London-based company remained relatively constant. The size of the companies did not protect them from financial loss; nor did their financial security increase their size. Admittedly, as the result of failed patronage or artistic inadequacy, some of the smaller troupes of the 1570s and 80s floundered and folded.[10] Nonetheless, more substantial groups could potentially go bankrupt and be forced to disband, as the example of the Pembroke's Men attests.[11] Somewhat to our surprise, the construction of the first Globe playhouse did nothing to alter the size of the company responsible for its finances. The company did not expand to compensate for the steep costs in house construction, land rental, or the purchase of staging properties. The lease for the site of the First Globe conveyed the grounds to seven lessees (1598). After the theater burned down, the initial estimate of the cost to rebuild a new playhouse (1613) was based upon a levy of £50 or £60 for each seventh share of the moiety.[12] There is, of course, a strong correspondence between the sharers and the players who inhabited the First Globe. The epilogue to *Every Man Out of His Humor* (1599) suggests that there were six "principall Comoedians" in the company: Richard Burbage, John Heminges, Augustine Phillips, Henry Condell, William Sly, and Thomas Pope.[13] Although these are not precisely the same as those who leased the playhouse site a year later (William Shakespeare and Will Kempe replaced Sly and Condell, and Cuthbert Burbage was added), the full-time players justified their investment by serving as its principal supporters. They did not recruit additional players or outsiders to cut their risks or provide greater funding for the venture.

There seems to have been an interest in maintaining the size of a company within certain limits, probably so that the player-shareholders could retain majority influence. Therefore determining the number of players necessary to constitute a majority of the Lord Admiral's Men, for instance, raises essential questions of company membership. Furthermore, it is difficult to judge exactly when and how shares were distributed. A simple count of company members is inconclusive because company size apparently fluctuated, in part, with production demands; also, the five extant plots from which we derive our count of participating actors may not provide a reliable basis for such inferences. (At best, we can rely on them to reflect the composition of a cast at a specific time when a play was produced. They do not record cast changes or variations in a play-text that may have occurred during the course of production.) Even with these reservations in mind, it is still consequential that the earliest extant plot, for *Frederick and Basilea* (June 1597), names twenty-two actors, five of whom had been principal actors in the troupe for several years. *The Battle of Alcazar* (March 1598–July 1600) lists nine actors, possibly only the most important. Since the company actors could double roles, few hirelings would have been needed to fill minor parts—certainly not as many as thirteen men, the difference between the size of this troupe and the company maintained earlier in 1597. The procession in *I Tamar Cam,* staged following Alleyn's transfer of the book to the company on 2 October 1602, called for the extravagant number of twenty-eight players.[14] Complicating any attempt to derive an accurate count is the suggestion that not all players in a company acted in every play. Thomas Heywood, who signed a bond with Henslowe in 1598 (agreeing to play at the Rose), is not among those who played in *Troilus and Cressida* (1599) or *Fortune's Tennis* (1600). Neither is William Bird, who agreed to three years' service in 1597. John Singer, an established player, was a significant enough member of the Lord Admiral's Men in 1597 to bear legal witness for two players who were signing bonds with Henslowe. Still, he was not among the cast of *Frederick and Basilea,* as the plot written that year attests.[15] Whether Singer was a sharer and could collect a full share of the profits, without acting in every play, is worthy of speculation. It would seem as if he could since he was continually on the lists of players in Henslowe's *Diary* who assumed financial responsibility for the company during this period.[16]

If any characteristics define the sharer's status from the late 1590s to the end of 1603—the period that can be documented by Henslowe's account book—they depend upon a connection between professional quality and financial responsibility. A sharer's status was not totally a matter of honorifics, as W. W. Greg hypothesized:

> the distinctive "Mr." of the Plots does indicate a sharer, either explicitly or because all recognized servants of the lord were sharers. In a few exceptional cases a sharer appears without the honorific, but no non-sharer is ever graced with it.[17]

What we can infer most confidently from the *Mr.* is something about the professional status of a player; that is, we can conclude that *Mr.* was an abbreviation for *master,* a title bestowed on players of high capability. The company was divided into "master players" and "adult players."

When these titles, as they were employed in the Lord Admiral's Men, are coordinated with the lists of men responsible to Henslowe for the repayment of loans, it can be demonstrated that master players were not the only shareholders in the company; moreover, they did not necessarily own shares. Using the plot of *Frederick and Basilea* as a test case, we note that its author named five "master actors": Edward Alleyn, James Tunstall, Edward Juby, Martin Slater, and Thomas Towne. These players were backed by seventeen "adult actors," three of whom were boy players. The company, as outlined by the plot, employed twenty-two players for the performance, and five were singled out for major roles. In contrast, in October 1597 (four months after the play opened for performance), Henslowe wrote up a list of ten players responsible for "all such money" that he had laid out for the company.

Out of the "master actors" in the plot of *Frederick and Basilea* Henslowe listed Juby and Towne. He did not mention Alleyn, Tunstall, or Slater. In a subsequent group of players who acknowledged company debts five months later (in March 1598), Juby had also been dropped from the ranks. Obviously, there was a large discrepancy between the "master actors" of June 1597 and the players who bore the financial responsibility for the troupe approximately nine months later.

Several of the omissions from Henslowe's lists can be explained by chronology. *Frederick and Basilea* opened in June 1597, and, according to Henslowe's *Diary*, Slater left the company in July. The plot had to be drawn up before his exit, Henslowe's list afterwards. During the next three months, Tunstall must also have left company service. Thomas Downton, his replacement, was hired immediately, and so he appeared in the October list as a full sharer. Of all the inconsistencies in Henslowe's accounts, then, only the disappearance of Edward Juby is a mystery. He was performing managerial duties for the company in July 1598 (again, according to Henslowe), and he continued as a company member until 1618.[18] As for Edward Alleyn, as I will discuss later, he seems to have held a share until his death in 1626, whether he appeared in Henslowe's lists or not.

Nevertheless, chronology does not completely explain the difference between the plot and Henslowe's accounts. Gabriel Spenser, listed in the *Diary* as bearing financial responsibility in 1597 and 1598, does not appear in any of the plots for plays produced before he was slain by Ben Jonson in September 1598. Robert Shaw does not appear in them either. On the contrary, Humphrey Jeffes and Anthony Jeffes were among the "adult actors" throughout their careers and yet consistently on the lists of those who were expected to repay company debts. (Greg cites the Jeffes case as the one exception to his generalization, an instance in which adult actors held a share between them. The proof for this unusual arrangement is doubtful. Henslowe is particularly attentive to a debt of £3 in 1598 for "humfreye Jeaffes hallffee share";[19] however, the sum is so small as to rule itself out as constituting a half-share in the company. Henslowe may have been justifying the payments to cover a part of some other debt owed him by Jeffes. Or alternatively, he may have been referring to the final instalment toward the payment for a half-share.)

Indeed the breaking up of shares in the early stages of the company's development is impossible to verify, especially with respect to the involvement of Humphrey and Anthony Jeffes. At the beginning they may have held part-shares, but both the 1612/13 patent for the Palsgrave's Men and the actors' list of 1610 seem to indicate that Humphrey ranked equally with the established master actors.[20] Under these circumstances, we would expect him to have been entitled to a full share and to have purchased one, although there is no factual evidence to support such a hypothesis; and in fact Anthony's decision to leave the troupe around 1609 may indicate that neither expected to advance to an improved rank in the troupe. Of Anthony's later career as a brewer we know that he made an impressive income, one that allowed him to donate sizable amounts to the Brewers' Company's charitable fund.[21] Had he stayed on, there was no guarantee that he would have become a full sharer. Not every well-known player held a share or made a fortune. As I will demonstrate later, some (such as William Bird) who acted long and well died poor.

The involvement of Richard Jones and Thomas Downton in Francis Langley's Swan Playhouse suggests even more strongly that neither seniority nor honorifics were reliable indicators of a shareholder's status. Until Henslowe signed bonds with players in 1597/98, there seems not to have been a sharers' system of the kind that we envision as traditional in the Lord Admiral's Men. From 1594 to 1597 (perhaps earlier), Jones and Downton were "master actors" at Henslowe's Rose; their activities included financial, performance, and managerial duties. As the result of some unknown influence, they left to join Pembroke's Men at the Swan where they provided an initial bond of £100 apiece and agreed to stay in residence for twelve months. The disturbance that their departure caused at the Rose was reflected by a hiatus in Henslowe's regular accounts; but oddly, Henslowe did not mention among his records having returned to the two men, upon their departure, a sum to cover the deposit that they had laid down for their shares. Therefore it is unclear whether they were ever sharers in the Lord Admiral's Men according to standard definition. At the Swan, circumstances were similarly unusual: Langley was the one to lay out £300 for costumes and equipment, as if Pembroke's Men, together with Jones and Downton, had failed to bring with them any costumes of their own. Barely six months later, owing to *The Isle of Dogs* incident, Jones returned to the Rose. Again Henslowe did not record a deposit on a share from him although, theoretically, Jones would have been resuming a share in the company. Instead, Jones signed a bond to stay with the company for three years at the penalty of one hundred marks upon default. When Downton rejoined for a term of two years, he agreed to accept a penalty of £40 should he default; and there is no entry in the *Diary* for his share. The legal consequences of the breakup with Langley led to an extensive lawsuit, the details of which have been discussed substantially elsewhere.[22] For our discussion, what ought to be noted is the players' complaint that Langley never handed over the apparel for which they had paid him out of their half of the gallery receipts. Presumably, they in turn defaulted on their bonds to Langley, possibly without penalty. Were Jones and Downton sharers at the Swan? Certainly not in the sense in which Chambers has defined those arrangements. Henslowe's ensuing caution and preparation of bonds testify to an increased need for control over the players. The three players who came from Pembroke's Men along with Jones and Downton were bound to Henslowe and the playhouse, as were the rest of the players in the company, including those who were recently appointed members of the Lord Admiral's Men and had never been involved in *The Isle of Dogs* incident. There is only one exception to this trend: Greg states that in December 1597 when Alleyn "left playing," he received £50 as reimbursement for his share in the company.[23] Still, after the Swan affair Henslowe learned to cover the Rose by making sure that the company to which he rented would stay intact. With few exceptions they did so, even after the players' bonds ran out.

Even though an enumeration of the players in the company or the "master actors" does not in itself prove conclusive, those men listed by Henslowe as responsible for "money laid out" are those we should most appropriately associate with the term *sharer*. Still, on the authority of Henslowe's lists and supplementary supporting materials, the number of sharers apparently varied. In 1597 Henslowe named ten players (each of the Jeffes singly); in 1598, ten; in 1600, eleven; and in 1601, nine. The patent of 1606 lists eight players.[24] In the cases where ten sharers were declared, Henslowe and Alleyn could have made up two shares for a total of twelve. Where fewer were declared, either Henslowe and Alleyn controlled a greater number of shares (as many as four), or the company temporarily operated on fewer shares. It is a vexed question; however, Alleyn's personal vacillation throughout his career between active playing and retirement seems not to have hindered his claims.

In conclusion, a reconsideration of the sharers at the Rose and Fortune in the context of company size and composition helps to delineate the source of the enduring strength underlying the "business" of shareholding. As financial arrangements developed and settled, there was an increased emphasis upon the players' professional values; their responsibilities were extended as well. It was quite a change from the period before the playhouses were built when companies collected "rewards" or "gifts," a form of rhetoric echoed by those who opposed the players in London. (Their purpose in repeating these phrases was, of course, to debase the players' art as a kind of frivolous, indigent servitude. For instance, Thomas Newton's translation of Danaeus' *A Treatise Touching Dice Play and Prophane Gaming* (1586) emphasized: "Augustine forbiddeth us *to bestow any money* for the seeing of stage plays and interludes: or *to give anything* unto the players" [italics mine].)[25] But within the confines of the playhouses, players gained newfound financial control over their enterprise. The players at the Rose and the Fortune playhouses "gathered" admission fees. And by 1622 those who held shares in the playhouse itself would be able to advertise an additional elitism both in terms of their capabilities as players and by their willingness to "venture" money in support of the building in which they performed. The shareholder-householders then found themselves in a financial deadlock, forced to make their investment in the playhouse pay off. But even earlier, when the players' investment was limited to costumes and playbooks, they possessed an incredible financial autonomy in comparison to London guildsmen. Indeed, a company of actors was not, as M. C. Bradbrook has stated, "a horrible parody of a trade guild."[26] Rather, their unique financial power lay in their prerogative (under royal or aristocratic patronage) to create a discrete corporation that was impervious to external governmental control, unlike any trade guild. As long as the sharers were fellow players, they were bound to reach agreements only with other members of their company; and the corporation could continue as long as the sharers were willing to contribute their support.

II

Were it not for the players who occasionally left a company's service and sold their shares or the few whose widows received settlements, we would know absolutely nothing about the value of shares. In 1597, as cited earlier, Edward Alleyn may have sold his share for £50. Richard Jones and Robert Shaw (Alleyn's fellows) received £50 each in 1602; and by 1613 a sharer in the company could sell out for £70. In comparison, around the same time a Queen's man would be paid £80 for his share.[27] The similar prices evidenced by this array of information would suggest three broad conclusions: that the initial investments necessary to form major companies were fairly equal; that the companies' expenses—whether for rent or costuming—were similar; and that the increase in their costs, over almost a twenty-year period, remained relatively consistent as well. Upon reconsideration, however, it is clear that this analysis is misleading in its implications. We cannot assume that the finances of the major companies were consistent with one another. Moreover, we will never be able to determine accurately their gains or expenditures.

Essentially, the consistency in the sale value of shares is part of a larger account-ing problem, the basic premise of which is that a share's sale value could not have reflected a calculable portion of the total value of a company. In other words, if there were ten sharers in a company, the actual value of the company did not equal £500 (at £50 per share). We must realize that no theatrical corporation, no matter how stable, could have had a stable, calculable value. To begin with, the value of tangible assets was in constant fluctuation. Old costumes were sold to help purchase new apparel. Even costumes that were put in storage after a production closed must eventually have depreciated from their purchase value. At the same time, the number of playbooks varied—old ones being retired as new ones were acquired. Or, alter-nately, an old play was rewritten and revived for performance at a fraction of its original cost. With such constant variation in the company's storehouse, how can an assessment of their "actual worth" be made?

Hypothetically, the sole way to ascertain the value of a corporation would have been if one had closed down completely and its assets had been liquidated. Of course, extant records never document such an event. And only John Chamberlain's account of the fire that destroyed the first Fortune playhouse in 1621 hints at the value of a company's storehouse: "It [the playhouse] was quite burnt downe in two howres, & all their [the players'] apparell & play-bookes lost, wherby those poore companions are quite undone."[28]

Moreover, another variable inherent in the structure of the players' finances renders the company's value indeterminable, that being the changing practices in-volving the ownership of costumes and plays. Although, theoretically, nothing pre-vented a player from purchasing his own costumes or playbooks, joint ownership among company members was the rule by the 1590s. This was a significant departure from former practice when arrangements were more tentative. In 1588/89, for example, Richard Jones sold his "Share parte and porcion of playinge apparrell*es*

playe Bookes, Instrument*es* and other comodities" (owned jointly by Jones along
with Edward Alleyn, John Alleyn [Edward's brother], and Robert Browne [another
player in the same troupe]) to Edward Alleyn alone for £37. 10s.[29] This purchase may
or may not have signaled an alteration in company organization as Chambers suggested.[30] Yet that line of inquiry is not as fruitful for our purposes as the fact that
the buyer constituted only one of Worcester's Men (with whom all of the men
played) and only one of the company's sharers. This was a purchase made by a single
sharer to be owned by him alone. Had Alleyn purchased Jones's property on behalf
of the company, the terms of the contract would have differed. Each of the new
owners would have been dealt a portion of the sale price. Possibly Edward made the
purchase on behalf of his brother and Browne, and he may have subsequently
collected a fee for the company's use of the properties. Assuredly, all of the items
mentioned in the sale, with the exception of the playbooks, would have depreciated
in value immediately and had to be put to use. As far as Alleyn's interest was
concerned, the mere ownership of the properties would have been useless without
a way for the investment to repay itself; but in this instance it is unclear whether
he purchased the properties to increase the number of his own shares, for personal
use, or with the intention of renting them to his fellow players. What is of direct
concern to us is his mode of purchase.

In a wholly different sense—also unaccounted for in the sale value of shares—
the sharers who remained with a company for a considerable time built up a kind
of unquantifiable equity in the parts that they mastered. For the most successful
players this would have made it difficult to move from troupe to troupe without
jeopardizing both professional and financial status. Thus groups of sharers generally
cohered for long periods of time.

The Rose and Fortune companies typify this pattern. Between 1597 and 1598,
Anthony Jeffes and Edward Juby were replaced temporarily by Charles Massey and
Samuel Rowley. Two years later, Jeffes and Juby returned; but the size of the
company thereby increased by only one player since, in the interim, Gabriel Spenser
had died. Substitutions still maintained the company's size. In 1610, a decision
allowed the company to swell to fourteen in order that seasoned players would be
established when older players retired. The lessees of the Fortune in 1618 included
ten players. The dimensions of company size were always predictable, in part, due
to the players' stable personal and professional commitments. Documents from 1622
show that six of the most prominent players—and sharers—had worked with the
company for four years, and none of the eleven players who comprised the company
then ever seem to have held shares in other troupes before their involvement in the
Fortune. Perhaps the chance of achieving a sharer's position alone attracted the
players, and in consequence, many of them stayed on for a lifetime. Downton
remained for twenty years; Juby, for twenty-three; Cartwright and Bird, for twenty-
five; Massey, for twenty-six.

Furthermore, when players left service, it was a final, decisive move. Fully
one-third of those counted among the Admiral's Men in 1597 were no longer active

by 1603; but they did not alter their loyalties to competing companies. John Singer became an Ordinary Groom of the Chamber. Richard Alleyn disappeared totally from contemporary theatrical records. Richard Jones possibly returned to the Continent, to wherever he had been before in Germany. Thomas Downton and Anthony Jeffes took up trades. Of all of the players in the Lord Admiral's Men, two were exceptions. Thomas Hunt, who appeared first in 1602 and was seemingly a member of the Admiral's Men, signed articles of agreement with Henslowe in 1611 as a Lady Elizabeth's Man. (He may not have been a sharer in the Admiral's Men.) Martin Slater, a player who did change companies several times, was heavily involved in theater management, probably not "sharing" in a traditional sense, but in an administrative capacity.[31] The restrictions that applied to players who held shares may not have applied to him.

On the basis of these trends, we are probably safe in assuming that, for the actors, part of the worth and guarantee of a share was determined by their active participation in performance, but that a share guaranteed only an equal portion of the return on performance takings. A letter from Charles Massey to Edward Alleyn written in 1613 seems to confirm this hypothesis. Massey was careful to point out in his letter that Anthony Jeffes was paid £70 when he left the company, but that the widows of Thomas Towne and William Pavye got £50 upon their husbands' deaths. (The difference between payment upon retirement and that given upon death is nowhere explained. We might conjecture that a player's participation counted as part of the worth of his share.) Massey's letter also made clear that a player could, under unusual circumstances, borrow money against his share. He requested £50 of Alleyn explicitly for the purpose of paying debts. In return, Massey offered two alternatives for repayment: Edward Juby (in his capacity as business manager) could reserve for a year all of Massey's gallery receipts and a quarter of his house money; or, were that insufficient, Juby could reserve all of the returns on Massey's share, except a mark per week.[32] Could Massey's annual salary have totaled slightly more than £50? Probably there was no steady, predictable income from a share if we take into account the natural variation in daily performance returns. Hence, Massey pleaded that the second, more extreme plan for repayment could be undertaken "if in [six] monthes J sawe the gallerye mony would not dow." Then, realistically, a duality was built into the sharers' system: Massey could conceivably work for twelve months and not earn the value of his share, although he could leave company service at any point during that inauspicious year and receive £70. For reasons of safety he was requesting the lower sum (£50), what could have been collected upon his death.

Besides this, other consequential inferences can be drawn from Massey's request. The market value of a share was essentially indeterminable:

> Ser J beseche your pardon in that J made boulde to wryte to you word*es* consernynge my selfe, and Jt may be distastfvll to you but nessessete hath no lawe. . . . J ever shall reste e[ver t]o be c[omman]ded by [you] ne[ve]r wovld J desire you shovld hasard the [losse of] one p[enny] by me, for ser J know [you] vnd[er]stande th[at ther] is [the] compositions betwene ovre compenye that if [any] one gi[ve] over wth consent of his fellowes, he is to

r[ece]ve thr[ee] score and ten povnd*es*. . . . Ser J besech howsoeuer pardon me, in that
bovldly J have presvmed to wryt vnto you.

Massey's longstanding service, including fifteen years of acting coupled with managerial responsibilities, was insufficient security for an assured loan, even while his
commitment to the company went unquestioned. His attempt to recall his "lytt[ell]
moete" was not easily won. The tone of the letter is most thoroughly desperate: "J
dow it not wth ovte my wiffes consenn[te] she wilbe willinge [to] set her hand to any
thinge that myght secvre it to to [*sic*] you." In short, a share was, most precisely, a
combined interest in time, skill, and capital, valued more in the preservation than
in the selling, at which time it was worth whatever a player could get for it.

By analogy, a player could acquire a share, or a portion thereof, on the promise
of performance. This could explain why Henslowe required bonds of the players in
1597. Not all the players may have been able to afford a share upon their entrance
to a company. The bonds would have served in place of loans from the company
manager. So Richard Jones, in a request to Henslowe for a loan of £3 to pay for a
suit of clothes and a cloak at pawn, adds, "J am to go over beyond the seeas w^{t}
m^{r} browne and the company but not by his meanes" (February 1592).[33] Browne was
experiencing his own difficulties mounting a company, "for he is put to half a shaer,
and to stay hear, for they [the troupe that he formerly played with] ar all against his
goinge." The half-share which Browne owned evidently belonged to a London
company that hesitated to release to him the value of the portion that he was "put
to." In consideration of Jones's statement, it seems as if Jones had no share to collect
from Henslowe, but, at best, a minimal living: "fo^{r} hear J get nothinge, some tymes
J have a shillinge aday, and some tymes nothinge, so that J leve in great poverty
hear." Prospective sharers could "venture" on the promise of talent and past
experience.

The final query follows logically: who "ventured" the greatest risk—the players
or the playhouse owners? Before shareholders began to assume responsibility for the
playhouses as "householders" (the Second Globe of 1613 was the first such establishment), their personal risks did not extend anywhere near the total liability for any
theatrical enterprise. Failed companies could recoup part of their losses by selling
all playbooks and costumes when they disbanded, or they could regroup to form new
or altered companies. Potentially, the players' mobility was insurance for their
self-employment. It was the playhouse owners who hazarded the greatest loss. The
term "privileged share" as Chambers employed it—a share held by a non-player
whose financial contributions were minimal and discontinuous[34]—misrepresents the
burden and involvement of persons like Henslowe and Alleyn whose responsibilities
(as accountants or financiers) were a trade-off for services that they did not render
in theatrical performance. (The Burbages, who held partnerships in both house and
company, were in an unusually advantaged position.) Those "privileges" given to
Alleyn were not commensurate with the value of his involvement in playhouse
activities, even during his temporary retirement from the stage. Any portion of

Henslowe's *Diary,* or Alleyn's own account book (kept from 1617 until 1622), or many of the Henslowe papers will verify the playhouses' ongoing upkeep, land rental, taxes—all indicators of the financial ruin that Henslowe and Alleyn could have suffered had the company folded or left their houses.

Further, owning a share did not automatically secure wages in direct proportion to services rendered. From within the troupes that inhabited the Rose and the Fortune emerged certain players who shouldered duties additional to those incurred in the normal routine of rehearsal and production. William Bird, Edward Juby, and Thomas Downton divided literary and financial tasks from 1597 to 1602, when William Bird stepped to the forefront of affairs. By 1616 or thereabouts, Charles Massey and Richard Gunnell predominated, and in 1622 Gunnell and Francis Grace were in charge.[35] None of these men received extra financial compensation as far as sources show. They did not own—nor were entitled to—larger shares than the other players in the company.

To summarize, whereas a single, all-encompassing financial arrangement prevailed in the Lord Admiral's-Prince's-Palsgrave's Men, the sale of Richard Jones's properties indicates that individual purchases were permitted within the company's early economic framework. Conversely, the fellowship of players that evolved later seemed to feel more comfortable with group ownership. In return, the company was obligated to pay a sharer a return upon his investment if he surrendered his share, although that return did not reflect the fluctuation in the actual value of the company. Within limitations, it would seem that the number of shares in a company made little difference when the sum that a sharer received in selling out was an agreed-upon amount, indicative of nothing except the consensus of previous sharers who had initiated the fee structure. We may then be left wondering why the early companies were so adamant about buying back (that is, paying off) the shares owned by players who left company service. Simply put, selling a share back to a company was more a matter of financial security for the company than for the sharer since it cleared the company of any future financial claims by a player or his widow. It also reinforced the solidarity of the troupe and ensured a group prerogative. The decision-makers *owned* the corporation. Given this structure as a controlling influence, we would be inclined to imagine a company of the early seventeenth century as a rather democratic unit. From what we can tell, it was. But as the specifics of Francis Grace's will imply (see Section III of this paper), the financial structure at the Fortune playhouses altered radically after 1622. Suddenly key players could promote or destroy the well-being of the entire company, especially when shareholders became householders, and testators were allowed to bequeath shares to non-players, whose best interests might not always coincide with the company's.

III

Exactly when it became permissible for testators to leave shares to their heirs, instead of selling them back to their companies, is debatable. The change seems peculiar to

the period after 1622. It seems also to have been provoked by the changeover from
sharers to shareholder-householders and the new practice of selling shares to non-
players. Before this innovation, the playhouse lessors could claim only property
interests in their wills, even if they held shares as well. When Henslowe died in 1616,
for instance, his younger brother and his nephew instigated a formal complaint
against Edward Alleyn over the first Fortune playhouse. The plaintiffs argued that
Henslowe had bequeathed the playhouse to his wife but that Alleyn had taken
advantage of her advanced age to secure the lease for himself. In all their claims they
concentrated on what could legitimately be passed on—the lease to the building—
not Henslowe's share in the Palsgrave's Men.[36] (Henslowe's wife, who died during
the next year, did not specify anything about shares in her will either.[37]) In circumstances wherein a landlord who was not a player owned the playhouse, this manner
of proceeding was the norm. It continued into the 1630s. And many prestigious
players who were active to their deaths never left their heirs a continuing financial
interest in their companies. Such a group of men would include Thomas Towne
(1616), Richard Burbage (1619), William Bird (1623), Nicholas Tooley (1624),
Henry Condell (1627/28), Thomas Basse (1635), and Thomas Taylor (1636).[38]

The earliest known will—to this date—that documents the transition of inheritable shares has been John Underwood's (proved 1 February 1624/25), although the
arrangements made for the collection of the proceeds from his share were tentative.
He left for his children

> all the *right, title,* or *interest, part or share,* that I haue and enoiy at this present by lease
> or otherwise, *or ought to have, possesse or enoiye in any manner or kinde at this present,*
> *or hereafter* within the blackefryars London or in the Company of his Maties: Servants my
> Loving and kinde fellowes in their house there *or* at the Globe on the Banckeside And also
> that my *part and share or due in or out of the playhovse* called the Curtaine. . . . Provided
> allwaies that my Executors shall not *alienate change or alter by sale* or otherwise directly
> or indirectly any my part . . . in the said playhouses.[39] (*italics mine*)

In sharp contrast, wills written during the next decade were very explicit.
Christopher Beeston divided up and passed on four shares (1638). William Browne
bequeathed the profits proceeding from the Red Bull, "whereof I am a member"
(1634). John Shank defined precisely "Two Eight parts in the Blackfryers Playhouse," and "Three Eight parts in the moity of the Globe Playhouse," for the
"Terme of Nyne yeares from Christmas last which I bought, and paid deere for"
(1635/36). John Heminges left "the moiety or one half of the yeerely benefitt and
profitt of the severall partes . . . of the Globe, and Blackffriers" (1630).

With specific reference to players in the Lord Admiral's-Prince's-Palsgrave's
Men, we are limited by a paucity of information. Few of the actors in these companies died in company service. Of those whose wills are extant, only Thomas Towne's
adds to our consideration. (Gabriel Spenser was stabbed by Ben Jonson in 1598 and
died intestate. William Bird's estate was paltry.) The amounts that Towne dispersed
totaled about £35, a sum that falls within the £50 fee which Charles Massey verified

as having been paid to Towne's widow. Probably Towne relied on the return from his share in making out his will.[40] But, unfortunately for historians, many bequests are formulaic, and so we cannot be sure exactly what properties testators owned. The language of bequests commonly refers to property as "leases and worldly estate." They rarely detail individual properties. Therefore, there has been no convincing proof that shares were inheritable before John Underwood referred to his in 1624/25.

Francis Grace's will (proved 31 January 1623) is the first piece of specific evidence to indicate an earlier date for this change in financial procedure. It begins: "*It is my will and desire* that the benefitt / of my share wch is to continew for two yeares after my decease / shalbe disposd in this manner."[41] (See Appendix for the full text.) Still, we may wonder if the change to inheritable shares did not occur even earlier, with the move to the second Fortune playhouse. Unhappily, this question is not so easily answered. Two factors confuse the issue. First, Grace was not mentioned among the sharers who signed the lease for the Second Fortune in 1622. Second, Alleyn had been trying to shift financial arrangements in the company as early as 1618, partly for his own gain.

The following is an attempt to clarify the financial arrangements at both Fortunes and to determine exactly where Grace fit into the structure. In 1618 there were ten sharers at the First Fortune. All were players and Grace was among them. Alleyn, we assume, owned two shares, bringing the total up to a conventional group of twelve. More importantly, Alleyn was the sole lessor of the land on which the playhouse stood. He also owned the playhouse, which was eighteen years old. Probably because of its advanced age the playhouse needed repair—or it needed to be rebuilt entirely—and Alleyn decided to invest no more money in it. Instead he offered the sharers a lease on the Fortune, along with the taphouse attached to it and a small piece of ground that constituted a passageway on the south side of the playhouse. The lessees would hold the properties for a term of thirty-one years at an annual rent of £200, or £20 from each of the ten lessees.[42] We are uncertain whether this lease was executed. If so, the agreement should have relieved Alleyn of his responsibility for the upkeep on the building, while he could have retained the lease on the land and his share of the performance takings.

From the markedly different arrangements made on the Second Fortune four years later, however, we would deduce that Alleyn's formal proposal had been rejected by the company. This time there were twelve sharers who agreed to rent the land for £10, 13s., 10d. for 51 years. Fewer than half of the sharers were players, and Alleyn carefully reserved one share for himself. (Over the next two years some shares were turned back and resold. Alleyn eventually acquired and kept two full shares.[43]) He retained an interest in the Second Fortune probably because it was new and because it was built of brick to last longer than the first house. William Prynne also stated that it was substantially larger than the First Fortune.[44] In contrast to the arrangement for the construction of the First Fortune, Alleyn decided not to carry the entire expense of the Second Fortune himself. This innovation cost the sharers dearly, just over £83 per share,[45] with the consequence that a share in the house and the land ran about £94. The expense of a share had therefore almost doubled in ten years. It should not be thought unusual then that significantly fewer players could afford to invest.

Because Grace is not listed as a sharer in the two series of extant leases preceding his death, he too may have found the cost prohibitive. Afterwards he obviously reconsidered his position and bought the share to which he referred in his will. Even so, we must yet account for the origin of his share and its value, neither of which is as settled a fact as it would seem. All the shares were presumably sold out in 1622; furthermore, the total of the "benefitt" that Grace expected comes to about £32, £10 less than the value commensurate with a half-share of the playhouse (without an investment in the land on which it stood).

The most tenable explanation for these curiosities relates to a change in Charles Massey's holdings. On 20 May 1622, Massey purchased one whole share according to one lease and one twenty-fourth part (a half-share) according to a separate lease made out on the same day. He surrendered the whole share to Alleyn on 14 March 1622/23, and on 1 August 1623, Alleyn parted with a half-share to Margaret Gray. The standard assumption has been that these changes left Alleyn with his own share plus one half-share that had formerly been Massey's. But events seem to have progressed differently. Between Massey's surrender of his whole share and Grace's death ten months later, Grace had to have purchased his half-share from Alleyn. This was all that was available if we trust a bill in Chancery some years later (in 1647) that implied strongly that the group of sharers named in 1622 remained intact for a long time. Certainly we know that those who parted with full shares did so after Grace's death. In this situation he had to take what he could get, and it is not impossible that he purchased the half-share actually expecting his imminent decease. A half-share was good insurance because it was large enough to cover a few modest bequests and his funeral expenses.

Aside from these practical considerations, Grace's will implies a noteworthy change in company policy, one that concerns the continuance of his share's value for two years after his death. We must remember that Massey's 1613 letter to Alleyn suggests that a player's active participation in performance weighed something in the value of a share. By Grace's death, this notion seems to have been discarded. Grace's heir could collect on Grace's half-share after the player's death; and Grace's will implies that he expected full value for that half-share.

But, finally, what did Grace own a half-share in? A half-share in the land and the playhouse would have come to nearly £57; a half-share in the playhouse, almost £42. There is no way to come to a sound conclusion, except to realize that the lease written in 1622 indicates that the players who financed the playhouse would also have taken on a share in the lease to the land. We must then favor a conclusion that Grace owned a half-share in both land and playhouse. Interestingly, owing to the large proportion of non-players who purchased shares, a player's participation in the company as an actor can no longer be understood as contributing to the value of his share; the basis of that value shifted entirely with the arrangements conceived for the Second Fortune. Nonetheless, some of the players were forced to become house-holders, venturing the same risks as former landlords like Henslowe, in order to have some part in control over the playhouse.

Besides this revised understanding of shareholding at the Second Fortune, there are biographical details to be culled from Grace's will that augment our knowledge of the Fortune company. First, Grace was possibly a gatherer at the playhouse. He left the benefit of his "gathering place" to Tomazin Tomson. Second, Richard Grace (Francis's brother) has traditionally been viewed as a hired man at the Fortune from 1623/24, when the clerk who kept the parish register at St. Giles Cripplegate began to style him "player," instead of "yeoman," his former title. What seems truer is that Richard acquired a more esteemed position after his brother's death. (The suit filed in the Court of Requests by Gervase Markham against thirty-nine men, chiefly players, draws attention to Richard as one of the more notable of Palsgrave's Men [1624/25].) Francis names his brother recipient of whatever is left over after his debts and benefactors have been paid; so Richard earned a comfortable income. (Francis apparently never married.[46] He does not mention a wife or children.) Third, the "[blank] Rhodes" herein named was most probably John Rhodes, who owned part of the Second Fortune in 1637 and 1648 and who succeeded Richard Gunnell as manager sometime after 1634. If Grace is in fact alluding to this man, then Rhodes was associated with the company much earlier than theater historians have imagined.[47] Fourth, Andrew Cane is numbered among both the Palsgrave's and Lady Elizabeth's Men in 1622, the understanding being that he transferred to the Second Fortune. Indeed, his career from 1622 to 1631 is an enigma; yet Grace's will would lead us to believe that Cane was active with the Palsgrave's Men (possibly until 1631) and served as the business manager. The payments derived from Grace's share are "to be disposd to em, by Andro Kene."[48]

Grace was confident enough of his company's security at the time of his death that he depended upon their continuance for two years, devastated though they were by the fire that had struck the First Fortune.[49] The number of plays licensed for the company between 1622 and 1625 was impressively large, but we would be mistaken to interpret this fact as signaling a formidable comeback. As events turned out, the plays were not very good, and subsequent factors—especially the plague of 1625—militated against the players' success. It is Bentley's impression that the plague of 1625 decimated the company's ranks—that, in 1626, an amalgamation of several companies emerged that styled itself the King and Queen of Bohemia's Company.[50] Grace could not, of course, see into the future to predict this downfall; he may have wanted to believe that the company would prosper enough to pay his heirs, and so he did not attempt to liquidate his half-share for its value before he passed away. To him, the company's future was the better risk. As for Andrew Cane, he may or may not have been responsible for the company's precarious financial position throughout the 1620s. As late as 1654 he was defending the prominent Palsgrave's Men—Grace's fellows—against the charge that, when the going got rough, they left the Fortune and broke the company to protect their own interests.[51]

IV

It is all too often taken for granted that the playhouses were the players' domain because it was the power of their performance that drew the crowds that either made, or broke, the playhouse owners. Yet a reexamination of the sharers' arrangements in the Lord Admiral's-Prince's-Palsgrave's Men shows that their situation is not so easily delineated. Finances altered throughout the company's history, and these changes did not always work in the players' best interests. Essentially, the sharers at the Rose playhouse invested in each other. They owed their fellows cooperation while in service, and they expected a standard fee in return if they left the company.

Henslowe's ties to the company were vastly different. He provided the physical structure necessary to their financial success, and he benefited both from the returns on his house and, possibly, from a percentage of the performance takings if he owned a share. All he owed the players was stipulated by the terms of their lease and on the pages of his account book. As far as his monetary advances to the company were concerned, they could be taken care of by adequate reimbursement. The players owed Henslowe no greater responsibility. Henslowe could not complain as long as they cleared their debts. He could not tell the players which plays to purchase. He could not dictate how many days of the week they were to play or the amount of money that they could spend on costuming. At this point in the evolution of the players' corporation, they enjoyed something of a "world apart" from external control. Therefore, were a landlord in Henslowe's position to attempt to exert control over the players, we can well imagine that his self-assertion would have put the company on the defensive; ultimately, negotiations between them may have been confrontational. This conjectural reconstruction of their dealings is, however, only a portion of the picture that is often painted. We are used to accounts of Henslowe's tight-fisted business dealings. Yet, as particular as he may have been about balancing his books, he always risked finding himself without lessees, especially during this early period. The players were in majority control, at least in one sense; if their skill can be viewed as a commodity, then their right and ability to perform constituted most of the value that they invested in. Theirs was a portable skill. The players who left the Rose for Francis Langley's Swan are evidence enough that the freedom to exercise that prerogative was important.

The players of latter-day fame did not enjoy as much freedom. On 4 April 1604 the Privy Council issued a warrant authorizing the Prince's Men to play only at the Fortune. This guaranteed the players a house and it extended to them the privilege of royal patronage, as one of three authorized companies; but, concurrently, it restricted them to a playing arena that they did not own. Later on, in 1618, the Fortune's players had to contend with Alleyn's proposal for incorporation, which included ownership of the first house. This seems to have been drawn up for reasons relating to his own financial security, not the players'. Then they were apparently successful at maintaining their autonomy, although the fire that destroyed the playhouse in 1621 was equally destructive to the established sharers' system.

Under the new shareholders-householders plan at the Second Fortune, the players were immediately disadvantaged by the high price of shares. Fewer of them could afford to remain sharers, and fewer of them invested. The change probably brought with it a sharp division within the company. At the very least its influence increased the player-sharers' authority over their business. But instead of having to respond to one or two landlords, they now had to answer to a group, only some of whom were their fellows. The basis for determining a share's value had also been transformed in the process. No longer was it tied loosely to the goods in the tiring house and variable performance returns. It was linked strictly to land and buildings, with the performance takings reduced to subsidiary importance. As long as the Second Fortune continued to exist, a share in it could be passed on to one's heirs—perhaps until all the shares passed into the control of non-players.

Appendix

Will: Francis Grace, Guildhall Library, MS. 25, 626/4, fol. 230^r—

(1) *It is my will and desire* that the benefitt/of my share wch is to continew for two yeares after my decease/shalbe disposd in this manner to the payment of my debt*es*∼/as farr as the two yeares profitt of it doth come to wch is to Margo/

(5) =re[tt] Goborne the som*m*e of twentie two poundes. To Robert∼/Gibbs the some of fortie six shilling*es*, to [blank] Rhodes the some/of fortie shillinges. To Richard Witton the som*m*e of six∼/pound*es*. To Edward Cobrone the som*m*e of three pound*es,* and to/ be disposd to em, by Andro Kene, in an equall proportion and/

(10) my gatheringe place ((the benefit of it)) [in my—crossed out] for the/*two* yeares, I give vnto∼/ Tomazin Tomson as allso all that is mine in her house & if my/share do amount to more then the satisfaction of these debt*es*∼/aboue specified, I give it vnto my brother Richard Grace./Franck Grace. Wittnesses to this, [will—crossed out] John Peirson,/

(15) John ffishe, Edw: Knight.//./

[Proved 31 January 1623: John Goborne, creditor]

NOTES

1. E. K. Chambers, *The Elizabethan Stage,* 4 vols. (Oxford: Clarendon Press, 1923), I, 348; Chambers's history will be cited hereafter as *ES.* A preliminary version of this paper was prepared for the Shakespeare Association of America conference in Ashland, Oregon (1983). I wish to thank the Colgate Research Council and the National Endowment for the Humanities for providing the support that enabled me to carry out this work. This paper is dedicated to Lisa, whose first publications are just in the offing.

2. See as the standard sources, "The Actor's Economics" in *ES,* I, 348–388; Edwin Nungezer, *A Dictionary of Actors* (New Haven, Conn.: Yale University Press, 1929) cited as "Nungezer"; Gerald Eades Bentley, *The Jacobean and Caroline Stage,* 7 vols. (Oxford: Clarendon Press,

1941–68), II, 343–628, cited hereafter as *JCS*. Another source, used frequently throughout this essay, is Walter W. Greg, ed., *Henslowe Papers* (1907; rpt. New York: AMS Press, 1975), cited as *HP* hereafter.

3. *ES*, I, 453–454.

4. Andrew Gurr, *The Shakespearean Stage, 1584–1642*, 2nd ed. (Cambridge: Cambridge University Press, 1980), p. 66; M. C. Bradbrook, *The Rise of the Common Player* (Cambridge: Cambridge University Press, 1962), p. 40.

5. *ES*, I, 352.

6. *ES*, II, 79.

7. Mary Susan Steele, *Plays and Masques at Court* (1926; rpt. New York: Russell & Russell, 1968), pp. 85, 182.

8. *Malone Society Collections, VII*, ed. Giles E. Dawson (Oxford: The Malone Society, 1965), pp. 14–17.

9. *ES*, II, 86, 106.

10. For instance, Lord Abergavenny's Men, Sir Robert Lane's Men, or Lord Vaux's Men (*ES*, II, 92, 96, 103).

11. Karl P. Wentersdorf has estimated eleven adult actors, four boy players, and about five hirelings made up Pembroke's Men ("The Repertory and Size of Pembroke's Company," *Theatre Annual*, 33 [1977], 74).

12. *ES*, II, 417, 423.

13. Later on the number of shares was expanded. According to the *Sharers Papers* (1635), the Globe had been "formerly" divided into sixteen shares, and the changed nature of the shareholding system admitted many sharers who were not players (*ES*, II, 425). For a clarification of the shareholding system at the Second Globe see Herbert Berry, "The Globe, its Shareholders, and Sir Matthew Brend," *Shakespeare Quarterly*, 32 (1981), 339–351.

14. *HP*, pp. 135–142; 144–148. I am not challenging the dates assigned to the plots by W. W. Greg, "The Evidence of Theatrical Plots for the History of the Elizabethan Stage," *Review of the English Studies*, 1 (1925), 257–274.

15. *ES*, II, 152–153.

16. R. A. Foakes and R. T. Rickert, eds., *Henslowe's Diary* (Cambridge: Cambridge University Press, 1968), p. 84.

17. W. W. Greg, *Dramatic Documents from the Elizabethan Playhouses*, 2 vols. (Oxford: Clarendon Press, 1931), I, 38.

18. Foakes and Rickert, eds., *Henslowe's Diary*, pp. 60, 84, 87, 93, 328–329; *ES*, II, 325.

19. Foakes and Rickert, eds., *Henslowe's Diary*, p. 71; Greg, *Dramatic Documents*, I, 38–39.

20. *JCS*, I, 136.

21. Guildhall Library (London), Records of the Worshipful Company of Brewers, MS. 5442/Vols. 5, 6/n.p., and 5445/Vols. 12, 13, 14/n.p. Although Bentley notes that Anthony Jeffes is one of the players in Prince Henry's Household Book in 1610 (*JCS*, I, 136), Jeffes was not active as a player in his company. His participation in the Brewers' Company is evident from 1609 on. See my article, "Anthony Jeffes, Player and Brewer," in *Notes and Queries*, n.s., 31 (1984), 221–225.

22. *ES*, II, 131–133; 152–153, and "The Isle of Dogs" in William Ingram, *A London Life in the Brazen Age* (Cambridge, Mass.: Harvard University Press, 1978), pp. 167–196.

23. Greg, *Dramatic Documents*, I, 39. I cannot locate the support for Greg's claim in Henslowe's *Diary*, although Chambers mentions the same fact (*ES*, I, 352).

24. *ES*, II, 187.

25. As quoted in Bradbrook, *Rise of the Common Player*, pp. 75–76.

26. Bradbrook, *Rise of the Common Player*, p. 74.

27. *ES*, I, 352; *HP*, pp. 64–65.

28. *ES*, II, 442.

29. *HP*, pp. 31–32.

30. *ES*, II, 224.

31. *ES*, II, 117, 247; *JCS*, I, 155; see *JCS*, II for individual player biographies.

32. *HP*, pp. 64–65.

33. *HP*, p. 33.

34. *ES*, I, 353–354.

35. *ES*, II, 149–150, 156, 190 list principal members of the companies to 1613. I have determined the predominance of certain players in the companies from the nature of their involvement as documented in Henslowe's *Diary* and the later Henslowe-Alleyn Papers.

36. For a fuller discussion of the circumstances, see John Briley, "Edward Alleyn and Henslowe's Will," *Shakespeare Quarterly*, 9 (1958), 321–330.

37. Philip Henslowe's will, formerly 6 Cope, is now PCC, PROB 11/127, fols. 45^r–45^v; Agnes Henslowe's, formerly 72 Weldon, is now PCC, PROB 11/130, fols. 67^r–68^r.

38. See *JCS*, II, 631–651 for all transcriptions, with the exception of Edward Alleyn's (in J. Payne Collier, *The Alleyn Papers* [London: Shakspere Society, 1843], pp. xxi–xxvi; in manuscript, formerly 146 Hele, now PCC, PROB 11/150, fols. 291^v–292^v); Thomas Townes's (in Gerald Eades Bentley, "The Wills of Two Elizabethan Actors," *Modern Philology*, 29 [1931/32], 110–114; and William Bird's (in manuscript, formerly as 3 Byrde, and now PCC, PROB 11/143, n.f.).

39. *JCS*, II, 651.

40. See note 38 for the source of Towne's will.

41. In the transcription of manuscript materials, I have followed rules of standard, conservative diplomatic transcription. Only abbreviated symbols for which there are no modern printer's equivalents have been extended. I use square brackets for deletions and alterations or to suggest entries for letters or words that are quite illegible or cut away. Scribal interlineations are reproduced in double parentheses. Italics indicate bold script; a single slash the end of a line.

42. *HP*, pp. 27–28.

43. *HP*, pp. 28–30, 112; *JCS*, I, 144.

44. *JCS*, VI, 154; Bentley finds Prynne's report "vague." It would seem, however, that the "two olde Playhouses" that were "enlarged" could only have been the Second Fortune and the Red Bull.

45. *JCS*, I, 144.

46. *JCS*, II, 448–449, 682–683.

47. *JCS*, II, 544–546 gives the background on Rhodes; *JCS*, II, 457 refers to the lawsuit in which Cane reported that Richard Gunnell died in 1634.

48. *JCS*, II, 398–401; Nungezer, pp. 82–85.

49. *JCS*, I, 145, 152–153.

50. *JCS*, I, 153.

51. *JCS*, II, 399 (see the entry dated 30 April 1624).

The Prison-House of the Canon:

Allegorical Form and Posterity

in Ben Jonson's *The Staple of Newes*

DOUGLAS M. LANIER

> In the meane time perhaps hee is call'd barren, dull, leane, a poore Writer (or by what
> contumelious word can come in their cheeks) by these men, who without labour, judge-
> ment, knowledge, or almost sense, are received, or preferr'd before him. He gratulates
> them, and their fortune. An other Age, or juster men, will acknowledge the vertues of
> his studies: his wisdome, in dividing: his subtilty, in arguing: with what strength hee doth
> inspire his Readers; with what sweetnesse hee strokes them: in inveighing, what
> sharpenesse; in Jest, what urbanity he uses. How he doth raigne in mens affections; how
> invade, and breake in upon them; and makes their minds like the thing he writes.
>
>   (*Timber: or Discoveries,* ll, 781–793)[1]

    Two facts of literary history have set the course for the study of Ben Jonson's
late plays. The first, John Dryden's label "the dotages," has encouraged critics to
apologize for or attempt to rehabilitate the late plays, in effect to speculate as to just
how much blood got to Ben's brain in the final decades of his life. The second event,
though less acknowledged, is the more influential, for it not only determined the
criteria for judging Jonson's final works but also set up for Ben Jonson himself a series
of literary problems that his final plays seek unsuccessfully to solve. That event was
the publication of Jonson's *Workes* in 1616, the first printed edition of an author's
works supervised by the author himself, a landmark in English literary history.[2] The
publication met with derision from not a few of Jonson's contemporaries[3]—notably
Thomas Heywood and John Suckling—for it was an extraordinary act of artistic
self-consciousness and self-confidence, down to its classical spellings and footnotes.
The title *Workes,* on which Jonson's detractors fastened, and the care with which
Jonson prepared the text reveal a writer aware of his dramatic writings as printed
texts and not merely as words-to-be-performed—here was a volume designed to be
read, not merely heard.[4] Jonson modeled his volume on Renaissance editions of
classical playwrights, in effect placing himself in the pantheon of immortal classical
writers whom he admired and emulated.

    Certainly then it was on the 1616 Folio that Ben Jonson quite consciously hoped
his reputation as dramatist would rest.[5] With its publication, Jonson sought to
establish his position as the satirist of Elizabethan and Jacobean London. In its
prefaces, letters, prologues, and epilogues, it set forth Jonson's theories about drama,

specifically his theory of the comedy of humors, the subgenre that he had developed. Above all, the Folio was designed to preserve nearly all the plays that continue to be reckoned as Jonson's masterpieces—*Every Man in His Humor, Volpone, Epicoene,* and *The Alchemist.*[6] We should note that Jonson quit the public stage the year the Folio appeared and did not write for popular audiences again for nine years. As Herford and Simpson remark (I, 72–73), Jonson's interests in his 1619 conversations with Drummond touch rather little on drama. The implication is that Jonson felt that his literary career for the popular stage was complete, his reputation assured by his *Workes.*

However, by the time Jonson decided to return to the public stage in 1626, the Folio had proved in a sense too successful, for it not only set the terms of Jonson's reputation but also became the measure by which all Jonson's subsequent stagework was to be judged. Simply put, Jonson had erected a reputation as a particular type of dramatist, a contemporary satirist; to continue to write and build a career, Jonson would have to compete with his own *Workes.*[7] Because Jonson was acutely aware of creating a unified canon, a body of "workes,"[8] it was both within and against his own self-created dramatic tradition that Jonson wrote *The Staple of Newes. Staple* reorients Jonson's own earlier humors drama to accommodate his new understanding of the nature of literary reputation, both the ephemeral and the lasting qualities of printed texts, and the continual problem of audience misreading. That Jonson anticipated and addressed the failures of *Staple*'s experimental form in the play itself testifies to his extraordinary sensitivity to the problems of reputation, genre, and interpretation.

The themes of *The Staple of Newes,* abuse of money and language, are of course no news at all to readers of Jonson, for these are the governing obsessions of all his earlier plays;[9] it is the form that surprises. Oddly, Jonson uses the humanistic mortality play as his model, a dramatic form radically out of fashion in the late Jacobean and Caroline periods. Jonson arranges his allegorical characters schematically, the three Pennyboys representing Prodigality, Miserliness, and Moderation, each a wooer of Pecunia the Maid of Money. Lest his point be missed, Jonson uncharacteristically compels one of his characters to spell out the moral of the play's action in the final scene:

> And so *Pecunia* her selfe doth wish,
> That shee may still be ayde vnto their vses,
> Not slaue vnto their pleasures, or a Tyrant
> Ouer their faire desires; but teach them all
> The golden meane: the *Prodigall* how to liue,
> The *sordid,* and the *covetous,* how to dye:
> That with sound mind; this, safe frugality.

> (*V.vi.60–66*)[10]

Unlike the supporting characters of Jonson's earlier comedies, those of *Staple* are not clearly differentiated by their humors or their use of language. The jeerers, for example, act as a group rather than as individuals and are distinguished not by quirks of character but only by their occupations.[11] These departures from Jonson's characteristic dramatic style serve to emphasize not the topical manifestations of vices (the humors) that plague his age, the specific ways in which individuals abuse money or language, but rather the universal themes of the Jonsonian canon itself, the abuse of money and language *per se*. Linked with this broadening is the conspicuous absence of another Jonsonian staple, the catalogue of contemporary details. More than any other rhetorical device, the Jonsonian catalogue serves to root his earlier plays and poetry in Renaissance London, to give the vices that Jonson rebukes a gritty substance and up-to-the-moment relevance. Catalogues in this play appear in three speeches only, Cymbal's vended "news," Pennyboy's description of Canters' College, and Lickfinger's description of his city made of food, a striking contrast to the incessant cataloguing that marks *Volpone, The Alchemist*, or *Bartholmew Fayre*. Once again, Jonson seems to restrain his penchant for mimetic and copious detail. Why? Why turn from topical humors comedy, on which his dramatic reputation was based, to the abstract world of the morality play? It is not enough to assert that Jonson had been writing masques exclusively for ten years and that the allegorical mode was now second nature to his playwrighting. Herford and Simpson remind us (II, 170) that, from 1620 on, Jonson's masques show an increasing attraction to the comic realism of the popular stage and antimasque. Rather, we should view Jonson's choice of form as an experimental solution to artistic problems—problems that sprang ironically from Jonson's self-fashioned stance as a professional writer of comedy.

Jonson's effort to assure his reputation by printing an authoritative edition of his works derives in part from a familiar Renaissance poetic trope: the author's text preserves for posterity his self and reputation, thereby denying the power of Mutability. Jonson ends his dedicatory poem on the Droeshout Shakespeare portrait with a witty version of this commonplace: "Reader, looke / Not on his Picture, but his Booke."[12] The trope dominates Jonson's dedicatory and elegiac verse;[13] its very frequency suggests that Jonson linked the survival of texts and the survival of the author's voice—well-written poems might cheat the Reaper by transmitting the author's reputation to the future. Throughout his career, Jonson heaped scorn upon those who pandered to their readers, for such writers not only destroy the moral quality and reputation of true poetry but also risk exchanging current literary fame for eventual oblivion.[14] Jonson advises Donne that "A man should seeke great glorie, and not broad" (*Epigrammes* XCVI, l. 12). As my epigraph from *Timber: or Discoveries* makes explicit, Jonson distinguishes between the judgment of his peers and that of posterity, between fleeting notoriety and permanent literary significance. "If I thought my iudgment were of yeeres" (*Ungathered Verse* XXVI, l. 27), Jonson remarks as he praises Shakespeare in his famous dedicatory poem to the Folio, aware that the passing of time confounds all contemporary assessments of reputation and that no single man but rather the "yeeres" judge the value of an author's corpus.

When Jonson prepared to return to the public stage with *Staple* in 1626, he was
the grand old man of the London theater, father to a generation of literary "sons,"
yet in the midst of his celebrity, there was much to remind him of his own mortality.
The plague was once again ravaging London. Since his last public play, his most
famous dramatic contemporaries, Shakespeare, Beaumont, and Fletcher, had died—
Fletcher the year before. Much of Jonson's verse from 1619 to 1626, particularly his
many elegies and epitaphs, reveals the poet's growing awareness of death. A number
of poems focus on the poet's failing flesh or faltering poetic voice, and the verses
Jonson penned after 1626 elaborate upon this theme.[15] As well, in the years after his
farewell to the popular stage, there was much to remind Jonson of the fleeting nature
of literary creations and the reputation that they maintained. In 1623 Jonson's
library had burned. At the head of the catalogue of destroyed texts that makes up
"An Execration upon *Vulcan*," Jonson lists some "parcels of a Play, / Fitter to see
the fire-light, then the day" (*Vnder-wood* XLIII, ll. 43–44). Important here is not
the play's identity but the morbid irony of the line—Vulcan has rendered nil Jonson's
efforts to preserve his work for posterity, and in an uncharacteristic gesture of futility
Jonson punningly consigns his play to the flames as not worth keeping anyway.
Moreover, he links Vulcan's fire to the public's misjudgment of his writing and the
burning of his books to the destruction of his body:

> Thou should'st have stay'd, till publike fame said so.
> Shee is the Judge, Thou Executioner:
> Or if thou needs would'st trench upon her power,
> Thou mightst have yet enjoy'd thy crueltie
> With some more thrift, and more varietie:
> Thou mightst have had me perish, piece, by piece,
> To light Tobacco, or save roasted Geese,
> Sindge Capons, or poore Pigges, dropping their eyes;
> Condemn'd me to the Ovens with the pies;
> And so, have kept me dying a whole age,
> Not ravish'd all hence in a minutes rage.

> (*ll. 46–56*)[16]

In lines 101 and 106 he exclaims over his "twice-twelve-yeares stor'd up humanitie
. . . All soote, and embers!" That the poem laments only the loss of Jonson's writings
and the books lent to him by friends and not the other possessions which presumably
the fire destroyed might suggest that Jonson realized that his literary works, and the
reputation they might establish, could perish utterly: despite any efforts to codify and
preserve his canon for posterity, books are vulnerable to time or the whims of Vulcan.
If we set this list of texts beside the Latin and Greek classics that Jonson indefatiga-
bly worshipped, *opera* that had successfully cheated time, the weight of Jonson's
recognition of the transcience of books and reputation recorded in "An Execration
upon *Vulcan*" becomes clearer. Jonson depicts Vulcan as Mutability itself, as an
effacer of theater (the Globe, the Fortune, Whitehall), of history (the court rolls

in the Chancery Office), and, with a pun on the Globe's name, of the world itself: "See the worlds Ruines!" (l. 137). The superficial mock-anger of the verse only partially conceals an anxiety that informs the later works of Jonson: the fear of death, of not surviving through his art. Because the law cannot bind Vulcan, all Jonson can do is register an impotent "civill curse" and imply that his lost texts, like the razed buildings, "were burnt, but to be better built. / 'Tis true, that in thy [Vulcan's] wish they were destroy'd, / Which thou hast only vented, not enjoy'd" (ll. 166–168).

It is ironic then that the great Folio edition of Shakespeare's works should appear in the same year, for soon it became the standard of dramatic achievement against which Jonson must have measured his own works. Although Jonson thought himself the better dramatist—he never lauded Shakespeare without some qualification—in the next years Shakespeare's reputation waxed as Jonson's waned, and the vagaries of contemporary fame loomed large once again. In Jonson's dedicatory verse for the 1623 Folio, he seats Shakespeare, despite his "small Latine, and lesse Greeke," in the company of Aeschylus, Euripides, Pacuvius, Accius, Seneca, Aristophanes, Terence, and Plautus. Was Jonson's dramatic work, despite its learnedness, merely of topical interest and not of lasting importance, mere "news" and not *Workes,* as Jonson styled them? Such a question rises as well out of Charles I's early indifference to Jonson. The poet's prestigious and lucrative position as the unofficial poet laureate under James was by no means secure under James's son. Jonson's masques were conspicuously absent from the court in the first five winters of Charles's reign, and Jonson was forced to petition the new king for money.

I have sketched Jonson's distinction between two types of reputation, one for contemporaries, one for posterity, and his connection between the survival of texts and the survival of the author's self to suggest the background of anxiety against which Jonson may have played out his return to the popular stage, newly isolated from royal patronage, wary of shifts in contemporary opinion, aware of the physical and critical perishability of texts, yearning for an enduring place in English letters. Thus we might view *The Staple of Newes* as Jonson's attempt to address not only Renaissance London but literary posterity as well, an attempt to establish his place as a dramatist of lasting and not merely topical importance. To do so, Jonson consciously chose to eliminate as much as possible those details that would mark him as a dramatist of his age. Instead he chose allegory, a deliberately universalized form, a timeless mode in which he might cast the characteristic themes of the 1616 Folio for all ages.[17]

Staple reflects Jonson's distinction between the ephemeral and the classic work of literature in two ways. Most obviously, in *Staple* Jonson inveighs against the dangers of news, ephemeral bits of information fastened upon for their novelty and not for their enduring moral significance. Jonson had earlier derided news-mongering in "An Epistle answering to one that asked to be Sealed of the Tribe of Ben" and *Newes From the New World Discover'd in the Moone,* and in *Staple* he returns to this theme.[18] However, Jonson also seems to recognize that plays themselves, the latest dispatches from the poet's brain, are also regarded as a sort of news. The gossip

Tattle, at the theater for entertainment and not moral instruction, specifics that "your *Newes* be new, and fresh, M*ʳ*. *Prologue,* and vntainted," or, she threatens, "I shall find them else" (Induction. 24–25). Never grasping Jonson's dicta on money, language, and man's corruptible nature, the gossips instead fasten upon the surface of the play, its spectacle, action, and dialogue. They whine that it is boring, predictable, a confusing morality play in modern garb; they long for a devil or a fool and, like George and Nell in *The Knight of the Burning Pestle,* invent alternate events to enliven the story line. Jonson has to cope with the disadvantage that much of the audience's pleasure in his dramatic work derives from the novelty of the content, his gibes against the current fashion or latest exchange of wit and not his judgments on man's moral essence. Indeed, Jonson's catalogue technique, by including contemporary events, places, fads, and persons in his earlier plays, whetted his audience's appetite for the ephemeral. Ironically, the comedies of the 1616 Folio established Jonson as the master of staged yellow journalism, veiled versions of the latest satirical pamphlet directed at some current figure or fashion. For these reasons, in *Staple*'s "Prologue for the Stage," Jonson warns those who hang on such meaningless details as the number of coaches in Hyde Park or the tavern with the best wine that the stuff of drama is not "newes." Explicitly Jonson states that "the Stage might stand as wel, / If it did neither heare these things, nor tell" (ll. 16–17).

Rather, in this play Jonson offers such moral guidance as can "steere the soules of men" (l. 23). He directs his audience's attention to "his *wayes,* / What flight he makes, how new" (ll. 27–28, italics mine), highlighting that the "newes" here will be Jonson's departure from his traditional "wayes," the comedy of accumulated detail and civic humors. The "Prologue for the Court" is even more explicit: "Wherein, although our *Title,* Sir, be *Newes,* / Wee yet aduenture, here, to tell you none; / But shew you common follies" (ll. 9–11), the lines stressing that *Staple* focuses on the moral failure of human nature ("common follies") and not the fleeting forms that such failure can take. Both Prologues maintain that the reader or viewer should judge those events that the text presents, apprehending "The *sense* they heare" (Court Prologue, l. 7, italics mine) and not lingering over the bright details by which that sense is delivered. Cymbal's Staple of Newes feeds upon the same readerly weaknesses as do those poets who seek immediate fame: a hunger for the latest, newest literary entertainment. Ironically then, the proper understanding of the play is threatened by the very vice that it seeks to chastize. With an allegorical approach, Jonson attempts to shift his public's gaze from the details of the play's surface to its enduring moral verities.

Although in *The Staple of Newes,* Jonson sets out to universalize observations about the corrupting power of money and language, his allegorical form raises two new artistic problems that threaten this artistic strategy—problems that Jonson foresees and seeks to avert in the play itself. First, allegory opens up new opportunities for misinterpretation, in particular "application," the art of construing the play's events or characters as allusions to contemporary events or persons. Jonson was particularly sensitive to such misinterpretations, not the least because he had spent time in prison for his part in *The Isle of Dogs* and *Eastward Ho* and had been summoned before the Privy Council for *Sejanus*. For example, in the prefacing letter to *Volpone*, witness the protest that he registers against such intended "application." Once Jonson has set in motion an allegorical strategy of interpreting the play, he must somehow control his audience's interpretive process, lest they read into his allegory meanings that Jonson never intended. The impulse to "apply" is particularly tempting in *Staple* because readers of *The Workes* would expect an abundance of contemporary allusion and topical satire from a Jonsonian comedy. For those in the theater, Jonson counters the impulse to "apply" by directing his audience's attention from the visual spectacle onstage to the spoken lines in which that spectacle is made clear. Although Jonson was not to quarrel with Inigo Jones for another five years, the complaint that spectacle, mere "shows," instead of moral poetry had become the heart of drama had already surfaced in the Induction to *Bartholmew Fayre*.[19] This complaint appears once again in both Prologues to *The Staple of Newes* as a distinction between those who merely "see" and those who "heare." The gossips observe that, to the eye, the allegorical characters are "attir'd like the men and women of the time"; only in the characters' speeches do we learn, for example, that the maiden-queen pursued by several suitors is Pecunia or that Pennyboy Junior's costume changes reflect his spiritual condition as well as his financial fortunes. For those who read the play, Jonson adds an unorthodox address to the Reader prefacing Act Three. The address applies the principle of allegorical reading to a specific episode, the dispensing of news items by the Staple itself in III.i. Jonson reminds the audience that "the *Newes* here vented, [is] none of his *Newes,* or any reasonable mans; but *Newes* made like the times *Newes*" (ll. 8–10), news that should not be read as anything but an exemplum of man's "owne folly, or hunger and thirst after . . . *Newes*" that have "no syllable of truth in them" (ll. 12–14). Jonson punctuates his instructions to the reader with an Horatian epigram: "Ficta, voluptatis causa, sint proxima veris." The poet does not create a real world of detail; rather he only feigns things that approximate truth in their moral significance. The address thus insures that the reader construe the news dispensed in III.i not as pokes at contemporary figures but rather as an indictment of Gossip.

However, for both playgoer and reader, Jonson's primary "audience-proofing" device is the frame tale of the gossips that precedes each act. In part, the Induction functions to undercut the audience's suspension of disbelief, to force viewers and readers, by hindering an empathetic response and instead encouraging judgment with esthetic distance, to experience the play as a text that instructs and not as a cathartic event.[20] For example, in the Induction, the gossips interrupt the Prologue and force him to break character, to have them seated, to explain the lighting conventions of the private theater, and to clarify that he is merely an actor playing the Prologue among many other actors who are about to enact "a thing call'd a Play" (Induction, 55). As well, the Prologue is compelled to remind the audience of the "stew'd Poet" in the tiring house from whose mind the drama sprang and who manipulates the events that they are about to see. After each act, the gossips remind the audience of the artist behind the play as they mercilessly criticize him. Jonson's thereby unavoidable presence serves two ends: first, it places into view, albeit in caricature, the poet's anxiety over his work's reception and, in the gossips' misguided attacks on his artistry, plays out how misunderstanding may endanger a poet's reputation; second, it ironically and confidently asserts Jonson's own poetic authority—throughout the play Jonson reminds us that *he* is the author, that his vision informs the work we view or read, and that the reader or viewer is obliged to recover the playwright's intent accurately from the text or stage.

In recovering Jonson's intent, the gossips are hopelessly (and delightfully) inept, for they consistently misunderstand the moral significance of his characters and their actions. For example, in the Second Intermean, Expectation and Tattle reveal that they have not yet recognized the vice-figures of the play. They cannot judge properly without such visual cues as the Vice's conventional wooden dagger or "Iuglers ierkin," for they react to the stage spectacle and not to the text. As Mirth explains Jonsonian humors characterization to her friends, it becomes clear that she understands it not as a moral reconception of character but merely as a change in costuming: "That was the old way, Gossip, when *Iniquity* came in like *Hokos Pokos,* in a Iuglers ierkin, with false skirts, like the *Knaue* of *Clubs*! but now they are attir'd like men and women o' the time, the *Vices,* male and female!" (II Intermean, 14–17). Predictably, Censure misinterprets Mirth's explanation, viewing it as evidence that the play targets specific individuals, particularly the Spanish Princess. Mirth replies that the Princess (and by implication the other characters) should be read not topically but allegorically:

> Take heed, it lie not in the vice of your interpretation: what have *Aurelia, Clara, Pecunia* to do with any person? do they any more, but express the property of *Money,* which is the daughter of earth, and drawne out of the Mines? Is there nothing to be call'd *Infanta,* but what is subiect to exception? Why not the *Infanta* of the Beggers? or *Infanta* o' the Gipsies? as well as *King* of Beggers, and *King* of Gipsies?
>
> *(II Intermean, 27–34)*

As these examples suggest, the gossips function as an anti-chorus. By following their exaggerated misinterpretations in the Intermeans, the audience can check its own misplaced curiosity, expectation, or censure and gloss Jonson's allegory properly. (Problems arise when Jonson uses the gossips to compensate for defects in the play's workmanship—for instance, when the gossips complain that Jonson introduces the Staple only to drop it abruptly in Act Four.) As faulty critics, the gossips force the audience to confront the problem of properly interpreting the play by anticipating the audience's misunderstandings and parodying them.

Why the gossips cannot grasp *Staple*'s point stems directly from Jonson's distinction between the ephemeral and the universal, "news" and allegory. His onstage audience—the gossips Mirth, Tattle, Expectation, and Censure—are themselves allegorical projections of the failings that have led audiences to demand "news." The gossips' entrance emphasizes that they have come to the theater "to see and to be seene"; they view their very presence as a newsworthy event, for they announce themselves as "persons of quality . . . and women of fashion" and insist upon sitting on the stage, in the process interrupting the Prologue's admonition to glean "judgment" from the play. Instead of extracting Jonson's moral instruction from the play, Censure intends to look for such ephemera as "who wears the new suit today, whose clothes are best penn'd whatever the part be, which actor has the best leg and foot, what king plays without cuffs and his queen without gloves, who rides most in stockings and dances in boots." As Renaissance philistines preoccupied with tyrannies of the moment, transient details of fashion, status, and rumor, the gossips cannot understand the peculiar nature of fiction—enduring universal truths given a fleeting local habitation and a name. As Jonson puts it in the Court Prologue, his play aims to reveal the "common follies, and so knowne, / That though they are not truths, th' innocent *Muse* / Hath made so like, as Phant'sie could them state, / Or *Poetry*, without scandall, imitate" (ll. 11–14). Unfortunately, the gossips never fully see that the characters before them point to moral issues beyond the characters' particular situations. Instead, the gossips react to the characters as they would to real people, liking or disliking the fictional creations but never judging the meaning of their actions. Indeed, Censure goes so far as to speak of Zeal-of-the-Land Busy from *Bartholmew Fayre* as if he were a real Puritan minister. The play's frame tale does far more than caricature the audience that Jonson imagined he had. By reducing species of misunderstanding to absurdity and holding them up for ridicule, the gossips' exaggerated misperceptions stress those distinctions that an audience should properly make, distinctions between a story and its moral significance, character and human being, allegory and "news."

The second problem introduced by *Staple*'s allegorical form also grows out of the distinction between reality and the fictive world of allegory. Jonson chose allegory, I have argued, because it allowed him to universalize his particulars, to broaden humors characters into human types that approximate personified abstractions. In such a hybrid form Jonson could state his ideal of rational moderation broadly and directly, addressed to all eras. Yet such a universalized statement, exemplified by Pennyboy Junior's transformation in Act Four, is so abstracted from human experience as to be inapplicable to the morally ambiguous world of Realpolitik. The ideals of moderation and restraint that Pennyboy Canter espouses at the end of Act Four are unquestionably noble, but how might they be put into action in the machiavellian court? Are such universalized moral imperatives confined to allegory, in which man's behavior may be easily schematized and idealized, and not useful in the realm of actual human conduct? Jonson was too close an observer of human foibles not to be confronted with such doubts as he penned the transformation of Pennyboy Junior at the opening of Act Five, and I suggest that Jonson includes the further adventures of the Pennyboys in that final act as a recognition of the need for ethical pragmatism as well as idealism in a world where "all men are canters."

The final act has disappointed many critics, who have felt that the action is anticlimactic and reminiscent of the gullery and double-dealings of the middle

comedies that had been so conspicuously avoided in the preceding acts. Tattle herself
complains that the catastrophe falls too early, in the fourth and not the fifth act (IV
Intermean, 1). However, this backward glance at the middle comedies allows Jonson
to consider the unidealized means by which a moral man must hold to his principles
in a deceitful and greedy world. Pennyboy Canter, if he is to disguise himself and
test his son's ethics, must trust Picklock, who, as his name suggests, is the inheritor
of the role of the Vice, the worst kind of canter and disguiser. By manipulating words
and feigning trust,[21] Picklock can manipulate the law, the chief social institution
governing ethics, to his own advantage, threatening the moral standards implicit in
Pennyboy Junior's reformation. Are men to reform and embrace moderation only to
be swindled by men of policy? Pennyboy Junior's thwarting of Picklock's double
swindle emphasizes the dubious means by which moral men must act in a duplicitous
world.[22] In a play that attacks pretenses and cheats, it can be no accident that
Pennyboy Junior uses a lie to swindle the swindler. Not only Picklock but also the
audience are momentarily taken in by Pennyboy Junior's deceit—like Picklock, we
are led to believe that Pennyboy Junior has returned to cant and policy by allying
himself to the crooked lawyer's scheme. When we learn that Pennyboy Junior
has lied to entrap Picklock, we may hear an echo of the moral pragmatism of
Catiline, in which Cicero claims that the moral man must use questionable means
to achieve the proper ethical end.[23] By accenting the means of Picklock's overthrow,
Jonson can stress that Pennyboy Canter's ideal of moderation *is* possible, that the
moral man need not be vulnerable to men of policy if he approaches the question of
moderate action pragmatically. Jonson seeks to avoid any sort of moral legalism, the
mechanical application of the ethical rules that his allegory seems to sketch out. As
in his earlier humors comedies, he values the character who can skilfully improvise
upon a situation to get what he wants, the character who cleverly bends the rules.
This is why Pennyboy Canter presents the reader with a problem of divided sympa-
thies when, in his speech at the end of Act Four, he appears much like Pennyboy
Senior in his rigidly legalistic approach to morality. We know that what Pennyboy
Canter says is true, but the moralistic vehemence of his soliloquy, its overblown and
pharisaical rhetoric hints that the father does not understand the problem of moral
action in the world in all its complexity; he fails to see that good men may be used.
His entrapment by Picklock confirms this hypothesis. It becomes the son's function
to teach the father the potentially reforming power of guile in a world of disguises.

In this light, the madness of Pennyboy Senior seems to extend the critique of
moral legalism stressed in the Pennyboy Junior/Picklock episode.[24] Throughout the
play, Pennyboy Senior stresses that he is a "just" man—for him right conduct is a
series of rules that exclude all forms of festivity.[25] Our final view of Pennyboy Senior,
without human company, absurdly and pitifully questioning his dogs, arbitrarily
convicting and forgiving them for breaking rules that have no rational basis, demonstrates how dubious legalistic "logic" and ethical ranting are. Just as Picklock has
the legal right to confiscate Pennyboy Canter's deed of trust, so Pennyboy Senior has
the legal right to punish his servants or dogs, but neither is morally on safe turf. The

final act of the play then qualifies the idealism implied by the allegory of Pecunia in the preceding acts: in this world, one cannot assume that moral means lead to moral ends; the idealized standards of conduct codified by the allegory of the Pennyboys in the first four acts cannot tell the reader how to approach a moral problem in the complex world outside of the play, although they do serve as standards.

I am not arguing that *The Staple of Newes* succeeds as a unified dramatic piece. Jonson never seems able to commit himself wholly to a thoroughgoing allegorical play.[26] The recurrent impression in the criticism that the life of the play resides in the Staple and Apollo scenes is certainly justified. Pecunia, like her attendants but unlike the Pennyboys or the jeerers, seems marooned in a nether world between play and humors comedy, never fully a palpable princess or a moralized abstraction. Thus the play must rely too heavily upon metatheatrical devices to enforce an allegorical conception of its details. Indeed, that Jonson felt the need for such devices underlines how the play as written does not compel such an interpretation without some commentary from the wings. Jonson's dramatic genius seems inextricably wedded to "news," despite his attempt to address posterity in a play less dependent upon the particular.

As a generic experiment (and the play cannot be convincingly salvaged as a parody of allegorical drama), *The Staple of Newes* offers the reader a peek into how the aging Jonson conceived of himself as an artist and how his return to the public stage works from that conception. As Jonson addressed the problem of his canon with allegory, he found himself caught up in new problems of audience misunderstanding and of abstraction from the moral realities of the court, problems that *Staple* anticipates and tries to tackle, finally without success. Jonson himself may have sensed his failure, for the plays that follow, *The New Inne, The Magnetick Lady, The Tale of a Tub,* and *The Sad Shepherd,* strike out in new generic directions. As the subtitle of *The Magnetick Lady* suggests, the final plays seek to reconcile humors comedy, a morally static form because the characters cannot change without violating their essential humor, with the transformative possibilities of romance. In those plays, too, Jonson had to do battle with the canon that he had so carefully established. Such a conception of Jonson's career helps explain his sincere anguish over the failure of *The New Inne,*[27] for this failure signaled the persistence of a (mis)conception of his dramatic career that, it may be argued, lives to this day. Habitually Jonson's final plays have been measured in terms of the dramatic achievements of the 1616 Folio and thereby have come to be regarded as feeble comedies of humors that beg for some sort of critical apologia, rather than being regarded as Jonson's attempt at recasting the artistic identity that he had crafted for himself. The authority of the 1616 Folio tempts even Jonson's most sympathetic audience to become the type of audience that he most feared. Thomas Carew's "To Ben. Iohnson. Vpon occasion of his Ode of defiance annext to his Play of the new Inne," written several years after *The Staple of Newes,* clearly illustrates Jonson's dilemma as an aging laureate playwright. Although a Son of Ben, Carew admits that Jonson's "commique Muse from the exalted line / Toucht by thy *Alchymist,* doth since decline / From that her Zenith" (ll. 5–7).[28] Hence, the poor reception of *The New Inne* (and by extension Jonson's final plays as a group) springs not so much from the play's own dramatic failings as from audience expectations that Jonson's 1616 Folio had fixed—from, in Carew's terms, a "quarrell ... Within thine owne Virge" (ll. 47–48):

> The wiser world doth greater Thee confesse
> Than all men else, than Thy selfe onely lesse.
> *(ll. 49–50)*

As a student of the classics and as the first English writer to issue his own *opera*, Jonson was uniquely attuned to the power of the printed text to preserve the writer's voice and authority. It is therefore ironic that he should be made aware of the negative capabilities of his self-fashioned "classics," the text's uncanny ability to imprison the living author behind his own lines of print.

NOTES

1. All quotations from Jonson's works are from *Ben Jonson,* ed. C. H. Herford and Percy and Evelyn Simpson, 11 vols. (Oxford: Clarendon Press, 1925–52), hereafter referred to as H & S. H & S, VIII, 587-588.

2. Richard C. Newton discusses the significance of the 1616 Folio for English literary history in "Jonson and the (Re-)Invention of the Book," *Classic and Cavalier: Essays on Jonson and the Sons of Ben,* ed. Claude J. Summers and Ted-Larry Pebworth (Pittsburgh, Pa.: University of Pittsburgh Press, 1982), pp. 31–55.

3. See Richard Helgerson, "The Elizabethan Laureate: Self-Presentation and the Literary System," *ELH,* 46 (1979), 206–207, and *Self-Crowned Laureates: Spenser, Jonson, Milton, and the Literary System* (Berkeley: University of California Press, 1980), pp. 145–147, on the status of printed drama within the literary system of the day.

4. Jonson seems, in *The Staple of Newes* as never before, aware of the play as a written text as distinct from a performance and takes care to keep that awareness in the foreground of the play. The edition of 1631 is a text consciously addressed to readers and not to spectators. In addition to the address "To the Readers" between Acts Two and Three, Jonson added marginal glosses to the text that restate the dialogue or action; worth noting here is that the notes to Act Five make clear Pennyboy Junior's strategem to recover Picklock's deed of trust, a strategem rather confusing on the stage and even more confusing to a reader. Most interesting, however, is Pennyboy Junior and Cymbal's discussion of the difference between written and printed news—Pennyboy Junior notes that "Vnto some, / The very printing of them, makes them *Newes,* / That ha' not the heart to beleeue any thing / But what they see in print" (I.vi.51–54). Jonson seems exceptionally attuned to the power of print, and such awareness cannot but reflect upon his notion of the power of his own carefully printed 1616 Folio. Some characteristics of "readerly" texts and differences between written and printed texts are mapped out admirably in Walter Ong's *Orality and Literacy: The Technologizing of the Word* (London: Methuen, 1982), pp. 117–138.

5. See W. David Kay, "The Shaping of Ben Jonson's Career: A Reexamination of Facts and Problems," *Modern Philology,* 67 (1969–70), 224–237.

6. *Bartholmew Fayre,* a play that most commentators would include in the roster of Jonson's finest works, was not included in the 1616 Folio probably because Jonson had already begun editing the volume before the play was produced in 1614. In a study of William Stansby, the printer of Jonson's

Folio, James Bracken deduces that the Folio went to press in early 1615 and was completed early the following year. "William Stansby's Early Career and the Publication of Ben Jonson's Folio," Diss. University of South Carolina, 1983.

7. In this connection, it is significant that *The Staple of Newes* had to compete with the growing reputation of Jonson's own work in repertory, notably *The Alchemist* at court in 1623 and *Volpone* in 1624. H & S, IX, 196 and 225.

8. Kay, p. 236: "[Jonson] attempt[ed] to interpret himself to his age as a writer whose individual works formed a unified corpus animated by his conception of the poet's function."

9. Modern commentators on Jonson's work have tended to view the play as a summary piece. Typical examples are Robert E. Knoll, *Ben Jonson's Plays: An Introduction* (Lincoln: University of Nebraska Press, 1964), pp. 172–177; C. G. Thayer, *Ben Jonson: Studies in the Plays* (Norman, Oklahoma: University of Oklahoma Press, 1963), pp. 177–178; and Larry Champion, *Ben Jonson's "Dotages": A Study of the Late Plays* (Lexington: University Press of Kentucky, 1967), p. 75.

10. H & S, VI, 381. All subsequent citation from *The Staple of Newes* will be taken from H & S, VI and will be cited parenthetically by act, scene, and line number.

11. Although Jonsonian names usually indicate a character's humor or essential nature, the names of the jeerers (except for Cymbal) reflect only their jobs. Cymbal's name may recall I Corinthians 13:1, where St. Paul makes a crucial distinction between mere eloquence and moral action ("charity"), a distinction that *Staple* insists upon as well.

12. H & S, VIII, *Ungathered Verse* XXV, ll. 9–10. All subsequent citations from Jonson's poems will be taken from H & S, VIII and will be cited parenthetically by poem and line number. See also Jonson's coupling of Shakespeare's "Booke, and Fame" in the second line of "To the memory of my beloved, The AVTHOR Mr. William Shakespeare" (*Ungathered Verse* XXVI) and lines 22–24: "Thou art a Moniment, without a tombe, / And art aliue still, while thy Booke doth liue, / And we haue wits to read, and praise to giue."

13. In addition to the pieces quoted above, examples include *Epigrammes* CXI (l. 11); *Epigrammes* CXXIII (pun in line 1); *Epigrammes* CXXXI; *Vnder-woods* LXXVIII (especially ll. 25–26); *Vnder-woods* LXXXIV, 4 (ll. 17–24); *Ungathered Verse* [*UV*] I (ll. 30–31); *UV* VIII (ll. 11–16); *UV* XXI (ll. 1–13); *UV* XXIV (ll. 2–3).

14. In addition to Jonson's burlesques of poets in the plays, see the preface to *Volpone* (H & S, V, 21, ll. 129–146), the preface to *The Alchemist* (H & S, V, 291, ll. 2–27), the letter to William, Earl of Pembroke, prefacing *Catiline* (H & S, V, 431, ll. 1–6), and the Induction to *Bartholmew Fayre* (H & S, VI, 134, ll. 1–57). See also *Epigrammes* CXXXI, especially ll. 13–14: "Then stand vnto thy selfe, not seeke without / For fame, with breath soone kindled, soone blowne out," and *UV* VIII, especially ll. 14–16: "thy murder'd *Poeme:* which shall rise / A glorified worke to Time, when Fire, / Or moathes shall eate, what all these Fooles admire." The last example anticipates the connection in "Execration" of fire and literary mutability.

15. Early examples of this anxiety are the two poems that Jonson sent to Drummond in 1619 (*Vnder-woods* VIII and IX). Both fix upon the image of death and physical decay. The former, "The Houre-Glasse," adapts a Latin poem by Amaltei and shifts its focus from a Petrarchan commonplace toward a *memento mori*. The latter, entitled "My Picture Left in Scotland," paints a portrait of the aging poet himself, gray-haired, obese, aware that he is physically past his prime and that his eloquence cannot make up for his failing flesh. One must be cautious in equating the persona of Jonson's poetry with Jonson the man; however, these pieces testify that mortality was at least on the poet's mind. Other examples from 1619 to 1626 include *Vnder-woods* II, i (ll. 3–6 and 20–24); *Vnder-woods* XII (ll. 35–36); *Vnder-woods* XVI (ll. 6–7); and *Vnder-woods* XLII (ll. 1–8). See also John Lemly, "Masks and Self-Portraits in Jonson's Late Poetry," *ELH*, 44 (1977), 248–262.

16. The final couplet reveals Jonson's anxiety over an unintended direction that his reputation might take, the possibility that posterity might long remember him as a bad poet.

17. This shift in form actually begins with *The Divell is an Asse,* Jonson's last play before the hiatus in his writing for the public stage. The play's extraordinary allusiveness to earlier Jonson plays suggests that Jonson, as he placed the final touches on the Folio in 1616, was already glancing backward and recasting old material in new form. The humors chastized by *Divell* are somewhat standard Jonsonian fare, but the setting of the first scene is wholly uncharacteristic—the court of Hell. The opening scene in Hell and the devil Pug's presence throughout the play do more than establish a running joke on the play's sententious title: they establish a more universal context (the pan-historical evil that Satan creates and embodies) for the contemporary London evils that the play indicts. Jonson places what might be dismissed as passing fancies in vice in the context of universal Sin. Unfortunately, Jonson has as usual marshaled a mass of detail from contemporary London in service of his moral and thereby overwhelms his own strategy. Although in this devil play we might expect fire and brimstone, we get rather little, an indication that Jonson remains uncomfortable with subject matter not rooted in the realities of this world. See also Eugene M. Waith, "Things As They Are and the World of Absolutes in Jonson's Plays and Masques," in *Elizabethan Theatre* IV, ed. G. R. Hibbard (London and Basingstoke: Macmillan, 1974), p. 112.

18. Note Richard Peterson's comments in passing on the dangers of "news" in *Imitation and Praise in the Poems of Ben Jonson* (New Haven, Conn.: Yale University Press, 1981), pp. 134–157.

19. Jonson's differentiation between the effects of the written and visual arts tends to clarify why Jonson balked at increasingly elaborate visual spectacles on the stage. In *Timber: or Discoveries,* he writes of *Poesis and Pictura:* "Yet of the two, the Pen is more noble, then the Pencill. For that can speake to the Understanding; the other, but to the Sense" (H & S, VIII, ll. 1514–1516). That is, visual arts can only describe, impart raw experience to the senses; one must turn to language for analysis and moral judgment. A similar distinction between the arts runs throughout sections 3 and 4 of "EUPHEME; or the Faire Fame Lefte to Posteritie," (*Vnder-woods* LXXXIV). In *Timber: or Discoveries* Jonson specifies that "*Speech* is the only benefit man hath to expresse his excellencie of mind above other creatures. It is the Instrument of *Society*" (ll. 1881–1883). See also Wesley Trimpi, *Ben Jonson's Poems: A Study of the Plain Style* (Stanford, Calif.: Stanford University Press, 1962), p. 160.

20. In "Jonson and the Loathed Stage," Jonas A. Barish examines Jonson's suspicion of theatricality, although he focuses for the most part on the early and middle plays and the masques (*The Antitheatrical Prejudice* [Berkeley: University of California Press, 1981], pp. 132–154). Robert W. Witt, in *Mirror Within a Mirror: Ben Jonson and the Play Within,* Jacobean Drama Studies, No 46. (Salzburg: Inst. für eng. Sprache & Lit., 1975), pp. 55-56, underestimates the effect of the frame tale on the remainder of the play. It is the only frame that Jonson saw fit to develop throughout a play.

21. *Trust* is a key word in the final act. It occurs only in the fifth act and there twenty times, plus a pun on "truss'd" in V.iii.15.

22. Alexander Leggatt, *Ben Jonson: His Vision and His Art* (London: Methuen, 1981), p. 149. My reading of the final act differs from Professor Leggatt's in emphasis but not in principle.

23. Discussed at length in Leggatt, pp. 150–155.

24. Jonas A. Barish notes the legalist parody in "Feasting and Judging in Jonsonian Comedy," *Renaissance Drama,* n.s. 5, ed. S. Schoenbaum and Alan C. Dessen (Evanston, Ill.: Northwestern University Press, 1972), p. 32.

25. See Devra Rowland Kifer's Introduction to her edition of *The Staple of News,* Regents Renaissance Drama (Lincoln: University of Nebraska Press, 1975), pp. xix–xxi.

26. Leggatt, p. xv: "While Jonson's art seems to move at times toward morality-play abstraction, he is never finally content with such abstraction; there is an awareness of the solidity and complexity of life, a respect for particular realities that prevents him from being as schematic or reductive as some recent criticism has made him out to be."

27. See Jonson's "Ode to Himself (Come Leave the Lothed Stage)," H & S, VI, 492–493 and the replies by Owen Feltham, Thomas Randolph, Thomas Carew, and John Cleveland collected in *Ben Jonson's Plays,* ed. Felix E. Schelling, Everyman Library, 2 vols. (London: Dent, 1910), II, 498–504.

28. *The Poems of Thomas Carew, with his Masque 'Coelum Britannicum',* ed. Rhodes Dunlap (Oxford: Clarendon Press, 1949), pp. 64–65. Line numbers are cited parenthetically.

Three Charges against Sixteenth-
and Seventeenth-Century Playwrights:
Libel, Bawdy, and Blasphemy

DAVID McPHERSON

Many of the charges against theater favored by opponents of the stage in Shake-speare's time had little or nothing to do with alleged abuses in the scripts. Hence there was hardly any way in which purging the scripts could have reformed such abuses. Playwrights, for example, could have done nothing, *qua* playwrights, about the economics of theater; if plays were indeed a waste of time and money, no moral reformation of scripts could have alleviated the problem.[1] If the theatrical medium itself is corrupt because it is a kind of living lie (worse than mere fiction because its spectacle makes it all the more appealing sensually), no purification of scripts could have corrected this "evil."[2] The argument that a higher moral tone in scripts would perhaps have had a long-term beneficial effect upon the social milieu of the playhouse (where actors allegedly misbehaved and whores picked up trade) is not wholly implausible, but the effects would have been so slow and indirect as to be problematic at best.[3]

But there were three oft-repeated charges that, because they concerned the scripts themselves, had great importance for playwrights: libel, bawdy, and blasphemy. Ben Jonson, for example, is at special pains (in the dedicatory epistle for *Volpone*) to defend himself from these three charges (although in reverse to the order in which I have named them):

> For my particular, I can (and from a most clear conscience) affirme, that I have ever trembled to thinke toward the least prophanenesse; have lothed the use of such foule, and un-wash'd baudr'y, as is now made the foode of the scene. And, howsoever I cannot escape, from some, the imputation of sharpness . . . I would aske . . . Where have I beene particular? Where personal?[4]

We will be in a better position to understand the effects that the attack on the stage might have had on playwrights if we examine carefully the nature of the opposition to libel, bawdy, and blasphemy. The great bulk of the evidence used in my examination here has been employed for similar purposes by earlier scholars; what is new here, I hope, is the method. While earlier scholars have studied both the attitudes of the various arms of the government and the attitudes of the pam-phleteers who opposed the stage, I believe that fresh perspectives are gained by comparing and contrasting the attitudes of those two groups. A word about terminology: I use *puritan* with a lower case *p* to refer to those with a strict moral attitude toward the stage, whatever their political affiliations; I use *Puritan* with a capital *P* to refer to that very loosely knit political group composed of those who did not think that the reformation of the Church had proceeded far enough away from Rome.[5]

I

One particular court case illustrates how broadly the term *libel* was defined legally. The case, known as *De Libellis Famosis,* was decided in 1605 in Star Chamber.[6] The published report of it ought to have put fear in the heart of any dramatist who had satirized an individual or was contemplating doing so.[7] The facts are that one "L.P." had confessed to composing and publishing what Justice Coke, who wrote the report, calls "an infamous Libel in verse" against Whitgift and Bancroft. The offender had couched his satire in "circumlocutions and descriptions, and not in express terms" (Coke, p. 489). On the one hand, playwrights like Jonson could take comfort because the convicted offender was probably of the Puritan party (since he was attacking the Bishops); satirists attacking the Puritans could presumably count on greater leniency. On the other hand, one notes that the libel was in verse and that it was not explicit—both dangerous precedents for playwrights.

Coke makes a very interesting distinction between libel against a private man and libel against "a Magistrate and publick person." Libel against a private man, he holds, "deserveth a severe punishment, for although the Libel be made against one, yet it inciteth all those of the same family, kindred, or society to revenge, and so may be the cause of shedding of blood, and of great inconvenience." But Coke continues:

> If it be against a Magistrate, or another publick person it is a greater offense; for that it concerneth not onely the breach of the peace, but also the scandal of government: for what greater scandal of government can there be then to have corrupt and wicked Magistrates to be appointed and constituted by the King to govern his subjects under him? and greater imputation to the State it cannot be, then to suffer such corrupt men to sit in the sacred seat of Justice.
>
> *(p. 489)*

Libel of a magistrate then, as Lucio discovers in *Measure for Measure,* is tantamount to sedition.

The breadth of the definition may be seen in other points made by Coke. For instance, he says that "it is not material whether the Libel be true, or whether the party against whom the Libel is made, be of good or ill fame," since private revenge might be attempted regardless of truth or reputation. Further, libel for Coke could be spoken as well as written. Written libel may occur "when an Epigram, Rime, or other writing is composed or published to the scandal or contumely of another." The spoken word may constitute libel if it is "maliciously repeated or sung in the presence of others." Finally, a libel need not even use words as its medium: a scandalous picture or sign "as to fix a Gallows, or other ignominious sign at the parties door" may constitute libel (p. 489). Under this definition a play might be held libelous even if the dialogue was innocent; gestures alone might suffice.

As for punishment, the court ruled that "if the Case be exorbitant," the offender might be sentenced to the pillory and to the loss of his ears. The most famous case in which this severe penalty was actually enforced is that of William Prynne, whose criticism in *Histriomastix* of females who appear on stage was taken personally by Queen Henrietta Maria. At this first offense his ears were merely cropped, but upon his second conviction—this time for libeling Laud—the hangman took the rest of the ears and burned on his cheeks the letters "S.L." for "seditious libeller."[8]

The word *seditious* is crucial; Prynne was accused not only of libel but also of treason. In practice, libel thought to be unaccompanied by sedition was rarely prosecuted and lightly punished. But one cannot say that the censors ignored the libel of private men altogether. It seems reasonably clear that fear of disorder caused by libel was the chief motive behind the famous book-burning order of 1 June 1599. Almost all of the proscribed books were either satires or epigrams, and the list is followed by the express proviso that "noe Satyres or Epigrams be printed hereafter."[9] Plays were on the suspected list also; the order specifies "that noe playes be printed excepte they be allowed by suche as have aucthorytie." What did the Bishops dislike about satires, epigrams, and plays? Some of the books on the list contain a good deal of obscenity, it is true. But Thomas Cutwode's poem *Caltha Poetarum* seems extremely chaste, whereas its curious fable seems obviously allegorical and must have been suspected by someone of containing either libel or sedition "by circumlocution and not in express terms," to use Coke's phrase.[10] The idea that libel was the target of the order is further supported by the provision "that all Nasshes bookes and Doctor Harvyes bookes be taken . . . and that none of theire bookes bee ever printed hereafter." It is easy to imagine a censor reading the violent rhetoric of Harvey and Nashe and concluding that the quarrel could very easily pass from words to blows.[11]

Despite the censors' crackdown, however, we know that dramatists continued to write personal satire during the early years of the seventeenth century and that they did not suffer much for their indiscretions. Chapman libeled the private citizens John and Agnes Howe in the lost play "The Old Joiner of Aldgate" (1603); yet he does not seem to have been punished.[12] Indeed, his involvement in the trouble concerning *Eastward Ho* (1605) and *Byron* (1608) suggests that any punishment that he received for transgressing in "The Old Joiner" was not sufficient to persuade him to mend his ways. Another case in point: in 1624 Dekker, Rowley, Ford, and Webster were accused in a lawsuit of libeling private citizens in "Keep the Widow Waking"; again no mention is made of their having been punished (Sisson, pp. 80–124).

Despite the government's leniency in practice (when only private citizens were being victimized), we should not underestimate the danger that Jonson and his fellow satirists ran. Every time that they engaged in personal satire, they were flirting with Lady Disaster. The legal precedents were there.

Standing in marked contrast to the government's extreme, if largely theoretical, sensitivity toward libel is the relatively cursory attention given to this abuse by the puritan attackers of the stage. Stephen Gosson, who had himself been ridiculed on the stage (Ringler, p. 67), makes a strong argument that "no private mans life ought to be brought in question or accused, but where hee may pleade in his own defence and have indifferent judges to determine the cause."[13] He notes that ancient Roman writers had used the stage not to correct manners but to get personal revenge, and he asserts that the provision of the Law of the Twelve Tables against libel was included to halt this abuse. Munday argues that if anyone is to reprehend vice publicly (private correction is more Christian), it ought to be the magistrate rather than a filthy player (sigs. H8^V–I2). But neither author dwells on the subject, and authors such as Northbrooke, Stubbes, and Rainoldes hardly touch it at all. This neglect of the issue we could perhaps attribute to the fact that libel did not become a staple of the stage until the heyday of the child actors. But the anonymous *Refutation of the Apology for Actors,* published in 1615 (just after the apex of satiric comedy), contains no condemnations of libel by name, although it does say that "to speake malliciously" is the "chief subject of our Commedies now" and asserts that they are "full of rayling, reviling, backbyting, quipping, taunts, and evill speaking" (sigs. G3, G4).

The reformers could not afford to lay too much stress on the libelous tendencies of comedy and satire because the reformers so often bordered upon committing this abuse themselves. We should read the pointed remarks that several of the pamphleteers addressed to the authorities in the light of Coke's dictum that libel of a magistrate is the worst sort of libel. Magistrates do not always take kindly to being told how to do their jobs; but Munday, for example, reminds them that their "warrant ... to forbid plaies is great, and passed unto them by such a Prince, whose auctoritie is above al auctorities of earthlie governors" (sig. E5^V). The magistrate is "not to shrinke in the Lordes cause ... because of some particular men of auctoritie"—almost an open invitation to lesser magistrates such as Justices of the Peace to defy openly the orders of superior political bodies such as the Privy Council. As if this were not enough, Munday goes on to attack noblemen who protect players (sig. F4).

As the Tudor era gives way to the Stuart, the admonitions become more and more pointed. Alexander Leighton in 1624 gives sharp advice not to magistrates and noblemen, as Munday had done, but to the King himself: "*David* and all his, must not onely turn away his eyes from beholding the vainity of Stage-plaies, and other idlements; but he must whip out, with *Augustus* that counterfeiting rabble that God never made."[14] In asserting that "the abhorring or liking of Stage-plaies was holden amongst the Romans for a note, of a bade, or a good Emperour" (sig. Pp4), Leighton is implying that since James likes plays, he is a bad monarch. In arguing against Sunday plays at court ("yea, it is fearfull on the Lords day to make them a part of princely intertainment" [sig. Pp4^V]), he is getting dangerously specific. Hence we are not surprised to learn that he got into trouble for this book and that in 1630, because of another book of his, he preceded Prynne in having his ears cut off, nose slit, and face branded (*DNB*). Leighton's attacks on the Bishops and the Queen were far more important in bringing on this punishment than his admonitions to the monarch concerning plays, of course; but these admonitions are certainly consistent with the bellicose tone of his other writings. It is no wonder that men like Leighton said little against the playwrights' use of libel. Nevertheless, we should realize that the pamphleteers did oppose libel, even if less zealously than they opposed blasphemy and bawdy.

II

The puritan assaulters of plays reached white heats in their denunciations of sexual and scatological references, and I deduce from the number and intensity of their complaints that they must have defined the term very broadly. The strategy of the attackers was to base their case on the Bible. No biblical text condemns theater, and so they were thrown back upon those that condemn sexual lust. The attackers relied heavily on the seventh commandment of the Decalogue: "Thou shalt not commit adulterie" (Exod. 20:14, Geneva Version), which they defined very broadly indeed. Calvin writes, "For in forbidding aduoutrie, God not onely forbiddeth the act it selfe . . . but also . . . in effect al unchast behaviour."[15] To the English attackers, playgoing was classified as unchaste behavior because the viewer's morals were bound to be affected adversely by the unchaste content of plays.

Commentaries on the Ten Commandments became astonishingly popular in England during Jonson's time, and almost all such commentaries contain at least one antitheatrical passage, which is usually included either in the discussion of the seventh commandment or in the discussion of the fourth commandment ("Remember the Sabbath"), or under both headings. But one finds it under the seventh more often. Thomas Becon's early Elizabethan exposition of the commandments, written before the establishment of the Theatre and the Curtain, asserts that the seventh commandment forbids by implication "vayne pastymes" but does not (at that point) name plays specifically. Later, however, Becon does attack plays by name and entirely on the ground that they promote unchaste behavior:

> not onlye idlenesse is to be exchued of those Maidens, which entend to prove godlye and vertuous, but also the runninge about unto vain spectacles, games, pastimes, playes, enterludes, &c.: where rather vice than vertue, sinne then soule health, wickednesse than godlinesse is to be learned. Let them remember what chanced to Dina Jacobs daughter through going abrode to se vaine sightes. Was she not deflored: & lost her virginity. Virginity ones lost, what remaineth safe & praise worthy in a maide?[16]

The commentaries of Bishops Babington and Andrewes, written in the 1580s, name theater specifically in discussions of the seventh commandment.[17] William Perkins includes in his discussion of the seventh commandment the heading "Effeminate wantonnesse wherby occasions are sought to stirre up lust." His sixth occasion is "Lascivious representations of love matters, in playes and Comedies."[18] Among the most popular of these Decalogue commentaries was that of John Dod and Robert Cleaver. Under the familiar heading of the seventh commandment, they comment: "Those also have offended in wantonnesse, that give themselves libertie to be present, and see such things as be practices of wantonnesse, as stage playes, which serve for nothing but to nourish filthinesse; and where they are most used, there filthinesse is most practiced."[19] New commentaries continued to pour from the press throughout the period, but neither the heading under which the attack appears nor the wording of the strictures varies appreciably from the pattern already established.[20]

In England, the argument against theater was based on even better Scriptural evidence, namely, on Deuteronomy 22:5: "The woman shal not weare that which perteineth unto the man, nether shal a man put on womans raiment: for all that do so, are abominacion unto the Lord thy God" (Geneva Version). The habit of making this verse the keystone of the argument against theater goes back, like so many other habits of the attackers, to the Church Fathers. Tertullian, for instance, is notably absolute in his interpretation of the verse; he will have no truck with the idea that the prohibition was not meant to include special occasions such as theatrical performances: "that thing is no where, nor at any time lawfull by the word of God which is not ever, and every where lawfull."[21] Some commentators noticed that the biblical context does not give a rationale for the prohibition of cross-dressing; so they supplied one. The Geneva Bible's marginal comment is as follows: "For that were to alter the order of nature and to despite God." Calvin, the major influence behind this Bible, connects the Deuteronomy verse with the seventh commandment, arguing that the former is "onely an exposition" of the latter.[22] He specifically condemns the cross-dressing common in folk plays and celebrations: "For they that love to go so disguised, do despise God: as for example, in these maskings & mummings, when men put themselves into womens apparel." Calvin goes on to assert that "such disguisings are but inticements of baudry," especially when "they attire themselves like brides" and "seeme to be sorie that God made them not women" (sig. Ttt3).

This interpretation of Deuteronomy 22:5 by Calvin is the basis for an interesting argument that developed in England. Quoting both the verse in question and Calvin's interpretation, John Rainoldes goes on to argue that the practice of using boys for female roles in England actually promotes homosexuality: "[who knows] . . . what sparkles of lust to that vice the putting of wemens attire on men may kindle in uncleane affections, as *Nero* shewed in *Sporus, Heliogabalus* in him selfe."[23] Others, Rainoldes argues, "grew not to such excesse of impudencie, yet arguing the same in causing their boyes to weare long heare like wemen" (sig. C2).

Rainoldes's fellow-professor William Gager, his principal opponent in the debate, took the reference to homosexuality personally. Gager's academic drama *Ulysses Redux,* the immediate pretext of the whole controversy, had been acted by his

own students in Christ Church, Oxford, and he protests his and his students' innocence:

> As for the danger of kissinge of bewtifull boyes, I knowe not howe this suspition should
> reache to us. . . . We hartely pray you, Sir, to make a great difference between us, and *Nero*
> with his *Sporus* or *Heliogabalus* with hym selfe . . . or them that cause their pages to weare
> longe heare like weemen . . . we hartely abhorr them; and if I could suspecte any such
> thinge to growe by owre Playes, I would be the first that should hate them, and detest my
> selfe, for gyvinge suche occasion . . . we thanke God owre youthe doe not practyse suche
> thinges, thay thinke not of them, thay knowe them not.[24]

Rainoldes in his turn replies that he spoke only of men with unclean affections, and
why should Gager wince unless his jade had been galled? (*Overthrow,* sig. E3^V).

Rainoldes's ideas about drama and homosexuality are remembered and quoted
frequently by Prynne, who develops the notion (as he develops all his notions) at
astonishing length.[25] Like Rainoldes, Prynne bases his argument on Deuteronomy
22:5. But his pages make more interesting reading than Rainoldes's because Prynne
moves from biblical theory to specific examples. He quotes with hearty approval a
passage from Stubbes's venerable *Anatomie,* the most popular of the early tracts that
contained attacks on plays. Stubbes had written:

> marke the flocking and running to Theaters & curtens, daylie and hourely, night and daye,
> tyme and tyde to see Playes and Enterludes, where such wanton gestures, such bawdie
> speaches: such laughing and fleering: such kissing and bussing: such clipping and culling:
> Such winckinge and glancing of wanton eyes, and the like is used as is wonderfull to
> behold. Than these goodly pageants being done, every mate sorts to his mate, every one
> bringes another homeward of their way verye frendly, and in their secret conclaves
> (covertly) they play the *Sodomits,* or worse.
>
> (*sigs. L8–8^v*)

Whether the actors play the Sodomites with the other actors, aroused spectators with
other spectators, or the actors with the spectators is not made clear. Prynne characteristically assumes that the accusation includes the spectators: "Players and Play-
haunters in their secret conclaves play the Sodomites" (sig. Ee2).

Prynne for his part adds "some moderne examples of such, who have been
desperately enamored with Players Boyes thus clad in womans apparell, so farre as
to sollicite them by words, by Letters, even actually to abuse them" (sigs. Ee2–
Ee2^V). As evidence supporting this charge Prynne offers the following marginal note:
"This I have heard credibly reported of a Scholler of *Bayliol* Colledge, and I doubt
not but it may be verified of divers others" (sig. Ee2).

Prynne is particularly bothered by the question of whether it is worse for boys
to act the women's roles or for women to act them. He is aware that "they have now
their female-Players in Italy, and other forraigne parts," and he is scandalized that
"they had such *French-women Actors,* in a play not long since (in Michael. Terme,
1629) in *Blacke-friers Play-house,* to which there was great resort" (sig. Ee4). He

first challenges those who believe that actresses are preferable to prove "an irrita-
tion, an inducement to Sodomy . . . a lesser sinne, a more tollerable evill, then
mannish impudency, or a temptation to whoredome, and adultery: whch none can
evidence" (sig. Ee4). He then changes tactics:

> Secondly, admit men-Actors in womens attire, are not altogether so bad, so discommend-
> able as women Stage-players; yet since both of them are evill, yea extremely vitious, neither
> of them necessary . . . the superabundant sinfulnesse of the one, can neither justifie the
> lawfulnesse, nor extenuate the wickednesse of the other.
>
> (*sig. Ee4*)

I have been arguing that many of the English attacks on obscenity rely heavily
on biblical authority. Even the argument about homosexuality is related, as we have
seen, to the Deuteronomic prohibition of cross-dressing. Once Prynne admits (even
as a possibility) that watching an actress might produce a moral effect worse than
watching an actor dressed as a woman, he is demonstrating considerable indepen-
dence from biblical justification because such a view renders Deuteronomy 22:5
largely irrelevant.[26]
    The relative indifference of the English censors to sexual and scatological
references is a well-established fact in modern scholarship. Writing in 1908, Virginia
Gildersleeve was herself shocked at the bawdy passages in plays that got by the
censors: "Scenes which to our modern sense of propriety seem inexpressibly offensive,
the Master [of Revels] passed over without a misgiving."[27] Although *our* "modern
sense of propriety" in the latter twentieth century is quite different from the one
prevailing when Gildersleeve wrote, we can still see her point. The indifference of
the censors was not, however, complete. Sir Henry Herbert, for instance, commends
Shirley's *The Young Admiral* (1633) for being "free from oaths, prophaneness, or
obsceanenes" and asks that the play be an "example to all poetts, that shall write
after the date hereof." As Master of the Revels, Herbert is clearly concerned principally because "the quality . . . hath received some brushings of late"—undoubtedly
the brushings were connected with the publication of *Histriomastix* in that same
year, an event that probably rallied the antitheatrical forces in London. Again in the
same year, 1633, Herbert seems to have censored some passages in Fletcher's *The
Woman's Prize* because of their obscenity (Gildersleeve, pp. 124–127). Nevertheless, the concern of the censors is minimal, especially when it is compared to the
obsessive concern of the reformers.

III

The subject of blasphemy may be divided into three parts: (1) satire against preachers and Puritans, (2) biblical references, and (3) profane oaths. The mildest censure
of the attackers of the stage fell upon satiric references to godly folk such as preachers
and Puritans. Such satire was sometimes construed as blasphemous, at other times
as merely impious. But there is no doubt that most of the attackers thought all

biblical allusions in plays to be outright blasphemy, regardless of the context. Their bitterest opposition, however, was to profane oaths. I shall consider in turn each of these three charges.

The hostility between stage and pulpit goes back, like so much in the sixteenth- and seventeenth-century attack, to the Church Fathers. Saint John Chrysostom, for example, writes: "I correct, the Player corrupts: I administer salves to thy disease, he ministers the cause of the disease: I extinguish the flame of nature, he kindles the flame of lust. What profit is there, tell me? one edifying, and another pulling downe?" (Quoted in Prynne, sig. Iii4^V). Saint Augustine, too, sees the pulpit and the stage in direct competition. He notes, for example, that church attendance is worse if a performance has been announced at the theater and praises the people for standing at church by pointing out that a theater audience would not have stood.[28]

The earlier Elizabethan attackers, who borrowed so much from the Fathers, were also very much aware of the rivalry. *The Second and Third Blast of the Trumpet* points out that if people will not reform because of words "uttered by the mouth of the reverend Preachers," why should we assume that they will reform because of the evil examples given them in plays? (sig. H7^V). Stubbes regards the very comparison of plays and sermons as blasphemous: "Oh blasphemie intollerable: Are filthie playes & bawdy enterluds comparable to the word of God, ye foode of life, and life it selfe? It is all one, as if they had said, bawdrie, hethenrie, paganrie, scurrilitie, and divelrie it self, is equall with the word of God" (sig. L7^V). Richard Schilders, in his Preface to *Th'Overthrow of Stage Plaies,* censures "the gentlewo- man that sware by her trouth, *That shee was as much edefied at a play as ever she was at any sermon*" (sigs. A3^V–4). Prynne, quoting (in part) from an earlier tract, adds that the competition is not only spiritual but economic: "How many hundreds ... spend more, daily ... at a Play-house to maintaine the Devils service ... then they disburse in pious uses, in reliefe of Ministers, Schollers, poore godly Christians. ... How many ... contribute more liberally ... *to Stage-playes, then to Lectures; to Players, then to Preachers.*"[29]

As the dramatists began to counterattack by satirizing puritan preachers, the attackers replied by blasting the satire. The preacher William Crashaw, father of the poet, takes the unusual step of making a reference so specific that we can identify the play to which he is objecting: the anonymous comedy *The Puritaine.* Crashaw asserts: "for now they bring religion and holy things upon the stage.... Two hypocrites must be brought foorth; and how shall they be described but by these names, *Nicholas S. Antlings, Simon S. Maryoveries?*"[30] Crashaw is scandalized because Saint Antlings and Saint Mary Overies were the names of two prominent and Puritan-leaning parishes in London. The anonymous *Short Treatise Against Stage-Plays* (1625) complains that "the word of God and the ministers thereof, are now and then taxed and taunted" (sig. C2^V). But it is Prynne (as usual) who is most prolix on the subject; he argues that "Stage-Playes are for the most part satyrically invective against the persons, callings, offices and professions of men; but more especially against Religion *and Religious Christians"* (sig. Q4^V). One of Prynne's diatribes on this subject may even contain a glancing allusion to Ben Jonson. That Jonson had suffered a stroke about 1628 was well known because of the point that he made of it in his notorious ode "Come Leave the Loathed Stage." Prynne, writing shortly thereafter, says, "When God sends his judgements, crosses, or tormenting mortall diseases upon such who were most bitter Satyrists against Puritans all their lives before . . . they send for those very Puritan Ministers whom they before ab-horred" (sig. Kkkk4ᵛ). Could this passage be related to Isaac Walton's report that Jonson "was (in his long retyrement, and sicknes, . . .) much aflickted, that hee had profain'd the scripture, in his playes"?[31]

That profanation of Scripture was a more serious offense to the attackers than satire against the godly may be seen clearly in Schilders's Preface. Schilders first protests that playwrights, whom he calls "humourists" (surely a reference to Chap-man and Jonson), "have not been afraid of late dayes to bring upon the Stage the very sober countenances, grave attire, modest and matronlike gestures and speeches of men & women to be laughed at as a scorne and reproch to the world, as if the hypocrisie of Judas (if it were brought upon the stage) could any whitt disgrace the apostles of our Saviour Christ." He continues: "And yet if these men [that is, the humorists] had but thus farre exceeded, kept themselves there, and gone no farther to the foule prophaning and abusing of the holy Scripture of God, their sin had not bene half so great as it is" (sig. A4).

Thomas Beard, known for his blistering denunciation of Marlowe, reaches a similar heat of invective in alleging that "the holy and sacred scripture ordained to a holy & sacred use, is oftentimes by these filthie swine prophaned to please and to delight their audience."[32] William Perkins, whose rhetoric is more moderate, never-theless notes that "all such jests, as are framed out of the Phrases & sentences of the scripture, are abuses of holy things."[33] Considering the number of editions that Lewis Bayly's *The Practice of Piety* went through, no one can doubt the wide dissemination of the charge concerning the profanation of Scripture. Bishop Bayly's famous devo-tional manual argues that at plays one hears the actors "scoffing *Religion, & blasphe-mously* abusing phrases of holy *Scripture* on their *Stages,* as familiarly as they use their *Tobacco-pipes* in their *bibbing-houses.*"[34]

Profane oaths were regarded as the worst kind of blasphemy because they were so clearly in violation of the Second Commandment of the Decalogue. Northbrooke, inveighing against blasphemy in plays, cites cases in which blasphemers have been struck mad or blind (*Treatise,* sig. K[1]). His horror stories, although ancient in origin, are related to popular pamphlets such as Edmond Bicknoll's *A Sword Against Swearyng* (1579), which was still being reprinted well into the reign of King James.[35] Bicknoll cites, for example, the story of "An[n] Averis wyddowe," who dwelt "in Ducke Lane . . . in the Parysh of S. Bartholomewe . . . by Smythfielde." She is said to have been struck down while swearing volubly at a shopkeeper who had caught her in the act of shoplifting: "downe she fell in the shop, and became speachlesse, never able to ryse without helpe" (sigs. E3, E4). My favorite pamphlet of this type, perhaps because of the accompanying woodcut, is the story of Anthony

Figure 1. Anon. *Anthony Painter, the Blaspheming Caryar.* (*STC* 19120).
By permission of the Bodleian Library, shelfmark:
4° C.16 AABs (48) T/P.

Painter, "the Blaspheming Caryar," who, as the title-page informs us, "sunke into the ground up to his neck, and there stood two days and two nights, and not to be drawne out by the strength of Horses or digged out by the help of man: and there dyed the 3 of November, 1613."[36]

The disapproval of oaths in plays was so strong that Parliament passed the important 1606 Act which provided a ten-pound fine for those who "in any stage play, interlude, show, May-game or pageant jestingly or profanely speak or use the name of God or of Christ Jesus, or of the Holy Ghost or of the Trinity."[37] Here, for once, the attackers and the government were in some agreement. But this law is remarkably narrow in its scope: (1) it does not significantly restrict biblical subject matter, references, or quotations; (2) it does not even outlaw the forbidden names absolutely—the adverbs "jestingly" and "profanely" provide a possible line of defense for a poet or player in the dock; and (3) although the ten-pound fine would have been a very large sum for most poets and players, the penalty is astonishingly mild compared to the penalty for libel. Nevertheless, the very existence of the Act, mild though it may have been, is evidence that the attackers were influential enough to get legislation passed. And there is evidence that, unlike the libel laws, the 1606 Act was fairly effective in practice. There is manuscript evidence that Sir George Buc, otherwise a rather permissive Master of Revels, felt obliged to delete some oaths from a particular script.[38] Sir Henry Herbert, a later and much stricter Master of Revels, even disagreed with King Charles himself on the subject of the oaths in Davenant's *The Wits*: "The King is pleased to take *faith, death, slight,* for asseverations and no oaths, to which I do humbly submit as my master's judgment; but, under favor, conceive them to be oaths."[39]

Despite the government's effort to enforce the Act, however, the attackers of the stage were not satisfied. The author of the *Refutation of the Apology for Actors* is still complaining in 1615 that plays are full of "othes, and blasphemies, cursing" (sig. G4) and Prynne is still asserting in 1633 that plays contain "prophane or scurrill Jests, . . . heathenish oathes and execrations" (sig. Cccccc2^V).

IV

In summary then, we may say that the Crown and its courts considered almost any utterance that they did not like to be libel, whereas the puritans—often guilty of libel themselves, from the Crown's point of view—were less touchy on the subject. The reverse is true of bawdy: the puritans seemed obsessed by it, whereas it was given scant attention by the government's censors. Both puritans and censors opposed blasphemy, although the puritans had much the broader, more inclusive definition. All in all, the pressures on playwrights, both legal and moral, were intense, although—because of laxity in the enforcement of laws—hardly crushing. Given the strength of these pressures, I am surprised that extant scripts contain as many apparent instances of libel, bawdy, and blasphemy as they do. But demonstrating that last proposition is a task for another time.

NOTES

1. On the economics, see Russell Fraser, *The War Against Poetry* (Princeton, N. J.: Princeton University Press, 1970), pp. 52–76.

2. On objections to theater as medium, see Jonas Barish, *The Antitheatrical Prejudice* (Berkeley: University of California Press, 1981).

3. On alleged corruption in the social milieu of the playhouse, see Philip Stubbes, *The Anatomie of Abuses* (1583), sigs. L8–8ᵛ.

4. *Ben Jonson,* ed. C. H. Herford and Percy and Evelyn Simpson, 11 vols. (Oxford: Clarendon Press, 1925–52), V, 18 (ll. 43–48, 56–57). In quoting from this and all other old-spelling texts I silently modernize *i* and *j, u* and *v.*

5. Scholars are currently divided concerning the usefulness of the time-honored term "The Puritan Attack Upon the Stage." Barish, to my mind the leading authority, still uses it. But William Ringler long ago pointed out that Gosson, one of the leading antistage pamphleteers, was no Puritan politically; and Margot Heinemann has recently shown that many political Puritans actually supported the stage. See *Stephen Gosson: A Biographical and Critical Study* (Princeton, N. J.: Princeton University Press, 1942), p. 80, and *Puritanism and Theatre: Thomas Middleton and Opposition Drama Under the Early Stuarts* (Cambridge: Cambridge University Press, 1980), pp. 18–47. Hence my compromise (the little *p* and big *P*), an idea based on the two main definitions in the *OED.*

6. Frederick S. Siebert, *Freedom of the Press in England, 1476–1776* (Urbana: University of Illinois Press, 1952), pp. 119–120. See also William S. Holdsworth, *A History of English Law,* 17 vols. (1903–22; rpt. London: Methuen, 1966), V, 208, 211.

7. For the law French, see *Quinta Pars* (1605), ff. 125–126. I quote, however, from *The Reports of Sir Edward Coke . . . Faithfully rendred into English* (London, 1658), sig. Ss 3. The law French was reprinted in 1606, 1607, 1612, and 1624 (see *STC*).

8. William Lamont, *Marginall Prynne 1600–1669* (Toronto: University of Toronto Press, 1963), p. 39.

9. Edward Arber, *A Transcript of the Registers of the Company of Stationers of London, 1554–1640 A.D.,* III (London: privately printed, 1876), 677.

10. Whatever the suspicion, it was cleared up, since the book was probably not burnt after all; see *Stationers' Register,* III, 678.

11. The prohibition against epigrams and satires was for several years surprisingly effective, as O. J. Campbell points out in *Comicall Satyre and Shakespeare's "Troilus and Cressida"* (San Marino, Calif.: The Huntington Library, 1938), p. 3.

12. Charles J. Sisson, *Lost Plays of Shakespeare's Age* (Cambridge: Cambridge University Press, 1936), pp. 12–79.

13. Arthur F. Kinney, ed., *Markets of Bawdrie: The Dramatic Criticism of Stephen Gosson,* Salzburg Studies in English Literature, no. 4 (Salzburg: Inst. für eng. Sprache & Lit. Univ. Salzburg, 1974), p. 163.

14. *Speculum Belli Sacri* (1624), sig. Pp4.

15. *The Sermons of M. John Calvin Upon . . . Deuteronomie,* trans. Arthur Golding (1583), sig. Ttt3ᵛ.

16. *Works* (1564), I, sig. BBb2.

17. Gervase Babington, *A Verie Fruitfull Exposition of the Commandments* (1583), sigs. U6ᵛ–U7; Lancelot Andrewes, *The Moral Law Expounded* (1642), sig. Cccc5.

18. *A Golden Chaine* (1591), sig. H4ᵛ.

19. *A Plaine and Familiar Exposition of the Ten Commandments* (1604), sig. Aa3. By 1635 this work had reached its nineteenth edition, of which fourteen (according to the old *STC*) survive.

20. See, for example, Osmund Lake, *A Probe Theological* (1612), sigs. R6, S6–8^V; the anonymous *Covenant Between God and Man* (1616), sigs. Bb7–8; Edward Elton, *God's Holy Mind* (1625), Part 2, sig. S7^V; and John Downam, *The Summe of Sacred Divinity* [1630?], sig. O6.

21. I quote from Gosson's (unacknowledged) translation. See *Markets of Bawdrie,* ed. Kinney, p. 176. For the Latin, see *De Spectaculis,* XX, trans. T. R. Glover, Loeb Classical Library (London: Heinemann, 1931), p. 280: "nusquam et nunquam licet quod semper et ubique non licet."

22. *Sermons . . . Upon . . . Deuteronomie,* trans. Arthur Golding (London, 1583), sig. Ttt3^V.

23. *Th' Overthrow of Stage Plaies* (1599), sig. C2.

24. Karl Young, "William Gager's Defence of the Academic Stage," *Transactions of the Wisconsin Academy of Sciences, Arts, and Letters,* 18 (1916), Part II, pp. 624–625.

25. *Histriomastix* (1633), sigs. Aa^V–Ee4^V.

26. Puritanical critics of the stage in countries that permitted actresses got along well without Deuteronomy also; yet they, like their English brothers, insisted on the importance of the sexual issue. See my article, "The Attack on the Stage in Shakespeare's Time: An International Affair," *Comparative Literature Studies,* 20 (1983), 168–182.

27. *Government Regulation of Elizabethan Drama* (New York: Columbia University Press, 1908), p. 89.

28. F. Van der Meer, *Augustine the Bishop,* trans. Brian Battershaw and G. R. Lamb (London: Sheed & Ward, 1961), pp. 174–175.

29. Sig. Tt. Edmund S. Morgan considers the rivalry to be the key to the entire attack: see "Puritan Hostility to the Theater," *Proceedings of the American Philosophical Society,* 110 (1966), 340–347. Another excellent, though brief, discussion of the rivalry is Stephen Hilliard, "Stephen Gosson and the Elizabethan Distrust of the Effect of Drama," *English Literary Renaissance,* 9 (1979), 235–237.

30. *The Sermon Preached at Paul's Crosse, Feb. xiiij, 1607* (1608), sig. Y^V. The offending passage in the play is at the beginning of I.iii; see *The Shakespeare Apocrypha,* ed. C. F. Tucker Brooke (Oxford: Clarendon Press, 1918), p. 224.

31. The accuracy of Walton's report is not beyond question. First, it was sent to John Aubrey by Walton in 1680, when Walton was 87 years old; even Walton did not get it firsthand but had it from George Morley, Bishop of Winchester in 1680. Morley had allegedly been with Jonson often during the sickness in question. See H&S, I, 181.

32. *Theatre of God's Judgements* (1597), sig. Aa6^V.

33. *Cases of Conscience,* 1606 ed., sig. Oo6.

34. According to the old *Short Title Catalogue,* the third edition (1613) is the earliest now surviving. I have used the 1620 edition (the twelfth) in The Folger Shakespeare Library, sigs. A3–3^V.

35. The work went through at least four editions. The second (old *STC* 3050) is undated. The third and fourth, both of which are mistakenly attributed in the old *STC* to Alexander Nowell, are dated 1611 (new *STC* 18743) and 1618 (new *STC* 18743^a).

36. This anonymous pamphlet is listed under the name of its central character (*STC* 19120); see Figure 1.

37. *Statutes of the Realm,* ed. T. E. Tomlins *et al.* (1810–28; rpt. London: Dawsons of Pall Mall, 1963), Vol. 4, Part 2 (1819), p. 1097. E. K. Chambers prints this law in full in *The Elizabethan Stage,* 4 vols. (Oxford: Clarendon Press, 1923), IV, 338–339.

38. Frances Shirley, *Swearing and Perjury in Shakespeare's Plays* (London: George Allen & Unwin, 1979), pp. 13–15.

39. Quoted in Gerald Eades Bentley, *The Profession of Dramatist in Shakespeare's Time 1590–1642* (Princeton, N. J.: Princeton University Press, 1971), p. 185.

The Chester Cycle:
Review Article

LAWRENCE M. CLOPPER

R. M. Lumiansky and David Mills's *The Chester Mystery Cycle: Essays and Documents*[1] was originally designed to be the introductory chapters to the second volume of their Early English Text Society (EETS) edition of the Chester mystery cycle. Owing to space limitations in that volume, these introductions had to be published separately from the textual notes. The authors are fortunate in having found in the University of North Carolina Press a publisher amenable not only to publishing the book but also to printing it so elegantly and so free of error. The book has five chapters, of which the first, "The Texts of the Chester Cycle," and the fourth, "Development of the Cycle," are the most dense and are likely to prove the most controversial. Since the other chapters are simpler and more straightforwardly informational, I should like to provide a brief guide to their contents before addressing the issues advanced in Chapters One and Four.

In Chapter Two, "Concerning Sources, Analogues, and Authorities," the authors indicate that they will provide a review of proposed sources but focus on the issue of the evocation of authority within the cycle. They take a very guarded approach to analogues and sources, whether ultimate or immediate, because (1) it is often impossible to distinguish among the three; (2) the number of variants (many unpublished) of a single source does not allow substantiation of claims; and (3) much of the material is common and appears in many forms, with the result that it is difficult to assign a specific source. On the other hand, Professors Lumiansky and Mills are interested in showing how the Chester playwrights altered possibly close analogues or sources in order to make the plays fit the cycle.

The review of proposed sources yields the following observations: the authors are highly sceptical of Baugh's argument that the Chester plays were a translation or remaking of a French original. To this observation one might add that the whole theory arose from the assumption that Chester was the earliest cycle and that, like other early Middle English works, it derived from a French original. But if the extant texts are sixteenth century, as the authors argue in Chapter One, then the initial assumption is invalid and the whole theory collapses. A late date for the extant texts argues against a French original.

On the relationship between Chester and other dramatic versions, for example, the Brome *Abraham* and the three versions of the *Christ and the Doctors,* the authors take the position that it must remain uncertain whether the borrowings are direct or through common exemplars because of the revisions that were made to make the play fit the needs of the cycle. They do not rule out the possibility that the cycle is indebted to the *Stanzaic Life* with its dependence on the *Legenda aurea* but point to the fact that the playwright might not have been restricted to one text or version of that text. He may have synthesized several versions.

Lumiansky and Mills would shift attention away from the identification of sources to the recognition of the function of materials gathered from a variety of sources and traditions. In the second part of the chapter, they point to the emphasis on the authoritativeness of the cycle. There are citations of the Bible in the text that they believe to be scribal insertions rather than texts to be spoken in performance. There is an insistent evocation of authority in the Banns, in the use of prophetic passages that foreshadow later events, or simply within plays. They argue that this emphasis on authority, which they believe to be characteristic of Chester, suggests that "due credit should be given to the playwright for integrating material from various sources into a coherent whole" (p. 110). I do not believe that by this statement, Lumiansky and Mills are arguing that there is one Chester playwright (see, for example, the usage on p. 108); rather, I think they would have us understand that there was one playwright who went through the cycle at one point adding, adapting, and altering to make it a coherent whole, and that it was his concern "to stress [the cycle's] reliance on authorities" (p. 110).

The chapter contributed by Professor Richard Rastell will prove of interest to literary scholars for its lucid presentation of the role of music in the cycle. The chapter far surpasses Carpenter's famous early essay, and, drawing in part on Dutka's monograph, it conveys to the non-specialist like myself the richness of the musical presence.[2] Rastell begins with a consideration of the structural and practical functions of music as a way of enlarging our understanding of the text. He points out that earlier critics had argued that the music was emotive—rather, one suspects, in the Cecil B. DeMille mode. To the contrary, he claims that the music is representational. For example, the heavenly music of the first two plays expresses the harmony of the divinely created universe and thus represents the Divine Order. A different kind of music, as a consequence, can be used to suggest disorder; the heavenly music can reinvoke the harmonious order; and the songs of mortals can be used to imply that the mortal is in tune with the Divine Will (as in the case of Mary's singing of the *Magnificat*). Iconographical evidence, plus clues in the texts, suggest that certain instruments were used to define character and role; thus trumpets (*buisines*) were symbolically associated with kingship, especially with the king as judge, and so they are appropriate to the *Last Judgement* (24/40+SD). The music has structural functions as well: (a) to cover the movement of characters about the acting areas; (b) to mark entrances and exits; (c) to indicate the passage of time; and (d) to draw attention to a new location. These functions are structural in the sense that they mark divisions of the play.

The remainder of the chapter considers the evidence for music in the cycles. On pages 138–142 Professor Rastell provides a convenient list of all musical items mentioned in the play manuscripts, the Late Banns, and the guild records with a description of the type of music, its function, and its title, where known. The three succeeding sections provide more detailed discussions of each item of liturgical or other kind of music, citing the source, the type of chant, musical range and pitch, or other relevant information. These sections have a practical value, for they can be used to design a production of the plays. The chapter as a whole, however, has the major effect of demonstrating the existence of the rather large quantity and variety of music.

Chapters One and Four address themselves to two important issues: the character of the extant play-texts and the development of the cycle. The first chapter resolves the mystery of the relationship that obtains among the extant manuscripts and thereby comes to the, at first, astonishing conclusion that "the Chester cycle" "is a convenient abstraction" and that the text which the editors produced in the EETS series is a "cycle of cycles," not the definitive edition of a single dramatic work. Unlike the other cycles, the Chester plays exist in five complete or nearly complete manuscripts as well as in three fragments. It might be expected that this quantity of manuscript material would result in an editor's being able to produce an authorial text using the best of these manuscripts as a base text and collating it with the others. However, this has turned out not to be the case. First, it was determined that four of the manuscripts were more closely related to each other than to the fifth; these four are referred to as the Group manuscripts, composed of MSS HmARB, and the fifth as MS H. This simple grouping nevertheless disguises numerous divergences one from another. Without going into minute detail, let me instance the case of the scribe George Bellin, who copied two complete manuscripts (A and R) as well as Play XVI (MS C). As might be expected these manuscripts show numerous similarities, and yet it was recognized early on that none could have been copied directly from any of the others. Furthermore, MS R, which was copied after MS A, contains a scene at the end of Play XVIII that appears only here and in the non-Group manuscript H. There are so many instances of this sort, as well as a bewildering array of cross-variants, that W. W. Greg was led to conclude that none of the manuscripts descended directly from any of the others and that each of the Group manuscripts was descended from a different, now missing, intermediary.[3] F. M. Salter, on the basis of the fragments, established an even more exotic stemma that Greg succeeded in disputing without coming to any firmer conclusion than that an editor would do well to use MS Hm as a base text.[4]

Professors Lumiansky and Mills have taken a fresh—and I believe convincing—approach to the problem. Building on the ideas that inform the editions of *Piers Plowman* by Professors Kane and Donaldson, the editors of "the Chester cycle" postulate that since all the manuscripts contain demonstrable common errors, these errors must have existed in a copy that they term the Exemplar. They distinguish the Exemplar from its precursor or precursors without speculating further on the nature of the precursor or its descent. They argue that all the scribes of the extant manuscripts, with the possible exception of the one who produced MS P, had recourse to the Exemplar and that the extant manuscripts are the record of what the scribes understood the Exemplar to say.

The Exemplar, it is argued, could produce such varying texts because it was a working text that contained corrections of previous scribal errors and alterations, both insertions and cancellations, not only of individual words but also of entire scenes. In addition the Exemplar had marginal production notes in English (musical cues, cues for action, and so on) that the scribes at times treated as stage directions, or ignored, or, in the case of the scribe for MS H, translated into Latin. A variety of material was before the scribes when they made their texts; consequently, each scribe was faced with the necessity of making choices. The scribes, some more conscientious than others, had to decide which readings were accurate, but when they came to alternative scenes or stanzas, they had to choose which to include. The responses, even among individual scribes, run the gamut: in some cases a scribe seems to have chosen one variant over another, but in other cases he may have transcribed both variants or both alternatives. The state of the Exemplar thus makes more explicable the variations in George Bellin's manuscripts; rather than being derived one from another, they were all derived from the same source (although A may have been used as well in producing R). However, Bellin had to make the same choices the second time that he made the first, with the result that he decided to include the end of Play XVIII in one instance but not in the other.

Lumiansky and Mills draw several conclusions from their analysis of the extant texts. First, they insist that the Exemplar does not represent a definitive cycle; instead, it is a record of alternatives among which the city authorities and the guilds would have had to choose their text. This suggests not only that individual plays might differ from year to year depending on which scenes were chosen for production but also that the cycle might differ from year to year depending on whether it was decided to present all of the possible plays. I do not believe that Lumiansky and Mills are trying to suggest that there were unlimited possibilities represented by the Exemplar; rather, there were instances in which decisions had to be made. For example, the Cappers had to choose to present the Balaam scene or the Procession of Prophets; the Painters had to decide whether to include the Shepherds' apprentices; and some decision had to be made about the text for the Passion, which is ascribed to two companies but which was probably reckoned to be one play. There is external evidence for alternative scenes; for example, in the Late Banns Christ's appearances to the Mary's is said to be part of Play XIX, whereas the scene referred to is probably the one that appears at the end of Play XVIII in MS RH, and in 1575 the Smiths presented two versions of their play before the Mayor so that he could choose the better of the two.

There are major implications in these findings for literary scholars. The edition of MS Hm printed in the EETS series is not an edition of any cycle ever performed in the city of Chester. It is instead the record of one scribe's understanding of the Exemplar. Lumiansky and Mills say that they chose to print this text, not because it has priority of date over the other manuscripts or that its readings are stylistically or semantically better than the others, but because "it has fewer unsupported readings than any other manuscript" and because the evidence suggests a "high degree of conservatism on the part of its scribe" (p. 58; the characteristics of each of the manuscripts and their scribes are described on pp. 57–86). Nevertheless, Lumiansky and Mills insist that this scribe made alterations, emendations, corrections, and other choices when he copied the manuscript. Literary scholars who wish to assess the literary, artistic, and dramatic qualities of "the Chester cycle" therefore are going to have to make choices as well.

The stated purpose of Chapter Four, "The Development of the Cycle," is "to evaluate the external evidence for the cycle in order to suggest a context for the extant texts of the cycle" (p. 165). The two contexts under consideration are the historical and the dramatic, the former of which involves the development of the cycle and the latter of which describes the mode of presentation (chiefly, pp. 182–189, 192–194). The description of the dramatic context reviews what is known about the production of cycle plays with special emphasis, of course, on the unique features of Chester and with reference to Chester records (the important documents are appended in the chapter that follows.). This survey is a good succinct introduction for the general reader, but since it offers little that is controversial, I will not repeat its points here. The discussion of the historical context, on the other hand, advances an interpretation that differs from my own and that of Salter; so I would like to rehearse the argument in order to highlight the main areas of agreement and disagreement.

The reconstruction of the history of the cycle is impeded by the fragmentary records before the sixteenth century; indeed, the records do not become plenteous until mid-century. We know that the cycle was in existence by 1422 because there is a copy of a guild dispute over responsibilities in the play that year. The records for the remainder of the fifteenth century and the early decades of the sixteenth are similar in that they are records of guild disputes or agreements or rentals for carriage houses and the like. There is a consensus that these records indicate that the cycle was originally produced on Corpus Christi day in one location (at St. John's outside the city hall), that *circa* 1521 the cycle was shifted to Whitsunday, and that *circa* 1531 the cycle was shifted to three days in Whitsun week and probably began to be performed at several locations within the city.

The most important document for the reconstruction of this early history is the Early Banns. Our only copy of this document is in BL (British Library) Harley 2150, a collection made and partially annotated by Randle Holme. Two scribes wrote the extant copy: the first of these, probably in the late sixteenth century, copied all but lines 136–210 (comprising the descriptions of the pageants from the Mercers and Vintners' *Magi* through the Fishmongers' *Pentecost*). In the seventeenth century Holme copied in the missing lines and made a number of annotations in the margins. The text is written in the same *rime couée* stanza as the majority of the cycle text. Most of the guilds receive a half-stanza for the purpose of describing their play; however, several pageants are given a complete stanza (the Tanners' *Lucifer,* the

Wrights' *Nativity,* the Vintners' *Magi,* the Goldsmiths' *Slaughter,* and the Shermen's *Prophets of Antichrist*). Two guilds have quatrains for which there is no matching half-stanza (the Painters' *Shepherds* and the Wives' *Assumption*), and one guild has eleven lines, probably a defective twelve lines (the Mercers' *Presentation of the Magi*). Salter argued, and I concurred, that the variations indicated revisions or changes in the cycle.[5] Lumiansky and Mills argue that there was no necessity for the Banns-writer to have used a systematic scheme of equal distribution and that the variations therefore can tell us nothing about the composition of the cycle or changes in it. They conclude that the cycle had reached its full state by 1521 and that the shift from Corpus Christi to Whitsunday occasioned the composition of the Banns. Further, they believe that the copy with its variants provides a record of the cycle as it existed at that time.

The issues are whether the variations indicate revision, an issue not significant in itself, and, if they are signs of revision, whether they tell us anything about the history of the cycle. My analysis of the document and the other evidence led me to the conclusion that the Corpus Christi play had been primarily a Passion play and that the Chester play did not achieve cyclic form until the sixteenth century; if this was the case, we should expect to find late evidence of the admission of Old Testament and Nativity plays in the sixteenth century. Lumiansky and Mills believe that the cycle took its form in the fifteenth century and that the Early Banns, written *circa* 1521, describes that cycle. The key element in their argument is that the Banns-writer may not have sought any consistent pattern of distribution of lines for the pageant descriptions. They point to the fact that the cycle itself is not consistent but shows similar instances of variation of stanza form. In addition, they assert that many of the eight-line descriptions are for plays having double actions or that the unusual length, especially in the case of the Mercers' Magi play, points to the Banns' emphasis on spectacle.

The conclusions are plausible—except that they are not formed with regard to all of the internal and external evidence. The Painters' half-stanza and the Mercers' defective twelve-line stanza are crucial in the evaluation of the document. Lumiansky and Mills argue that a half-stanza (aaab), or a quatrain as they prefer to call it, is a legitimate verse form in the Chester cycle and that the Banns-writer simply used this verse form to describe the Painters' pageant, and eight-, twelve-, and eight-line stanzas, respectively, for the succeeding three pageants. The argument is not convincing for several reasons. First, the basic stanza for the cycle as a whole is an eight-line *rime couée* (either aaabaaab or aaabcccb). *Rime couée* stanzas are expandable, and one often finds instances of twelve-line stanzas in tail-rhyme poems in which the base is an eight-line stanza. But the smallest *rime couée* unit is a six-line stanza (aabaab) because any further reduction would result in simple alternate rhyme (abab). In an appendix, "Stanza-Forms in the Cycle," Lumiansky and Mills list approximately forty instances of their quatrain form (aaab); in the discussion, they single out eight of these, presumably the best examples, to press their case for the existence of the quatrain. Of these eight, four appear at points where the verse

pattern changes in the immediate vicinity of the quatrain (3.233–236; 7.324–327,
584–587; and 23.377–380). In the first instance the text is in *rime couée* to line 224,
then there are two quatrains in abab followed by the cited quatrain (aaab), and then
a return to the regular *rime couée*. Following the line of reasoning outlined in
Chapter One, one might argue that the abab quatrains are alternatives to the *rime
couée* stanza and that the scribes did not note the cancellation of the whole *rime
couée* stanza and so copied half of it; alternatively, someone may have substituted
the abab quatrains for the first half of the *rime couée* stanza. The half-stanza at
7.584–587 provides an even more obvious case of a remnant left from the production
of alternative texts. There are numerous irregularities in the stanzas between lines
552 and 596; nevertheless, it is clear that two distinct rhyme schemes are present,
abab and eight-line *rime couée*. Stanza 105 (lines 556–562) is a *rime couée* stanza
lacking one line. Line 567 is probably the missing line—"stare" would rhyme with
"bowre" and "succour"—but it appears at the beginning of stanza 107, where it is
the ninth line in an otherwise complete eight-line stanza. Interspersed through this
section are abab stanzas (stanzas 104, 106, 108, 109, 111). Lines 584–587 (stanza
110) fall between two of these abab quatrains. The pattern suggests the conflation
of two versions of this scene in which half of stanza 110 was cancelled or could not
be read in the Exemplar. One of the other cited examples (I.56–59) also appears
amidst a group of abab stanzas, and it could be made an abab stanza simply by
transposing the last two words in the second line to achieve the rhyme "-full" /
"-angelle." That leaves us with only three instances of a Chester quatrain aaab, and
I think that the reasonable conclusion is that such quatrains are remnants of the
regular *rime couée* stanzas.

But there is also internal evidence in the Early Banns to suggest that the
Painters' description was not originally intended to stand by itself as a quatrain. The
Mercers have eleven lines in the pattern aaabcccxddd. The omitted line is undoubtedly line twelve and this line may have rhymed with x, but the x-rhyme clearly does
not rhyme with b, "skyle," and no rearrangement of either line will produce a rhyme.
We have then a half-stanza and a defective eight-line stanza. The possibility exists
therefore that Holme copied alternative passages, a cancelled half-stanza and an
eight-line stanza. There is some evidence to support this conclusion in the fact that
the b-rhyme of the Painters' quatrain, "wyll," matches that in the Mercers' quatrain,
"skyle." The conclusion to be drawn is that the Painters and Mercers/Vintners
originally shared a stanza, that when the Vintners and Mercers separated their Magi
plays, an eight-line stanza was written for both. When Holme made his copy, he
transcribed the Vintner's stanza and both versions of the Mercers' description.
Indeed, the original may have been in such a state that the first scribe, in the
sixteenth century, left this section uncopied because he was confused by the manuscript.

There is also external evidence that links the variations in the Early Banns with
possible revisions in the cycle. Two of the plays described in eight-line stanzas, the
Tanners' and the Painters', are primarily in abab and variants, not *rime couée*. The

Tanners' play is demonstrably a late addition; the Painters' *Shepherds* is first referred to *circa* 1515. Secondly, the most common stanzas in Chester are aaabaaab and aaabcccb, the latter of which predominates because it is the easier to achieve. Plays VI (the Wrights' *Nativity*), VIII (the Vintners' *Magi*), and IX (the Mercers' *Magi*) show a predominance of aaabaaab by a ratio of three to one or more. All three are described in eight-line stanzas in the Banns. We do not have the text of the Wives' *Assumption,* and the plays X (the Goldsmiths' *Slaughter*) and XXII (the Shermen's *Prophets of Antichrist*), both described in eight-line stanzas, have a more normal distribution of aaabcccb against aaabaaab; however, the eight-line description of X would seem to be an insertion because there is no remnant of a half-stanza for it to have been attached to (and it includes material relevant to the two "Magi" plays that precede it), and the description of XXII follows the half-stanza devoted to the Wives' *Assumption,* so as to suggest that the eight-line description was substituted for the missing half-stanza.

The weight of the evidence, it seems to me, suggests that the Early Banns was originally written in eight-line *rime couée* stanzas in which each half-stanza contained a description of a pageant. The eight-line descriptions indicate that new plays were added, old plays divided, or that other alterations took place subsequent to the writing of the Banns. I believe that these Banns were originally written while the cycle was undergoing significant change from a Passion play to a cycle. There is some substantiating evidence for this conclusion in the extant texts. The New Testament section is the most regular, having either an even balance of the two forms of the Chester stanza or a preference no greater than a ratio of two to one (the exceptions are Plays XVI, XXI, and XXIV). Plays showing an almost exclusive preference for one form are all in the Old Testament or Nativity sections (III–V, VIII–IX). In addition, plays lacking the Chester stanza are confined to these sections as well (I, VII, and the Doctor's portion of Play XI). There is evidence, then, in the extant texts for the addition or revision of all the Old Testament and Nativity plays except for Play II (*Creation and Fall*) and X (*Herod*), and the eight-line stanza in the Early Banns and external evidence suggest that X was revised, if not added. The only evidence against this line of argument is the supposition that the Carpenters/Wrights, who are referred to in the 1422 document, had the Nativity play at that time. But this is a supposition. There is no specific reference to any Old Testament or Nativity play until 1505–21, when the Cappers presented their petition about the Balaam play. Furthermore, the dispute in 1422 was over whether the Fletchers *et al.* were to aid the Ironmongers or the Carpenters in the Corpus Christi play. The Fletchers claimed that they were obligated to neither because they had their own play of the *Flagellation* up to the *Crucifixion,* for which the Ironmongers were responsible. The Fletchers also disclaimed responsibility to the Carpenters for the latters' (unspecified) pageant. It is certainly not clear why this dispute should have arisen if the Carpenters had the *Nativity* and the Ironmongers the *Crucifixion,* especially since the Fletchers assert that their portion of the play goes *up to* the *Crucifixion.* It seems more likely that all three plays were contiguous and that it was unclear where one segment ended and the other began.

I have carefully scrutinized Lumiansky and Mills's volume and noted only one oversight—a reference to an article by Stemmler (p. 168) that is not cited in the Bibliography. Perhaps it should be pointed out that the documents in Chapter Five do not have complete scholarly apparatus. I do not mean that they are not accurate transcriptions—generally they are—but some features of the text are not indicated. For example, the editors print the Early Banns without noting the changes in scribal hands. The evidentiary value of the document is therefore not apparent. But I suspect that this section was prepared with a broader audience in mind and was included chiefly to aid comprehension of the discussion in the preceding chapter. Scholars who wish to use the Chester records are referred to the volume in the Records of Early English Drama series. It is good to have this volume of introductory material, and it is to be hoped that the notes volume for the plays will soon be available from EETS so that scholars of the medieval drama can at last have before them reliable texts with an intelligent line-by-line commentary.

NOTES

1. (Chapel Hill: University of North Carolina Press, 1983).

2. Nan C. Carpenter, "Music in the *Secunda Pastorum*," *Speculum,* 26 (1951), 696–700; JoAnna Dutka, *Music in the English Mystery Plays,* Early Drama, Art and Music Reference Series, 2 (Kalamazoo, Mich.: Medieval Institute, 1980).

3. W. W. Greg, " Bibliographical and Textual Problems of the English Miracle Cycles: II—The Coming of Antichrist: Relation of the Manuscripts of the Chester Cycle," *The Library,* 3rd ser., 5 (1914), 168–205.

4. *The Trial and Flagellation with Other Studies in the Chester Cycle,* ed. W. W. Greg (Oxford: The Malone Society, 1935).

5. Salter, "The Banns of the Chester Plays," *Review of English Studies,* 15 (1939), 432–457; 16 (1940), 1–17, 137–148; Clopper, "The History and Development of the Chester Cycle," *Modern Philology,* 75 (1978), 219–246.

REVIEWS

Renaissance Drama, New Series, IX, edited by Leonard Barkan. Evanston, Ill.: Northwestern University Press, 1978. Pp. x + 236. $22.95.

Reviewer: ROBERT E. BURKHART

As the editor of this volume (the topic is "Renaissance Drama in the Theater") notes in somewhat different terms, the concept of performance as a significant aspect in studies of drama has clearly come of age. All ten essays in this collection combine in some form the theatrical with the literary elements of drama, and most are in fact theatrical in orientation.

The opening essay, Bruce R. Smith's "Toward the Rediscovery of Tragedy," deals with Seneca in sixteenth-century England. Smith uses three productions that are chronologically well-spaced to provide a sampling of Seneca in the second half of the century: Alexander Nowell's manuscript prologue for *Hippolytus* (Westminster School, *ca.* 1546); Alexander Neville's translation of *Oedipus* (printed in 1563 and perhaps produced at Trinity College, Cambridge); and William Gager's Latin additional materials—prologue, epilogue, and two scenes—for another production of *Hippolytus* (Christ Church, Oxford, in 1592). Smith's point is "that Seneca as a text for study was not at all the same thing as Seneca as a script for performance" (p. 8).

Smith shows how Nowell's prologue, which presents Phaedra as the "calculating temptress" of a saintly Hippolytus, springs from a medieval English understanding of drama. Neville's translation of *Oedipus,* moreover, transforms Seneca's terseness into expanded morality. Smith also notes in Gager's additions the Renaissance love of variety by Englishmen whose own dramatic traditions did not include a really clear notion of classical tragedy. In short, Smith does a fine job of reminding us not only of Seneca's importance to the Elizabethan idea of classical tragedy but also of how native dramatic traditions affected English productions and the response of audiences to them.

Two of the essays touch upon the audience in other contexts. In "The Logic of Elizabethan Stage Violence," Alan C. Dessen questions whether the realism often assumed as necessary to satisfy a critical audience is the only criterion to be applied to stage combat. He suggests that symbolic or patterned staging may also be possibilities, and he wisely concludes by noting that undisputed evidence is limited. The focus of Marjorie Garber's contribution is the role of the audience in Shakespearean tragedy. Probably no one would take issue with the conclusion that the audience's role is to be a kind of actor who has survived the tragic spectacle and must testify about the experience.

Essays by G. K. Hunter and Maurice Charney are hybrids that present something of a problem. Hunter's contribution on the *Henry VI* plays is partly a review article of the 1963 and 1977 Royal Shakespeare Company productions and partly a study of the plays. While the elements are obviously related and many worthwhile comments are made along the way, an attempt to deal with two productions of three plays seems a difficult task for a relatively brief article. Charney's "Hamlet's O-groans and Textual Criticism" reveals its dichotomy in the title. Charney rightly and convincingly argues that a chain of O's looking foolish in a text may well represent a significant piece of acting, but—as he realizes—the ultimate argument on the issue, the textual one, is only touched upon.

Three essays on Jonson all involve ideas of stagecraft. Patrick R. Williams ("Ben Jonson's Satiric Choreography") approaches the understanding of Jonson's plays in the literary sense through the theatrical movement of characters. Frances Teague takes a somewhat similar approach with the original production of *Epicoene* as her specific focus. R. B. Parker surveys more than fifty years of *Volpone* productions (1921–1972) and finds it "a work that is peculiarly dependent on the dimension of performance" (p. 149).

R. B. Graves uses *The Duchess of Malfi* as the basis for his interesting and sensibly argued comparison of the Globe and Blackfriars in terms of lighting. He uses the dead hand of IV.i to demonstrate that the scene would be equally effective indoors or out. Clearly he is on firm ground in asserting that, regardless of where played or what the dramatic intention, the scene required sufficient lighting for the audience to see the action.

Graves also argues convincingly that the Blackfriars hall need not have been artificially darkened. His evidence for starting time and playing time indicates that the scene could not "have taken place much before 4 P.M.—just the time of London's winter sunset" (p. 199). He also reminds us that even a situation of general illumination and pretended darkness ultimately depends upon the effectiveness of the actors.

Finally, Ejner J. Jensen points out the shortcomings of past Elizabethan revivals by Charles Lamb and William Poel and asserts that the revival of the last thirty years is genuine because of our kinship with the vision of the playwrights. It remains for a scholar of a future generation to reveal our lapses.

The World's Perspective: John Webster and the Jacobean Drama, by Lee Bliss. New Brunswick, N. J.: Rutgers University Press, 1983. Pp. x + 246. $20.00.

Reviewer: CHARLES R. FORKER

The post-romantic, alienated, and iconoclastic temper of our own age increasingly gives rise to literary studies that emphasize the alleged modernity of the past. As

Eliot reminded us some decades ago, our relationship to the great literature of earlier
times is one in which we inevitably modify tradition even as, co-responsively, it
modifies us. Nowhere is this cultural mutuality more obvious than in recent commentaries on Jacobean drama—a body of plays in which we are forever discovering
twentieth-century concerns and perspectives and to which we are magnetically
attracted because of the multiple opportunities that they offer us to see unlovely
characters (Flamineo, Bosola, and Romelio, for instance, or Vittoria and Leonora)
as stage representatives in antique dress of our own psychic isolation, moral confusion, or diminished stature. Lee Bliss's interpretation of Webster embraces these
opportunities with evident gusto and without a trace of historical embarrassment.
Her Webster is a dramatist for whom mockery, farce, and relentless satirical deflation
so undercut tragic grandeur and moral security that human dignity itself (if Webster
does not wholly annihilate it through irony and other techniques of detachment)
becomes problematic, limited, and of doubtful or, at least, of qualified validity. In
Bliss's view, Websterian tragedy is a form that progressively defines itself through
a process of critical self-scrutiny, a genre in which modish parody and comic self-
reference either command the stage or lurk in the wings threatening to unsettle and
disrupt what we might otherwise be tempted to mistake for high passion or moral
fervor, and to confront every naive response with the knowing smirk of the cynic or
the bemused smile of the skeptic.

Similar in point of view and in some of its most astute observations to Jacqueline
Pearson's *Tragedy and Tragicomedy in the Plays of John Webster* (1980; reviewed
in these pages a year ago but apparently unavailable to Bliss), this book is rather
more ambitious in scope. The stress falls upon questions of knowledge and self-
knowledge in Webster's principal characters rather than on formal techniques of
dramatic structure, and Bliss offers us detailed readings not only of Webster's three
major dramas but also of Marston's *Dutch Courtesan,* of Chapman's *Widow's Tears*
and *Bussy D'Ambois,* and of Shakespeare's *Antony and Cleopatra* and *Coriolanus*—in
her opinion Webster's most influential esthetic antecedents. Like Pearson, Bliss
emphasizes the experimental nature of Jacobean drama, its constant toying with and
intermixing of established genres, and she sees satiric comedy (the staple of Jonson,
Marston, and Middleton) as more and more tending to enclose or overwhelm tragedy in the period. All the dramas that she examines, including Webster's, become
witty attempts to reformulate or call in question old definitions of social, religious,
or personal value so that, in her handling, they emerge as problem plays somewhat
in the manner of *Measure for Measure.*

Two long introductory chapters examine the distancing techniques and effects
of Jacobean tragicomedy and tragedy. The characteristic detachment of these works,
the author argues, springs from an acute sense (felt both inside and outside the play)
of man's divorce from nature, of his assertive ego in perpetual and unresolved tension
with conventional notions of moral responsibility and social harmony; and the in-
triguers who tend to dominate the action and control theatrical response often
combine cleverness with a kind of solipsistic refusal (as in the case of Shakespeare's

Vincentio) to acknowledge the deeper implications and consequences of their own willfulness, however benign their motives. In tragicomedy the manipulated solutions of the plot jar with our need for adequate moral solutions so that the happy endings seem factitious and are robbed of conviction. In tragedy the idealists and absolutists lack true inwardness and are incapable of exploring or testing the supposed verities for which they stand. Unable to accommodate their virtues to social reality, they increasingly isolate themselves in ways that limit their awareness and therefore their humanity. Coriolanus, Antony, and Bussy, for instance, are all heroic solipsists who "dissolve, try to remake themselves, and are finally remade through others into a self they originally neither foresaw nor desired" (pp. 93–94). The self-knowledge of heroes and villains alike in these plays remains tenuous, uncertain, shallow, of dubious worth—and Bliss, of course, is at pains to suggest that the problems that characters experience in attaining to meaningful self-understanding reflect an impoverished spiritual universe pervaded by epistemological failure, frustration, and futility. Even when a character does possess or achieve some awareness of a more profound identity, he tends to pursue the knowledge for political or utilitarian purposes rather than for its own sake. The self disengages itself cynically from social commitment out of a need for psychological defense or in order to maneuver or dominate others.

Not surprisingly Bliss gives special prominence to the bitterest and most alienated of Webster's figures, especially to Flamineo, Bosola, and Romelio. She finds Webster's dramatic universe nasty and emotionally constricting—"a world where egoistic detachment allows a calm acceptance of any misfortunes but one's own and where men, like animals, helplessly yet ruthlessly pursue appetite's satisfaction," "a world of farce run mad" (p. 101). In *The White Devil* Bracciano's "potential complexity" is "progressively simplified" (p. 125), and "death leaves Vittoria tritely moralistic" (p. 137). Francisco "is a farceur, his wild justice a series of practical jokes" (p. 122), and in the mock-suicide scene "we are *delighted* [emphasis mine] when [Flamineo] pops back to life" (p. 129). In *The Duchess of Malfi* the naiveté of the heroine and her husband characteristically renders them "comically inept" (p. 147), the "self-deluding fools" or "comic dupes" (p. 148) of a genre antithetical to tragedy, and Bliss stresses the Duchess's domestic, as opposed to her regal, nature, condemning her "foolish[ness]," her "infuriating refusal to pursue heroic stature" (p. 169). "Bosola's mocking voice bars our fully sympathetic involvement" (p. 168) with the ruler of Amalfi. As for Ferdinand's remorseful speeches after her murder, these are "hypocritical and laughably inappropriate" (p. 156).

It is only fair to point out that Bliss allows Webster's characters considerably more depth and subtlety than these quotations, plucked from their contexts, would suggest. If I exaggerate the comic side of her interpretations, I do so because this will strike the generality of readers as the most important and controversial aspect of her book. Much in this volume is thoughtfully formulated, and Bliss's command of a wide range of challenging plays as well as of the massive scholarship that surrounds them is impressive. Her writing is densely concentrated, intellectually strenuous, and rather highly colored—perhaps too much so for the soberest tastes. The chapter on

The Devil's Law-Case seems to me especially suggestive, partly because this notoriously difficult play resists satisfactory analysis and partly because its tragicomic mode seems most responsive to the author's granitic, fiercely antisentimental approach.

What I miss in Bliss's book is an old-fashioned appreciation of Webster's poetry and of the passion that this surely implies—in other words a sense of deep emotional engagement with the plays that she so mercilessly dissects and to which her tone seems so often condescending. My caveat need not be taken as a rejection of her critical premises. I grant many of the effects of detachment, irony, and horrid laughter to which she points (although I believe she invents some of them), but one would never guess from her book that Webster is a great lyricist as well as an ironist-farceur, that he is the poet of the moving dirges, or of the haunting meditation on ruins, or of those terrifying silences and moments of stabbing pathos that sometimes punctuate the arrogant posturings and theatrical grotesqueries of his stage. Pity and terror seem to have been surgically excised from Bliss's Webster to be supplanted by a withering and all-pervasive contempt. No one can deny that ironic self-consciousness is a Websterian specialty, but in the theater effective irony presupposes that at least some things must be taken straight. Bliss invokes the word *naive* so often that, in her usage, the term begins to take on a special opprobrium almost as though direct and open emotions such as sexual passion and family affection and hatred and fear were manifestations of mental weakness or sentimentality. Webster's characters regularly generate doubt, particularly when it comes to assessing their complex and often obscure motivation, but in Bliss's disillusioned readings, they almost never reap the benefit of such doubts. Specialists in Jacobean drama will need to take *The World's Perspective* seriously as a work of scholarship, but the book will be less enthusiastically received by readers who believe that there is more fire than ice at the heart of John Webster.

The Dramatic Works in the Beaumont and Fletcher Canon, vol. 5, gen. ed. Fredson T. Bowers. Cambridge: Cambridge University Press, 1983. Pp. viii + 670. $99.50.

Reviewer: WILLIAM PROCTOR WILLIAMS

On 2 January 1965 Professor Fredson Bowers wrote, in the Foreword to this edition, the first volume of which was published in July of the following year, that although each play conventionally assigned to Beaumont and/or Fletcher and others was to be edited by an individual editor, under the supervision of the General Editor, he hoped that the compromise and interconnection would result in "some uniformity" while there would be "sufficient free play" for each editor to ensure individuality. And so was launched one of the largest projects in the editing of English Renaissance drama in the twentieth century. Published in that first volume were *The Knight of the Burning Pestle* edited by Cyrus Hoy, *The Masque of the Inner Temple and Gray's Inn* edited by Bowers, *The Woman Hater* edited by George Walton Williams, *The Coxcomb* edited by Irby B. Cauthen, *Philaster* edited by Robert K. Turner, and *The Captain* edited by L. A. Beaurline. Four years later (1970) Volume II appeared containing *The Maid's Tragedy* (Turner), *A King and No King* (Williams), *Cupid's Revenge* (Bowers), *The Scornful Lady* (Hoy), and *Love's Pilgrimage* (Beaurline). Six years later (1976) Volume III contained *Love's Cure* (Williams), *The Noble Gentleman* (Beaurline), *Beggars' Bush* (Bowers), *The Tragedy of Thierry and Theodoret* (Turner), and *The Faithful Shepherdess* (Hoy). A short three years after that (1979) Volume IV had *The Woman's Prize* (Bowers), *Bonduca* (Hoy), *The Tragedy of Valentinian* (Turner), *Monsieur Thomas* (Hans Walter Gabler), and *The Chances* (Williams). Now, only three years later, we have Volume V with *The Mad Lover* (Turner), *The Loyal Subject* (Bowers), *The Humorous Lieutenant* (Hoy), *Women Pleased* (Gabler), and *The Island Princess* (Williams). The edition has then gone forward at an average of one-and-one-half plays per year over more than two decades as the work of only six editors—a remarkable accomplishment. But even more remarkable has been the steep escalation in the prices of the volumes. Volume I appeared at the relatively moderate price of £5.00 but Volume V tips in at £55.00. I leave it to the reader, who probably will not be a buyer, to calculate the percentage of increase, and Cambridge has boosted the prices of the older volumes as well so that Volume I no longer sells for £5.00.

But finances aside, what can be said of this edition and its most recent volume? First, as most of us know, the editorial method set forth by Professor Bowers in the first volume, along with his general textual introduction to his edition to Dekker (1953), has become what can only be called the "standard" method for producing old-spelling editions of English Renaissance dramatic texts and, to some extent, for Renaissance texts generally. I know of many an editor who keeps photocopies of both those textual introductions to hand and uses them as handbooks. Bowers set forth what one might call the elegant form of old-spelling editing—pure and uncorrupted by critical introductions, historical introductions, and general commentary notes. Bowers set for his task, and that of his editors, the production of rigorously edited texts of all the plays in the Beaumont and Fletcher canon and only that. Perhaps Bowers felt that this task was more than enough, and he may have been right. But one thinks of the recent Edwards and Gibson edition of Massinger from Oxford University Press that not only presented all the works of Massinger all at once in old spelling but also provided at the same time the critical and historical apparatus that the Cambridge Beaumont and Fletcher will provide later (one can see what "later" means when one notes that the Dekker commentary has only recently appeared in print).

Is there an advantage to the all-at-once form of production as opposed to the bit-by-bit form? Well, for the user who is alive and active when it all comes out I suppose the answer is "yes"; but if one has a look at the introductory matter to the Massinger edition, one will see that the time of preparation stretches back many decades during which no part of the edition was generally available. However, the relatively rapid production of volumes by Bowers and his team of editors outlined above means that scholars have had some of Beaumont and Fletcher available for many years now, even though they have had those portions available as text and textual apparatus only. On balance I think I must come down on the side of the question which says that perfection and completeness are not always possible and that it is better to present the scholarly world with what one has rather than to make it wait for a long time for something one may have. The Edwards and Gibson Massinger edition is lucky to be here, and we all know of other large editions that have foundered, or are foundering, and that may never see either completion or the light of day, if cast in the all-at-once mold.

But there is one curiosity in this question of the temporally extended publication of a scholarly edition. Scholarship does not, should not, stand still. As the first section of "The Text of this Edition" in Volume I (1966)—the very material I said many have used as a sort of editing handbook of the last two decades—Bowers has "The Copy-Text and its Treatment." What Bowers sets forth in this section is the orthodox doctrine of copy-text as handed down by W. W. Greg in his "The Rationale of Copy-Text" in 1950 and as supplemented by Bowers in two articles and the essay he published in *The Aims and Methods of Scholarship in Modern Languages and Literatures* (New York: MLA, 1963). For good or for ill, that comfortable orthodoxy has taken a considerable battering over the last decade, and I was struck by the peculiar situation of Bowers and his fellow editors locked into an editorial process that they cannot easily change (should they want to, as I doubt) or even properly defend within the confines of the Cambridge Beaumont and Fletcher edition. It will be interesting to see if some sort of revised editorial statement will be issued when this edition is completed. Since I am in nearly full agreement with Bowers's theory and practice in editing English Renaissance texts, I am distressed that this magnificent, indeed stately edition is supported by an editorial statement based upon textual theories currently under attack. I might be expected to keep up with the articles on this debate in the pages of *Studies in Bibliography, The Library, Papers of the Bibliographical Society of America, Analytical and Enumerative Bibliography,* and even in non-bibliographical journals, but would we expect the usual scholarly, or non-scholarly, reader to do so? I would hope that the next volume of this edition might, in some way, take account of the current "state of play" on the issues of copy-text, accidentals and substantives, and the like.

It is certainly the case that none of the plays in the Beaumont and Fletcher edition will need editing again for a good long time, for Bowers and his fellow editors have extracted very nearly all the textual and critical information they can from the physical evidence and have applied it, along with a conservative but acute critical sense, to the texts before them. For example, those who like to view the work of modern bibliographers and textual critics as that of harmless and/or harmful drudges (the Edmund Wilson and William Empson school of textual evaluation, one might say) would no doubt object to the amount of care lavished by Robert K. Turner on the text of *The Mad Lover* since there is such a small amount of textual change, save for the emendation of the pointing and spelling changes of an apparently minor nature. But the answer to such cavils is to ask the counter question, "how many instances of punctuation and spellings without authority must there be before the texture, the authoritative texture of the play is altered?" We must always bear in mind the cumulative effect of those minor features of a text, what W. W. Greg called "accidentals," and an editor must take as many pains with them as with the more obvious and interesting "substantives." Turner has certainly taken pains, but he has not allowed these to make his textual work stuffy. I cannot resist quoting his textual note to V.iv.8, which exemplifies this appropriate scholarly lightness of touch: "8 friends] As Bond notes, Chilax is addressing his buttocks, which received 'a cruell, a huge bang' (line 5) and probably replied in kind" (p. 111).

Turner has an unusual problem in *The Mad Lover* in that the lyrics found in F1 (the First Beaumont and Fletcher Folio) have lived a textual life separate from that of the text of the play. Four were printed in 1653 in Beaumont's *Poems* and six (including the four in the 1653 printed edition) appear in as many as seven seventeenth-century manuscripts or as few as one. Turner has chosen to treat the textual history of these lyrics in an appendix to his edition since the inclusion of the material in the edition itself would have been confusing and would have made the apparatus of the edition unnecessarily difficult to use. Both here and in the Textual Notes Turner provides much more in the way of commentary for those readings that he must explain than anyone has a right to expect. Not only is his editing of this play a model of conservative old-spelling editing, but it is also a model of how scholars should write prose.

Fredson Bowers has a much easier textual situation for his edition of *The Loyal Subject*; "the text of F1 is relatively clean," as Bowers says. I noted, in particular, one emendation early in the play deriving from Colman's eighteenth-century edition, "Ancient" for F2's "Ensign" in the "Persons Represented in the Play" (p. 157). (F1 omits this section.) This is an interesting conservative old-spelling emendation made more timely by Gary Taylor's recent translation of Ancient Pistol to Ensign Pistol in his 1982 edition of *Henry V* in the modernized Oxford Shakespeare. We could hardly invent a more pointed contrast between the aims, methods, and results of editions aimed at a scholarly audience (not the same thing, I might add, as an audience only of scholars) and editions aimed at some other audience. Clearly Bowers is correct to emend his text to a form that would have been current in Fletcher's time and with Fletcher, although Bowers does not argue for the emendation in his Textual Notes. He is also right not to emend "fate" to "faith" in II.i.162 and "bodies" to "bodice" in II.i.323, the latter reading showing the richness of indefinite, or hovering, meaning that is available to the readers of old-spelling texts accurately and conservatively edited. As Philip Gaskell has said in his *From Writer to Reader: Studies in Editorial Method* (Oxford: Oxford University Press, 1978):

> The deliberate modernization of the spelling, punctuation, etc. of an early text is undesirable because it suggests that the modern meaning of the words of the text is what the author meant by them; because it conceals puns and rhymes; because it causes the editor to choose where the author was ambiguous; and because it deprives the work of the quality of belonging to its own period.
>
> (*p. 8*)

(However, for a recently dissenting view see John Creaser, "Editorial Problems in Milton," *Review of English Studies,* n.s., 34 (1983), 279–303 and 35 (1984), 45–60.) Although Bowers does not need to emend his text frequently—there are only thirty-five substantive emendations in the entire text by my count, and several of these exist only to supply omitted material—and his Textual Notes are not as enlightening as are Turner's, this is a sound edition.

Cyrus Hoy has a very unusual textual situation in his edition of *The Humorous Lieutenant,* for it exists not only in the usual printed editions, beginning with F1 in 1647, but also in a manuscript, Brogyntyn MS 42 in the library of Lord Harlech at Brogyntyn, Oswestry, which is a private transcript made by Ralph Crane for Sir Kenelm Digby and is dated 1625. The play's title in the manuscript is *Demetrius and Enanthe.* Hoy says that the F1 text represents the play as cut for theatrical production whereas the Brogyntyn manuscript, according to Hoy, comes virtually uncut from Fletcher's own papers. Hoy says that, "given the virtual certainly [*sic*] that F1 is at least two removes from the author's original papers, which have been (1) transcribed to produce the manuscript that eventually became F1 copy, and (2) set in type by the F1 compositors," he has "no reason to suppose that Crane's manuscript is any more than one remove from Fletcher's original papers" (p. 297), and he chooses F1 as his copy-text but emends freely from the manuscript. But he has said earlier that both the manuscript and F1 derive from a common original, and the evidence is, in part, that both texts are divided into acts and scenes and that one scene (III.vii) is unmarked in both F1 and the manuscript and was therefore unmarked in the common ancestor (Fletcher's papers?). Such evidence as this would seem to me to argue that Crane and F1's three compositors were working at exactly the same number of removes from the common ancestor or, rather, that we cannot know and need not speculate on such matters. What can be said is that F1 is a shortened acting text; the manuscript provides a fuller version of the play with no less authority than F1; and Hoy is perfectly correct to emend his copy-text (F1) two hundred times from the manuscript. But he may do this without speculating about "removes" from Fletcher's papers, just as editors of *Romeo and Juliet* are correct to adopt various "theatrical" emendations from the "bad Quarto" of that play because those readings in the "bad Quarto" show us how the play was staged during Shakespeare's lifetime.

Indeed, Hoy does have an interesting and difficult editing task. Unlike Bowers, who rarely emends copy-text, Hoy must emend F1 from the manuscript an average of about three times per page in his edition, these emendations ranging from a single word ("ye" for "you" at a number of places in the play) to several lines. There are also a number of instances where the uncorrected state of F1 agrees with the manuscript and thirteen places where the corrected state agrees with the manuscript. Hoy says these latter instances are independent witnesses "to the reading of the now-lost Fletcherian original that lies behind both [that is, F1 and the manuscript]" (p. 295). But what of the former instances? How could the corrector be wrong so many times? Let us look at a few of these readings. At I.i.389 the manuscript and the uncorrected state of F1 read, "*Leontius*. Let's away Gentlemen, / For sure the Prince will stay us," while the corrected state of F1 reads "stay on us." II.iii.26 in the manuscript and uncorrected state of F1 reads, "Those kinde are subtile," while the corrected state of F1 reads "These." Even more curiously, Hoy has accepted the reverse situation (corrected F1 and manuscript against uncorrected F1) only three lines earlier. In these and other instances it seems to me perfectly possible to believe that F1 was normally corrected by reference to an authoritative document and to hold that in those instances where the manuscript and the corrected state disagree, we have two independent and *different* witnesses to the readings in two authoritative documents deriving, by whatever paths, from a common ancestor, the scribes of both being equally likely to nod from time to time. I feel that Hoy, presented with the unusual situation of a Ralph Crane manuscript done twenty-two years before the first printed edition, has been rather too ready to accept its authority without fully thinking the matter through. If the manuscript did not exist, would Hoy still have selected those uncorrected readings from F1? I think not. I am not sure that I would, in the end, handle the text very much differently, but I hope I would not adopt the attitude that whatever the manuscript has, it must be right and try to maintain such an attitude even at the risk of inverting a textual argument that I have just made.

Women Pleased, or *Women Pleas'd,* as it appears throughout Hans Walter Gabler's Textual Introduction, presents almost no textual problems: thirty-three textual notes at the foot of the pages of text in all, four textual notes, and no stop-press corrections (but more on this later). Gabler leaves his text alone and good for him! There are only 149 emendations of accidentals, not counting the act and scene conversions, and a good many of these concern only the moving of stage directions to appropriate positions, and the adding of exits and entrances as needed. Almost the only problem with Gabler's edition is the odd confusion about what the play's title should really be.

George Walton Williams's edition of *The Island Princess* is also a very straightforward affair. However, he has the added problem of a revival of the popularity of this play after the Restoration. Although his discussion of this fact in the Textual Introduction is brief, clear, and informative, he quite rightly says that while he has consulted these revival texts, they play no part in his collation. Williams is a little better than the other editors in placing the play in its later stage history, but he has a play that has a somewhat more extensive stage history than do the others in this volume. But even here one does miss the rather full treatment of the stage history of plays that one finds in the Edwards and Gibson Massinger edition. Perhaps the Bowersian formula of old-spelling editing is a little too elegant? In the end Williams produces an edition along the conservative and sound lines that we have come to expect from him and from the Bowers edition of Beaumont and Fletcher.

I began this review by quoting Bowers on the matter of the control of the General Editor over the entire edition and the freedom permitted the individual editors. Certainly Bowers meant the control of the General Editor to extend over such matters as the consistency of work and approach by each editor to his play while allowing each editor full freedom in the actual editing of the play so long as that was done responsibly and according to the editorial policy of the edition. This policy sounds very proper and scholarly. However, as I looked more carefully at this volume I was struck by a glaring lack of consistency in at least one aspect, and I hope it does not represent the sort of lack of control by the General Editor that it might. It has to do with the number of copies of the copy-text collated and the method of referring to them.

All the plays in the volume under review have as their copy-texts F1. Therefore all five editors should be working with very nearly the same material, save for Turner's manuscript songs and Hoy's 1625 manuscript. Now Bowers had never said that all editors had to consult the same copies when using F1 as their copy-text. What he did say was, "plays first printed in the 1647 folio have been collated in several copies" (I.x). Well, we can all decide what "several copies" means, and we can all decide just how much the General Editor should insist that all editors deal with technical matters, such as copies to be collated, in the same way. I will not trouble you with the names of the copies collated but offer some totals. For *The Mad Lover* twenty-nine copies of F1 were collated; for *The Loyal Subject* eighteen were collated, seventeen of these being among those collated for the previous play; for *The Humorous Lieutenant* nineteen copies were collated, eighteen being the same copies as those used for the two other plays; for *Women Pleased* we do not know how many or what copies were collated since there are no press variants and Gabler makes no statement about the matter in his Introduction; for *The Island Princess* sixteen copies were fully collated and three copies partially collated, seventeen being the same as those used for the other three plays. Put another way, not counting the three partial collations of *The Island Princess,* thirteen copies were used for all four of the plays (note that we do not know what copies the fifth play used), five copies were used for three of the plays, one copy was used for two of the plays, and thirteen copies were used for only one play.

The location of the copies is also curious. Copies at the British Library and Huntington Library were used by only one editor each; the same Bodleian Library copy was used by two editors. If one studies the locations geographically it is clear that selection was, at least in part, based upon where the editors were located, so that the copies most frequently used were those at the University of Virginia (two copies), the University of Wisconsin-Milwaukee (four copies), the Newberry Library, and some large university libraries of the north- and southeast United States. Notable omissions in this volume are copies from the Folger Shakespeare Library, Harvard, Yale, New York Public Library, and the list could go on.

Now no one would ever claim that F1 is a scarce book, and I suppose that there might be something to be said for spreading the F1 use around as much as possible, but what we have here is neither consistency of copy use nor diversity. All the editors used thirteen of the same copies, yet one editor used in addition thirteen copies used by none of the others (admittedly, Turner's use of *seven* University of Texas copies skews the statistics a bit), and there seems to be no plan of approach that I can discover; there is certainly no stated plan. Furthermore, each editor's method of citing the copies used is slightly different from that of the other editors. Some give a few shelfmarks and use superscript numbers to distinguish among multiple copies at a given library; others give no shelfmarks but only library names and, in the case of multiple copies, such statements as "University of Wisconsin-Milwaukee (four copies)"; only Williams gives full shelfmark information for nearly all the copies he used. Of course, Gabler saves himself this sort of difficulty by not listing any copies used at all! Somehow, one would have expected a more careful and/or clear plan of attack than what we have, particularly in this edition.

However, I have no evidence that this method, or lack of it, has any bad effects on the final product—the edited texts—and I am sure that we all look forward to the next instalment of this, the "standard edition" of Beaumont and Fletcher in another three years' time. But I hope that this excellent edition might improve and/or regularize some of the minor matters of presentation, and that the General Editor and the other editors might see their ways clear to offering a further explanation, if not a defense, of their method and theories in light of the scholarly discussions about editing that have taken place over the last twenty years.

The Privileged Playgoers of Shakespeare's London, 1576–1642, by Ann Jennalie Cook. Princeton N. J.: Princeton University Press, 1981. Pp. x + 316. $22.00

Reviewer: STEPHEN BOOTH

This excellent, widely useful book is evidence both for and against the all-but-proverbial proposition that, as a sound scholarly article usually attempts to carry matter enough for a book, the matter of a sound scholarly book is usually sufficient for a sound scholarly article. Seven years before *The Privileged Playgoers,* Ann

Jennalie Cook published "The Audience of Shakespeare's Plays" (*Shakespeare Studies*, 7 [1974], 283–305)—a belated review of Alfred Harbage's then thirty year-old and, in 1974, still putatively definitive *Shakespeare's Audience* (New York: Columbia University Press, 1941). With energy, evidence, and precision such as might have made Cataline glad he had a mere Cicero to contend with, the essay took out after Harbage's thirties-hatched thesis that the audience majority at the Globe and at comparable other Renaissance London playhouses was—unlike the supposedly very different clientele of the so-called "private" theaters—"working class" (a term by which Harbage usually seemed to refer to all of what we would call the lower middle and "middle middle" economic classes, but a term that also takes in their often Croesus-like employers).

Harbage had rested his thesis on (a) the assertion that craftsmen and retailers (both masters and men) constituted a majority in the population of Elizabethan London; (b) the assertion that admission charges for public theaters were designed to fit the pocketbooks of that working class, and (c) the careless assumption that enough craftsmen and retailers had enough afternoons off to have regularly made up the majority in audiences at the public theaters. Dr. Cook's article carefully set up (a), (b), and (c) and then painstakingly dismantled them: (a) there is no evidence that craftsmen and retailers constituted a majority in London's population on any given day—and considerable reason to think they did not; (b) the least that the least desirable place—standing room—cost at any time during Shakespeare's working life was a penny, and a penny would have been a lot of money to a journeyman or to a typical apprentice (as it would have been negligible to most employers); moreover, groundlings were inevitably a minority in any audience: since higher-priced places—seats in the galleries—far outnumbered spaces for "understanders" in the yard around the front of the stage, a majority of Shakespeare's audiences at the Globe would have spent at least 2d.—a considerable sum when 4d. was the usual daily allowance for a wage earner's meals; and (c) no wage earner or apprentice would often have been free to leave work to see a play; performances were given only in daylight, and by statute all wage earners worked from dawn to dusk, six days a week (holidays were increasingly rare after the break with Rome, and from 1586 on playhouse performances were illegal on Sunday).

Early in the 1974 article, Dr. Cook said that her intention there was only "to reexamine the hypothesis of a working-class majority" in Shakespeare's audience—not to argue that "some other group was in the majority" (p. 284). And, having completed her devastating reexamination, she concluded the essay with these two sentences: "Either no group dominated the audiences, or else a new group can be proposed as preeminent. However, establishing a new majority is a task demanding enough for a separate study." *The Privileged Playgoers* is that separate study, and its title identifies the new majority it establishes. However, despite its supposedly negative, limited results, the 1974 essay embodied—if only by implication—the complementary, separate study it proposed for the future.

The evidence in the essay left no one to fill Shakespeare's theater except "the privileged": people who could afford the time and money necessary for playgoing. Moreover, the evidence in the essay was more than sufficient to remind the mass of *Shakespeare Studies* readers that—antitheatrical Puritan polemics aside—most contemporary references to London theatergoing between 1576 and 1642 are by or about theatergoers of wealth and substance. Furthermore, in the course of questioning Harbage's assertion that the audience must have been "working-class" because of their "great numerical superiority," the modest essay that so carefully pretended to limitation profitably spent a good deal of space listing the affluent groups living in London or visiting it on business. All in all, for the scholars and Shakespearean aficionados it reached in *Shakespeare Studies* in 1974, the essay made *The Privileged Playgoers of Shakespeare's London* unnecessary.

However, to say that is not to reason away need for the book.

For one thing, the book is much more than a counter-argument to Harbage's. In fact, its mode is not argumentative at all. In the 1974 essay the focus was Harbage's thesis and its shortcomings, and the essay was occasionally shrill—as it was when Dr. Cook sarcastically summed up Harbage's "working class": "This class is highly skilled and is possessed of innate good taste, as witnessed by its preference for the theater—just exactly the sort of playgoers required to support that broader thesis concerning the Shakespearean audience's superiority to the coterie audience" (p. 286). In *The Privileged Playgoers* Cook is like the Roosevelt administration fifty years ago: after they took office in 1933, the New Dealers never mentioned the Hoover administration at all. After page 10, Harbage's name never appears in *The Privileged Playgoers* again. Moreover, like the 1974 essay, the first pages of the book make it clear that Cook is not so much Harbage's adversary as his successor in a continuing effort to displace the still critically convenient and therefore still entrenched misconceptions about Shakespeare's audience that were wished into being by self-consciously modern, chronologically smug commentators in the late seventeenth and early eighteenth centuries (commentators whose most potent ally was Hamlet, Prince of Denmark, who should have been more precise when he tossed off the line about groundlings).

There is a great difference between supporting a thesis and doing what Dr. Cook does in *The Privileged Playgoers*. The book folds its reader into the society in which Shakespeare's plays were first performed. Cook has 316 pages at her disposal, and she crams them with facts and figures from recent work in historical demography (notably that of Lawrence Stone) and with long, rich contemporary quotations familiar to professional Shakespeare scholars. Cook's fellow Shakespeareans do not need to reread acres of quotation from Stow, the large percentage of *The Gull's Hornbook* scattered across the book, or the several swaths from William Harrison's familiar (and always treacherous) *Description of England* from *Holinshed's Chronicles*. What they *do* need—and what this book forces upon them—is to see all that familiar information in the context of the curiously isolable, traditionally isolated topic of Shakespeare's audience. (The isolation of "facts about Shakespeare" from other scholarship is a phenomenon worthy of study. Shakespeare is special, and Shakespeare scholarship has been special too. All sorts of half-truths, easy schoolroom explanations based on casual, traditional pseudo-scholarship, and pure, outdated theories remain vital and virulent in Shakespeare studies—even for scholars who would never think of packing unexamined freight into studies of, say, Hooker or Spenser or Milton. And conversely, unlike other kinds, Shakespeare scholarship customarily sails grandly past decades of profitable modern research by historians—or chooses to acknowledge historical discoveries selectively, when and if they appear convenient.)

I said earlier that *The Privileged Playgoers* is not argumentative, and that is true. On the other hand, the book is splendidly open about the fact that it is out to demonstrate the justice of a proposition stated right at the start: the proposition that the privileged were not only included among the playgoers of Shakespeare's London but that—aside from a few anomalous interlopers (what Roger Tory Peterson would call "casuals")—they *were* the playgoers of Shakespeare's London. Dr. Cook has no qualms about the validity of the evidence she presents, but she does fear that her revolutionary conclusion may be too sweeping.

I admire her caution, and—in a way—I share it. I say "in a way" because I have fewer doubts about Cook's conclusions that she herself appears to have. What sells me on her thesis is the high socio-economic status of the people who mention their own playgoing and the similar status of the people they and other contemporary writers tell us were also patrons of the public theaters. As Cook forcefully points out, after Sunday performances were banned in 1586, even the tirades of Puritans imply affluence in the audiences endangered by playgoing. There seems to have been no appreciable difference between the audiences at the large public theaters and those at the smaller more costly "private" ones. Although I accept Cook's thesis, I am nervous about the statistical evidence she brings in to bolster her case. I am not dubious about the statistics themselves. I have neither reason to question them nor the capacity to make a good job of it if I did have reason. What troubles me is the persistent reminder the statistical evidence presents of the fact that what makes sense is not necessarily true. That fact is particularly urgent to sensible conclusions based—as Cook's is not—on statistics, altogether trustworthy statistics.

Consider these examples. On the night of Wednesday, July 22, 1934, it cost twenty-five cents to see *Manhattan Melodrama* at the Biograph Theater in Chicago. The theater is said to have been crowded. Given the American economy in that year (when an average Chicago family's weekly income was about $21), does it not make sense to guess that—like John Dillinger, who was shot as he was leaving the theater—the mass of other patrons at the Biograph that night were also economically privileged? And yet Americans bought 3,640,000,000 movie tickets in 1934. It seems improbable that the vast majority of those tickets could have been bought by people who could not afford them, but we know very well that that was indeed the case. And in 1936 (the first year for which we have attendance figures for regular-season, major-league professional baseball), the most conservative of estimates—one that allows for large Sunday crowds, larger holiday crowds, people who worked nights, and a handful of night games played at Crosley Field in Cincinnati—says that at least four million of the eight and a half million admissions sold that year were for games played on the afternoons of working days. Are we wrong in our confident belief that the majority of spectators at professional baseball games were then, as they are now, adult, working-class males? Probably not. Who had the time and the money (about fifty cents) to go to those afternoon games in 1936? Common sense says, the "privileged"—the employer class. Common knowledge says otherwise. Ask your parents and grandparents. Better yet, look at the impression thirties writers who make casual mention of major-league baseball give of its clientele.

I would be the last to deny the wisdom and justice of the foregoing demonstration of the folly of assuming that one set of facts will reflect others in the ways that reason dictates. Bear in mind, however, that my digression on discrepancy between truth and probability was only that: a digression, pertinent perhaps but—because the conclusions Dr. Cook so persuasively presents in *The Privileged Playgoers* do not depend on the economic information that, perhaps fortuitously, reflects them—pure. Given the other information to which Cook calls our attention, there would be no reason to suspect that Shakespeare performed for audiences of journeyman shoemakers and plasterers even if somebody were to turn up documentary proof that every employer gave every employee two afternoons off a week with tuppence in pocket money. If that is understood, I will go back to praising the book.

At the point where I digressed, I had noted the book's healthy openness about its avowed thesis and its caution about overstating its case. One of the book's primary graces derives from Cook's insistence that her readers resist the book's rhetorical weight and go no further with its author than her evidence permits. She insists that her readers think about her evidence and argument as they read. That insistence and the candor with which Cook rejects the common, kittenish tactic whereby—in mystery-story fashion—author and reader arrive at the same time at precisely the stunning conclusion that the author reached before he began serious research make *The Privileged Playgoers* something rare and wonderful in literary scholarship: a thesis-driven book that is also safe for sophomores and graduate students.

What is more, the book is not only safe for students new to the study of English Renaissance literature but also valuable to them—generally valuable, valuable beyond its special topic. To read this book is to have been a particularly thorough tourist in Renaissance London, one who has come as close as scholarship can bring its clients to understanding the day-to-day life of a city four hundred years distant from them. A student who reads this book will be as immune as students ever can be to the conventional luxury of isolating inviting bits of information about life in "the olden times" from the less convenient, much larger body of other facts. Although the book's focus is always and only the probable constituents of audiences in the public and private London theaters between 1576 and the closing of the theaters in 1642, students who read *The Privileged Playgoers* for a Shakespeare course will find themselves more at home with other late sixteenth- and early seventeenth-century English literature—dramatic and nondramatic—than they would otherwise be.

Academic publishers are always on the lookout for specialized properties that also have a better chance than a thesaurus of Mandarin Chinese has of being widely adopted for classroom use. Representatives of university presses are heartbreakingly dear when they inquire whether one's eight hundred-page monograph on the uses of *apud* in Ovid is likely to find a large market in the kind of undergraduate Humanities course that is curricularly obligatory everywhere from Tantamount College to the University of California at Chicago Circle. Publishers' representatives have an awesome capacity to be newly surprised by the obvious and usual response such innocent inquiries evoke. Their faces collapse. *The Privileged Playgoers* suggests that the book for which they quest can sometimes be found.

Wooing, Wedding, and Power: Women in Shakespeare's Plays, by Irene G. Dash. New York: Columbia University Press, 1981. Pp. 295, illustrated. $24.00.

Reviewer: Elaine Upton Pugh

Irene Dash's *Wooing, Wedding, and Power* is a work that is contemporaneous with several notable studies of female characters and gender-related issues in Shakespeare's plays. A collection of essays entitled *The Woman's Part: Feminist Criticism of Shakespeare* ed. Carolyn Ruth Swift Lenz, Gale Greene, and Carol Thomas Neely (Urbana: University of Illinois Press, 1980), Marilyn French's *Shakespeare's Division of Experience* (New York: Summit, 1981), and Linda Bamber's recent *Comic Women, Tragic Men* (Stanford: Stanford University Press, 1982) are a few examples of work resulting from the upsurge of interest in women in Shakespeare. These three books, unlike Irene Dash's, contain arguments that may be said to revise the view of Shakespeare presented by Juliet Dusinberre in *Shakespeare and the Nature of Women* (London: Macmillan, 1975). In the main, Dusinberre's study aims to render Shakespeare as a feminist in that he, according to Dusinberre, rejects misogynistic views of women as well as the false idealization of them. Although French and Bamber's specific concerns are different, both show that whereas Shakespeare gives sympathetic portrayals of women, he is by no means always free of the Renaissance social and political views that make women less significant than and subject to men. French explains that even when supportive of allegedly feminine qualities, Shakespeare "never abandons belief in male legitimacy" (p. 17). The editors of *The Woman's Part* observe that "despite the presence of matriarchal subtexts, patriarchy seems to prevail throughout the canon of Shakespeare's plays" (p. 5). These editors tell us that Shakespeare's relation to the oppression of women is a complicated matter. "The extent to which Shakespeare aligns himself with patriarchy, merely portrays it or deliberately criticizes it remains a complex and open question, one that feminist criticism is aptly suited to address" (p. 6).

However, in *Wooing, Wedding, and Power* Dash expresses little doubt about Shakespeare's attitude to patriarchy in the plays. Rather, she makes the general claim that his plays "challenge accepted patterns for women's behavior," patterns such as "compliance, self-sacrifice for a male, dependence, nurturance, and emotionalism." She implies that an omniscient Shakespeare stands behind the plays and outside the system of male social and political dominance and that his "varied, multi-faceted portraits of women" show him to be keenly aware of the way patriarchy stereotypes and restricts women (p. 1).

To demonstrate what she calls Shakespeare's "infinite variety" in his portrayal of strong female characters, Dash devotes chapters to the *Henry VI–Richard III* tetralogy and to six other plays—*Love's Labor's Lost, The Taming of the Shrew, Romeo and Juliet, Othello, The Winter's Tale,* and *Antony and Cleopatra.* She examines patterns of courtship, sexual behavior, marriage and political activity as seen in the heroines of these plays and their relationships to males. It strikes me as odd that a study of Shakespeare's variety in depicting strong female characters who challenge the norms virtually ignores or only scantily refers to Rosalind of *As You Like It,* Viola and Olivia, Isabella, Helena, Imogen, Portia of *The Merchant of Venice,* Beatrice, and Lady Macbeth. It is difficult to understand why a chapter is devoted to the relatively undistinguished and indistinguishable women of *Love's Labor's Lost* rather than to the versatile, agile, and singular Rosalind of *As You Like It,* especially when Dash's subject is wooing, courtship, and oath-taking. It seems that Rosalind does more to undermine the male habit of swearing loyalty and devotion in love than does, for example, the Princess of France, who exhibits a relatively straightforward and superficial mistrust of the value of men's oath-taking.

Troublesome is Dash's frequent use of long superseded Shakespearean criticism and her frequent and almost myopic reference to the Victorian philosopher John Stuart Mill. Mill's impressionistic views about the condition of women may be generally provocative, but Dash's arguments might gain in force and credibility if she were to rely more upon or debate more often with a historical researcher such as Lawrence Stone, to whom she refers less frequently than to Mill. Dash's handling of long dead or superseded critics is problematic insofar as she does not always find what is useful or refreshing in writers such as Alexander Pope, Charles Lamb, Edward Dowden, and Anna Jameson. When she counters the misogynistic view of older critics, Dash often is superfluous. And surely she does not need to rely upon Irving Ribner to remind the informed reader of Shakespeare or of any great writer of what is by now a truism, that is, that Shakespeare's attitudes are not to be found in the didactic speeches of individual characters but rather in the larger design of the play. Yet Dash does show that, even in relatively recent criticism, often blatant and unfounded indictments of Shakespeare's female characters are to be found. For example, as late as 1971, Hugh M. Richmond in *Shakespeare's Sexual Comedy* (Indianapolis: Bobbs-Merrill, 1971) sees female characters as neurotic and as "the prime sources of disaster in Shakespeare's plays" (p. 71).

In Dash's examination of how Shakespeare challenges traditional patterns of male-female behavior in courtship, she gives a slippery and unconvincing reading of *The Taming of the Shrew*. She opines that Petruchio's misogynistic words are often heavy with irony and that this irony is part of the play's questioning of women's subjection to men. But one looks in vain to find the place where, as Dash says, Petruchio's words to Kate are undercut by his actions. His speeches and Kate's final speech of submission can hardly be explained as ironic when the play provides no other viable alternative to Kate's submission in marriage.

Dash is more convincing in her readings of the *Henry VI–Richard III* tetralogy and *The Winter's Tale*. She explains that in the tetralogy women can see power only in male terms and thus are finally powerless. Dash sees Shakespeare reversing masculine and feminine stereotypes in *The Winter's Tale*. Paulina and Hermione appear as agents of reason and courage, whereas Leontes is irrational and unreliable, qualities traditionally associated with females.

Perhaps Dash's major contribution in *Wooing, Wedding, and Power* is her use of promptbooks and stage history to show how actor-managers and directors have frequently revised, excised, and adapted plays so that women appear as morally and rationally inferior to men. As in her essay in *The Woman's Part*, "A Penchant for Perdita on the Eighteenth Century Stage," Dash herself shows a penchant for enlightening us about the representation and misrepresentation of female characters on the stages of Theophilus Cibber, David Garrick, Henry Irving, and twentieth-century directors.

One might wish that Dash would devote more time to stage history and less to overworked generalities about women's strength and power or lack of power. True, Shakespeare creates a variety of assertive females, but then in saying this, Dash hardly offers a new or refreshing insight. As several critics, male and female, have shown, Shakespeare is not a univocal presence consistently challenging patriarchal systems. His portrayal of women and men in sexual, marital, familial, and political contexts shows what Coppélia Kahn and Murray Schwartz in *Representing Shakespeare* (Baltimore: Johns Hopkins University Press, 1980) term either Shakespeare's "unresolved ambivalence" or his "continual openness to dramatic interplay at many levels" (p. xv). In an ambience of contemporary Shakespearean criticism such as the best essays in *Representing Shakespeare* and *The Woman's Part,* studies that find challenge or delight in Shakespeare's ambivalence, ambiguity, and openness, it is difficult to see any profound value in *Wooing, Wedding, and Power* except in the parts that discuss performance records of various centuries. These parts have the potential for increasing critics' sensitivity to the theatrical dimension of the plays and for increasing awareness of the sometimes subtle, sometimes overt restriction of women on stage as well as off.

Radical Tragedy: Religion, Ideology and Power in the Drama of Shakespeare and his Contemporaries, by Jonathan Dollimore. Chicago: University of Chicago Press, 1984; Brighton, Sussex: The Harvester Press, Ltd., 1984. Pp. viii + 312. $20.00.

Reviewer: HARRY KEYISHIAN

Jonathan Dollimore's challenging and already much discussed study might best be thought of as two separate works, for besides being a sweeping reinterpretation of Jacobean tragedy, it is also a lucid exposition and defense of Marxist theory. Although there is reason to quarrel with much—perhaps most—of what is said here, both "works" deserve and reward attention.

The virtue of Marxist theory, for Dollimore, is that it "decentres" man (I adopt his British spelling and his use of *man* for *humankind*) and denies that the individual has some pre-social essence, nature, or identity which gives him autonomy (p. 250). Dollimore cites Marx's assertion that " 'the essence of man is not an abstraction inherent in each particular individual' "; rather, " 'the real nature of man is the totality of social relations' " (p. 153). When we—and in that "we" is to be included not merely the interpretive community concerned with Renaissance drama but also human consciousness in general—cast off our "essentialist" notions and demolish what Louis Althusser has called "the myth of man," a number of benefits follow: we become aware of the forces that form us; the bases of racist thought are undermined; we understand the ways that ideology functions, both in its "cognitive" aspect, as a conspiracy of those in power, and in its "materialist" aspect, as it exists in the social practices that constitute people's lives. When man is decentred, we will be able to see him in terms of potentiality rather than essence; we will speak of cultural differences rather than "the human condition"; we will not feel under the control of destiny but instead seek "collectively identified goals" (p. 271).

These are high stakes indeed and the implications for criticism are considerable. For one thing, we cannot, if we accept Dollimore's prescriptions, assume that there is some "transhistorical" plateau where value and meaning exist separate from their particular material contexts. For another, "essentialist" or humanist tragedy loses its eminence, for not only does it incorrectly preach an indestructible essence in man, but it also assumes, wrongly, that suffering is necessary and redemptive. On the contrary, says Dollimore, citing Raymond Williams: while it is true that we often do not avoid suffering and are broken by it, suffering is in fact avoidable and it need not break us (p. 158). Again, essentialist tragedy wrongly assumes that dispossession and displacement cause redemptive suffering. They do not, although suffering may cause recognition of the truth of social relations, as when King Lear learns, while on the heath, that power controls justice. And further, essentialist critics assume the flaw in tragedy to be in the protagonist, when in fact, as J. W. Lever has argued in

The Tragedy of State (London: Methuen, 1971), it is in the world (p. 194); hence they wrongly deny tragic status to *Death of a Salesman* because its hero's fall is shown in sociological rather than essentialist terms (p. 263).

How did our misunderstanding of Jacobean tragedy come about? Dollimore says that we have viewed the plays from the perspective of an essentialist humanism which did not come into existence until the Enlightenment and which taught that individuals are autonomous, unified, substantial, and self-generating (p. 155). We impose this presupposition on Jacobean tragedy and thereby distort it. In fact, Dollimore says, the prevailing view of the time did not consider the soul to be autonomous, but rather to be "metaphysically derivative" (p. 155)—a distinction not pursued in sufficient detail for my understanding, I confess. In any case, it was this latter view that Jacobean tragedy challenged, just as Marxism today challenges essentialist humanism.

Marxism also challenges *existential* humanism, which, Dollimore shrewdly observes, has become for literary criticism a "surrogate or displaced theology." It is, in his view, "merely a mutation of Christianity and not at all a radical alternative" because its vision is one of man bereft of Absolute and Essence, forlorn and regretful because he "understands his world only through the grid of their absence" (p. 195). For Dollimore, on the contrary, the "vision of decentred subjectivity" is a "vision of liberation" (p. 271). He cites Levi-Strauss's assertion that " 'the ultimate goal of the human sciences' is 'not to constitute, but to dissolve man' " (p. 257); he quotes Jacques Derrida on the need for an affirmation which " *'determines the noncentre otherwise than as loss of the centre'* " (p. 271: Derrida's italics, from *Writing and Difference,* trans. Alan Bass [London: Routledge, 1978], p. 292).

Dollimore maintains that the plays which he discusses—selected works of Shakespeare, Marston, Chapman, Webster, and others—"were more radical than has hitherto been allowed" (p. 3). They subjected English institutions to "sceptical, interrogative and subversive representations" (p. 4); they demystified political and power relations, provided a critique of ideology, and decentred man. Thereby they contributed to the English Revolution.

We have difficulty seeing this, according to Dollimore, both because of our essentialist orientation and because the dominant tragic conception of our day, deriving from Bradley and Eliot, ascribes "to Jacobean drama an ultimate ethical and/or metaphysical coherence revealed in and through dramatic structure" (p. 59). But that coherence is absent, Dollimore says: the closure in Jacobean tragedy is usually "perfunctory" (p. 60). Rather, Jacobean tragedy is to be understood in terms of Brecht's epic theater, in which drama ends in contradiction rather than closure or transcendence and in which characters are systematically demystified. The "disconnectedness" (p. 67) of Jacobean plots reflects the playwrights' aim of focusing on the radical distinction between appearance and reality. Indeed, "literature becomes internally dissonant because of its relationship to social process, actual historical struggle and ideological contradiction" (p. 68).

Because of censorship, among other causes, the drama did not explicitly repudiate the so-called Elizabethan world view; rather, it subverted that set of beliefs by showing that ideology is misrepresentation. Citing Montaigne, Machiavelli, Marlowe, Bacon, and Hobbes, Dollimore demonstrates contemporary awareness of the ideas he discusses. (W. R. Elton's *King Lear and the Gods* [San Marino, Calif.: The Huntington Library, 1966] is appropriately cited as a significant supporting study.) The attitude expressed in Marlowe's quip that " 'the first beginning of Religion was only to keep men in awe' " (p. 9), for example, and the general insight that "truth" is not absolute but relative to custom and culture turn up in many authors. Even Luther and Calvin are quoted for their contributions to the undermining of "providentialism" (pp. 104–105).

Dollimore's "anti-essentialist" band of playwrights did their work of subversion by promoting political and social realism; they showed the powerlessness of individuals and demystified the social order; they demonstrated that social process determines identity; they reflected and exposed the contradictions of society; and when they portrayed inversions—son over father, woman over man, subject over prince—they may, depending upon the occasion and the context, have stimulated rebellion (pp. 26–27).

Dollimore finds support for his line of thought in Stephen Greenblatt's *Renaissance Self-Fashioning* (Chicago: University of Chicago Press, 1980), which likewise argues that the human subject in the Renaissance was " 'the ideological product of the relations of power in a particular society' " (p. 181). Jacobean tragedy had developed away from the didactic and prescriptive earlier drama, which conceived a universe divinely controlled. It moved toward becoming "a form with empirical, historical and contemporary emphases" (p. 71). Didacticism ("idealist mimesis") would, for example, assume the reality of justice in life; "realist mimesis," on the other hand, "represents an actuality which obviously differs from the providential order" (p. 73). In Renaissance critical theory, it was recognized that justice belonged to the fictive realm only and not to real life, and Jacobean tragedy moved to fulfill the function of history rather than poetry.

Marlowe's *Doctor Faustus,* an important precursor of Jacobean drama, provokes subversive questioning by locating Faustus in relation to the contrary and antagonistic forces of God and Lucifer, who between them destroy him. The audience identifies subversively with the "alien" through the travesty of cherished orthodoxy that occurs in Faustus's blasphemous reaffirmation of his pact: *"Consummatum est."* The play, by affirming that God has created evil as well as good, subverts divine authority. God becomes a god of power, not goodness; He destroys Faustus in order to reaffirm His credibility but by the same act compromises it. The play demonstrates that "if human beings perpetuate disorder it is because they have been created disordered" (p. 118). Dollimore concludes that "the concept of 'heavenly power' interrogated in *Dr Faustus* was soon to lose credibility, and it did so in part precisely because of such interrogation" (p. 119).

In Dollimore's view, Faustus rebels not because he is arrogant or in error but out of insecurity about the knowledge that he possesses; he consciously transgresses limits out of a wish to escape irresolution. Unfortunately, Dollimore's interpretation seems to require the wrenching of certain lines from their apparent meaning: where the play seems to say that Faustus is being shortsighted or is pursuing false logic and contradiction, Dollimore sees subversive questioning; when the play exposes weaknesses in Faustus's moral character, as when he wishes ill to the old man who has tried to save him, we are apparently to shift the blame from Faustus to the God who, in creating him, gave him the capacity for error and evil. That *Faustus* promotes sympathy for its erring hero and interrogates its stern God is probable; but Dollimore's seeming implication that Faustus is merely the "site" of a power struggle between God and Lucifer rather than an implicated, complex tragic figure is not so convincing.

But Faustus only foreshadows the figures that Dollimore wishes to discuss. The true prototypes for the socially rather than religiously "radical" plays that he deals with are Marston's *Antonio* plays and Shakespeare's *Troilus and Cressida*. In these works, characters "are not defined by some spiritual or quasi-metaphysical essence, nor, even, a resilient human essence; rather, their identities are shown to be precariously dependent upon the social reality which confronts them" (p. 29). When they take revenge, it is not a working out of divine vengeance but "a strategy of survival resorted to by the alienated and dispossessed" (p. 29). Because they have no "essential" self to resort to—as the Stoic characters in the plays discover when their philosophical defenses break down—they are limited to merely social restoration of their identities by forming a "subculture" of revenge. That ghastly ritual slaughter that ends *Antonio's Revenge* is their way of "re-engaging" with society.

Again, Dollimore's comments are suggestive but perhaps off center. The breakdown of Stoicism, in the *Antonio* plays, *Hamlet* (I am thinking of Horatio's final passion), and elsewhere, does not necessarily demonstrate the lack of an essential core of being but the folly or limitation of one philosophical ideal. The revengers in *Antonio's Revenge* seem more interested in restoring personal wholeness and stability than in integrating themselves into society. They do form a "subculture" of revenge, and their companionship does aid their individual efforts to restore wholeness, but in the end they must and do separate themselves from society at large. The play—a difficult one to interpret, to be sure—seems to indicate that what they have found, through regenerative violence, is precisely some essential self that protects them from dissolution.

In *Troilus and Cressida,* as in the *Antonio* plays, "the disintegrating effects of grief are resisted not through Christian or stoic renunciation of society but a commitment to revenge—a vengeful re-engagement with the society and those responsible for that grief" (p. 40). The plays dispose of essentialist myths about providential governance and resilient human essences; in them the contemplation of defeated human potential does not (as it does in essentialist tragedy) confirm that potential, Dollimore says, and the protagonists do not learn wisdom through their suffering. Antonio and Troilus lack "essentialist self-sufficiency" (p. 49); they are "the prototypes of the contradictory Jacobean anti-hero: malcontented—often because bereaved or dispossessed—satirical, and vengeful; at once agent and victim of social corruption" (p. 50), and they always bring to mind the social conditions of existence.

Dollimore strongly associates himself with W. R. Elton's exposition of the disintegration of providentialist belief (in *King Lear and the Gods*) and traces an Elizabethan and Jacobean atheistic tradition from Marlowe onwards. Dollimore rejects approaches that would make of Shakespeare either a believer in "the crude idea of retributive intervention from above" or an "immanent providentialist" (p. 90). Rather, Dollimore feels that in *King Lear* "the concept of nature is interrogated and its multiple meanings, often contradictory, laid open" (p. 91). But the playwrights are not seen as "offering a simple atheistic repudiation of providentialist belief"; more effectively, "they play upon the contradictions and stress-points within it. In effect they inscribe a subversive discourse within the dominant one" (p. 92).

Again, Dollimore rejects both the Christian *Lear,* which conceives of the tragic protagonist as atoning for an evil world, and the humanist *Lear,* which credits human nature with an undefeatable spirit of health. Rather, he suggests that the play repudiates essentialism and decentres man "in order to make visible social process and its forms of ideological misrecognition" (p. 191). Lear's madness is not truly a divine furor; rather, his ravings are mere "incoherent ramblings" that reveal "just how precarious is the psychological equilibrium which we call sanity, and just how dependent upon an identity which is social rather than essential" (p. 195). The King does not, as essentialist critics maintain, fulfill "the notion of man as tragic victim somehow alive and complete in death" (p. 202); *Lear* refuses the autonomy of values that humanist critics see in it.

Dollimore's dismissal of Lear's "ravings" seems an unfortunate lapse. One might as well argue that Lady Macbeth's sleepwalking soliloquy is unconnected to the murder of Duncan as suggest that Lear's multilayered, imaginative, antic running commentary is without deep and brilliant connection to his situation, even as it dramatizes the fragility of the King's mental balance. He may not attain his fullest vision on the heath, but surely he is passing through meaningful stages toward recognition.

To Dollimore, "*King Lear* is, above all, a play about power, property, and inheritance" (p. 197). The wielders of power in the play, the ones obsessed with inheritance, are Lear and Gloucester. Edmund falls prey to their obsession, but he does not introduce it into their world. Because he has been excluded from power, Edmund gains insight into his society's "dominant ideology of property and power" (p. 201). He is evil, Dollimore concludes, but his philosophy is not (p. 198)—a distinction I confess I found hard to sustain.

This is a modern *Lear* indeed, with an Edgar who delivers his lines about his father's blinding ("The gods are just . . . ") with a "wince" (p. 203), since they make divine justice unintelligible. Dollimore acknowledges that characters at the play's close do try to "recuperate" their society—Edgar's victory, Edmund's repentance, Albany's allusions to heavenly judgment all contribute to that—but they do so in the very terms that the play has subverted and undermined. The deaths of Cordelia and Lear finally "sabotage the prospect of both closure and recuperation" (p. 203).

In *The Revenger's Tragedy* the providential idea of a vengeful god is parodied, reduced to stage effects, as Vindice adopts the *persona* of playwright and "cues" the thunder. While respecting the rhetoric of providentialism, Vindice subverts its spirit, and the ironic tone of the play casts doubt on the sincerity of its moral framework. Because "peripeteia and poetic justice are construed in terms of a villainous aesthetic delight" (p. 143), the play inverts the standard principles of moralistic drama.

The Revenger's Tragedy emphasizes the futility of each character's struggle for power. Their senseless activity, whether sexual or social, seeks "self-fulfillment through domination of others" and, at the same time, is a "process of inevitable disintegration: dissolution and death seem not in opposition to life's most frantic expression but inherent within it" (p. 146).

While most of the characters in the play live obsessively, Vindice realizes, in moments of stasis, how self-stultifying the expenditure of energy is and "articulates the tensions and contradictions of his world." Paradoxically, his vindictiveness is a "desperate" bid for reintegration into a society which he is trying to destroy, but without which he cannot survive. The play's "vital irony" and "deep pessimism" are held together not in esthetic unity but through a sensibility of "subversive black camp" (p. 149). Finally the play is "beyond—or before— 'tragedy' " because in it "no one . . . is allowed the role of heroic despair: in relation to no one is human suffering made to vindicate human existence" (p. 150).

In the later Jacobean plays that Dollimore discusses—*Bussy D'Ambois, Coriolanus, Antony and Cleopatra,* and *The White Devil,* among others—man has no "essence": he is "decentred to reveal the social forces that both make and destroy him" (p. 168). Thus the plays are potentially, and sometimes actually, revolutionary. By demonstrating the absence of teleological design in the universe—in Dollimore's reading of Bussy's last lines, the character dies repudiating the existence of the soul—Chapman reveals the social relations that govern character.

Antony and Coriolanus discover identity to be "radically contingent": the latter, for example, has been socialized by his mother to need the plebeians as "objects of inferiority without which his superiority would be literally meaningless" (p. 222). In *The White Devil* the tragic subject is utterly decentered: state power and ideology are demystified as we come to see how policy acquires ideological sanctions. As characters get nearer the court and learn the truth about that world, they grow vicious: sexual and social exploitation are a continuing concern in the play and family bonds "here, as throughout Jacobean tragedy, . . . collapse under pressure . . . because . . . they are shown to be not natural at all, but social" (p. 236).

Dollimore's challenging readings follow from his premises, but, as I have tried to indicate, they are not uniformly convincing. It is one thing to call these plays interrogative and to say that they thereby contributed to the breakdown of belief; it is another to describe them as intentionally subversive. More helpful and better grounded in historical and psychological probability is Stephen Greenblatt's approach in *Renaissance Self-Fashioning,* which suggests that plays like *Doctor Faustus* and *Othello* subvert through excess—Marlowe through a "perverse" submission to divine authority and Desdemona through "excessive" submission to male authority. We need not make unverifiable assumptions about intentions when more plausible psychological strategies offer appropriate explanations.

Dollimore's readings may also be said to come under Richard Levin's interdiction, as set forth in *New Readings vs. Old Plays* (Chicago: University of Chicago Press, 1979), upon ironic interpretations in which a play is read as meaning the opposite of what it seems to say. Further, Dollimore's method, once applied, need not be restricted to Jacobean tragedy: for one thing, a "non-essentialist" reading of Shakespeare's first historical tetralogy would be as convincing as one applied to *The White Devil*. (Dollimore even seems to suggest as much—see p. 90.) For another, Dollimore's reading of *Antony and Cleopatra* as "anti-essentialist" appears to ignore the power of Shakespeare's verse, which seems rather to exalt the fallen lovers and their ideology of autonomy than to disprove it. Equally hard to accept is the idea that the ideology of the English Revolution is so closely linked to the subversive views that Dollimore discovers among his radical playwrights: the triumphant literary document of the Revolution, Milton's *Paradise Lost*, is, for all its antimonarchial sentiment, a strong defense of providentialism and male superiority.

Perhaps the point on which Dollimore is on the shakiest ground is his insistence that the playwrights intended rebellion in their work. It is not hard to see how interrogation can hasten the day of collapse for an ideological structure; we can easily see that an obsession with chaos can function either as a conservative or a progressive force (pp. 93–94); the argument that Jacobean tragedy lacks esthetic structure because it reflects reality rather than art is plausibly presented (p. 8); that Jacobean tragedy "interrogates ideology from within, seizing on and exposing its contradictions and inconsistencies" is easy to accept, but the clause following—that it offers "alternative ways of understanding social and political process" (p. 8) is less so.

It is frustrating to be critical of this study: its thesis is exhilarating and seductive, since it requires us to take these playwrights at their word and make them our ideological contemporaries. If they had, in fact, been doing what Dollimore thinks, they certainly were greater, more courageous, and keener than we have thought them. Unfortunately, even readers who share Dollimore's orientation are generally likely to be unconvinced by his readings of individual plays. Despite that, I must say in closing, *Radical Tragedy* is worth attention for its scope and for the freshness of its attack on the material it discusses.

The Poetics of Jacobean Drama, by Coburn Freer. Baltimore: The Johns Hopkins University Press, 1981. Pp. xxiv + 256. $22.50.

Reviewer: PAUL BERTRAM

This book sets out to renew our attention to the dramatic rhythms of Renaissance verse plays, and it locates and illustrates its subject within a good selection of intellectual and theatrical contexts. Argument and literary history are presented in the opening chapters and an Epilogue; between these Freer offers exemplary close readings of five major plays that were first written and produced between (roughly) 1605 and 1630: *The Revenger's Tragedy, Cymbeline, The White Devil, The Duchess of Malfi,* and *The Broken Heart.*

The opening chapter ("Poetry in the Mode of Action") is concerned with critical tradition and begins with a sober statement of professional dismay: "As far as the bulk of published criticism on English Renaissance drama is concerned, including criticism of Shakespeare, the plays might as well have been written in prose—highly figurative prose, but prose nevertheless" (p. 1). Freer cites Bacon's dictum that poetry is nothing but feigned history, "which may be stiled as well in Prose as in Verse," and then goes on to note recurrent manifestations of this bias in the course of a wide-ranging and generally fair-minded excursion through the critical literature. The narrative is bound at times to stress the negative:

> one recent example of a critical argument that locates the poetry of poetic drama almost entirely in rhetoric also happens to be one of the best. . . . Even here, though, where the reading is full of the most spacious insights, there is only passing acknowledgement of the fact that dramatic poetry begins in a sensuous apprehension through the ear—which the dramatists and the audiences of the time never forgot.
>
> *(p. 8)*

There is "no way or need," of course, "to divorce the rhythms of dramatic poetry from other elements of meaning, including metaphor, plot, staging, and so forth" (p. 10), but Freer is calling special attention to a culturally perverse attitude toward the verse in verse drama:

> reference to verse drama is difficult in some journals and presses, which quote the poetry as if it were prose, running on the lines one after another without even slashes to indicate line breaks, and with only a vestigial capital letter now and then to mark the start of a poetic line. Certainly this practice saves paper and typesetting costs, and certainly it focuses our attention more on the "content" of the poetry, which is supposed to be what the author was interested in anyway.
>
> *(p. 3)*

Freer's discussion takes up a variety of theoretical and practical issues, touching especially upon the different experiences of seeing and hearing a play in the theater and reading it at home in a presumably reliable text. Because the dramatic belief of an audience is "Both sealed with eye, and ear" (*Two Noble Kinsmen*), Freer is right to stress that Renaissance stages, relative to those of later times, made a greater demand on the ear.

This point is brought home in Chapter Two ("Contexts of Blank Verse Drama"), which is a deft review of salient attitudes toward poetic drama among Elizabethan and Jacobean playwrights and audiences. Readers of a journal on Renaissance drama need hardly be persuaded that London audiences of that golden age were somewhat more alive than those of our own day to the metrical orderings and the heard rhythms in the plays that they attended and read; the novelty of the chapter lies in the broad selection of supporting testimony that Freer has assembled from plays, poems, letters, prefaces, notes, ballads, satires, and from the writings of pedagogues and puritans as well as poets. Whether or not one agrees with all his comments on the Renaissance witnesses he calls, their testimony is more than sufficient to show that "the dramatists here studied are writing for what John Webster called 'an understanding auditory'.... Even when social and economic pressures regularly urged plays into print, the reader was still regarded as a type of listener" (p. xvii). The central part of the chapter presents "the player and his art" from the viewpoints of Elizabethan and Jacobean observers (pp. 41–50); it ought to be a welcome text in drama schools that do classical theater, and it also leads up to a more general reminder about the metrical pulse that links acting with reading:

> The paradox of performance as literature is inherent in all those metaphors used to describe the actor's basic job of work. Meters or "numbers" in the poetic text become a kind of music in the delivery of the actor, or in the mind of the reader. The process of mediation begins in the poet's mind, and ends in speech that occurs on stage or in the mind of the reader; the second is a sensible apprehension as well as the first, because the residual core of poetry in poetic drama allows the reader himself to re-create the play.
>
> (*p. 48*)

By posing against modern critical neglect a strong Jacobean awareness of this "residual core of poetry in poetic drama," Freer's opening chapters are thus able to raise some teasing questions:

> How can poetry assume the center of an extended argument? Can every line of a play be analyzed and coordinated with every other line, as if the whole were a mammoth lyric, some sort of poetic dinosaur? How can even the most tireless reader respond to every line in a play? The challenge seems impossible, but Paul Alpers has assured us that each of the 4,000 stanzas of *The Faerie Queene* is addressed directly to us as readers; if we can rise to that occasion, then we ought to be able to stand up and walk through plays like a man.
>
> (*p. 11*)

These questions resist abstract analysis, but they underlie all the specimen readings in the later chapters.

Each of these chapters deals with the poetic design of one play (two in the single chapter on Webster) and, while hardly treating "every line," follows the movement of the play by tracing the roles of two or three leading characters, discriminating with great sensitivity what Freer calls "the intellectual and physical rhythms by which the characters lived" (p. 48). These readings, richly rewarding in many ways, are difficult to summarize or exemplify briefly, since they consistently relate details of rhythmic stress to a more fully orchestrated consideration of the dramatic scenes; to illustrate them fairly would require several uninterrupted pages of quotation. Each reading is self-contained, and any reader who prefers to bypass the literature-as-performance argument of the opening chapters and go directly to its practical application might find the thirty-three-page chapter on *Cymbeline* an absorbing place to begin; its focus is on the voices of Iachimo, Posthumus, and Imogen, the "central triangle" of the main action, and it incorporates a fascinating demonstration of Iachimo as "a kind of living nightmare through which the other characters have travelled" (p. 135).

Freer attributes *The Revenger's Tragedy* to Tourneur "for convenience's sake" (p. 231), tactfully keeping the ongoing authorship debate isolated from his immediate focus, an illustrated discussion of Vindice's poetic-dramatic progress. Freer is naturally concerned with questions of textual authority, especially the verse-arrangements in the original texts (all five of them good ones) and their later editorial preservation or rearrangement. With regard to four plays, only in rare cases (as in restoring an alexandrine from the Folio to a citation from the Arden text of *Cymbeline*) is he obliged to call attention to textual transmission, but the text of *The Revenger's Tragedy* is more problematical—notorious for its abrupt shifts between verse and prose and for the varying length of its verse lines, both in the original Eld Quarto of 1607 and also, after many adjustments and rearrangements, in many modern editions. Freer offers a succinct and penetrating analysis of the lineation problem, scanning both the bibliographical hypotheses and the variant reconstructive surgeries of editors, to show that adhering to the basic arrangement of the Quarto text (following Allardyce Nicoll) makes equally good sense editorially and dramatically (pp. 86–93). Elsewhere Freer comments, always interestingly and more often than not persuasively, on Webster's dramatic development (including an incisive comparison between Bosola and Flamineo) and, in the longer view taken in the Epilogue, on the place of 1590s closet drama and of the plays of Fletcher and Shirley in the development of Renaissance poetry and theater to the Restoration. The central chapters on the five plays are nevertheless the heart of the book, an original and refreshing experiment in critical reading that is also a distinguished act of historical recovery.

Renaissance Self-Fashioning: From More to Shakespeare, by Stephen Greenblatt. Chicago: University of Chicago Press, 1980. Pp. 321. $20.00.

Reviewer: ALAN SINFIELD

Stephen Greenblatt began writing *Renaissance Self-Fashioning* with the intention of understanding "the role of human autonomy in the construction of identity" but found instead that the human subject is "the ideological product of the relations of power in a particular society" (p. 256). This changing perception evidently resulted from his assimilation of Althusser, Geertz, and Foucault, and the importance of the book results as much from that as from its brilliant critical and historical analyses. The prominence of Marxist, anthropological, and post-structuralist approaches in current literary studies is not just academic fashion (self-fashioning). In the wake of what Greenblatt at one point calls "the heady manner of the late '60s" (p. 174), intellectuals have felt obliged to ask themselves urgent questions about power and autonomy, ideology and culture; about how far they are the victims of the exercise of power by government, and how far they are implicated through their roles in the production of ideology in the continuation of an unsatisfactory society. *Renaissance Self-Fashioning* represents and promotes a current tendency in intellectual life, and I shall take it partly at that level of seriousness.

No forcing is required to locate in the Renaissance period questions about the implication of writing and power, although Greenblatt achieves a salutary shock of recognition when he compares Henry VIII to Stalin. Literature then was written by people closer to or more dependent upon centers of power, and patronage and censorship suggest that it was taken seriously as an element in the construction of ideology. Criticism has traditionally regarded such matters as peripheral—the circumstances that the text transcends in order to justify its consideration as literature. It is the program of Greenblatt's "cultural anthropology" to reverse this tradition by attending precisely to the relationships between writing and the structures of power in society. So the Marlowe chapter begins with a contemporary account of the destruction of a village in Sierra Leone: "If, on returning to England in 1587, the merchant and his associates had gone to see the Lord Admiral's Men perform a new play, *Tamburlaine the Great,* they would have seen an extraordinary meditation on the roots of their own behaviour" (p. 194). And the demolition of Acrasia's bower is found to be related, in detail, to the destruction of Irish and North American Indian lives and cultures—to be based similarly on the exercise of power to achieve identity, the demonization of aliens and apostates, and the compulsion to smash seductive images that cannot be contained within dominant ideas of an ordered society. Greenblatt holds, following Geertz, that *The Faerie Queene* is "one manifestation of a symbolic language that is inscribed by history on the bodies of living beings" (p. 179).

Greenblatt's main focus is the predicament of the individual who strives to fashion his or her self in such a society. It seems that there is more than one possible emphasis to the book's title. Sir Thomas More had some scope for maneuver: he "was always aware of the tension that underlay the seemingly effortless performance, and the mingling of this tension with his evident delight makes his self-consciousness as a player both compelling and elusive" (p. 30). *Utopia,* Greenblatt argues, may be seen as "More's strategy of imagined self-cancellation" (p. 45)—the construction of a shame culture in which there is very little of the personal inwardness that was the ground of More's anxiety. More then knows what the problem is, he has a *modus vivendi* over which he has some control, he gains some pleasure from the necessary manipulations, and he is able to write a book that is the imaginary resolution of his real contradictions.

Other figures in *Renaissance Self-Fashioning* seem to have less autonomy. Wyatt "cannot fashion himself in opposition to power and the conventions power deploys; on the contrary, those conventions are precisely what constitute Wyatt's self-fashioning" (p. 120). Here Greenblatt develops, more definitely, the position of Foucault that the human subject "must be stripped of its creative role and analysed as a complex and variable function of discourse" (*Language, Counter-memory, Practice* [Oxford: Blackwell, 1977], p. 138). Even rebels, on this kind of analysis, can only reproduce the structure against which they would rebel, and this is what Greenblatt perceives in Marlowe's plays: "For the crucial issue is not man's power to disobey, but the characteristic modes of desire and fear produced by a given society, and the rebellious heroes never depart from those modes" (p. 209).

The concluding explanation of how Greenblatt began to write about autonomy but found instead the determinations of power is given in a little story, but of course the whole of *Renaissance Self-Fashioning* is his story in the way that he remarks of *The Faerie Queene*: "If Spenser told his readers a story, they listened, and listened with pleasure, because they themselves, in the shared life of their culture, were telling versions of that story again and again" (p. 179). An underlying theme of this book is the powerlessness and perhaps complicity of intellectuals in a repressive social structure. Behind the sixteenth-century colonialists' destruction of people and cultures, it is easy to see the shadow of Vietnam; violence resulting from the English colonization of Ireland is still with us. Greenblatt's Renaissance figures invite comparison with the range of identities that it is now possible to envisage for intellectuals. One may, like Spenser, co-operate with state ideology, or like More, one may cultivate a playful detachment. Like Tyndale and Marlowe, one may attempt resistance, although this will be futile if we are constructed within discourse to the point where even rebels afford "unwitting tributes to that social construction of identity against which they struggle" (p. 209).

The last, most limiting possibility must be entertained in relation to *Renaissance Self-Fashioning* itself: its own operation is liable to be contained within the structures it would criticize. In one way at least, this is what happens: for all Greenblatt's insistence upon the effects of power upon heretics, Indians, and the Irish, his focus is finally upon the states of mind of his group of relatively privileged writers. Thus his analysis may be not uncongenial to his likely readership, especially to the frustrated rebels, whom he slips into romanticizing when he writes of Marlowe and his characters facing "the tragic limitations of rebellion against this culture" (p. 209) and taking "courage from the absurdity of their enterprise" (p. 220). State power may seem less objectionable to some readers when it appears as the necessary tragic precondition for the existential-heroic intellectual.

Actually, there is something of all Greenblatt's sixteenth-century figures in his own enterprise—certainly the ludic More and also Tyndale, to whom I shall return—and Greenblatt is not trapped within the tragic Marlovian version of the story that he explores. But the sources of power do become somewhat blurred and dispersed in his book, and their scrutiny mainly through the psyches of individuals allows the reader to side-step some of the political implications. This is in large part a consequence of Greenblatt's use of Foucault. The idea, for instance, that "the ruler's social identity seems to be absorbed into his personal being," that the punishment of traitors is made especially brutal and protracted so that it shall "correspond fully to the incorporation of power in the body of the prince," and that this is connected with the use of sexuality in punishment (p. 140) is probably correct, and certainly Greenblatt uses it effectively in his discussion of Wyatt. But in seeking to go beyond mere empiricism, Greenblatt dangerously abstracts power from its specific political applications. Compare the allied but slightly different emphasis of British "cultural materialism," as represented by Raymond Williams's *The Country and the City* (London: Chatto & Windus, 1973). Greenblatt uses this too when he invites us to "remind ourselves that the estate to which the poet retreats from power is the reward for royal service and that the pleasant acres are swelled with confiscated monastic lands" (p. 132). But his more typical move is into the mind—for instance from the manipulative strategy by which Spanish colonialists exploited Indians and Elizabethan monarchy exploited religious symbolism to the interpersonal operation of such a strategy by Iago in *Othello*. The theoretical underpinning of this move is the perception of structural homology that characterizes anthropological criticism, and certainly it is justified by the quality of the resulting analysis of *Othello*. But by directing attention finally to an instance of personal relations, Greenblatt restores criticism and his intellectual readers to the realm where they feel safest and most effective, and the Indians may be forgotten.

The most frightening model in *Renaissance Self-Fashioning,* although not explicitly acknowledged as such, is More, for he may be loosely translated in modern terms as the liberal intellectual who becomes, in office, intolerant, vindictive, and oppressive. Greenblatt rather flinches from this rendering of More, for it emerges only gradually that even in *Utopia* More's position relied upon an underlying certainty of faith and that when this was radically challenged the questioning spirit was abruptly repudiated; and the fact that More was personally involved in the persecution of Protestants is left until the chapter on Tyndale. The sequence is familiar enough in modern institutions, not least universities; anyone taking on official responsibilities experiences pressures to sustain an imperfect system by suppressing challenges that seem to entail intolerable instability.

There is a straightforward radical in the book: Tyndale, with his undeviating commitment to publishing the Bible in the vernacular and his view of "the existing church as a conspiracy of the rich against the poor, the educated against the ignorant, the priestly caste against the laymen" (p. 113). We may discern Greenblatt here also, but somewhat regretful about the apparent absence of interiority in Tyndale, feeling that "More's life seems richer and fuller" (pp. 107, 109). Greenblatt speaks for many more than himself through his implicit preference for the early More, not yet forced by radical challenge into reaction and repression, able to sustain through playful detachment a certain autonomy, freedom from responsibility, and space within which to explore in writing the contradictions of contemporary power structures.

Tyndale is the one figure in the book who is shown to have been effective as a writer in the world: the effects of printing the Bible in English are convincingly analyzed. Elsewhere Greenblatt's concentration upon the ideological construction of the writer tends to obscure the extent to which his work was complicit in the maintenance of an unjust political system. Ideological factors are presented as feeding powerfully into the text, but it is less clear what comes out the other side. Spenser is credited with an understanding of the role of culture in sustaining hegemony and identified as questioning art "precisely to spare ideology" (pp. 187, 192). But although Shakespeare's relation to the oppressive structures disclosed in his work is acknowledged to be that of a "dutiful servant, content to improvise a part of his own within its orthodoxy" (p. 253), his language and themes are said to be caught up "in unsettling repetitions, committed to the shifting voices and audiences, with their shifting aesthetic assumptions and historical imperatives, that govern a living theatre" (p. 254). On that analysis we need not worry too much about what we write—it will all be subject to shifting assumptions and historical imperatives. Again, if, as is said of Marlowe's plays, attempts at rebellion "simply reverse the paradigms" (p. 209), then it all comes to the same thing. Yet Tyndale's career does suggest that writing can contribute to social change.

Greenblatt's hesitation over the role of literature in the production of ideology may be traced, speculatively, to two contradictory elements in the current constitution of intellectual life in the West. One is an assumption of powerlessness. In the United States especially, intellectuals have appeared to be important—when they were accused of un-American activities, when Kennedy drew them into the White House, during opposition to the Vietnam War. But that importance seems to have passed, perhaps to have been insubstantial. The idea that writing may help to make things happen is now difficult to sustain. Second, power entails responsibility: if the literary text is a story that is being told again and again in the culture (p. 179), then at least it can do no harm. We can concentrate on fashioning ourselves through the free play of the mind. This is, at any rate, one tendency that emerged in the 'seventies: "Where the word was, the pun shall be. The reality-reference of literature is subdued to intertextual allusions, omnivorous flowers of speech, metaphors, devices" (Geoffrey H. Hartman, *Saving the Text: Literature/Derrida/Philosophy* [Baltimore: Johns Hopkins University Press, 1981], p. 79).

If Greenblatt hesitated over the role of literature in the production of ideology in *Renaissance Self-Fashioning,* that was part of a complex, demanding, and immensely stimulating exploration of possibilities. His subsequent work has gone further towards identifying the terms within which resistance to Renaissance ideology could be thought, the possibilities of the presence of genuinely subversive elements, and the scope of containment. Moreover, he has addressed explicitly the role of sixteenth-century texts in current intellectual life, distinguishing between what may once have been subversive and what we do with it now: "we locate as 'subversive' in the past precisely those things that are *not* subversive to ourselves, that pose no threat to the order by which we live and allocate resources. . . . There is subversion, no end of subversion, only not for us" ("Invisible Bullets: Renaissance Authority and its Subversion," *Glyph,* 8 [1981], 52–53). Here is a challenge to intellectual complacency that will prove very hard to evade.

Renaissance Drama & the English Church Year, by R. Chris Hassel, Jr. Lincoln: University of Nebraska Press, 1979. Pp. ix + 216. $16.95.

Reviewer: ALICE-LYLE SCOUFOS

Some knowledge of sixteenth- and seventeenth-century English society and a modicum of common sense should have led us long ago to suspect that the secular entertainment given at the royal court on church holidays, during the period from 1510 to 1640, was related thematically to the holy days of the church calendar. But it is only with R. Chris Hassel, Jr.'s careful study *Renaissance Drama & the English Church Year* that such a suggestion has been turned into well-evidenced fact.

Armed with the basic information about dates of performance gathered in E. K. Chambers's *The Elizabethan Stage* and in G. E. Bentley's *The Jacobean and Caroline Stage,* Professor Hassel has examined a majority of the 560 dramatic works performed at court during this period and has found that almost 400 of the plays and masques have some thematic, narrative, and/or imagistic elements that correlate with the doctrinal ideas and images of the religious holidays. Choosing ninety-six works to analyze in detail, Hassel categorizes the correlation as extensive or moderate, slight or none. He has refined his study so that certain patterns emerge: seventy percent of all recorded court performances took place on the eleven traditional religious festivals. Hassel suggests that in many instances there is more than a recognizable adaptation of festival themes, that some of the plays "are repeatedly, intensely, and self-consciously redolent of those occasions" (p. 183). Although acknowledging the complexity of the secular works, the author points out that the Elizabethan and Jacobean audiences would have been familiar enough with the traditional characteristics of the religious festivals to recognize the religious themes and images in the secular presentations.

Among the numerous plays that were presented at court on Saint Stephen's Day (December 26), for example, are *Measure for Measure* (1604), *King Lear* (1606), *The Island Princess* (1621), and *The Duchess of Malfi* (1630). Noting that the Saint Stephen's Collect stresses, "Graunt us, O Lorde, to learne to love our enemies, by thexample of thy Martir sainct Stephen who praied for his persecutours," Hassel points out the applicability of that idea to *Measure for Measure* with its central theme of learning to love one's enemies. With even more precision he examines the strikingly apposite elements to be found in Beaumont and Fletcher's *The Island Princess* (pp. 25–27).

The records of the festival of Epiphany (January 6) are especially rich in evidence: it was the holiday most frequently graced by dramatic performances. Perhaps one good reason for this abundance of entertainment is that the central spirit of Epiphany (enlightenment, peace, concord) lies close to the central idea of Renaissance romantic comedy. This spirit also correlates closely with the idealistic subjects and images of numerous court masques. The discussion of Ben Jonson's masques, their "high aesthetic, political, moral, and even mystical seriousness," is an especially valuable section of the book (pp. 59–69).

The dichotomous characteristics of the Shrovetide plays and masques, entertainment that frequently concentrates upon the "Battle of Carnival and Lent," are investigated with care and perception, and Hassel concludes that the elaborate parallels with the Easter themes attest to a well-established tradition of festival entertainment at court. Indeed the author suggests that such a relationship may have been the genesis of the traditional antimasque-masque structure that dominated the seventeenth-century masques in the Jacobean court (p. 139).

I cannot give in this limited space an assessment of each play; let it suffice to say that the eleven festival days, Saint Stephen's, Saint John's (December 27), Holy Innocents' Day (December 28), New Year's Day, Twelfth Day (January 6), Candlemas (February 2), Shrovetide (Sunday, Monday, and Tuesday before Lent), Easter, Saint Bartholomew's Day (August 24), Michaelmas (September 29), and Hallowmas (November 1), together with their dominant festival themes, are carefully compared with the major themes and images developed in the plays and masques presented at the English court on those religious holidays. The growing body of evidence is convincing: many of the extensive liturgical parallels are so overt in the secular works that it is possible to say that many authors consciously selected their themes and developed characters to emphasize the scriptural and doctrinal messages associated with the festivals. Few readers of Chris Hassel's study today will disagree with his scholarly conclusions.

In addition to the overwhelming abundance of thematic, narrative, and imagistic parallels tabulated in this study, there are also some fascinating statistics on the
major authors of the day. The works of Shakespeare, Jonson, and Beaumont and
Fletcher dominate the list of plays and masques to an extraordinary degree. Of the
fourteen Shakespearean plays included in the listing, all have some correlation with
the festival themes and images, and ten of them contain extensive correlation.
Moreover, the "affinities are also usually more obvious and more profound than in
the other dramatists" (p. 180). Ben Jonson's twenty-four works on the list include
twelve with extensive correlation, and of Beaumont and Fletcher's eighteen works,
sixteen have at least slight correlation with the liturgical themes.

This study is important even for what it does not find: the plays of Tourneur,
Marston, and Ford are missing from the list. It would seem that these authors did
not embody in their art the festival spirit of the liturgical holidays; these dramatists
are "oblivious to that universe" (p. 183).

Finally, this study raises some pertinent questions: were the suppression of the
mystery cycle of liturgical plays and the rise of the new secular drama consciously
related occurrences? Perhaps even more fascinating: were the continental court
dramas of the Reformation designed upon similar patterns? Is there a closer relationship between the earlier French romantic dramas and the English "comedy of
forgiveness" than scholars have thought? These and other forward-looking studies
are suggested by Hassel's valuable research into the relationship between the English
church festivals and English Renaissance drama. It is easy to conclude that this
pertinent study of the Renaissance dramatic traditions will have a resounding impact
upon future literary studies in this area.

Milton's "Comus": Family Piece, by William B. Hunter, Jr. Troy, New
York: The Whitston Publishing Company, 1983. Pp. xvi + 101. $15.00.

Reviewer: PHILIP B. ROLLINSON

This little book is mandatory reading for all students of *Comus*. It collects a decade
of Professor Hunter's work (some previously published, some not) on the historical
and dramatic origins of the performance of *Comus*. Its approach then sharply differs
from the usual literary focus, and the results are most illuminating—giving convincing historical answers for Milton's emphasis on chastity and, through a sound examination of the probabilities of staging and performance, the best discussion I have seen
of the textual variants, particularly the transposed song ("From the Heavens now
I fly") of the Attendant Spirit.

The first chapter reviews "The Problem of *Comus*." The second investigates Milton's composition of *Arcades* and its historical occasion. Chapter Three examines the background of the Bridgewater family using Barbara Breasted's important article of 1971, "*Comus* and the Castlehaven Scandal" (Dissertation, Rutgers, 1970). Chapter Four discusses the family's relationship to Lawes and his role as the Attendant Spirit, and Five traces Milton's creation of the literary text in the context of all the information that Hunter has assembled. Chapter Six presents "A Tentative Promptbook for *Comus*"—text with a sensible introduction, which could be, and I hope will become, the basis of new performances. Finally, a brief appendix on "The Date and Occasion for *A Midsummer Night's Dream*" applies Hunter's method of dating *Arcades* in Chapter Two (matching apparent allusions to readings in the Prayer Book to their respective dates in the church year) to Shakespeare's play. The results are more convincing for *Arcades* than for *MND*, because the former case is simpler, more direct, and requires (in terms of Ockham's razor) fewer supporting hypotheses (see especially the middle paragraph of p. 97 on *MND*).

Ben Jonson: His Vision and His Art, by Alexander Leggatt. London: Methuen, 1981. Pp. xvi + 300. $35.00.

Reviewer: SCOTT COLLEY

Much critical writing about Ben Jonson brings to mind the story of the blind men who try to describe an elephant. Which part of this massive figure is the real Ben Jonson? Playwright, deviser of masques, poet, satirist, literary critic, classicist, lyricist, Jonson confounds critical attempts to simplify him. He is at once the determined know-it-all who declares confidently that comedy must chronicle "deeds and language such as men do use" and the insomniac who spent at least one night imagining the Romans and Carthaginians doing battle around his knobby great toe.

Alexander Leggatt accepts T. S. Eliot's contention of half-a-century ago that we need an "intelligent saturation" in Jonson's work "as a whole." In looking at the entire Jonson, Leggatt produces one of the best studies written to date about this enormous and rare figure. Tracing patterns, themes, and preoccupations throughout the prose works, poems, masques, and plays, Leggatt is able to describe the achievements of a poet who is not above self-contradiction but who labors always to respond honestly to what he recognizes as a complex and sometimes contradictory world.

To Leggatt, the rationalist Jonson is obsessed with the clash between ideals created in the imagination and the shocking reality of noise, filth, and corruption:

"The organizing mind admits the disorder around it, and seizes what victories it can. The struggle to live by high ideals is matched by a ruthless honesty about the world as it is; yet sometimes, in a small poem or casual gesture, we can see an ideal become reality" (p. 279). Leggatt's Jonson is not as morose and desperate as other portraits would have him. This Jonson does not deny the narcotic appeal of nonsense in the fallen world: Volpone's songs, Face's unending resourcefulness, and the puppets of *Bartholomew Fair* beckon those of us in the audience to share momentarily in the excitement of folly. And yet Jonson's steady moral sense warns us simultaneously of the deadness at the center of so many of his tricksters and rogues.

By reading in all of Jonson's works, one discovers alternate worlds to the brazen cosmos of the satires and comedies. Jonson affirms human potential and accomplishment in certain vivid and yet scattered moments. Where Spenser and Shakespeare seek "their great images of order in celebrations of love, marriage, and the family, Jonson turns more to the public institutions of society" (p. 74). Indeed Jonson's image of Penshurst is among his fullest realizations of a just, balanced society, a little world that more than matches the best achievements of Caesar Augustus' Rome. Penshurst is not merely an idealization of a society that functions well but is "based on reality that can be documented from other sources" (p. 112). Jonson feels it is in small things that one can measure the worth of the world: 'How a host treats his guests, what a man thinks of poetry, whether words are used as they ought to be" (p. 118). Jonson does not seek perfection from his world; he simply looks for true signs of civilization.

Some of his characters are not as flexible as Jonson himself in dealing with fallen humanity. Genuinely good and yet innocent characters have a hard time making their way through the snares and nets of life as it really exists. A key to Jonson's thoughts about innocence comes in the "Epode" (*The Forest,* XI) in which he declares:

> Not to know vice at all, and keepe true state
>   Is vertue, and not *Fate*:
> Next, to that vertue, is to know vice well,
>   And her blacke spight expell.

Celia and Bonario in *Volpone* have been thought of as ninnies and objects of Jonson's scorn, but Leggatt thinks of them as victims of a world that does not allow virtue to operate effectively. They are like the Germanican faction in *Sejanus* who can do nothing but "protest, retreat, or die" (p. 141). Jonson depicts "virtue adrift in a hostile world, made vulnerable and even laughable in its context, but not despicable in itself" (p. 140). Most figures of authority have a hard time of it in Jonson's works—the Avocatori in *Volpone* and Waspe and Busy in *Bartholomew Fair* come to mind—but some figures of authority and orthodoxy are treated with delicacy. Old Knowell in *Every Man in His Humour* and Justice Overdo in *Bartholomew Fair* are two. Indeed Overdo's discomfiture recalls Celia's, for both characters are decent persons who are ill prepared to function in a context that is more corrupt than they could ever have anticipated.

Leggatt's best chapter is "The Poet as Character," in which he deals with the tricky interplay of an author and his work. Raphael had painted himself in *The School of Athens*; a character named Chaucer told a minor story to the Canterbury pilgrims; and Milton portrayed an old blind poet in *Paradise Lost*. Of the English playwrights, only Shaw figured as importantly in his own plays, "and Shaw never matched the rich variety of uses to which Jonson put the device of self-portraiture" (p. 199). The Jonson who emerges from his poems and plays is not a single figure but one who fills a variety of roles. He is not there for the sake of vanity but appears so that he can engage with "the same problems as . . . the purely invented characters—the attempt to live by ideals when the world is fallen . . .; the tensions between retreat from the world and continued involvement with it; the dangers, responsibilities and delights of creation itself" (p. 215).

Jonson has a sense of humor about himself, twice joking about his brush with hanging (p. 200) and openly admitting his bad temper, his girth, his love of food and drink (pp. 201–204). Leggatt thinks that the playwright's candor about his weaknesses (and to be sure, his strengths) is a part of Jonson's full vision of the multiple possibilities for art and experience: "As each Jonson we meet is to some extent a mask, rather than the true man, so each declaration about art is a statement of an ideal, a possibility, rather than a literal description of what a particular play or poem actually achieves. . . . It is not that Jonson is uncertain how to handle his material; rather, he is determined to see as many of its possibilities as he can. Idea and achievement are at odds; but instead of undercutting each other, they combine to create a larger and more comprehensive vision" (p. 227).

Leggatt makes a recognizable elephant out of the blind men's several reports and does not deny the paradoxical appearance of the result. The separate Jonsons seem to exist and at any moment threaten to cancel one another: at any reading, we are less likely to saturate our minds with all of Jonson's poems, plays, masques, and prose works than to concentrate instead upon the single vision of experience that confronts us. Celia and Bonario, taken as we find them, do look like ninnies, and it is good to be reminded by Leggatt that they are something else as well. It is good also to be reminded that the Jonson who seems always too well organized, the satirist who forces ill-tasting medicine upon us for our own good, also possesses intermittent powers of enchantment. It was Wordsworth, Dorothy tells us, who, after dinner, read some of Jonson's short poems, "which were too *interesting* for him, and would not let him go to sleep" (quoted p. 279).

The Revels History of Drama in English, Volume IV, 1613–1660, by Philip Edwards, Gerald Eades Bentley, Kathleen McLuskie, and Lois Potter, General Editor. London and New York: Methuen, 1981. Pp. lvii + 337, including 32 illustrations. $53.00.

Reviewer: CATHERINE M. SHAW

"The theatre fell with the monarchy, and it returned with it in 1660; without this simple fact of dependence there can be no understanding of what happened to drama in the later years of James, the reign of Charles and the Interregnum" (p. 3). Although not all of the contributors to this volume (or its readers, for that matter) will agree wholeheartedly with the thesis expressed here, this straightforward statement by Philip Edwards in the introductory essay to the first part, "Society and the theatre," sets a pace and a direction for the other of its three sections and anticipates a unity for the work as a whole—at least more unity than has been apparent in other volumes in this series and, perhaps, as much as can be expected in such an undertaking. Indeed, because Edwards raises specific and provoking questions and then offers such good answers, his contribution, "Society and the theatre," is the most interesting series of essays to read as a group. Of necessity, some shifts must be made between subject divisions—from "The nobility and the drama" to "The managers of the public theatres" to "The dramatists" and so on—but the focus in each is consistently on the texture of the times: on the people who governed the age and its theater and those who were governed by them.

Gerald Eades Bentley's section, "The theatres and the actors," on the other hand, is interesting and valuable because it divides easily into units of time. What were the theatrical conditions during the years in which Fletcher was writing? No jumping about; here they are. 1613–1625: an essay on "Private and public theatres" for those years is followed by summaries of the activities of each of the acting companies—who managed it, where it played, who the patrons were, and so on—then the same for 1625–36, 1637–42, and, finally, a concluding essay on 1642–60. Here, in fifty pages, is a nutshell version of the same material found in Chapters One, Two, Six and part of Seven of *The Jacobean and Caroline Stage* that, although serving magnificently their function as sources for research and detailed knowledge, can be pretty daunting. Again Professor Bentley deserves the gratitude of every scholar working in the field. Nowhere is so much information encompassed by so few pages.

Both of these first sections are written with surety and in styles that would bear imitating. Unfortunately, Kathleen McLuskie has neither a strong thesis nor convenient time-breaks to ease her task in presenting coherently the complex mass of material in "The plays and the playwrights: 1613–1642," which takes up nearly half of the book. Only when she separates out particular topics that have self-imposed critical guidelines is there the sense that she is writing confidently and with a clear purpose. On specific dramatic techniques, for example, and a step-by-step development from Fletcher to Massinger to Ford to Davenant, even though she pauses for individual idiosyncrasies, the progression is clear and convincing. Terms like *traditional, imitative, exploitative,* or *innovative* are never used inflexibly. The same is true for her discussion of generic changes and fusions, which are also handled sequentially. What she sees as "restrictions imposed by Caroline decorum," on the other hand, are illustrated by comparison of an early play with a late one—*The Duchess of Malfi* with *The Cardinal*. She is not the first to set these plays off against each other, but they serve her purpose admirably, so why not?

Her claim that the "demands of decorum" led to a "triumph of romance over satire" (p. 257), however, is not convincing. Indeed, in order to make the statement, she must exclude "the most successful comedies" of James Shirley, the major playwright of Caroline England, because he, she admits, "abandons the troublesome fervour of romance" (p. 252). A number of the plays of Richard Brome, on the other hand, must be forced to fit a predetermined romantic pattern. *The Northern Lass* may be predominantly romance, but to say that the song sung by Constance the southern whore that ends,

> The snake beneath me stirred;
> And with his sting gave me a Clap,
> That swole my Belly not my lap,
> (*1632; 14$^{r.v}$*)

"has all the pathos of Ophelia's madness" (p. 240) is surely rather excessive. Professor McLuskie's reading of Brome's *The Jovial Crew* as romance sides with Pepys and Swinburne and ignores modern criticism completely. R. J. Kaufmann rightly calls the play "a social parable for the times—full of a weary disenchantment ..." (*Richard Brome, Caroline Dramatist* [New York: Columbia University Press, 1961], p. 170).

In the main, however, Professor McLuskie is more willing to accept social criticism in the drama of the time than she is political significance. For me, a distracting element in her discourse is what seems to be an antipathy toward anything that smacks of new historical criticism. In her first essay it might seem that she is not necessarily disagreeing with Edwards's statement on the inseparability of theater and monarchy but asking for a more moderate view. Connections, she says, between "the Laurel and the Crown" must be "considered with care." They "fell together because they were part of the same establishment" (p. 129). About a third of the essay, however, then seems to be given over to challenging Chapter Seven of Edwards's *Threshold of a Nation* (Cambridge: Cambridge University Press, 1979) either indirectly with comments such as "[*Believe as You List*] cannot really be described as a political play" (p. 131), or directly: "*Perkin Warbeck* has been associated with a 'deep current of hostility to Charles,' but such a specific political position is blurred by the romance values in the play" (p. 136–137).

Later, George Sensabaugh is taken to task for overrating Puritan antagonism to the courtly cult of platonic love. The cult, says Professor McLuskie, was "a further manifestation of [the court's] European outlook" (pp. 145–146). It seems to me that the "European outlook" of the Caroline court was very much a source of political and religious tension, and to acknowledge that would not negate the "common theme of a contrast between passionate love and pure love" that Professor McLuskie offers.

I support wholeheartedly Professor McLuskie's insistence upon the eclecticism of Jacobean and Caroline drama and her warnings against unilateral critical approaches such as excessive politicizing of the drama at the expense of the plays themselves. I also sympathize with the problem of organizing even representative plays and playwrights to encompass that eclecticism. I do suggest, however, that too often a reaction against overrating political significance has led to underrating it.

In the last section of this book, Lois Potter has put together a very readable group of essays on "The plays and the playwrights: 1642–60," and, perhaps because her part is short, Professor Potter is more successful in integrating political significance with literary history. Particularly valuable, I think, is the essay "Towards a 'reformed' stage," which rounds out the book.

Regretfully, I must now come to errors in this volume, technical and substantive. Were this the Renaissance, the first could be blamed on an unidentified scribe; in modern times, the onus for all errors falls on the General Editor. After I had noted three or four, I contemplated making a thorough check, but time was against it. So I list just these and suggest a thorough proofing should a second printing be contemplated. P. xxx: the death of Gustavus Adolphus at Lützen was in 1632, not 1630; p. 156: Heywood's *Love's Mistress* is misdated 1632 in the text, but correctly dated 1634 in the Chronology Table; p. 161: Brome's *The Lovesick Court* is dated according to Kaufmann's guess 1633–34 in the text and 1639 in the Table; p. 181: *The Lovers' Progress* (1634), accepted as a thorough rewrite by Massinger of an earlier and lost play "The Wandering Lovers" (Fletcher, 1623), is discussed in the text under its later and published title but appears in the Table under the earlier title and date; p. 186, l.1: for *solider* read *soldier;* l.35: for Memnon's *friend* read *brother;* p. 187: for Fletcher's *The Chances,* 1613–1623 is the date suggested in the text, 1625 in the Table; p. 200: for Cleora's *lover* read *former suitor;* p. 204: l.17 has been omitted completely and l.22 repeated in its place; p. 273: for *Faithful Shepherdess* read *Banished Shepherdess* (the Index also needs correcting); *passim* is the quixotic spelling *never the less,* of which the *OED* (5b) says "Now *rare* or *Obs.*" Also *passim* is an annoying lack of indication whether a play date is of composition, licensing, performance, or publication.

Puritans and Libertines: Anglo-French Literary Relations in the Reformation, by Hugh M. Richmond. Berkeley: University of California Press, 1981. Pp. 401. $27.50.

Reviewer: WILLIAM EDINGER

Professor Richmond has written a revisionist history of Anglo-French literary relations in the sixteenth and earlier seventeenth centuries—a history that purports to reflect contemporary tastes and interests. Earlier histories of the subject naturally reflected the tastes and interests of their times. For Sidney Lee the Italian influence was paramount, whether transmitted to England directly or through the French; in his *French Renaissance in England,* Petrarch and the sonnet receive a heavy emphasis. For Lee, the importance of the Pléiade is guaranteed by Spenser; when Lee thinks of "an early great work" of the Elizabethan era, he thinks of *The Shepheardes Calender.* Holding no brief for the poetic merit of Du Bartas, he chronicles at length the Huguenot poet's vogue in England merely because it happened; but the period's libertinism, which also happened, is, when mentioned at all, touched lightly, with euphemistic discretion. Lee's Marot is for the most part a cheerful *naif,* a follower of Villon, a maker of *rondeaux,* more medieval than modern. His Ronsard is, like Saintsbury's, a neoclassicist, a theorist of poetry, an advocate of noticeably poetic diction, a sonneteer. Through all this we glimpse a taste formed in the Victorian era—when Lee does praise Du Bartas, he compares him to Victor Hugo. This taste survived in academic circles long after the best twentieth-century poet-critics (Eliot, Tate, Winters, *et al.*), rejecting it, had thoroughly revaluated sixteenth-century literature: one remembers C. S. Lewis's division of English poetic styles into the "drab" and the "golden."

Professor Richmond's revaluation is more up-to-date than that of the poet-critics. The ruling categories of his approach are Sex, Self, and the Reformation. The book's ruling notion is, roughly, that the Reformation vastly complicated thinking about Sex and Self by challenging Catholic moral and social orthodoxy. Luther's heterodox views on sex, marriage, and human nature called everything connected with these subjects (and they do not leave much out) newly into question, with the result that the wittier and more sophisticated minds of the time—including those who officially rejected Lutheranism, like Marguerite of Navarre—were prompted to examine moral experience with a new subtlety, curiosity, and open-mindedness. They found it, accordingly, more varied, complicated, ambiguous, and fuller of opportunity than Medieval and Catholic tradition, and the literature built on this tradition, were capable of allowing. Professor Richmond suggests that we may find in these sixteenth-century developments the beginnings of such current literary and social preoccupations as pluralism, individualism, and feminism, as well as that old stand-by, the unpredictability and incomprehensibility of human nature.

The literary history that these topics bring into focus certainly differs from Sidney Lee's. Libertinism—sexual and intellectual, in life and in letters—becomes fundamental; Marot, Marguerite (as author of the *Heptameron*), and Ronsard are now prized as sensibilities on which the new influences left a vivid mark and as cultural and literary explorers whose writing anticipates and helps to explain a variety of manifestations normally associated with the later Renaissance, indeed with the "counter-Renaissance" of Hiram Haydn. Sidney, Spenser, the sonneteers (excepting Shakespeare) are largely beside the point; of Renaissance golden worlds we hear nothing. Brazenness is everywhere. Professor Richmond's touchstones are Montaigne, Théophile, the "feminist" Shakespeare (creator of Portia, Rosalind, the masked ladies of *Love's Labor's Lost,* Cleopatra), the "dark" Shakespeare (of *Measure for Measure,* the late sonnets, and the corrupt sexuality of Iago's Venice), Jonson, the libertine Donne, Marvell, and, somewhat incidentally, Milton. The Marot who looks forward to these later figures is not a cheerful *Villonard* but a full-fledged Renaissance individualist, writing about his personality, tastes, and moods in great detail, keeping a proud distance from orthodoxies Lutheran and Catholic, in trouble with the authorities and with the difficult brunettes whom he prefers to bland Petrarchan blondes and whom he celebrates to inaugurate the Dark Lady tradition. Richmond's Ronsard is not a neoclassicist or elaborate stylist or even sonneteer but a master of the plain style (who remarkably anticipates Jonson), a pagan in temperament, a lover of French (not classical) gardens and fields, and a varied and subtle self-analyst and psychologist of love whose metaphysically tinged love poems look toward Donne's. His Marguerite is a pluralist, relativist, pragmatist, opportunist, feminist, and a good deal more. She is in some ways the book's central figure, inasmuch as the author, insisting upon a quite direct connection between art and life, sees in the courts of Marguerite and her brother Francis I workshops of the new feminism and new morality (or licentiousness) from which descended a long line of Dark Ladies destined to exercise and alter the feelings and the art of (male) poets from Wyatt and Marot to Donne and Shakespeare.

This is undoubtedly one tradition in sixteenth-century letters rather than *the* tradition, as Professor Richmond, believing as he does in the irresistible appeal of Renaissance libertinism to our modern sensibilities, sometimes seems to think, but it is undeniably interesting. To show us the life that influenced the art, Richmond is lavish with good gossip. We are told once more about Anne Boleyn, King Henry, and Wyatt; about an attempted rape on Queen Marguerite as elaborately plotted as one of her own *Heptameron* stories (and about the hapless would-be perpetrator, one Guillaume Gouffier de Bonnivet, whom Francis I once nearly caught in bed with one of his own mistresses and who, hiding behind a screen while the King took his place and his pleasure, was—inadvertently?—pissed on by his sovereign as the latter left the chamber); about the beautiful bosoms and bare-breasted fashions of the Valois courts; and about the naked dinner-parties and outrageous sexual politics of Catherine de Medici's *escadron volant*.

Less stimulating, but no less rewarding to contemplate, are many of the passages from the French poets that Richmond gives to show the range, variety, and sophistication of their times and also to suggest their influence upon British writing. The book is lavish with quotation and offers almost an anthology of Marot and Ronsard in particular; it ought to motivate many graduate students and others to know these poets better. Some of the quotations are worth having in the book simply for their own wit or beauty; many usefully document the author's contention that the French had developed attitudes, tones, and styles in the treatment of religion, love, and sex that English poets would approximate only decades later, almost certainly with the help of French examples; some offer striking analogues to particular English poems. It is interesting to be shown Ronsard's repeated use of *ombrages verts* and *pensers verts* in light of Marvell (especially since Ruth Wallerstein found quite different analogues); it is even more interesting to discover in Ronsard a mastery of the Horatian *sermo pedestris* and, in a poem in praise of his priory at St. Cosme, details so close to those in the opening lines of "To Penshurst" that one must wonder about a specific indebtedness on Jonson's part. Perhaps the widely accepted view that Jonson's own plain style is based almost entirely on Roman models needs some qualification. Other readers will no doubt be struck by other instances of this kind; the book may well prompt a number of more specialized inquiries.

Richmond is thoroughly familiar with the French writers whom he chooses to emphasize, and his knowledge of English poetry from Wyatt to Milton (including Shakespeare's plays as well as his poems) is both wide and detailed. The book sustains the impression that no analogue or parallel between the French and the English writers has escaped his notice—he is sensitive indeed to the remotest possibility of parallelism. Yet his book is on the whole unsatisfactory. I will try to explain why.

Conceptually, the book is very loose. Richmond's thesis—that the Reformation produced a social and moral upheaval which led, in literature and in life, to the development of individualism, libertinism, skepticism, and a deepening awareness of human complexity, first in France, then through French influence, in England—is merely asserted, not argued or explored. Since at face value the thesis may seem a massive commonplace—it is rather like saying that nineteenth-century English literature was affected by the Industrial Revolution—careful discussion is necessary. Richmond's citations of other scholarship on this subject are scanty and insufficient. But no amount of such citation would suffice: the coherence of his book demanded that Richmond makes his own case, at least to the extent of linking his explanatory generalizations to the particulars that they are supposed to illuminate (and vice versa); and such coherence would require a good deal more in the way of definition, clarification of premises, and discovery of middle terms than he is willing to provide. As it is, we are offered a small handful of very abstract explanations and a great many social and literary particulars. Presumably the particulars are examples; but it is often unclear what they exemplify.

Richmond's Reformation hypothesis, unsupported as it is, raises more questions than it answers. Are Renaissance individualism, libertinism, and so on primarily responses to Protestantism? Are there not sufficient sources of these phenomena in European Catholic traditions? Richmond almost wholly avoids the question of Italian literary influence, and he tends to treat Catholic social and even literary traditions as though they were on the whole old-fashioned and rather strait-laced—epitomized by Catherine of Aragon, say, rather than by the Rome of Leo X. And he sees the modernity of Marot and Marguerite as part and parcel of their sympathy for *Luthérisme*, so that the book's early chapters give the impression that Catholics are moral and literary conservatives and that any deviation toward attitudes characteristic of the later Renaissance will reveal Protestantism somewhere in the background. Yet Marguerite's acknowledged master in the *Heptameron* is Boccaccio, and we must wonder whether her alleged modernity really represents any sort of advance over the pluralism, pragmatism, libertinism, and the like of the fourteenth-century Italian. When we come to Ronsard, we are faced with an at least nominal Catholic and political conservative who is, morally and literarily, as up-to-date as anyone could wish; and it is now his Huguenot detractors who resemble Catherine of Aragon (or as Richmond suggests, Coriolanus) in their strict and reactionary moralism (p. 83). Some Huguenot sympathizers are libertine, others conservative; some Catholic writers are libertine, others conservative. What can be concluded from this diversity? Obviously, the Reformation had an impact upon Ronsard insofar as he became involved in its religious and political controversies on behalf of his king; but why should we suppose that the formation of Ronsard's art or temperament is more indebted to the presence of the Reformation in his background than to the many influences that we group under the term Renaissance Humanism, which were surely sufficient to produce him had the Reformation never occurred? Careful explanation is needed, here as elsewhere, when Richmond brings in the Reformation and its train of social disruptions as an all-purpose cause; but none is provided.

Sometimes the generalizing is not merely unsupported but careless. In the opening statement of the thesis Richmond remarks, "It is the contention of this study that while much remained to develop of our modern literary attitudes after this period, decisive steps were taken in providing psychological models for a more self-aware, integrated, and socially consistent type of personality" (pp. 1–2). Later on, however, we are told more than once that the influence of Protestant thinking typically appears in the "drastic human inconsistency [that] is a distinctive attribute of Shakespearean characterization"—an inconsistency that reflects "the stress of such Reformation theologians as Luther and Calvin on human fallibility and the abrupt compensating effects of heavenly grace" (p. 83). Richmond explains that several features of Shakespearean plotting and characterization which may seem improbable when judged by either a modern or a strict Aristotelian standard become acceptable once we realize that they are affected by Protestant notions of Providence and original sin (pp. 83, 126, and elsewhere). Richmond's second formulation doubtless does apply to parts of Shakespeare—one thinks of Leontes, Angelo, and, as Richmond suggests, of the sometimes offensive reconciliation of such vicious characters in *The Winter's Tale, Measure for Measure, All's Well,* and other plays. But what of the first statement? Who represents the "integrated, and socially consistent type of personality"? Presumably not Angelo. The dominant literary personalities of the book—Marot, Marguerite, Ronsard, Montaigne, the Shakespeare of the sonnets, Donne, Marvell—put one in mind of Whitman's "I am large, I contain multitudes" as a motto to which all might have subscribed. Perhaps their inconsistencies are integrated and, *au fond,* socially consistent; who knows? Richmond's generalizations are haphazard and do not lead to any clear overview of his material.

There is also a question of literary judgment. In the chapter on Marot, Richmond cites Ian McFarlane's warning that "we must not confuse literary archeology with critical appreciation," but in spite of this good advice, Richmond goes on, in his chapter on Wyatt, to confuse the question of Wyatt's relation to the more socially and morally "advanced" Marot with the question of Wyatt's poetic quality. Richmond seeks to determine "why Wyatt unexpectedly failed to do full justice to French literary models of his time" (p. 93), and this failure turns out to be artistic as well as (presumably) social and moral, inasmuch as, throughout the Wyatt chapter, Richmond treats Marot's more flexible and "sophisticated" attitudes toward love and sex as a standard that Wyatt should have met but for the most part failed to. Richmond is of two minds about Wyatt and admits that his morally severe and more conservative love poems have, at their best, more depth and "tragic force" than Marot's (pp. 167, 174). Yet he gives most of these poems short shrift, dismissing the fine "Farewell, Love" as "largely inaccessible to modern sympathy" (p. 160), construing "Blame not my lute" as "puritan" (Richmond does not mention Douglas Peterson's valuable analysis of Wyatt's love poems in terms of the moral psychology of Aquinas), and ignoring others (for example, "It was my choice, it was no chance") whose originality and sophistication of moral and psychological treatment should have won them a prominent place in Richmond's chapter. On the other hand, Richmond gives undue attention to demonstrably inferior poems whenever they seem to flirt with Marotic attitudes (see pp. 171–174). Throughout the chapter we sense the assumption that being up-to-date is a *sine qua non* of literary merit. But this has never been true. Wyatt's strict and rational approach to love and constancy was conservative then as it is now and probably seemed as unrealistic to his contemporaries as it does to many of us; but it is neither quaint nor obsolete: Corneille made similar attitudes the subject of his *La Place Royale* (1637), and in our own time they have been restated with a dignity and power approaching Wyatt's by de Rougemont and by J. V. Cunningham. However forbidding as a solution, Wyatt's characteristic position in matters of love clarifies permanent problems and brings universal values into play; to measure him either by a merely historical standard (here "up-to-dateness") or by any (necessarily uncertain) notion of what is pleasing to modern taste is to obscure his achievement.

Finally, there is the question of the book's overall method. Richmond explains, drawing again upon Ian McFarlane for support, that he is not interested in old-fashioned source-and-analogue hunting; indeed the narrow "study of demonstrable sources can be deeply misleading," since a Renaissance poet's specific verbal or technical indebtedness in particular works may tell us much less about him than his relation to a much deeper and broader *fonds commun* of religious, moral, social, and philosophical presuppositions which he shares with many other writers in the traditions that he is exploring (pp. 96–97). So stated, this position is unexceptionable, though commonplace; all literature can profitably be studied in this way, regardless of period. In practice, unfortunately, Richmond takes this cultural approach to warrant analogue- and parallel-seeking of the most abandoned sort. He does not, to be sure, limit himself to the identification of specific borrowings; he does not limit himself at all. Richmond's book is long; and by far the greater part of it is generated by the author's gift, when confronting a particular French text, for being reminded of English texts with a similar bearing. This is a real talent, and I have indicated earlier that it produces some suggestive and close parallels. But Richmond typically employs it—apparently in the name of mapping the *fonds commun*—without regard either to the probability of specific indebtedness (this would be old-fashioned) or to the opportunity that his parallels might provide for sustained discussion of the concepts, attitudes, or values on which his poets might be drawing. The multiplication of parallels becomes an end in itself; and many of the parallels are farfetched. Thus when Ronsard writes, "Il faut suivre par tout nostre vocation," we are reminded that Falstaff tells the Prince: "Why, Hal, 'tis my vocation, Hal. 'Tis no sin for a man to labor in his vocation" (pp. 187–188). A French lament for France devastated by religious wars puts Richmond in mind of the King's opening speech in *1 Henry IV*, then of John of Gaunt's lament for the passing of the old England in *Richard II*, then of a passage in which Marvell echoes Gaunt, then of Ulysses' speech on order and degree, then of Burgundy's lament for the devastated France of *Henry V*, and finally, by this sort of free association, of another French poem in which Lucifer engenders Atheism on Lady Pride, which brings in Milton's allegory of Sin and Death in *Paradise Lost*! All this to show that many writers shared anxieties about the "shattering of complex Renaissance social structures" and that "the allegories and interpretations of such Huguenot poets afford important precedents for parts of Spenser's and Milton's more artificially ambitious enterprises" (pp. 189–196).

Richmond makes much of the fact that the sentiment, "Happy is he who can do harm and does it not," occurs twice in the *Heptameron*; here, he ventures, is a specific source for Shakespeare's Sonnet 94—"They that have power to hurt and will do none" (pp. 59–62). This is one of the few times when Richmond speaks of a specific indebtedness. But what an odd example! Surely the sentiment that Shakespeare shares with Marguerite is universal: I can think of places where it occurs in writers as far apart as Juvenal and Tolstoy; and there must be dozens of others. There is no mapping such a *fonds commun*—it is boundless. In the *Preface to Shakespeare* Samuel Johnson jokes about the analogue-hunters of his day, recalling the Shakespeare scholar who thought that "Go before, I'll follow" was lifted from Seneca's *I prae, sequar*. Many of Richmond's parallels are only a little less extreme.

These licenses result from the above-mentioned lack of conceptual rigor: having no thesis to argue, no definite purpose to help focus his discussions, Richmond becomes merely the collector, not the interpreter, of the passages that he ranges so widely to find. Such collections have a long history, but the traditional place for them has been the lexicon, thesaurus, or annotated edition, where they are offered sometimes as curiosities, sometimes as the raw material of future research. Richmond's book has value—perhaps, over time, considerable value—as a kind of thesaurus of the Anglo-French "brazen Renaissance." But, read in the hope of something more, it is frustrating and fatiguing.

The Division of the Kingdoms: Shakespeare's Two Versions of "*King Lear*," edited by Gary Taylor and Michael Warren. *Oxford Shakespeare Studies*. Oxford: Clarendon Press, 1983. Pp. xiii + 489. $67.00.

Reviewer: GEORGE WALTON WILLIAMS

At the Congress of the International Shakespeare Association in 1976, Michael Warren read a paper entitled "Quarto and Folio *King Lear* . . ." in which he advanced the thesis that the two substantive printed texts of the play-book represent two versions of the stage play substantively different in artistic conception and in final dramatic effect and that the editorial conflation of the two into one produces a version that never was. Other scholars took their stand beside him four years later at the meeting of the Shakespeare Association of America. The electricity of that session, chaired by G. B. Evans, has charged the volume under review, for eight of the eleven authors included here were present there.

   In consequence, the volume proceeds on the assumption that the hypothesis of separate texts has validity. Most of the contributors do not seek to prove that hypothesis true—though they take pleasure in pointing to details that would strengthen such a proof; they concentrate rather on the characteristics observable from the separation of the texts—the division of the kingdoms. It is probable that the hypothesis is finally not provable, that no amount of brilliance in criticism can create certainty. In that state, the hypothesis is like the hypothesis advanced for the identification of Shakespeare's hand in "The Book of Sir Thomas More." Those who wish to believe either hypothesis will do so; those who do not will not. Perhaps time will tell: one day the believers may outnumber the unbelievers (of either hypothesis), though we well know that democratic action does not automatically by its nature find out truth.

   That *King Lear* may have existed in two different shapes cannot surprise:

examples gross as earth exhort us. Stanley Wells's introductory article in this volume cites analogues in Wordsworth's *Prelude* and in Wilde's *Importance of Being Earnest*. Other examples are readily available. Beckett's versions of *Endgame* vary with his productions of it, and Stoppard boasts of the changes he makes to accommodate English texts to American or Australian audiences. The problems are, then, not that there may have been two versions of the play but (a) that those two versions should have been preserved in two different texts separated by fifteen years in their printing (and yet inexplicably connected) and (b) that modern editions should attempt to conflate the two separate versions into one. The tradition of this conflation is here set out by Steven Urkowitz in his article on "The Growth of an Editorial Tradition." Pope was the first editor to combine the two texts in a single edition, and since his time all editors have followed his lead. As a result, present texts give us all that Shakespeare wrote under the general heading of "King Lear," but not necessarily all that should be read or produced at one time or accepted as a complete or integrated version.

The identical problem confronts those who would prepare a text of Handel's *Messiah*. It is well known that Handel from 1742 to 1759 directed many different performances of his *Messiah*, constantly varying, rewriting, transposing, and adapting the work to meet the needs and requirements of "the varying circumstances of the many performances"—notably, the demands of his soloists. The result is a large number of alternative versions, all "ratified by Handel's own performance." Modern directors in shaping a specific performance tend to draw variously from the many texts available, providing no doubt " 'the best of *Messiah*,' " but in the process creating a version "that Handel himself never heard." The danger of this approach is that "by a process of cutting and substitution we can completely change the shape of a work that Handel calculated with impressive accuracy each time he recreated it."[1]

The hypothesis to be proved, then, is simply this: did Shakespeare calculate with impressive accuracy each of the versions of *King Lear* that lie behind the two extant printed texts? The answer of this review is affirmative. Though difficulties, improbabilities, and implausibilities underlie that acceptance, the coherence of the arguments that have been advanced in earlier studies and by those presented here is persuasive.

Randall McLeod in "*Gon*. No more, the text is foolish"—a title as accurate as it is gamesome—attacks the conflated text as it bears on the characters of Quarto Gonorill and Folio Gonerill. Beginning as far as possible with an unbiased mind, McLeod analyzes the variants between the roles from the beginning to the end. After discussing several variants in the opening scene and recording the "thematic consistency" of each character to her version he observes: "if, as we proceed [through the play]..., we find more and more thematic consistency..., we will naturally decrease our suspicion of accidents and agents of transmission, and have to speculate in earnest about purposeful differentiation of Q and F" (p. 167). As he proceeds, he finds more and more (pp. 171–172), a discovery that will not amaze; but the impartial critic must acknowledge that each character has her own integrity in her own text and that the two consistencies cannot be the results of random or cloudy chance or of the vagaries of theatrical or compositorial tinkerings. "F offers a vision of somewhat greater moral ambiguity than does Q" (p. 171); "through its first two acts, F seems to retard both the coming of our convictions of Gonerill's evil, and . . . the cry of indignation against her; but Q speeds both along" (p. 185); in Acts Four and Five, the Folio Gonerill is "ever more self-possessed than her Quarto counterpart" (p. 185).

McLeod's primary interest seems to be in showing that the two characterizations of Goneril, differing from text to text, are coherent and consistent each to its own text. Other contributors seem to stress, rather, the differences in characterizations between the two texts and the effect of those differences on the perceptions that audiences and readers take from the two versions.

Michael Warren, extending his earlier studies on the realignment of Albany and Edgar that is visible in a comparison of the two prints, notices in "The Diminution of Kent" from Quarto to Folio a movement consistent with the increased vigor and prominence of Edgar in the Folio: "Kent's behavior [is] played down, to emphasize Edgar's triumph" (p. 70). As ancillary to that change, John Kerrigan in "Revision . . . and the Fool . . ." finds the role of the Fool in the Folio "more shapely overall [than in the Quarto version, and the addition of the Fool's final and enigmatic line in the Folio provides a] conclusion . . . clearly and movingly motivated. Moreover, the F Fool overlaps with Edgar and Lear much less than does [his counterpart in] the Q" (p. 230).

For the part of Lear, Thomas Clayton contributes "Revision in the Role of the King." Clayton examines the variation between the two texts, calling attention particularly to two passages absent in Quarto, present in Folio: I.i.49–50 "(Since now we will divest us both of Rule . . . State)" and III.iv.108–109 "Come, unbutton heere." Though Quarto contains at both these situations the imagery of clothing—"I doe invest you" (I.i.132) and "off off you lendings" (III.iv.108)—it is clear that both these extra Folio phrases lead directly to the conclusion (in both texts), "Pray you undo this button" (V.iii.310), with greater exactness and force than do their Quarto "equivalents." Investing someone else is not the same as divesting oneself, and as Clayton points out, the divesting in the Folio leads precisely to the unbuttoning of Act Three (not merely a sharper image than "lendings") and that in turn leads to the final unbuttoning of Act Five. The first unbuttoning is "a symbolic divesting associated with becoming painfully and self-knowledgeably human"; the final one is "the ultimate divesting—death and disembodiment" (p. 128).[2] These citations are not unknown to scholars, but scholars have not known to see them in the context of two versions in which the Folio suggests a coherence and integrity particularly resonant.

In concentrating upon Lear's final unbuttoning and his death, Clayton draws parallels from the comparable *pieta* of the Talbots, father and child, in *1 Henry VI* (IV.vii.17–32), and from the death scene of Cleopatra in *Antony and Cleopatra*

(V.ii.283–313). Against the thesis of conception and revision Clayton enlarges upon these parallels brilliantly as he presents the different views of Lear's death that the two versions give. He concludes this section of his argument by facing squarely the presumed anticipation of Lear's death in Gloucester's. The absence from the Folio of lines 215–219 gives "special prominence to the 'burst[ing] smilingly' of Gloucester's heart [line 200]," precipitates "the movement from Gloucester's death to Lear's and explicitly prepare[s] for it. . . . it is undeniable that the final show of lightening at Lear's death, however interpreted, in the Folio [is] closer to Gloucester's" (p. 137).[3] The absence of these lines enforces the parallel between Gloucester and Lear which is as vital in their death throes as it has been throughout the play.

One is tempted to say—at least in these instances—that the Folio's readings are superior to the Quarto's. Such superiority would customarily suggest that the Folio is the revised and later text. It is a curious omission in this volume, however, that the question of the sequence of the two texts is nowhere seriously considered. (The fact that Quarto precedes Folio in print does not necessitate that it should have preceded it in composition.) But the authors of the essays take it as a given of their hypothesis that because the Folio is superior, it is the later text, yet they acknowledge that in the sweep of English literature revised versions not infrequently seem inferior to their originals. *The Prelude* (1805/1850) comes again to mind, as does now "La belle dame sans merci" (1819/1820).[4] *The Importance of Being Earnest* is perhaps a useful exception: a production of the original four-act version evokes a reaction very different indeed from that of the three-act version. The question of relative merit may not, however, be appropriate. It is clear that Wilde is attempting to communicate in the two versions two different visions of life. The same is true of *King Lear*. G. B. Evans thinks that neither version of Shakespeare's play "can really stand on its own" as a complete and comprehensible text; for him some conflation is essential.[5] Other critics wish to see for themselves; not all the loss from the Quarto is gain. Stanley Wells indicates some passages present in Quarto but omitted in Folio—"the Gentleman's description of Cordelia's grief at her father's plight . . ., the compassion of Gloucester's servants after his blinding . . ., and Lear's mock trial" (pp. 18–19). Two productions of the Folio version have been staged in the last two years, of which one added material from the Quarto, one did not. Criticism soundly based on theatrical experience and editorial acumen will bring us nearer than ever before to Shakespeare's craft and art.

The contributors to the volume are satisfied that the revising hand was Shakespeare's and that the date of the revision was 1609–10 (p. 353).[6] This date immediately suggests the move into the Blackfriars as the provocative act that called forth the revision. One critic finds that suggestion provoking rather than provocative, considering it "charmless";[7] he may well be thinking of the unfortunate improvements that that displacement produced in, for example, *Macbeth*. (In 1978 the Olivier Theatre, not to be outdone by the Blackfriars across the river, served up Hecate on a fork lift.)

One may well wonder why a revision was necessary or advisable; maximum effort for minimum effect, it might seem.[8] The answer is perhaps now available. There is one characteristic of the move into the Blackfriars which if not beneficial (or charming) does explain the need for revision and, in fact, the kind of revision found in the Folio text. That is the decision to reshape old plays that had been written without intervals for the public theater into new plays with the five-act intervals that had been fashionable at the private theater.[9] While Shakespeare was still with the company, the players would, "no doubt," have turned first to him to divide his own plays. Such a request would have sent him back to his original copies (or to the Quarto) and would have necessitated a re-creation—a fresh artistic shaping—marked, we may well suppose, by an accuracy as impressive as that of the original conception. MacD. P. Jackson in "Fluctuating Variation: Author, Annotator, or Actor" argues persuasively that the changes between the Quarto and the Folio are precisely those we should expect in a revision necessitated by theatrical demands: "Authors . . . are understandably solicitous about the least nuances of beginnings and endings . . . [and dramatists about the obligation] to set a train of events in motion and bring them to a conclusion. . . . The first and last scenes of . . . *King Lear* [are] among the most variant" (p. 330). "Act Four, the most heavily cut act, is also the act to which least has been added, and this is precisely the point in any play where audience attention is likely to sag if the tempo drops" (p. 331). Close to that point is Act Three, scene six, which features the "mock trial." Roger Warren discusses "The Folio Omission of the Mock Trial," termed by Gary Taylor "the Folio's most surprising cut" (p. 89), and argues that though the scene can be played well, more often than not in actual performance effectiveness here in presenting the theme of madness will decrease the effectiveness of the later scene, IV.vi, Lear's "most extended scene of madness." "Shakespeare could have decided to eliminate the less successful treatment of mock-justice in its dramatically weaker position in 3.6 in order to guarantee it maximum impact by concentrating it all in one place in 4.6, at the same time intensifying its effect . . . by making various additions to it there" (pp. 49–50).

Cutting in this part of the play includes the passage already cited—"the compassion of Gloucester's servants after his blinding." But the loss of their compassion at the close of III.vii is not so serious as is the absence of reassurance given by the sudden entrance of Edgar, IV.i.1, a juxtaposition that the present reviewer has long regarded as one of the crucial situations in the play.[10] He is restrained from sympathizing with the remark of a scholar—"If Shakespeare cut the dialogue of the servants . . ., the less Shakespeare he" (p. 450)—only by accepting the theatrical necessity to concentrate the play at this point—the point where the new interval between Acts Three and Four would fall. As the insertion of the interval would nullify the effect of juxtaposing Edgar's appearance and the compassion of the servants, the dramatic utility of the dialogue would be reduced.

Another aspect of the variants between the texts that should encourage acceptance of the hypothesis of revision has been observed by E. A. J. Honigmann in an independent study of the Q and F texts of *Othello* (1622, 1623) in which he argues that the Folio *Othello* is a revision of the Quarto. He draws, of course, a parallel with

King Lear, but that parallel is much closer than he had expected it to be or that chance would afford. In both plays "metre, grammar or textual dislocations" indicate that passages unique to the Folio are later additions (not merely omissions from the Quarto); in both plays "strategies of revision . . . strengthen the play" in characterization and in plotting; in both plays the additions sharpen the morality; in both plays the variants consist of short passages scattered throughout the play. "The fact that Shakespeare is thought to have re-touched not one but two of his greatest tragedies, and to have strengthened both in similar (and unusual) ways, makes the 'revision theory' more compelling."[11]

Two essays in the volume examine the behavior of the compositors of the texts. Beth Goldring offers a small detail in *"Cor.'s* Rescue of Kent" that suggests the complexities that constitute the problem. At I.i.162 and 188 she notices "two seemingly minor changes [between Q and F] . . . concerning the use of the *Cor.* prefix" (p. 143). At line 188 Folio has *"Alb. Cor.* Deare Sir forbeare"; Quarto has no comparable line. Modern editions give the dialogue to Albany and Cornwall; arguing from compositorial practices in the Folio, Goldring demonstrates that there is no convincing reason bibliographically that *"Cor."* must be *"Cornwall."* "Dramatic logic, characterization, and appropriateness of language" unite to suggest that *"Cor."* is *"Cordelia,"* thus providing a staging that "would reverberate throughout the rest of the play" (p. 149). As the identification of these three letters has required nine pages of this book, we can imagine how many more pages will be required to adjust all the other letters of the text!

In "Folio Editors, Folio Compositors, and the Folio Text of *King Lear,"* Paul Werstine responds to the assumption of eighteenth-century editors that the printers of the two texts were responsible for the corruptions. As he points out, belief in this assumption has justified the conflation of the texts and brought us to our present dilemma. He begins his analysis of Folio *Lear* by close studies of Compositor B in *1 Henry IV* and of Compositors B and E in *Titus, Romeo,* and *Troilus,* passing from quantitative to qualitative analysis in errors of substitution, transposition, interpolation, and omission in those plays. By such indirections, he finds out directions in *Lear,* concluding forcefully that the variants between the Quarto and Folio texts in *Lear* cannot—with a few exceptions—be attributed to the two compositors; they cannot be attributed to printing-house editors; they cannot be attributed to a hypothetical interfering scribe. There is no bibliographical evidence to support any thesis other than that the variants are the result of revision, presumably by Shakespeare (pp. 287–288). To take the argument one step further: if not by Shakespeare, by whom? Or to quote Honigmann again: "Who, other than Shakespeare, was capable of dramatic thinking at this level?"[12]

The contributions of Gary Taylor, constituting about one-third of the entire volume, are two: ". . . *King Lear* and Censorship" and the final essay, ". . . The Date and Authorship of the Folio Version." In the first of these, as Werstine had done, Taylor seeks to reduce the number of candidates for the position of "reviser" responsible for the variants between the texts. He demonstrates by a close reading of social and political sentiments in James's court that only one passage (I.iv.140–155) can actually be supposed to have suffered from censorship by the Master of the Revels. The offending passage includes lines in which the Fool calls the King a fool and references to the King's giving away titles and granting monopolies. These, indeed, might have offended James, himself guilty of such irregularities. In one other place (I.ii.131), the expletive "Fut" (= by Christ's foot) has been deleted, perhaps by the players themselves. No other instances give indication that the play has been censored.

The essay that concludes the volume is by far the longest essay in the series. It serves as a kind of summing up for the whole, and it aims at offering solutions to the "simple" questions: "Were there two periods of composition? If so, when did the second take place, who undertook it, and why?" (p. 354). If the essay does not fully respond to the last question—"why?"—it certainly deals thoroughly with the others. Evidence is assembled from discrete "strategies" to present the case for the hypothesis that there were two periods of composition, that the second occurred 1609–10, and that the reviser was Shakespeare. Taylor analyzes first the press variants in the Quarto; they demonstrate that "someone began rewriting *King Lear* on an exemplar of the printed Quarto text" (p. 353). He then examines the sources of the play as it appears in the Quarto and those further and different sources that he finds behind the passages unique to the Folio. His third inquiry treats of the use of "rare words," a useful technique (as other scholars have demonstrated) to fix the date of a text. All of these investigations answer the first and second questions—"when?" Taylor answers the third question—"who?"—by an examination of image clusters and a survey of linguistic criteria, the results of which exclude all conceivable agents other than Shakespeare. He also answers the question—to what effect?—by considering the literary and dramatic differences between Quarto and Folio.

The arguments here assembled are the voices of eleven critics in New Zealand (1), Canada (2), the United States (4), and Britain (4), speaking with a unanimity rare on the global scale. Their essays are disconcerting; are they also persuasive? They persuade this reviewer; but, more to the point, they make it impossible for serious critics to consider any passage in the conflated text now without asking if it is in Quarto, in Folio, or in both. Even if new evidence should render untenable the hypothesis advanced here, the arguments for the two versions by Taylor and his associates will require fresh and most searching investigation of the spirit of Shakespeare's great artistic exercise. The impact of these essays will be permanent; this volume looks directly into the mystery of things.

NOTES

1. Christopher Hogwood, "G. F. Handel's *Messiah*," in guide to the recording published by Decca Record Company, London, 1976, p. 5.

2. Caught up in the cogency of this argument, Clayton has understandably seen the Quarto "O, o, o, o" (V.iii.308) as "groans of agony" (p. 133), but that specific interpretation is ill founded, as

he well knows, for E. A. J. Honigmann has argued that such letters are a "signal" to the "actor to make whatever noise was locally appropriate. It could tell him to sigh, groan, gasp, roar, weep" ("Re-enter the Stage Direction," *Shakespeare Survey,* 29 [1976], 123). The "signal" in *Lear* might have told the actor here to make a noise appropriate to the sentiment expressed in "Looke there, looke there." Having dismissed in a footnote Honigmann's caution, Clayton builds this part of his argument shakily.

3. Clayton's text here reads "has been brought closer to Gloucester's"; that verbal form, natural enough, assumes what is not yet proved and seeks to persuade. The simple copula, still accurate, does not beg the question.

4. See Stanley Wells's Introduction here and Andrew Gurr, "The Once and Future *King Lears,*" *Bulletin of the Society for Renaissance Studies,* 2 (1984), 7–18.

5. "Review of Peter W. M. Blayney, *The Texts of 'King Lear',*" *Modern Language Review,* 79 (1984), 901–904.

6. Compare P. W. K. Stone who in *The Textual History of "King Lear"* (Menston: Scolar, 1980) supposes a date of 1618 for the revision and Massinger the reviser.

7. Gurr, p. 15.

8. See *Shakespeare Survey,* 33 (1980), 209.

9. In a paper presented at the meeting of the Shakespeare Association of America in 1984 (cited in footnote 170, page 451), Gary Taylor discusses the propriety of the Folio *Lear* for the fve-act structure.

10. See also S. W. Reid, "The Texts of *King Lear,*" *Shakespeare Studies,* 15 (1982), 335.

11. E. A. J. Honigmann, "Shakespeare's Revised Plays: *King Lear* and *Othello,*" *The Library,* Sixth Series, 4 (1982), 142–173, esp. p. 171. See also *Shakespeare Survey,* 36 (1983), 189.

12. Honigmann, p. 155. See also Honigmann's review, "The New Lear," *The New York Review of Books,* Feb. 2, 1984, pp. 16–18. A recent confession of Stoppard's is appropriate here: "Every time a play comes back for a revival, I take the opportunity to tinker with it; it is almost impossible to leave it alone" (from remarks made at Duke University, 18 January 1985).

Index

(Included are the names of persons and titles of Renaissance and Medieval plays.)

351

Contents of Previous Volumes

Volume I (1984)

The Malone Society

The Malone Society was formed in 1906 to make accessible material for the study of pre-Restoration English drama. For thirty-three years its Honorary General Editor was Sir Walter Greg, and the posts of officers and members of the Society's Council have continued to be held by well-known scholars.

So far, the Society has published over 140 volumes. Most of these are facsimile reprints or diplomatic editions of sixteenth- and seventeenth-century plays, from printed and manuscript originals. The introductions are brief and factual, and are largely devoted to clarifying the nature of the texts reproduced. Annotation is confined to such matters as press variants, manuscript alterations and the listing of irregular and doubtful readings. Occasional volumes of 'Collections' — twelve so far — reproduce shorter plays or contemporary documents relating to the drama.

Malone Society publications provide a range of essential texts and source materials, most of which are not otherwise available without consulting original documents. They are noted for their high standards of scholarship and good quality of production.

Annual subscriptions finance new publications on a non-profit making basis. At present, one volume is produced each year and issued to members without further charge. Members may also purchase past volumes (as available) through AMS Press Inc., at a substantial 40 per cent discount on the list prices.

The annual subscription of £ 10.00 ($17.00) is a modest price for volumes as significant in their content and as scrupulously produced as Malone Society publications. Each subscription helps the Society to give a fuller and more economic service. We therefore hope that you will apply for membership, sending one year's subscription fee to the Honorary Membership Secretary or, if you live in the USA, Canada, Australia, New Zealand, or Japan, to the officer for that area.

Honorary Membership Secretary:
Dr. John Jowett
The Oxford Shakespeare
40 Walton Crescent
Oxford OX1 2JQ

Honorary Treasurer for the USA:
Professor Thomas L. Berger
St. Lawrence University
Canton
New York 13617

Honorary Treasurer for Canada:
Professor Anne B. Lancashire
University College
University of Toronto
Toronto M5S 1A1

The Japanese Officer of the Malone Society:
Professor Jiro Ozu
201 Toyotama Mansion
1–8 Toyotama Kita
Nerima-ku, Tokyo

Honorary Treasurer for Australia and New Zealand:
Mr. F. H. Mares
Department of English Language and Literature
University of Adelaide
Box 498D, GPO Adelaide
South Australia 5001